PENGUIN BOOKS

LOVERS AND STRANGERS

Irish Times International Non-Fiction Choice Winner 2017

'Absorbing, substantial and often scintillating ... Richly empathetic, marvellously vivid' Roy Foster, *Irish Times*

'The perfect post-Brexit book' Arifa Akbar, *Evening Standard*

'Her well-written, readable story evolves like a novel or film script with key characters ... Post-war migration has increasingly become part of the British story: this volume helps to cement its central role in British lives' Panikos Panayi, *Times Higher Education*

'Poignant ... a rich account' *Economist*

'An authoritative and exhaustive study of post-war immigration to Britain. For a book that carries such heft, not the least of its qualities is the freshness of her approach ... meticulously researched and detailed ... a treasure trove of telling detail and unfamiliar facts ... beautifully crafted' David Chater, *The Tablet*

'Wills mines sociology, community newspapers, demotic poetry and oral histories from Irish, Cypriot, Polish, Pakistani and other cultures to show people making new identities as well as sustaining old ones, and helping rebuild a war-shattered country. The Little Englander fantasists currently in their pomp would do well to take note' Roy Foster, *The Times Literary Supplement*, Books of the Year

'A fine history ... masterfully charts how people "made their own stories" in a "limbo" between here and there. By seeing the white heat of change with new eyes, she offers a vital prologue to today's fevered fixations on immigration and identity ... Wills' extraordinary book reveals the roots of modern Britain's troubled relationship with immigration. These are the stories of Britain's yesterdays, todays and tomorrows, and they could hardly be more timely' Christopher Kissane, *Financial Times*

'Packed with surprises: the exceptional Irish contribution to the story is seen in the context of later arrivals from ever more diverse backgrounds' John Bowman, *Irish Times*, Books of the Year

'Clair Wills brings a refreshing insider/outsider perspective to the history ... Wills keeps her multiple narratives on path in exemplary fashion, with dizzying examples from her exhaustive research ... *Lovers and Strangers* is not just a richly illustrated compendium of under-exposed immigrant lives, but also an empathetic exploration of the nervous entitlement of indigenous Britons "mourning their own imagined futures", struggling to hold on to a better version of an imagined past'
Colin Grant, *The Times Literary Supplement*

'She understands and documents the *Windrush* generation, but she is also interested in Latvians, Lithuanians, Cypriots and the largest immigrant group of them all: the Irish ... brimming with new archival sources, careful cullings of governmental documents and oral histories – the book encompasses poetry and fiction as well as sociological accounts' Sukhdev Sandhu, *Guardian*

'*Lovers and Strangers* presents a historically rich view of immigration to Britain. Wills writes with both humour and detail about the lives of thousands of single men from Poland, Ireland, the West Indies and South Asia' Burhan Wazir, Chatham House

'This absorbing work uses fresh sources to build a rounded picture of the subject' *Who Do You Think You Are?*

ABOUT THE AUTHOR

Clair Wills is a critic and cultural historian. She is the author of *That Neutral Island: A History of Ireland during the Second World War*, which won the PEN Hessell-Tiltman History Prize, *Dublin 1916: The Siege of the GPO* and *The Best Are Leaving: Emigration and Post-War Irish Culture*. She teaches at Princeton University and divides her time between the United States and Europe.

CLAIR WILLS

Lovers and Strangers

An Immigrant History of Post-War Britain

PENGUIN BOOKS

PENGUIN BOOKS

UK | USA | Canada | Ireland | Australia
India | New Zealand | South Africa

Penguin Books is part of the Penguin Random House group of companies
whose addresses can be found at global.penguinrandomhouse.com.

First published by Allen Lane 2017
Published in Penguin Books 2018
001

The author and publisher are grateful to the following for permission to reproduce material:

The Enigma of Arrival, copyright © V. S. Naipaul, 1987, and *Half a Life*,
copyright © V. S. Naipaul, 2001, used by permission of The Wylie Agency (UK)
Limited; *The Girls of Slender Means*, Muriel Spark, reproduced by kind permission of
David Higham; *Journey to an Expectation*, *The Emigrants* and *The Pleasure of Exile*,
George Lamming, reproduced by kind permission of George Lamming; *The Seventh
Man*, John Berger, reproduced by kind permission of Agencia Literaria Carmen Balcells;
An Irish Navvy: The Diary of an Exile, Dónall Mac Amhlaigh, reproduced by kind
permission of The Collins Press; *Free Association*, Steven Berkoff, copyright © Faber
and Faber Ltd; *Escape to an Autumn Pavement*, Andrew Salkey, Peepal Tree Press,
reproduced by kind permission of the estate of Andrew Salkey and Peepal Tree Press;
In the Ditch, Buchi Emecheta, Heinemann, reproduced by kind permission of the
estate of Buchi Emecheta; *Dead as Doornails* and *The Life of Riley*, Anthony
Cronin, reproduced by kind permission of Anne Haverty; 'Nirmohi Vilayat', Ranjit
Dheer, reproduced by kind permission of Ranjit Dheer; *Dukh Pardesan de*, Pritam
Sidhu, reproduced by kind permission of Surjit Sidhu; 'Black People, White Blood',
Sathi Ludhianvi, reproduced by kind permission of Sathi Ludhianvi.

Set in 9.35/12.5 pt Sabon LT Std
Typeset by Jouve (UK), Milton Keynes
Printed in Great Britain by Clays Ltd, St Ives plc

A CIP catalogue record for this book is available from the British Library

ISBN: 978-0-141-97497-2

www.greenpenguin.co.uk

In memory of Beryl Suitters Dhanjal, 1939–2016

Contents

PART 3

Pasts

Introduction

About fifty years from now, future historians – in Asia, in Africa and perhaps in England – writing about Europe in the nineteen fifties and sixties will presumably devote a chapter to the coloured minority group in this country. They will say that although this group was small, it was an important, indeed an essential one. For its arrival and growth gave British society an opportunity of recognising its own blind spots, and also of looking beyond its own nose to a widening horizon of human integrity. They will point out that the relations between white and coloured people in this country were a test of Britain's ability to fulfil the demands for progressive rationality in social organisation, so urgently imposed in the latter half of the twentieth century. And the future historians will add that Britain had every chance of passing this test, because at that period her domestic problems were rather slight by comparison with those of many other areas of the world.

Ruth Glass, Newcomers, 1960[1]

The historian seeks to abstract principles from human events. My approach was the other; for the two years that I lived among the documents I sought to reconstruct the human story as best I could.

V. S. Naipaul, The Enigma of Arrival, 1987[2]

Long ago in 1945 all the nice people in England were poor, allowing for exceptions. The streets of the cities were lined with buildings in bad repair or in no repair at all, bomb-sites piled with stony rubble, houses like giant teeth in which decay had been drilled out, leaving only the cavity. Some bomb-ripped buildings looked like the ruins of ancient

castles until, at a closer view, the wallpapers of various quite
normal rooms would be visible, room above room, exposed,
as on a stage, with one wall missing; sometimes a lavatory
chain would dangle over nothing from a fourth- or fifth-floor
ceiling; most of all the staircases survived, like a new art-form,
leading up and up to an unspecified destination that made
unusual demands on the mind's eye. All the nice people were
poor; at least, that was a general axiom, the best of the rich
being poor in spirit.

> Muriel Spark, *The Girls of Slender Means*, 1963[3]

You jacked in your part-time job digging ditches for the County
Council in Mayo, or helping out on your uncle's small farm in Galway, and bought your ticket for Holyhead. You queued – and
queued – in the refugee camp in Germany's British Occupation Zone,
for a place on one of the labour schemes which would bring you to a
job in a mill in Bradford, or a mine in Wales. You applied by post to
a hospital in Lincolnshire from Kingston, Jamaica, and when the letter of acceptance came you borrowed the fare. You sold your plot of
land in Jalandhar in the Indian Punjab and paid the money over to an
agent who arranged the ticket and passport which would land you at
Heathrow. Unless you were a refugee trying to find a way out of the
post-war German camps, and had no home in Poland or Latvia or the
Ukraine to go back to, you did not imagine spending more than two,
or at the most five, years in Britain. You thought of yourself as a
migrant rather than an immigrant. You were prepared to give up
day-to-day life at home in order to get the training or earn enough
money in England to make home viable again. But you did not return.
You became a long-term immigrant, a practised reader of the British
psyche, adept at living between two cultures, and an expert in geographical gains and losses.

The refugees and migrants who arrived in Britain in the immediate
post-war years had to develop new ways of making sense of their
lives. They gave up their everyday immersion in the ordinary world of
family, village and small-town life for the sake of a future which they
could only dimly imagine. They left familiar environments and,
as they disembarked at Tilbury, Southampton, Liverpool or London

Airport, instantly became strangers. They were marked as outsiders by their language, accents, clothes, customs and, sometimes, their skin colour. Even fifty and sixty years after their arrival in a still largely mono-cultural Britain it is rare to meet post-war immigrants who feel a straightforward sense of belonging, however happy and successful their lives have been. They will always be from elsewhere.

An immigrant history of post-war Britain is in part a history of foreigners, but of foreigners who have given up their place in their own national history in order to play a role in the history of Britain. When I began this book I intended to write an account of Britain in the 1950s and 1960s from the perspective of the many thousands who moved from Europe, Asia, Africa and the Caribbean to power the country's post-war recovery. I wanted to put the migrants back at the heart of post-war British reconstruction, where they belonged. But I quickly realized that to try to map the stories of immigrants against the established background of British politics and society was to miss something fundamental about migrant experience. Immigrants from Europe and the Commonwealth differed in all sorts of ways but what they shared was the experience of belonging securely neither to the places they had left nor to the place they had chosen to make their home. It was not simply that they lived between two cultures but that they lived in a third space – the limbo of migrant culture. This was a world which grew at the meeting point between the hopes, desires and strategies for survival of the immigrants themselves, and the opportunities made available to them. First-generation immigrants' lives were circumscribed in all sorts of ways which set them apart from mainstream British culture, and to simply add them in to the story of Britain's recovery from the war and the boom years of the 1950s would be to miss both what was unique about their experience, and the ways in which they transformed the mainstream.

The world of the post-war immigrant operated in what was not only a geographical but also a temporal limbo. Migrants left home because they wanted a better future, but they mostly imagined that future would be safely back at home, not in Britain. They thought of their present-tense, everyday lives in Camden, Southall, Birmingham or Bradford as a kind of interregnum, a period to be endured or enjoyed because it would make possible a future that was envisaged, as often as not, as a return to a past made viable again. We all plot our lives by projecting ourselves imaginatively into the future, but for those of us who stay in the culture into which we were born, the set of decisions we are called upon to make is relatively contained: this job or that job; this partner or that partner, or no partner at all; this way of life or that one. The decisions made by post-war migrants were similar, but vastly more grand: this world or that world. Living and working inside the domain of the migrant was in part a way of not having to choose. They effectively dwelled in several places at once, and in several time zones. This book is an attempt to describe the migrant worlds which came into being in Britain in the 1950s and 1960s, and the characters who lived in them. And like the migrants themselves, in order to write about them I have had to forgo the reassuring structures of standard national, public narratives and even the established chronology in which the past leads to the present and eventually the future.[4] The series of miniatures I offer here are close-ups of the disorienting and exhilarating novelty of the metropolis for the rural and small-town migrant, a kaleidoscope of the fragmentary experiences of metropolitan migrant life. But they are also accounts of the ways in which those experiences intersected and began to converge with the main current of British politics and society, and change it in its turn.

What has been called 'the Windrush generation' was comprised not only of people from the Caribbean, but also Poles, Latvians, Lithuanians, Ukrainians, Italians, Maltese, Cypriots, Indians and Pakistanis, plus the largest immigrant group, the Irish, who alone arrived at a rate of approximately 40,000 every year during the 1950s. The experiences of those 1950s and 1960s arrivals – those who were to form the vanguard of multi-culturalism – were as varied as the places that they came from. The post-war immigrants came as refugees, as economic migrants and, in the case of the 'European Voluntary Workers' – who were shipped in to man essential industries in the late 1940s – as something between the two. Forced labourers, victims of concentration camps, former prisoners of war, the millions displaced by the redrawing of boundaries in Eastern Europe – by the end of the war there were nearly 7 million displaced people in Germany alone, all searching for a place of greater safety. These were white Europeans, stranded in the heart of Europe. Yet the history of their resettlement – and deportation – does not easily dovetail with the comforting story Britain likes to tell itself of compassion and concern for the victims of war. For despite the work of the international relief agencies, the acceptance of refugees in Western Europe and the United States was rarely powered by humanitarian concerns. The vast bureaucratic machine developed to decide who would be sent back, and who welcomed, operated according to a kind of hierarchy of need. Just as refugees arriving in Greece today are advised to get rid of their Iraqi passports so they can claim to be Syrians, in order to access help more quickly, so Ukrainians pretended to be Poles, and everyone tried to claim Latvian or Estonian nationality, hoping for better treatment. In the end, however, the needs of the refugees were neither here nor there beside the needs of the countries offering refuge. People were accepted in so far as they would be useful to the economies of Britain, Belgium, France and the United States. In effect, asylum seekers were turned into economic migrants. Those who had skills were welcomed, so long as they were healthy. Those most in need (the old, the sick) were left behind.

Governments were wary of the refugees, and popular opinion was often fiercely antagonistic to the displaced. In fact, the bitter post-war arguments about how, or indeed whether, to share out the depleted resources of a near-bankrupt Britain formed one model for attempts to differentiate between 'genuine' refugees and economic migrants, in effect to grade the most and least deserving. Ironically, however, those deemed to be driven by work-hunger were favoured over the most desperate and broken refugees. For although Britain – together with the rest of Europe – was going through a period of crippling austerity in the late 1940s and early 1950s, it was also in desperate need of labour. And it was primarily for this reason that the new settlers from Europe and the former colonies were tolerated, and in some cases even encouraged.

As the migrants arrived, destined in the main for low paid, unskilled work, so others left. Throughout the late 1940s very large numbers of Britons packed the trains out of London, and the boats out of Liverpool and Southampton, intent on making the move to Canada,

Australia and New Zealand. In 1947 Winston Churchill blamed two years of socialist rule for the fact that 'half-a-million of our . . . most lively and active citizens in the prime of life' had applied to emigrate. 'We cannot spare you . . . at a time when we are scouring Europe for 20,000 or 30,000 or more of unfortunate displaced persons of the great war to come in and swell our labour force.' Nonetheless, they kept on going. Over 650,000 people left Britain, mainly heading for the white Commonwealth countries, during the 1950s. All over the world, people were looking for a better break.[5]

All this coming and going – especially the going – did not sit well with the image of a proud island nation rebuilding domestic life after the chaos of war. The rhetoric of the new Labour government put across the idea of the war as, among other things, an interruption in family life. The conflict had accustomed men and women across the globe to huge displacements, not only of refugees but of members of the armed forces: British, Nigerian and Indian troops fighting in Burma, for example; GIs in Europe and the Far East; Italian prisoners of war in Scotland. But the end of the war was supposed to mean the end of disorder and disruption – the return home to Britain captured in images of demobbed soldiers being greeted by waiting wives and children waving flags proclaiming victory, in front of terraced houses and pre-fabs which stood for a frugal and prudent security. For these were to be family homes re-made for the post-war world. The determination never to return to the poverty and unemployment of the 1930s was to require collective effort and sacrifice – rationing was tightened, and shortages of food and fuel increased in the two years after the war – but the rewards would be legion. Full employment, the 'social' wage, welfare reforms in education and health, an end to sub-standard housing – home was to be a place of comfort and refuge in a state which properly looked after its own.

'Really, they're just like us, they want a home of their own', read the pamphlets distributed to local residents to reconcile them to the several thousand Poles billeted in former army camps near Bedford and Leicester in 1946 and 1947.[6] It was an attempt to domesticate the aliens, and in the long run, as intermarriage became more common and social contacts increased, it worked. But all the talk of house and home masked the real nature of the social transformation which was under way. Although its imperial power was waning rapidly, Britain lay at the centre of a network of international relations that worked themselves out not only at the level of high politics but of everyday experience. The international character of everyday life was no longer limited for most people to admiring the 'red bits' on the map of the world, which signalled the king's imperial dominion, or to the availability of bananas, oranges and cloves – not to mention tea and sugar – in the shops. For a start, many of the men returning from war brought with them a familiarity with (and in some cases an understandable resentment of) far-off places and cultures which they would never have encountered otherwise. The legacy of war, and the beginnings of the Cold War, took physical shape in the thousands of 'displaced persons' unable or unwilling to return home to Soviet-occupied Europe. For the majority of Britons too, the shrinking Empire meant not less but more contact with elsewhere. Naturally, the overwhelming impact of Independence for India and Pakistan in 1947 lay in the region itself, where vast and violent population movements quickly transformed the social and political geography of the two states. But over the next fifteen years the effects would also be felt in London, Leeds and Birmingham as Mirpuris, Punjabis and Sylhetis all sought their livelihoods in Britain. The desperate search for wages by people living in rural poverty in southern Italy, Cyprus, Ireland and the Caribbean all meant the collapse of the boundaries between here and elsewhere.

It was true that the post-war migrants were 'just like us'. They wanted homes, a secure livelihood, and a brighter future. Their desires were in many ways minimal, as the title of a 1957 study of West Indians newly arrived in London put it: 'They seek a living'.[7] Yet what has struck me most forcibly while writing this book is the disappearance, buried under all the rhetoric, of any sense of the migrants as ordinary people, the near-universal contemporary focus on them as *unlike* us, as strangers, aliens and outsiders.

Histories of post-war Britain, and more detailed studies of immigration, have focused obsessively on two or three aspects of the story: the initial, distrustful, encounter with the strangers on their arrival in the late 1940s; the rise in ethnic tensions, culminating in racially motivated riots in 1958; and the subsequent development of restrictive racial legislation intended to curb immigration of non-whites. This focus cannot be separated from the tendency among contemporary historians to interpret post-war British social history through a framework set out for them by post-war British politicians – through the lenses of the Cold War, political consensus, austerity and affluence, the rise of welfarism, the growth of youth culture and the demise of deference. In this story about never-having-had-it-so-good the migrant appears incidentally, and always in the context of black–white race relations. Despite the work of oral historians we have ended up with a largely 'public history', emphasizing the politics of racial prejudice, assimilation, integration, multi-culturalism and, most recently, the failure of multi-culturalism.

The story of post-war immigration is indeed in part a story about race. The account I offer here begins in the late 1940s, as the United Nations Relief and Rehabilitation operations were being wound up in Europe, and the newly formed NHS began seeking Continental, Irish and, later, Caribbean workers. It ends in 1968, a landmark year, when the Labour government under Harold Wilson effectively ended the right of Commonwealth citizens to enter Britain by pushing through emergency legislation (in three days) limiting entry to those with a parent or grandparent born here. By the late 1960s the immigration debate had become limited to a debate about race, and colour, whether articulated by Enoch Powell, the Race Relations Board, or the British Black Panthers, in ways which would have been inconceivable twenty years before.

This political and legislative history clearly formed part of the way that migrants lived their lives. Legal milestones, such as the 1948 British Nationality Act, the Commonwealth Immigrants Act of 1962 and the 1965 Race Relations legislation, transformed everyday life, at what must have felt like the stroke of a pen. Domestic political issues also intervened, such as trade union struggles to maintain control over the shop floor and to bar immigrant labour, the growth of far-right groups and the Notting Hill riots, the 1964 Smethwick election result, which saw a safe Labour seat overturned by the Conservative Peter Griffiths, who ran on an explicitly anti-immigration ticket, or the rise of Enoch Powell. These all had real-life, and sometimes catastrophic, effects. But whether written from a sympathetic standpoint or not, the political history – and its social impact – tend to overshadow what migration might actually have felt like for those concerned.

Many of the popular assumptions about the lives of migrants get us no closer. It is only partly true, for example, that immigrants took the jobs that British people, basking in the new affluence of the later 1950s, did not want. That suggests a natural process, but what really happened was anything but natural. More often the mechanization of factories in the drive towards greater productivity created new, entirely unskilled labouring jobs. People were needed to heft coal and iron ore around the foundries, to back up men working the modern machines, and the unions fought bitter battles to ensure that immigrant workers were kept out of the better paid grades. Or take another common-sense assumption: that as the years passed, immigrants from the Caribbean and Asia became more assimilated into British culture. Again this is only partly true. For the first settlers from Sylhet and the Punjab, for example, it was common to have relationships with English women, and dietary and religious customs were often ignored by young men fitting themselves into Western culture as best they could. But perhaps the most striking thing about the people who came in the 1950s was that most of them didn't think of themselves as immigrants at all. As they did not plan on settling permanently, the question of assimilation did not arise. The clash between British political rhetoric about the immigrant problem and the immigrants' own experience could not have been greater.

Writing in 1960, in the immediate aftermath of the Notting Hill riots, the sociologist Ruth Glass – acutely conscious of the steadily rising tide of racial prejudice – noted ruefully how it could all have been so different. Precisely because Britain had escaped the devastation visited on much of the rest of Europe, because the economy quite quickly recovered and set in train the industrial boom of the 1950s, because manpower was needed, and because the migrants worked hard, there was no rationale for the panic over resources, and the suspicion of the newcomers made no sense. With so little economic foundation the crisis could have been avoided, if only people had been prepared to see things differently. This question of perspective – what the West Indian novelist and migrant George Lamming called alternative 'ways of seeing' – has been fundamental to the conception of this book. Beyond the calculation of economic costs and benefits, Glass argued that the post-war migrants were necessary to Britain because they provided an opportunity for reflection. Through the eyes of strangers Britons could look at themselves. They could see themselves from the point of view of others, and even attempt to live up to outsiders' expectations. It was a test of the values and organization of British society, and society – in large part – failed the test. As she puts it, Britons remained trapped by their own very limited perspectives, accepted their blind spots, and failed to look beyond their noses and take a broader outlook in which refugees and migrants – whatever their colour – could be welcomed into an expanding and thriving democracy.

Can hindsight offer a clearer perspective on those uncomprehending looks, and allow us to look not at but through the eyes of the stranger? It should be clear from these remarks that my interest in this book is in what V. S. Naipaul calls 'the human story', although my aim is to tell that story in tandem with the political history of post-war migration, and to investigate the multiple, local, immigrant worlds created both by the movement of European refugees and economic migrants, and the arrival of people from non-European former colonies. Naipaul's remark is embedded in a fictionalized memoir in which he reflects on the moment in 1950 when he arrived in London, an eighteen-year-old migrant from Trinidad, en route to Oxford, and bent on a career as a writer. As he gives his account more than forty years later, he berates his former self for searching for a 'grand' subject which would measure up to his expectations of England, and for ignoring the people he encountered every day, people who were at once too ordinary, and too strange. He regrets his 'way of looking':

> The flotsam of Europe not long after the end of the terrible war, in a London house that was now too big for the people it sheltered – that was the true material of the boarding house. But I didn't see it . . . and in the Earl's Court boarding house, as fellow guests or as friends of Angela's, there were at least ten or twelve drifters from many countries of Europe and North Africa . . . men and women, some of whom had seen terrible things during the war and were now becalmed and

quiet in London, solitary, foreign, sometimes idle, sometimes half-criminal. These people's principal possessions were their stories, and their stories spilled easily out of them. But I noted nothing down. I asked no questions. I took them all for granted, looked beyond them; and their faces, clothes, names, accents have vanished and cannot now be recalled.[8]

Recovering those stories, the local narratives which have become buried under the larger political history, has involved a process of excavation combined with something more like 'misreading', or 'reading from the inside out'. As far as possible I have tried to narrate the history of migrants' and refugees' encounters with Britain through the experience of the immigrants themselves, and through contemporary accounts of that experience: contemporary interviews, articles and letters in the local and community press; manifestos; short stories; autobiographies; political essays; as well oral poetry and folk songs ranging from Irish ballads to Trinidadian calypso, Punjabi *qisse* and bhangra lyrics. Some migrant communities are undoubtedly better served than others by this form of documentation. The first wave of post-war Caribbean migration included significant numbers of well-educated men and women, many on university scholarships, who were eager to turn their hands to all sorts of writing, whether for local papers, the Caribbean programmes on the World Service, or for more political and intellectual movements: the Caribbean Artists Movement, *New Left Review*, or the movement for a West Indian Federation. Polish, Cypriot, Italian or Maltese migrants lacked any kind of comparable cultural scene, yet, for example, letters sent by recent Italian immigrants to the newspaper of the Italian mission, asking whether dating a non-Catholic was permitted, or whether it was possible to get married by phone, offer some insights into the world of those first arrivals. And some excavation has taken me further afield. Punjabi letters, articles and short stories about the experience of migration were published in newspapers in India and Pakistan in the early post-war years, before several newspapers were founded in Southall and the Midlands in the mid-1960s that offered further outlets to a growing circle of short-story writers and essayists.

Letters and stories like these can take us back to the post-war smog, the overcrowded lodging houses, the cafés selling dried eggs and spam alongside curry and Indian sweets, the bombed areas and construction sites, the prostitution rackets and greyhound race tracks and, perhaps most alien of all to us now, the networks of small engineering firms, foundries, rubber factories, family owned mills, sweat shops and manufacturing concerns which were dotted throughout industrial cities in the 1950s and 1960s. Rural immigrants, so often described as 'pre-modern' or savage outliers to industrial society, not only lived in the negative underside of the new suburban affluence, they also powered it – building the roads, cars and goods which made English suburban lives possible.

But this writing needs to be set alongside official and quasi-official documents – the records of police constabularies investigating 'coloured' crime, reports of interracial tension inside government hostels, statements by police and the judiciary on the Notting Hill riots, parliamentary debates on immigration and race relations legislation, ethnographic and sociological surveys of attitudes to race in relation to the housing crisis, and employment. It is here that 'misreading' comes in to play. For these documents are saturated with stereotypes of migrants, both ethnic and racial; they are absolutely confident about migrants' 'unlikeness' to the home-spun British, despite a superficial (and sometimes deep) commitment to integration and inclusion. These records offer plenty of insight into and information about attitudes towards the newcomers. They are eloquent when it comes to blind spots. But in order to tell us anything about the immigrants themselves they need to be held up before a mirror, and interpreted for what they tell us but do not say.

The principal problem with these documents for the historian of migrant experience is that they approach the problem (and it is nearly always *as* a problem) from the perspective of 'us', discussing 'them'. And what is striking is that, however positive the take, this perspective has carried through into more recent histories: for example, accounts of the influence of traditional Irish music on the folk revival and 1960s counter-cultural movements, of Caribbean music and style on the mods, of Sylheti cooks on British cuisine. It is not that these influences, and confluences, are not interesting. They are. But they crowd out the story told from the perspective of the new arrival, which is rarely about what they bring to others but about what they gain – and lose – for themselves. The stories spilling out of those European and North African 'drifters' encountered by Naipaul were about their pasts, their families and the homes they had left behind. In this, of course, the migrants were indeed 'just like us'. They were undergoing the universal experience of being cut off from the past, but with far greater intensity. My focus is on the people who came to Britain during the relatively short-lived period of the Commonwealth 'open door', rather than on the hyphenated identities of their Black-British, Polish-Irish, or Asian-British children. Unlike today's immigrants, these frontiersmen arrived into almost entirely mono-cultural communities; of necessity theirs were pioneer settlements. The vast distances, the cost of transport, the unavailability of things we take for granted, such as phones, all meant that for most migrants home was irrevocably lost, and thus reinvented. These were inter-national journeys, but they were emphatically not taking place in the global village. And 'just like us', their lives in Britain were oriented towards an uncertain future.

In attempting to do justice to the migrants' post-war present, I have shaped this history around various characters – the lover, the scrounger, the troublemaker, the broadcaster, the bachelor, the dancer – which I try to interpret from both sides, from the perspective of the ordinary British person looking from outside in, and from that of the ordinary migrant, looking from inside out. My cast of characters is by no means comprehensive. Many facets of migrants' professional, religious and domestic lives are touched on only lightly here. But I offer this shifting kaleidoscope as a counterbalance to the tendency to see the history of post-war immigration in monochrome, as primarily a story of the relationship between black and white. Whenever I lost the thread I found myself returning to the wonderful passage which opens Muriel Spark's novel *The Girls of Slender Means*, where she paints a portrait of the poverty and destruction of post-war London. This never failed to remind me of two things: first that, cushioned or not by wealth, everyone experienced the same post-war Britain; *everyone* was us in that present of the 1940s and 1950s, wherever they had come from. And, secondly, that dismantling the wall between inside and outside, although it may make unusual demands on the mind's eye, can bring into focus a new understanding of the vernacular. How did the fabric of the blitzed city, what Spark calls a new art form, work its way through the fabric of people's lives, and how might we begin to read the fabric of post-war experience through those new urban art forms – the buildings, the documents, the reports, the stories and the songs that migrants and their hosts wrote about each other? The story is not of immigrants as 'dark strangers', or, still less, 'bloody foreigners', but of the lives lived and imagined by immigrants themselves. Put bluntly, not how did they appear to the British but what did the British, those white strangers, look like to them?

PART ONE

Futures

The men and women who came to Britain after the war, from Europe, from the Caribbean and from Asia, did so because they imagined a future which migration would make possible. The promises they expected to be fulfilled by migration differed in kind, if not in intensity, from one another. West Indian immigrants had been brought up to believe they were guaranteed a welcome in the 'mother country'. It may have been hard to leave home, but migrating was simply making good on a promise that had long been made to them as citizens of the Empire. It was an unwritten contract which had been stamped on almost every aspect of everyday life in the islands, engendering a loyalty and feeling of belonging which only deepened during the war as the islanders identified with Britain's struggle.

Moreover, now the British government seemed intent on writing out the contract in black and white, by passing the British Nationality Act, giving all members of the Commonwealth (including those from countries such as newly independent India which had renounced allegiance to the crown) the same rights of citizenship as people born in Britain. In July 1948 the home secretary, James Chuter Ede, took waverers to task in the House of Commons:

> I know there are also some who feel it is wrong to have a citizenship of the United Kingdom and Colonies. Some people feel it would be a bad thing to give the coloured races of the Empire the idea that, in some way or other, they are the equals of people in this country. The government do not subscribe to that view. We believe wholeheartedly that the common citizenship of the United Kingdom and Colonies is

an essential part of the development of the relationship between this Mother Country and the Colonies.[1]

Why should the 'coloured races of the Empire' have disbelieved him? The Act simply ratified the existing situation in which nationals of the United Kingdom, the Dominions and the Colonies shared a common citizenship. It clarified but did not create the open-door immigration policy. The fact that no voices to speak of were raised in warning against the possibility of an 'influx' of colonial and post-colonial immigrants suggests not that politicians thought of such an influx with equanimity, but that they could not conceive of it at all. The idea of the Empire and the Commonwealth as a family of nations was far stronger than the reality of what that might mean in a new era of global migration networks. Parliamentarians were more concerned about the effect of a restrictive definition of nationhood on Britain's relationship with Canada and Australia, than with the possibility of unrestricted immigration from the colonies and former colonies. Yet the fact was that until the immigration rules were changed in 1962, *all* Britain's imperial subjects and citizens of the Commonwealth – a staggering quarter of the population of the planet – had the legal right to live in Britain as British citizens.

By contrast, for the survivors of the war in Europe, the refugees encamped on the Continent, the chance of a new life in Britain was predicated, literally, on signing a new contract, in which work was exchanged for refuge. Their bargain was nothing if not clear. For the rural poor who travelled from Asia, Ireland, Italy and Cyprus to make good in the industrial boom, the terms of the contract were far more vague. Theirs were futures conjured out of hope, and sometimes fantasy, rather than contractual promises. And all these different forms of expectation would result in different forms of fulfilment, as well as disappointment. The promised land, flowing with milk and honey, offered no divinely appointed homecoming. It was only ever going to end up being what you could make of it.

I

Geographers

And now we were about to be anchored at Southampton, we
realised that we had no return ticket. We had no experience
in crime. Moreover our colonial status condemned us fortu-
nately to the rights of full citizenship. In no circumstances
could we qualify for deportation. There was no going back.
All the gaiety of reprieve which we felt on our departure had
now turned to apprehension. Like one of the many characters
which he has since created, Sam said on the deck: 'Is who
send we up in this place?'

George Lamming, 'Journey to an Expectation' (1960)[1]

That young man in the double-breasted suit and snap-brim trilby,
grasping the handrail of the ship at Tilbury Dock, those girls in their
crisp summer dresses, the men and women waiting in the Customs
Hall in Southampton with their possessions packed in straw baskets,
the expectant faces of the crowds piling off the boat trains in Paddington, Victoria, or Waterloo. The news photographs of the arrival
of migrants from the Caribbean in the early 1950s have become iconic
images in the history of post-war Britain, signalling the beginning of
the transformation of British national identity. For us now, the power
of the photographs lies in the contrast between what appears to
be the migrants' innocence, caught in the moment of waiting before
their new life begins, and our knowledge of the difficulties most
of them will face. They have dressed up for their arrival out of
self-respect, and a sense of occasion. They believe that they are the
beneficiaries of migration – even the beneficiaries of empire – not its
victims.

When the photographs were first published, they spoke less of innocence than exoticism. Like much of the writing about immigrants then and since, the focus was on the difference between 'us' and the 'dark strangers'. Either way, the photographs conceal far more than they reveal. They tell us nothing about the experiences these people brought with them: the fact that they were more likely to have left the cities of Kingston and Port of Spain than the rural Caribbean, that many of them were well educated and hoping for clerical or teaching posts, that they had begged, borrowed and saved up for months to pay for their passage on the steamship, and that for most of them there was no going back. Like George Lamming and Sam Selvon, two young, as-yet-unpublished writers who sailed for Britain from Trinidad in 1950, they were, for good or ill, condemned to the rights of full British citizenship.[2]

'England lay before us', said Lamming in his account of that 1950 journey, 'not as a place or a people but as a promise and an expectation.' His distinction pointed to the disturbing gap between the reality of migration, experienced in encounters with the place and its people, and the idea. It wasn't just that West Indian migrants had unrealistic expectations of life in Britain – although many of them did – but that those expectations were the result of a promise they believed had been made to them as citizens of the United Kingdom and the Colonies. That promise was the product of the long history of empire. It was a contract rooted in the past, but, like any contract, it carried with it expectations of fulfilment. The migrants on the deck turned their faces towards a future they believed was owed to them. More than the colour of their skin, it was this that set them apart from other immigrants in these early post-war years. Unlike Europeans and migrants from India and Pakistan, they thought they already belonged. Indeed they were told as much:

> There were adverts everywhere: 'Come to the Mother Country! The Mother Country Needs You!' That's how I learned the opportunity was here. I felt stronger loyalty towards England. There was more emphasis there than loyalty to your own island ... It was really the mother country and being away from home wouldn't be that terrible because you would belong.[3]

If we try to look out from behind the photographs of Caribbean migrants, what was it that England promised them? More than seventy years on from the Second World War, with independence for nearly all former colonial territories long achieved, it can be hard to make the imaginative leap that would make sense of West Indians' attitude to the 'mother country'. As Lamming ruefully acknowledged many years later:

> Migration was not a word I would have used to describe what I was doing when I sailed with other West Indians to England in 1950. We simply thought we were going to an England which had been planted in our consciousness as a heritage and a place of welcome. It is a measure of our innocence that neither the claim of innocence nor the expectation of welcome would have been seriously doubted.[4]

The idea of a parental relationship between metropolis and colony is difficult to take seriously now, unless we see parents as exploiters and abusers as well as nurturing presences. And it was obviously not the case that West Indian migrants trusted naïvely to the rhetoric of the Empire's 'family of nations'. Most of them were simply unemployed and looking for a start. Lamming recalled his travelling companions:

> The emigrants were largely men in search of work. During the voyage we had got to know each other very well. The theme of all talk was the same. It had to do with some conception of a better break. We lived between the deck – which was a kind of camping ground – and the communal dormitory where we slept, wrote letters, or simply wondered what would happen.[5]

Yet Britain meant far more than merely economic opportunity. School pupils were educated in the British system, and took British qualifications; political, social, cultural and sporting life was fed through British institutions; all forms of authority resided in England; all routes to advancement passed through it. The monarch's sovereignty over the islands may have been questioned by independence-minded activists but, in the late 1940s and early 1950s, it was not yet seriously contested – a fact that had less to do with political innocence than political pragmatism. And for the young generation that would form the majority of post-war migrants to Britain, the war itself had further consolidated the relationship between colony and metropolis. Through war service and war news the islands were imaginatively positioned not only within an imperial orbit, but also within a European one. Above all, the promise that England offered was that of an independent future. To grow up in the West meant leaving your parents and setting out on your own, but for the West Indian, ironically, striking out for independence and economic security meant travelling to the 'mother' country. England meant adventure, a broader canvas, and an alternative to the constricted environment of home. It was the obvious next step in thousands of coming-of-age stories. For increasing numbers of young West Indians, crossing the frontier of adulthood meant crossing the Atlantic.

None of this implies that they were naïve about what they would find when they arrived. They were simply in the dark. Their first encounters with England were to delight some and confound others, but all of them were changed by the journey, from which – like all adults cut off from their past – they would never be able to return. Over the months and years that followed they would wake to new understandings of themselves: as workers, neighbours, lovers, and family men and women, but also as West Indians, as black and as outsiders to post-war British culture. They were citizens of the United Kingdom – a legal identity enshrined in the 1948 British Nationality Act – but they were regarded as strangers. For the first generation of West Indian migrants it was this central contradiction, between estrangement and belonging, between being a colonial and being a citizen, which was to determine their experience.

Lamming's first job when he got to Britain was in a car factory, but within months he was taken on as a writer and reporter for the BBC's Caribbean Service. In June 1953 he found himself assigned to cover the Coronation, for broadcast over the World Service. Down in Parliament Square the evening before the ceremony, the pavements were crowded with makeshift encampments of loyal citizens, old women munching sandwiches, children, couples, all determined to wait through the night for a glimpse of the Royals. As it began to rain they pulled their blankets and raincoats up. When the rain came down hard Lamming boarded a bus that crawled past the huddles of spectators, who still had another twenty-four hours to wait. The downpour, the steamed-up windows, the general jam meant that he could no longer see them. But he could hear them:

> They were singing. At first a little sadly, as though they thought it unfair that this should happen. Later the voices, each encouraging the other, achieved a little more gaiety; and finally they soared above the rain in a calculated outburst of triumph. They were determined to stay put; and they were embarked upon an attitude that would annihilate the weather.

At this point a foreigner on the bus intoned, 'in the gravest voice he could summon ... "I shall always remember it as their wettest hour".'[6]

Lamming's enjoyment of this moment was the enjoyment of an outsider – he shares the joke with the foreigner – but one who knew the inside. His ironic distance turned the tables on Britain's compact with its Caribbean possessions, that distance was no barrier to belonging. For young West Indians were schooled early in geographical ironies. They knew all about belonging from afar. 'My father kept a cupboard in the schoolroom full of flags,' recalled an Indian emigrant from Trinidad, the son of the local primary school teacher:

> On the slightest provocation – a holiday, a Royal death, a British victory – he tore them out. Rule Britannia! Half-naked children, some without food, some sick, but all loyal, would come out to school. Their voices were loud and clear, innocence drowning the subversive rumblings in their empty tummies. In the dining-room of our school-house, there was a Manufacturer's Life map of the world which my father would unfurl after reading the papers, and on which he would, with the help of tacks, trace the British front lines. We sometimes had the Rhine and the Ruhrgebiet while we drank our soup.

They may have lived nearly five thousand miles from the Rhine but the war against Germany was their war, the European field of battle their field. Indeed, if it was the Empire which enabled West Indian migrants to migrate to Britain then the catalyst was the war. West Indians who had served in the British armed forces during the

Second World War were among the first to emigrate to Britain in the immediate post-war years. From 1944 more than 5,000 West Indian men had served in the RAF in Britain, along with women in the WAAF and ATS; a further 1,200 served in the Caribbean Regiment. Quite apart from historical ties of Empire, these numbers give some context to the schoolroom study of the Rhine and Ruhrgebiet.[7]

Some servicemen chose to stay in Britain when the war ended, but, for most of the 110 men (including 10 stowaways) who arrived on the SS *Ormonde* in 1947, and the 492 ex-servicemen on the *Empire Windrush* in 1948, the journey from Jamaica was a form of delayed demobilization. Half of the *Windrush* passengers had been posted in Britain but opted to return home after the war, where they quickly came to the end of their demob money and faced a future out of work. The opportunity to travel back to the by-now-familiar 'mother country' on an ex-troopship, which was offering cheap passages for people boarding in Jamaica, must have sounded tempting.

Vincent Brown, who had been repatriated by the RAF in 1945, was one of twenty-two stowaways on a banana boat from Jamaica. When charged at Bristol Crown Court with travelling without paying his fare he explained:

> We had to get work or starve. The economic conditions in Jamaica are deplorable and there is absolutely no work. I am married with five children and I have been unemployed for three years. My life savings are diminished and I have parted with all my personal belongings. I have been at home empty-handed, only to see my wife and children go to bed without food. That is why I stowed away – to come to England to find work. As British subjects we think we should be given prefer-ence for work in this country over Germans and Poles.[8]

But the war had an impact in the islands far beyond that of individ-ual service, shaping Caribbean society in ways that in turn were to encourage migration. For a start, from 1939 the British West Indies was subject to the Defence of the Realm Act, ensuring the regulation of prices, rationing and censorship throughout the region. But the 1940 bases-for-destroyers agreement between the United States and Britain undoubtedly had a greater impact on everyday life. To take Trinidad as an example, for six years from 1941 the base at

Chaguaramas played host to up to 25,000 American soldiers at any one time, who brought with them money, values, styles and a way of life entirely at odds with the hierarchical, conservative and slow-moving structure of colonial society. They built roads and revolutionized transport on the island. They employed more than 25,000 of Trinidad's half a million people in construction work, and in a variety of roles at the base – paying higher than average wages so that agricultural workers and domestic servants flocked to these new employers. The craze for the 'drape shape' trousers and knee-length jackets of the zoot suit, and the money to pay for them, were inseparable from the presence of the GIs. The Americans spent their money on women, not only those working in the hugely expanding commercial sex trade, but the women they fell in love with and sometimes married – undermining long-established racial hierarchies, and cutting out the poor Trinidadian male at the same time. And then they left:

> Well the girls in town feeling bad
> No more Yankees in Trinidad
> They going to close down the base for good
> Them girls have to make out how they could.[9]

It wasn't only the women who had to make out. The Yankee dollar had only exacerbated the problems of a society that offered few opportunities for work of any kind, and far fewer for a career. To a greater or lesser extent all the islands suffered from what was delicately called a 'surplus population', the result of decades of under-investment in agriculture and little or no investment in anything else. In a 1946 survey of 11 Jamaican towns, 30,000 men and women were actively looking for jobs and could not find them – nearly 16 per cent of all those over the age of 14. By 1948 the fear was of increasing, chronic unemployment, with the return of demobbed RAF and army personnel and the shutting down of the US bases. It wasn't hard to work out why people wanted to leave. They were looking for a better break, however minimal: 'broadly speaking it was little more than a desire to survive with a greater assurance of safety'.[10]

Still, the idea of industrial Britain as an alternative to grinding rural poverty took a while to get going. Up until 1950 there were a total of only six ship journeys to Britain, carrying a mere 1,800 migrants, with

Shipping advertisements in the Jamaican *Daily Gleaner*, February 1956.

a fair proportion of those coming on the *Empire Windrush*. This was despite the fact that the Caribbean, and Jamaica in particular, had long been a traditional emigrating community, with as many as a fifth of the men in the region working seasonally in Central and South America and the United States, on projects that had ranged from the Panama Canal to agricultural work and the building of US naval and air bases. In 1950 there was a drastic reduction in the US wartime agricultural labour programme, which had employed more than 60,000 seasonal workers. The Jamaica Colony Report of 1950 laments that that year 'only 1,345' Jamaicans had been contracted for US work. Two years later the situation worsened with the McCarran–Walter Act, which slashed the quota for Caribbean migration into the States.[11]

In 1950 an enterprising Jamaican, Ferdie Martin, set up a travel agency arranging for people to fly from Kingston to New York on a chartered plane and then travel the shorter journey to Southampton by sea – all for a cost of £90 (432 West Indies dollars). Two thousand relatively well-heeled Jamaicans took advantage of this route in one year, and slowly the numbers of Atlantic crossings crept up. In 1954 just over 10,000 made the trip to Britain by sea; by 1955 it had leapt to a startling 24,500.[12] Clearly the closure of the United States seasonal labour route was having an effect, but so too was the expansion in Atlantic shipping. Ironically this was a consequence of Europeans also wanting to leave home. In 1955 61 ships left Jamaica for Britain, carrying nearly 8,000 men and women. But a further 39 ships heading for European ports (Marseilles, Genoa, Vigo) carried over 10,000 more. These were passenger steamers returning home after taking European immigrants to Latin America. Italian government schemes attempted to solve the problem of rural destitution in the south of the country through a form of assisted passage to Argentina, and to the oilfields of Venezuela; Portuguese and Spaniards left their impoverished rural smallholdings for waged work in the cities of São Paulo and Buenos Aires. To fill the otherwise empty ships on the return journey, companies offered cheaper passage (£67 was the going rate in 1955) to those prepared to travel by sea to Spain or Italy and then take a train across Europe. Even those travelling through British government recruitment schemes could take advantage of these cheaper European routes. Hazel Watson was sixteen and had been looking for work for two years when she was taken on as a domestic by a hospital in Hertfordshire, with her fare paid for by a loan from the government in Barbados; she made the journey from Bridgetown to Victoria Station, via Tenerife, Barcelona and Paris.[13]

Trips like these could take up to three weeks. Shipping companies, eager to maximize their profits, often took roundabout routes through the islands to pick up as many passengers as possible. So you might start off in Jamaica but travel south to Barbados, itself a distance of 1,200 miles, before island-hopping north again and then setting out into the Atlantic. There was of course a big difference between travelling on a 'proper liner' or on a converted troop ship. George Lamming travelled from Trinidad in April 1950 on the same boat as Sam Selvon, both keen to make their mark as writers in the metropolis, though in Lamming's case the actual decision to leave was sudden. Hearing of an imminent reduction in the number of cheap passages he scrambled together the money from three different sources and set sail. The ticket cost £50, for a bunk on a French ship, stopping at Barbados, Martinique (wildly colourful, 'like a circus', compared to the more staid British islands) and Guadeloupe. Though expensive (over £1,000 in today's money) the trip was a relative bargain, not because the company was trying to fill empty accommodation but because the ship's main function was still carrying troops. In Martinique they

picked up a battalion, 'white and black men and those who represented all the shades of brown'. They were seen off by waving relatives
and a military band, on the first leg of a journey to the war in Indo-
china. 'Those people won't see those chaps again,' said one passenger,
of the waving women on the dock. The soldiers' journey was one
result of the French policy to use overseas rather than metropolitan
troops in Vietnam, to prevent the war from becoming too unpopular
at home.[14]

The soldiers were billeted on one deck, the migrants on another –
in a large C Class dormitory, stacked with metal bunks three and
four high. The white passengers took the cabined accommodation,
and were provided with deckchairs. Another would-be writer who
left Trinidad that same year, 1950, was V. S. Naipaul, but he got to
travel in some comfort. From Port of Spain he flew north on Pan
American World Airways to New York (changing planes in Puerto
Rico). The journey provided him with a lasting image of his own
estrangement. As the plane rose above his island he saw the local
fields, waterways and settlements, 'at ground level so poor to me, so
messy', suddenly unfold itself as 'a landscape of logic and larger pattern ... So that at the moment of take-off almost, the moment of
departure, the landscape of my childhood was like something which
I had missed, something I had never seen.' In New York he spent a
night in a hotel and then took a berth on a liner to Southampton. His
trip was paid for by the British Council as part of the scholarship he
was to take up in Oxford. He wrote to his father, 'tourist class is first
class on an American liner!' But in an autobiographical sketch of the
journey he tells the story of how he was actually moved to a first-class
cabin on the liner, the recipient of a form of 'ghetto' privilege. His
ticket having been booked for him by the Consul in New York, the
shipping company had not prepared themselves for a 'coloured'
passenger – and baulked at asking any of the all-white tourist clientele to share a cabin with him.[15]

Ironically, the most stylish way to travel – by banana boat – became
a racist cliché for barbarianism in later years, in part because of the
large numbers of stowaways. The boats were small and tended to call
into smaller island ports where stems of bananas, each weighing 60–
100 lb (27–45 kg), would be loaded by hand (mainly by women,

'carrying heavy loads of bananas on their heads, running at a jog trot to earn a few extra coppers whenever a banana boat is loaded'). Wallace Collins, who stowed away at Port Antonio, Jamaica, in 1954 remembered long lines of people 'in rags' relaying stems of bananas into the hatch of the ship. There might be as many as fifty passenger cabins but sometimes no more than twelve, and the ships were popular with well-off Europeans taking Caribbean cruises. In 1951 Lucy Burnham was nineteen when she boarded an Elders and Fyffe banana boat at Port Antonio. She was headed for Amersham General Hospital in Buckinghamshire, where a friend was nursing, and where she hoped she might be taken on. 'It was a small boat with 12 passengers. I was on the boat for 14 days. I was the only black person and I found it a little strange.'[16]

When Donald Hinds boarded the SS *Auriga* in Kingston, Jamaica, on 2 August 1955, he had a choice between a bunk in a cabin for six people, at £85, or one for £75, sharing with twenty-three others. (This was around 360 West Indies dollars, when the average daily wage for semi-skilled work was 3 dollars, and for unskilled as low as 1 dollar a day.) There were 1,100 Jamaicans on board; the SS *Castel Verde*, which sailed from Kingston a couple of days later, carried the same number again. The mid-1950s saw the height of West Indian migration to Britain, with a large preponderance of Jamaicans. The docks seethed with the thousands who came to wave off their relatives, and Hinds recalls that there was no sense of sadness about leaving. He was twenty-one years old and had never had a day's work, having tried for the police force, agricultural college and store-work after leaving school. 'By this time, almost every family had a representative in "the mother country".' His friends took the view that 'it was just a matter of time before they too would be journeying to Spanish Town to get their birth certificates and lining up outside the Passport Office'. The 1,100 were augmented by 200 'small island people' as the ship docked in Santo Domingo, Barbados, Dominica, Montserrat and St Kitts. Three of the six people in his cabin were going to join their mothers – apart from Hinds himself, whose mother was in London and paid for his passage, the others were a young man of seventeen and a boy of eleven, who was to negotiate the final leg of the journey from Plymouth to Liverpool, where his parents lived, alone.[17]

In 1947 Cunard expanded its Atlantic business, commissioning five new freighters and two cargo liners. 'Getting there is half the fun!' proclaimed the brochures specially targeted at the tourist trade in Canada, the United States and Britain. For the migrants lucky enough to travel on Cunard's routes there were restaurant waiters, cabin stewards, cocktail parties and dinner dances – these last to be observed at least, if not joined in on. And the whole trip took only five days across the Atlantic. Ten years later competition among the shipping companies for the lucrative human cargo had improved conditions across the board. The Italian boats carried the majority of migrants from Jamaica, and had the worst reputation for packing the migrants in like cattle, or – a far worse analogy – like the slaves shipped from Africa on the Middle Passage.[18] By the end of the decade they had upped their game, and were offering 'Free travel bags! Free Limacol! Free Citronge!' to their guests, and promising: 'The very best by test. On board our reconditioned and luxurious ships you will now be entertained to England by our Italian jazz band.' The aim was to get close to the Cunard cruise experience:

> Travel like a tourist on a pleasure cruise for a memorable holiday trip – free lottery prizes on board to cover passage – cabins for everyone. Recreational activities round the clock. Two orchestras (including steel band and calypso), swimming pool, moving pictures, free medical care at sea (tourist class only). Trained nurses. Organized sports. Practically unlimited baggage allowance.

Migrants were good business, financing mushrooming numbers of official travel agents with their networks of sub-agents, and sub-sub-agents, all of whom took a cut. By the late 1950s the Jamaican passport office could no longer cope with demand, and new agencies grew up around the thriving business of paperwork: birth certificates could be got, forms filled in, passports secured, all for a fee. The authorities in some islands attempted to persuade intending travellers to think twice. In Trinidad, the Labour Department interviewed everyone applying for a passport who said they were going to use it to get to England, and gravely outlined the real difficulties they would face finding work and a place to live. But the letters and remittances from Britain, the advertisements for jobs in newspapers and magazines, the sunny brochures offering luxury travel, and the efforts of all the sub-agents, touts and loan sharks whose livelihoods depended on the migration business, told a different story.

Very few accounts of the slow journey from the Caribbean make much of the jazz bands and swimming pools. Instead they describe the trip as a period of adjustment and taking stock. A very large proportion of men and women travelled alone. Many of these lone women were mothers leaving their children; it wasn't unusual for them to send for them only five or ten years later, when enough money had been saved up and they had somewhere settled for them to live. The women, and later their children, tended to travel on the regular shipping lines direct to British ports, or, from the early 1960s, on BOAC flights. The cheaper ships heading for European ports carried a large percentage of single men. For three weeks they were thrown together with hundreds of others, all with nothing to do except pass the time. There were fights and disagreements, shipboard romances, gambling rings, paid sexual encounters, political discussions. Many travellers stress the fact that this was the first time they had seen other Caribbean islands, and other islanders. From going ashore to eat snails in Fort-de-France, Martinique ('I nearly vomited when I heard what I had eaten'), to rubbing shoulders with other islanders for the two- or three-week voyage, this was a first opportunity for West Indians to take the measure of their region, and its relationship to 'the mother country'. Emigration brought the islands closer together but only in the moment of departure. In 1956, for example, the building of the Montserrat airstrip facilitated regular flights to Antigua. By 1961 more than 30 per cent of the population of Montserrat had used the route to emigrate to Britain.[19]

The long journey functioned as an interregnum, a decompression chamber between a familiar past and an obscurely guessed at future. It wasn't only the huge monetary investment in the ticket, but also the timescale imposed by ship travel, which meant that for nearly all these early post-war migrants, to go abroad was to say goodbye. Few of these travellers would be able to afford a return trip for many years. Though reunions might take place in London or Birmingham, as friends and family members followed one another's travels across the ocean, the door was closed on the lives they had lived at home. The journey through space became a journey through time, as the past was locked in the Caribbean. And, apart from the small minority who had been signed up through the government recruitment schemes for the NHS and London Transport in Barbados, very few had a clear idea of what they would do in Britain. The sense of being suspended in time was reinforced by having to stare out at the same sea day after day. The passing of time was marked by the ritual of turning the clocks forward – every few days an announcement that another hour had been lost from the day – and by the creeping onset of colder weather. Somewhere in the mid-Atlantic the crew changed their uniforms from white to black and passengers went to fish their woollens out of cases and baskets. The effect of staying so long at the crossroads, being stuck in transit, was – for a remarkably large number of people – a feeling of panic on arrival, of not wanting to disembark into the unknown.

Staying on board was not an option, however. And after three weeks at sea, the ships themselves had become less-than-dignified containers of human hopes and desires: victims of weeks of drunkenness, gambling, seasickness, or plain weariness swayed around vessels now stinking of sweat, urine and vomit. None of this is visible in the photographs of West Indians arriving into Tilbury, Southampton or Waterloo in the 1950s. They have saved their smartest clothes for the moment of arrival – determined to make an impression, on the relatives come to meet them and on 'England' in general. We get some sense of what things might have looked like from the other side of the camera in Donald Hinds' memory of his first sight of England, coming in to Plymouth harbour: 'From the deck could be seen knots of white people staring back at us. I had hardly ever seen more than twelve white people together before. I had always been a member of the majority race.'[20]

The shock of arrival. Again and again emigrant memoirs relive this moment as though transfixed by this first encounter. For a start there was the cold. An advice manual entitled *Going to Britain?* warned: 'Dress for the Cold!' Men were advised to wear woollen socks and underwear, a serge suit, sturdy shoes, a woollen sweater, scarf and heavy overcoat:

> Do not put on your best clothes for landing. You will have a lot of
> waiting and you will have to carry all your luggage yourself, and it is

quite likely that you will get marks of grease or dirt on your suit or dress so make sure that you are warmly dressed in good strong working clothes, and keep your best clothes for your first party in England.

Waiting friends and relatives crowded the stations carrying coats and scarves for the new arrivals. They were joined by a raft of officials from the Colonial Office, the Salvation Army, London County Council and the British Council, detailed to meet those arriving on recruitment schemes, to pair children up with parents, or to help those without any idea of where they were going. The crowds were swelled too by men on the look-out for women, housing racketeers hunting for tenants, and groups of people just eager to see whether anyone they knew had turned up in the new consignment from the islands. British Rail closed stations when the platforms became jammed. Passengers might be set down at Olympia hours after they were due at Paddington, and filtered through to the main station in batches, substantially adding to the chaos of misunderstanding and missed rendezvous.[21]

The cold was a shock, and so was the lack of colour. Travellers commented on the drabness of everything, from the clothes, to the houses, to the food; on the difficulty of understanding ordinary English speech; on their surprise at seeing the factories which made the goods advertised at home: Ponds Cream or Wilkinson Sword razors; on the size of the cities, with their rows of houses each with its own chimney, domestic chimneys not being a feature of tropical living. One repeated memory is of assuming that each of these chimneys was attached to a small factory – a whole nation spawning industry in every street. For their part, British officials registered their own amazement. Lamming recalls that in the customs hall in Plymouth the travellers were asked to declare their resources.

> Some of the men had just enough to pay the fare from Plymouth to Paddington. The officials asked what would happen after they reached Paddington, but no-one answered with conviction. It seemed a tragic farce. England of all places, they seemed to say. They were bewildered by this exhibition of adventure, or ignorance, or plain suicide. For a while the movies seemed truer than they had vouched for, the story of

men taking ship with their last resources and sailing into unknown lands in search of adventure and fortune and mystery. England had none of these things as far as they knew. Caged within their white collars like healthy watchdogs, they studied the emigrants as though they were to be written off as lunatics.[22]

But the single greatest shock, which recurs in emigrant reminiscences with the force of a primal scene, was seeing working-class Britons. The vast majority of the new arrivals modelled their idea of British people on the colonial officials and missionaries they had encountered in the Caribbean. They had met no others. A number of women, headed for nursing training, recall the shock of 'seeing ordinary white people doing ordinary work. You were sort of made to believe that they lived in a more aristocratic way, that they didn't clean floors and they didn't sweep streets. I couldn't understand any of what they were saying!' 'It was really strange to see white people sweeping streets and doing manual jobs. I had not seen that before.' 'We had white people pick up our luggage and that was one of the first shocks because in Guyana all the white people that we came into contact with spoke like Prince Charles and they were in very high positions.' For the men it was the same. 'My images of white people were of a race which had all the good jobs and therefore lots of money. A people whose menfolk work while their women stay at home or play tennis.' The novelty of being addressed as 'sir' by station porters and train staff would wear off. But the image of the white street sweeper was so powerful because it revealed to the migrants their new situation. If white people worked in such lowly jobs, then to seek any employment at all in Britain meant challenging those who already belonged.[23]

The shock of white hands doing 'nigger work', as Lamming put it, was the beginning of learning that whiteness in Britain was not a social category – defining a hierarchy of class and power, as it did in Jamaica, Trinidad and Barbados – but a political one, defining those who belonged and those who did not. 'One doesn't realise one is coloured until one comes into white society'; 'I became black in London, not in Kingston.' In the months and years that followed, the recognition of not being white, and what that meant, would come to shape the experiences of these migrant pioneers, and dominate their recollections. It went hand in hand with another realization: that whether you came from Barbados, Trinidad, Jamaica, Antigua or Guyana, there was more connecting you with other islanders than separating you. Writing in 1960, after ten years' experience of living in London, Lamming reflected that 'most West Indians of my generation were born in England'. They were born in their twenties, to a new collective consciousness of themselves as Caribbean, and as Black, and these new political identities were to shape the immigrant experience in the years to come. Theirs was a version of the universal story in which to leave one's home and one's parents is to begin new narratives, but – as for migrants everywhere – it was a particularly uncompromising version. Leaving home is always a one-way trip. There is no home to go back to because the past has been left behind, even if we cannot help but carry it with us as story and psychic burden. Like V. S. Naipaul, who only began to grasp the contours of his island as his plane rose over Trinidad's fields, rivers and valleys, for the post-war migrant the meaning of home was understood in the moment that it was lost.[24]

2

Survivors

... in 1950 in London I was at the beginning of that great
movement of peoples that was to take place in the second half
of the twentieth century – a movement and a cultural mixing
greater than the peopling of the United States ... Cities like
London were to change. They were to cease being more or
less national cities; they were to become cities of the world,
modern-day Romes, establishing the pattern of what great
cities should be, in the eyes of islanders like myself and people
even more remote in language and culture.

V. S. Naipaul, *The Enigma of Arrival* (1987)[1]

For those alert to geographical paradoxes, post-war Britain provided
a rich sampler. As the nation appeared to shrink in terms of world-
wide power and prestige, everyday life, particularly in the cities,
began to become more, not less, international. The local cafés'
empire-grown tea, coffee and sugar were increasingly being con-
sumed, and indeed served, by empire-born men and women; the
traumatized Displaced Persons (DPs) who were admitted to asylums
or TB hospitals were as likely as not to be cared for by other refugees
from the camps, by West Indians or by the Irish. But the new international grammars which began to structure everyday life in Britain
were not all equally visible, and perhaps especially not to the immigrants themselves.

Ironically, some of the displaced Europeans had arrived via the
Caribbean, and had even formed part of the human cargo of the
Empire Windrush. Before they set out from Kingston, Jamaica, into
the Atlantic in May 1948, the *Windrush* passengers were given a tour

of the Gulf of Mexico. The ship sailed to London via Mexico, Cuba and Bermuda. Among the passengers disembarking at Tampico, Mexico, were ten Polish DPs, who were joining family members already settled there. The Mexican Poles had covered thousands of miles by the time they got to settle in North America. Deported in cattle trucks to Siberia by the Soviets in 1940 (during the time of the Nazi-Soviet pact), they had been offered a brief amnesty a year later when Germany attacked Russia and the Soviet Union became an ally of the West. From across Siberia Polish families converged on Kitab in Uzbekistan, travelling by horse-drawn sleigh from the north, by train, by cart and sometimes on foot. There the majority of the men joined the Second Corps of the Polish Army and headed for Palestine, while women and children were shipped across the Caspian Sea to a transit camp in Iran, and from there to a tented city outside Tehran. Here the evacuees were divided up and dispersed by train and ship (from Karachi) to camps in Tanzania, Uganda, Rhodesia and India. One and a half thousand were ultimately offered shelter in Mexico.

At the end of the war there were 5 million Poles scattered across the globe. Refugee agencies faced the mammoth task of tracing surviving family members, putting them in contact, and sending them off on further journeys. So that just as ten Poles left the *Windrush* in Tampico, sixty-six others joined it. They were mostly travelling to join husbands demobilized in Britain as part of the Polish Resettlement Corps. Apart from one married couple in their fifties (who were accompanied by their sixteen-year-old daughter), there were no Polish men over the age of eighteen on the ship's passenger list. Thirty-seven-year-old Bronislawa Kot had managed to survive deportations, forced labour and the journeys through Central and Southern Asia with three sons, Stanislaw, Tadeusz and Jan, who were seventeen, fifteen and thirteen years old in 1948 – though we don't know whether other children had died on the way. They were headed for Longbridge Deverill Camp near Warminster. She was typical of international shipping's Polish cargo throughout the late 1940s. Eudakia Folta, aged forty-six, travelled with her children aged twelve and fourteen to Barons Cross Camp near Leominster; thirty-year-old Pelagia Potapowicz went with her eleven-year-old son Jerzy to 46

Renown St, Plymouth. The address seems exquisitely ordinary after a journey that had lasted eight years.

The '*Windrush* Poles' were relatively few. Up to a thousand at a time might be carried on ships leaving Mombasa, Bombay, Dar es Salaam, Cape Town, Durban, Port Said or Beirut and headed for Southampton, Liverpool or Hull. Some of these ships were on the return journey from Australia, where they had deposited British subjects emigrating on the Free and Assisted Passages Scheme to the 'Old Commonwealth'. The Poles who had sat out the last years of the war in camps in India and East Africa chose Australia and, later, the United States as their eventual destinations too. Some returned to Poland. But the majority of those who had been deported to Russia in 1940, and later joined the Polish Army, chose Britain. They were officially welcomed with fanfares. As Churchill put it in February 1945 (perhaps feeling guilty about his imminent agreement with Stalin over Polish territory): 'We should think it an honour to have such . . . faithful and valiant warriors dwelling among us as if they were men of our own blood.' By 1946 the Polish Army had been restyled the Polish Resettlement Corps, with some 115,000 personnel billeted in ex-POW and army camps throughout Britain, while their scattered, surviving families painstakingly travelled back to them. And some families were newly minted. From 1944 the Polish Corps had been stationed in Italy, where it fought alongside the Eighth Army. In November 1946, when the SS *Atlantis* left Naples for Britain there were 106 Poles on board, many of them women who had served in the Polish ATS. By the time the ship docked in Southampton a week later the numbers had swelled to 114 – 8 babies had been born on board.[2]

All these global journeys had at their root geography lessons of a different kind from those learned by West Indians: the redrawing of Europe's boundaries at the end of the war. For the displaced Poles the cause of their post-war suffering could be summed up in one word: Yalta. At the Black Sea conference, in February 1945, Churchill conceded the eastern Polish territories to Soviet Russia. Many of the Poles who had been deported to Siberia now found that the towns and villages they had left were no longer part of Poland, but had been absorbed into the Ukraine and Belarus. They literally had no homes to go back to. But many former residents of western Poland also felt they could not return, fearing that the Warsaw-based government of the newly established People's Republic of Poland was little more than a vassal state of Moscow.

For these victims of geopolitics the central traumatic event of their lives was forced migration. Their memoirs and recollections do not dwell on their new lives as migrants, but return obsessively to the moment when they became irrevocably cut off from the past, definitively shut out of the place and community which had been home. The Poles who chose to settle in Britain by definition rejected the Warsaw government, but our knowledge of this fact gives no sense of the anguish which accompanied such decisions. Poles in camps throughout Germany and Italy were subjected to propaganda from all sides: Russian radio broadcasts (in Polish) argued that the Polish émigré government in London was fascist; German radio put out reminders of the Katyn massacre; in the camps run by the Polish Corps soldiers were put under pressure not to repatriate, and ostracized if they chose to. The argument was that truly patriotic Poles should wait and regroup, until they could fight the Communist take-over of Poland. As one soldier in a camp near Naples described it:

> What was I to do? Grim news reached us from the homeland. Everyday newspapers and radio broadcast news of the terror in Poland, of the waves of arrests, court cases, sentences. Those who made their way from Poland added new snippets and career gossips magnified each small detail until they achieved the grandest proportions. Drop by drop the poison of fear which remained from Italy took hold. Nobody then was in a position to establish how much truth there was in all this and how much rumour. Everyone believed the worst. In our situation the rallying cry, 'Return! The homeland is being rebuilt and needs your help' – far from reaching our hearts, missed its aim. I turned down then the chance of returning to Poland, as did thousands of others. I became an emigrant out of fear![3]

Fear lay at the heart of the decision of more than a million people caught in European DP camps not to return home after the war. It was in these camps, and in the border regions of Eastern Europe, that the human cost of what was to become known as the Cold War was felt first and hardest. As well as Poles, the camps in the four German Allied occupation zones were home to displaced Ukrainians, Yugoslavs, Estonians, Latvians, Lithuanians and Jews. Most of them had been deported from their homes as a result of Nazi occupation and sent as forced labourers to work in German agriculture and heavy industry. Their numbers were swelled by soldiers who had been forced to join the German army, others who had joined voluntarily, former Russian prisoners of war, collaborators, suspected war criminals, and tens of thousands of people (Ukrainians, Poles and Balts) who had fled by various means before the advancing Soviet armies in 1943–44.

From the Latvian countryside families had made their way by horse and cart to Riga. From there they travelled north to Talinn or west to ports on the Baltic coast, looking for a ship to take them further west.

> We left home on 4 August and moved through Latvia bit by bit until 4 December. We had a horse and cart with our belongings and even cattle. [We] had brought along flour and barley and meat, what there was and up to the time we left Latvia we managed. The sheep were killed one by one and the heifers. We sold the last two cows just before we got on the boat to go to Germany and the horses as well.[4]

Refugees told stories of camping for weeks in the forest, finding shelter in deserted houses, in abandoned hospitals and factories. At the Baltic ports they queued for days to pile on to boats sailing at night (to avoid aerial bombing) for Danzig and Gotenhafen (Gdynia), where German refugees were also queuing to flee further west. The majority took to the roads and made their way slowly west by cart, or on foot, living with the dangers of rape, hunger and disease (TB, typhus, diphtheria), often without papers, or with the wrong papers. Those who crossed into Germany before the spring of 1945 were sent to Third Reich labour camps, where families were separated for work in munitions factories, agriculture and mining. As the war in Europe ended, the journey continued for many of the refugees from Eastern Europe, whose main aim was to get out of the Soviet occupied zone, to reach a DP camp on the right side of the newly drawn border.[5]

In 1945 this flotsam totalled nearly 7 million people in Germany alone. It fell to the Allies to disentangle these populations, repatriate those who were willing to be repatriated, and find new homes for those who could not return. It was a mammoth, and expensive, task. But if the conflict had caused the crisis of displaced peoples it also provided part of the solution, in the elaborate, centralized and reasonably efficient bureaucracy that had developed to further the cause of total war. About 80 per cent of DPs did not return home after the war. Schemes allowing for their resettlement in the United States, Canada, Australia and other countries were slowly pushed though government legislatures, and by 1950 nearly all the camps were closed (though some refugees remained stuck in the European camps until 1960). Eighty-five thousand came to Britain.

The messy story of the European refugees who were accepted as workers in the years immediately following the war has never featured very highly in the history of post-war Britain. There are some obvious reasons for this. It is uncomfortable to dwell on the assumptions about class and breeding which lay behind the processes by which they were chosen – so Baltic women, 'of the same racial background to us', were taken in preference to Jews, for example. The pragmatism with which individuals were chosen to fulfil specific labour needs was masked by a rhetoric of humanitarian aid which was hardly convincing. And although the numbers were certainly not small, the outwardly straightforward manner in which the former Eastern Europeans accustomed themselves to British mores, intermarried, bought houses and settled down has meant there has been no dramatic tale of crisis to be told.[6]

But it is also the case that the European aspect to the story does not fit with Britain's wartime and post-war image of itself. This may seem paradoxical, given the British obsession with the country's pre-eminent role in vanquishing Nazi Germany. The self-congratulatory nature of popular histories of the island nation's victorious isolation is in some measure well earned. Nonetheless, it also plays into the country's sense of itself as only partly European. The rest of the European war (and, in particular, the decisive role of the Red Army in the victory over Germany) features only grudgingly in British versions, which serve to emphasize that semi-detachment from the Continent which has become a principal feature of political debate over the European Union. In 1945 it still – just about – made sense to regard Britain as an imperial power rather than just another part of Europe. The legacy of empire, and, in particular, the history of migration from the colonies and former colonies, has assumed a far greater role in debates about the British population, both at the time and since. In terms of numbers, the emphasis on post-colonial migrants' transformation of British society is clearly understandable. But the story of the DPs is important not only for what it tells us about the European migrants themselves. The systems put in place to process the DPs provided models for later immigrant schemes from Italy and elsewhere. And they revealed racial priorities that were to shape the experience of immigrants to Britain, and attitudes towards them, throughout the post-war period. Moreover as DPs were transformed by British bureaucracy into 'European Voluntary Workers' (EVWs), they became a potent source of the confusion over whether a refugee could also be a productive member of society – a confusion which continues to dog debates about immigration in Britain today. The government led a campaign to convince Britons that the DPs were the respectable poor – hard workers who would amply repay Britain's investment in them. Inviting them in was a form of long-term asset management. The counter argument was all about saving, not spending. The country was poor and the newcomers would leach precious resources from the fledging and overstretched welfare state. And anyway, hadn't Britain already done enough for Europe?

Britons were of course right to emphasize their distance from continental Europe. The principal difference in 1945 was that, apart from the Channel Islands, the country had not been occupied. There were no scores to be settled with people who had sided with collaborative regimes. Indeed, the war years had engendered forms of national reconciliation and rallying together (the myth of the people's war was not entirely a myth) rather than the ethnic pogroms and civil wars which had devastated much of the Continent. And there was one further distinction. With the exception of a few cities such as Paris and Marseilles, the rest of Europe ended the war as a series of newly mono-ethnic and mono-cultural states, while Britain had become more rather than less ethnically diverse. The annihilation of the majority of the Jews in Central and Eastern Europe, and the emigration (primarily to Palestine) of those left was the most obvious example of ethnic cleansing. But the final months of the war in Europe had provided the excuse for a series of more or less violent population transfers across the Continent. Ethnic Germans were pushed out of the East; the new borders of the Ukraine now encircled Ukrainians; those of Poland the Polish. Hundreds of thousands of these displaced people ended up in the refugee camps in Germany. It was at this point that Britain's own ethnic priorities came into play, as the ministries responsible for organizing the entry of refugees from the camps drew up a more or less explicit hierarchy of tolerable 'types'. Refugees were chosen as workers on the basis of the vague category of 'assimilability', a catch-all cover for less publicly acceptable measurements such as class and 'breeding'. Racial theories and the labour requirements of the national economy cut brutally across the humanitarian aims of the international relief agencies at work in Germany.

There were 762 camps in Germany by June 1947, run by the United Nations Relief and Rehabilitation Administration (UNRRA) and the International Refugee Organization, and funded at huge cost by the Allies. In July 1946 Britain imported 112,000 tons of wheat and 50,000 tons of potatoes, paid for by US loans, to feed to the local population of its zone in Northwest Germany. The government spent $317 million in 1947 to sustain the DPs and refugees – a level of expenditure which clearly could not be sustained. Initial plans to force repatriation on reluctant Poles and Ukrainians were abandoned in 1947 and the policy shifted to absorbing the displaced into Britain, or at least those who could prove themselves economically useful.

The systems of population management and control that had developed during the war, and above all the assumption of the government's right and duty to exercise control which went along with them, shaped the group migration schemes in the early post-war years. The war had placed government at the heart of British everyday life, and people had become accustomed, if not reconciled, to the ubiquity of government planning. The Emergency Powers Bill of 1940 had 'authorised the government to direct anyone to do anything in the national interest, to control any property and assign any industrial plant to any national end it chose'.[7] For five years the Ministries of Labour, Food, Transport and Agriculture had mobilized, requisitioned, disposed, rationed and directed as they saw fit, and now they saw fit to import workers from the European camps. Britain's schemes were some of the earliest on offer, but they were work rather than resettlement programmes – their primary aim was to solve the country's labour shortage rather than alleviate the refugee problem. The DPs offered a ready-made pool of workers for the old and increasingly unattractive industries, such as mining, textiles, agriculture, steel and iron, and for low-grade work in hospitals, especially TB hospitals and mental institutions. Oddly enough domestic service was also classed as an essential industry at this point, and numbers of young female refugees found themselves scrubbing floors in large private houses as their route out of the camps.

Perhaps the most important sense in which the war impacted on European migration to Britain was by bringing the country to the brink of bankruptcy. By the end of the war the country was spending more than half its Gross National Product on the conflict. The debt to the United States under the Lend-Lease scheme stood at $650 million; this was written off under the new terms of the 1946 Anglo-American Loan for $3.75 billion, at 2 per cent interest – a loan which was eventually paid off in 2006. At the same time the government was committed to vastly increased levels of spending on social services and social security. Money was needed for the physical reconstruction of the cities, the provision of homes, the rebuilding of factories. But for this the country needed to produce, and industrial manpower was at an all-time low.

According to some early post-war reports, Britain's post-war recovery was being put at risk by attitude – there were workers but they weren't sufficiently willing. Women who had got used to higher wages and better working conditions in munitions factories during the war had no intention of returning to the old mills, without canteens or proper toilets, to work for less money. Men living in the Midlands weren't about to move to Wales or Yorkshire for the privilege of working in the mines. The government made various attempts to persuade and cajole people into work, including the gloriously nicknamed 'Spivs and

A Ministry of Labour advertisement published in *Wife and Home*, the 'Married Woman's Magazine', in 1947.

Drones Order', intended to deal with 'parasites', 'idlers', 'slackers' and 'social limpets' (street-traders, buskers, bookmakers, people who worked in night-clubs, or didn't work at all) and get them into productive employment. This attempt at industrial conscription followed on from the Control of Engagement Order, brought into force in 1947, which required that all appointments had to go through official employment agencies, and designated some industries as 'essential', meaning that workers could be compelled to take up those vacancies, particularly in mining and agriculture: 'To overcome this post-war trouble is a task so heavy that every man and woman who can do so must take a share in the national effort. All our resources, human or material, must be fully devoted to essentials in this time of emergency.'[8]

Then there was the attempt to get women into the factories and hospitals. The 'Recruitment of Women Campaign' ran through much of 1947, and was spectacularly unsuccessful. There were advertisements targeting women on bus panels, cinema slides and in film trailers. Ads taken out in the national press insisted:

> We can't get on without the women. And that means YOU
>
> We can't win back prosperity without the women's help. Our *man-power* is not sufficient. Britain is up against it. Try and free yourself for work, whole-time or part-time. In the next big effort, you can be one of the women who turn the tide of recovery.

Women were hailed in the streets by loud-speaker vans, and signed up on the spot – but then failed to turn up for work, in large numbers. Part of the problem was that many women with school-aged children could only work between 9 and 3 o'clock, which didn't fit with most shifts. There was a move to bring in evening shifts to get more women inside the factory gates. But this did little to deal with the real issue, which was that women had no interest in these jobs in the first place. The campaign was doomed to failure 'because no one had perhaps previously realised the depth of women's feelings in general on certain points. The truth probably is that, with many women, the strain of the past few years has been even greater than one could reasonably have been expected to suspect. One outlet for their feelings is to express disgust at the present campaign.'[9]

Women were disgusted, and judging by the patronizing tone of much of the publicity they were right to be. For a start, it was annoying to be asked to work at the same time as men were campaigning for shorter hours. They were not being offered equal jobs or pay but were being directed to 'women's jobs' that men do not 'take to', and paid less. The policy makers argued that this needed to be explained 'gently' in order to 'cause women to see things in a proper light and search their consciences more'. So George Isaacs, the Minister for Labour and National Service after 1945, put out a broadcast in June 1947 in which he patiently explained he only wanted six months' or a year's work out of women. Moreover, 'we are not asking women to do jobs usually done by men. During the war women showed that they were able to do anything from chimney-sweeping to boiler-stoking. Now the jobs are in work which it has always been usual for women to do.'[10]

None of this made an impression, and it appeared that the situation was only going to get worse. The school-leaving age rose from fourteen to fifteen in the spring of 1947, taking an entire cohort (370,000 young people) out of the work force with a stroke of the pen. The fall in the birth-rate during the 1930s was to have an effect on the working population from the late 1940s onwards. And the fear was that the new social insurance schemes would mean that people were simply less desperate for a wage, and so less willing to put up with the most unpleasant jobs.

As early as 1946 the Cabinet Foreign Labour Committee argued that the answer to injecting 'new blood into our economic system' was to get it from the European DP camps. After all, the great advantage of migrant labour was that it could be directed to where it was needed, at least for a time:

> I suggest that we should first turn our attention to the possibility of utilizing the services of bodies of foreign labour which are already in this country ... secondly we should consider the desirability of increasing further our resources of manpower by permitting and if necessary encouraging the entry of special categories of workers. Our primary need is no doubt for unskilled workers for the unattractive industries, but there may also be a case to be made for a certain intake of skilled labour.[11]

Arguing that 'there is no danger for years to come that foreign labour will rob British workers of their jobs', a government *Economic Survey* announced in January 1947 the intention to employ, first of all, the Poles who had been with the Polish armed forces stationed in Britain during the war (now demobbed into the Polish Resettlement Corps), and then expand to the displaced persons. And the need appeared to be clear enough to those still employed in the 'unattractive' industries. As one Bradford mill-worker recalled:

> Most of the women or whatever had gone into munitions or in the Forces or they'd got married. A lot of the fellows had been in the Forces and they didn't feel inclined to go back, you see, into the textile. They thought, well, I'll try something else ... that's when we got these what we used to call D.P.s. Displaced Persons. They'd neither

country, home nor nowt, you know. They'd been in these camps in Germany and places and they came.[12]

Of the 85,000 European refugees who arrived in Britain between July 1947 and the end of 1951, 8,000 were Ukrainian prisoners of war who had been drafted into the German army and brought to Britain from Italy, avoiding repatriation to the Soviet Union. Most of the workers were 'hand-picked' by Ministry of Labour officials who travelled to the British, American and French zones, looking for young (the age limits were 18–50 for men, 18–40 for women), single, physically fit persons willing to do manual labour. Once the plan was decided on there was a rush to get in early and have the pick of the 'best' on offer, and avoid those whose health had been broken by years of ill-treatment, starvation and disease. And there was a rush inside the camps too:

An official from UNRRA tallies refugees by nationality at a camp near Klagenfurt in Germany, 1946.

And they said, 'Who wants to go to England?' They was queuing *night and day ... Everybody. Night and day*, queuing, not just in day because if you go on you missed your place, and thinking 'Oh, if I miss that place I never go', they sit down and sleep and waiting, you see.[13]

Kathryn Hulme, who supervised a number of DP camps in Germany's American Zone (one of which catered for 20,000 refugees – a small town), recalled the scramble to try to qualify for the rival recruiting schemes as at once heartbreaking and humorous:

The camp bulletin boards listing all the current avenues of escape made you think of some kind of macabre stock market that dealt in bodies instead of bonds. The DPs read the job offerings and rushed to qualify. When, for example, we posted the advance news that Canada would accept qualified tailors, everyone who had ever sewed on a pants' button was a master tailor. Our DP nurses with diplomas from Leningrad, Warsaw and Kiev swore they had done a bit of tailoring before they studied nursing. Ace mechanics in our garages dropped their tools and lined up at our employment office to try to have their work-tested card changed from mechanic to tailor.[14]

The newly stateless refugees and forced labourers were 'a new kind of debris of modern warfare', one with which we have become all too familiar in the years since 1945. But in order to make them acceptable to British public opinion they were represented not as refugees but as productive workers, people who would be useful to post-war reconstruction. Leaflets handed out to people living near the reception and holding camps insisted that the Poles and other Europeans were 'just like us', all they wanted was a home of their own, but they were willing to work for it. The official line was that the newcomers deserved help to help themselves; they were neither going to leach resources from the hard-pressed government social services, nor take the jobs British people wanted. A *News Chronicle* article from July 1947 was typical in its attempt to square the circle between neediness and independence: 'England means an end to their wandering: All they ask is work.' The article outlined the terrible histories the EVWs had lived through, and insisted they were not scroungers: 'How they pray for the privilege of working to keep themselves.' This claim lay in considerable tension with the worries in official circles that it was going to be hard to shake the refugees out of their characteristic 'displaced person's mind'. This was a mind apparently rotten with apathy and lack of initiative. After years of lack of freedom, they had lost the spirit of self-reliance. They would wait around for help from official sources rather than help themselves. The aim of various education and training schemes was to turn them into 'responsible and independent members of the civilian community'. There was even a national hierarchy for self-sufficiency. It was apparently hardest to get the Poles to face up to their new responsibilities as, unlike the DPs from Germany who had opted for England as a way out of the camps, the Poles had got stuck in England by default, and had no investment in their new futures.[15]

None of the official paeans to the virtues of Eastern Europeans made much impression on public opinion. A 1948 article in the *Daily Mirror*, entitled 'Let Them Be Displaced', offers some insight into the prevailing mood:

> In taking Displaced Persons wholesale we have had a bad deal. Too many are living or working in some dubious way. Some, no doubt are in the Black Market. They live on our rations – and live very well. They add to our discomfort and swell the crime wave. This cannot be tolerated. They must now be rounded up and sent back.[16]

Many Britons viewed the German camps as breeding grounds for black-marketeering, corruption, quarrelling, spying and violence. In September 1945 a *Picture Post* article on the camps was titled 'Report on Chaos': the piece focused on vice and anarchy as much as suffering. To add to this were the conviction that Poles (in particular) were fascists (a conviction fanned as much as possible by the British Communist Party), residual anti-Catholicism, and a belief that all these foreigners must be depriving British workers of homes and jobs. TUC opposition to the bulk recruitment schemes had only been overcome with assurances that foreign workers could not compete against the domestic work force. Their contracts stipulated a minimum period of work for the designated employer – usually three years – and included a 'deportation clause' if they breached the regulations. One miserable young Polish woman, who found the isolation unbearable in her Oldham mill, was deported back to Germany in 1950 because she attempted suicide. Nonetheless the fear persisted that employers could undercut established pay and conditions by use of cheap 'Fascist Poles', 'collaborating' EVWs and 'enemy' Italians and Austrians. Much of the anger focused on the favourable conditions in which it was believed the Poles lived (since they were the largest group) and, particularly, the idea that people were getting extra rations and sending food parcels to Poland. In Monica Dickens' 1961 novel *The Heart of London*, the Poles, along with 'coloured' people, the Greeks and the Maltese, are certainly not thought of as hard workers by the white inhabitants of Notting Hill. Dickens describes the locals' 'automatic addendum to any mention of the Poles': 'them Poles that come over to get their mothers buried on the National Health – taking the bread from honest people's mouths'. In fact there was a minor crisis over burial space in 1947, with small parishes situated near large camps occupied by ailing Europeans complaining that because of the high death rate in the camps 'the ground is being occupied by Poles'. The problem of scarce resources was not even solved by death, apparently.[17]

The question was whether the newcomers were the deserving poor, who could be turned into responsible citizens if given the chance, or the irredeemably corrupt apples that would rot the whole barrel. It was a question which went to the heart of post-war welfare state planning. War had transformed the role of the modern state, but also the expectations which were placed upon it. The fundamental belief behind social planning was that the physical and moral condition of the nation's citizens was the responsibility of government. Arguments in favour of public intervention in the health of the nation – informed by race theory, eugenics and theories of degeneration – all fed into debates about population growth, and environmental and occupational well-being. It was these arguments that led eventually to the system of national insurance, the National Health Service, pensions and social security. The idea that people's health and happiness were the government's concern was a relatively new one, but it quickly created an expectation that citizens would be looked after – through both social service and social security. And in so doing it brought into play the debate about resources that has dogged 'welfare' ever since. National Insurance, by definition, meant that health stood for the nation's health, not other people's; security meant security for

EVWs receive their first pay at a hostel near Lowton, Lancashire.

British citizens, not foreigners. Welfare state planning helped define the distinction between British people and everyone else. If the DPs were to be accepted they needed to be thought of as givers, not takers, and crucially as people who wanted to and 'could' become British. It was important then for the government to rebut, robustly, complaints that Britain was getting 'most of the scum' from the camps, 'the cream' having already been skimmed off by other countries. They did this by arguing for a process of moral rehabilitation. It was possible to turn the 'slaves of the Nazi regime' into 'labourers suitable for democracies' by encouraging self-help and hard work. The DPs were assigned work inside the German camps not only in order to help their rescuers and defray the cost of their upkeep, but because labour would teach them how to behave in a democracy.[18]

Moral and physical health were at the forefront of these debates about immigration and citizenship in part because of the fear of the money running out. It was important to be able to prove that everything had been done to screen out the sick, the old, the infirm, the pregnant and the lazy so that the EVWs would not prove a drain on the country's coffers, but would instead contribute to them – through paying taxes, but primarily through doing the essential but unpleasant jobs that British people were unwilling to take on, many of them, ironically, in the National Health Service itself. But the health and physical condition of the refugees was an issue too – at least as far as officialdom went – for the future population of the country.

Successful interviewees passed through a series of medical tests before they got the final go ahead. The British tests were evidently not as rigorous as those suggested by the Canadian industrialist who arrived in a DP camp in Germany looking for one hundred single Roman Catholic girls for his spinning mill in a small Quebecois town – the proviso being that they had to be virgins. At least one young Latvian woman was working in a mill in Oldham before the Ministry of Labour knew she was pregnant. ('The doctor asked me when my last period was. Well, I knew then that I was pregnant but I didn't tell him. I just lied and said I was regular as clockwork.') The symbolism of the first scheme's name, 'Balt Cygnet', bringing young women from Latvia, Lithuania and Estonia specifically to work in textile mills and as hospital domestics, had a peculiarly creepy ring to it – as though the ugly ducklings rescued from the camps would turn into quasi-English swans in the Lancashire mills and the isolated wards of TB hospitals and asylums. It was remembered by one refugee as 'that white swan thing'.

Balts were the first choice for the schemes, as they were considered 'more easily assimilated than other foreign immigrants'. Baltic women were 'an exceedingly good type of woman', 'of good appearance', 'scrupulously clean', 'exceptionally healthy and fit'. In a 1947 Parliamentary debate the EVWs in general were described as 'ideal immigrants', 'first-class people, who if let into this country would be of great benefit to our stock', whose love of freedom signalled 'the spirit and stuff of which we can make Britons'. It was a market in bodies, a piece of social and demographic engineering in which British officials aimed to solve both the labour and population crisis by controlling the entry of pure, clean, strong Europeans. In practice the DPs were as likely as not to be hungry and dirty, with loose teeth, scabies, lice, TB, and quite often pregnant. Ironically the premium placed on 'good stock' meant that the hierarchy of those deemed most easy to assimilate into British society mirrored the system of racial stratification for German forced labour. This parallel was uncomfortably evident at the time. The British system was 'a slave market . . . horribly reminiscent of another similar offer made by the Germans not very long ago'. 'We all had armbands in national colours.' The preference for Balts over Poles and Ukrainians, who were judged as more dirty and less civilized, was in effect a preference for what was vaguely assumed to be a more educated, middle-class type over a rural peasantry. Nationality was coded as class.[19]

The fear of miscegenation lay not very far below the surface of these comments. In the early post-war years Britain was gripped by a population panic, a fear that unless the birth-rate could be hiked up it was only a matter of time before the country's labour force must shrink irretrievably below acceptable military and economic levels. But, as the report of the 1949 Population Commission spelled out only too plainly, at the same time the government had better be choosy about who it let in: 'Immigration on a large scale into a fully established society like ours could only be welcomed without reserve if the immigrants were of good human stock and were not prevented by their religion or race from intermarrying with the host population and becoming merged with it.'[20] Where religion might present a barrier to intermarriage it is hard to see how that could apply to race, but the crucial phrase here is 'becoming merged' – intermarriage was alright so long as it was invisible, between Europeans.

The officials who formulated these policies, and the men and women who operated them on the ground, were taking common-sense views of the conditions for assimilation; language proficiency, a favourable social environment and everyday contact with British people would all help to bring about mutual understanding. 'We want them to be "Englishized" as soon as possible', explained one official who objected to 'labelling' the EVWs with uniforms and badges. Members of the Women's Voluntary Service who organized tea parties, clothes sales and language lessons, explained: 'What we wanted was to help foreigners see with our own eyes.'[21]

Did the British immigration planners get it right, managing the arrival of the newcomers in such a way that they could effectively disappear? Thirteen years later the sociologist Sheila Patterson attempted to assess attitudes to immigrants in South London, on a scale of relative acceptability. While West Indians and the Irish were, apparently, considered barely respectable, other white strangers had fared better:

> The Cypriots, Maltese and Italians are often held to infringe the criteria of neatness and quietness, but most are thought to live respectable family lives, or at least to keep themselves to themselves. This also applies to the Poles who, after a doubtful start, have earned respect as conformists and solid householders interested in conserving and even improving their property.[22]

The memory of that doubtful start has long faded. The Second World War Poles who settled in Britain are remembered, when they are remembered at all, as the men of the Free Polish Army. In fact three-quarters of Poles who came to Britain had endured Soviet deportation. The far-more-numerous ranks of these displaced, the men and women who were at the time regarded with suspicion, not admiration, by their neighbours, have disappeared from view. But this had little to do with what the planners judged to be qualities of assimilability. Their policies reduced the identity of the refugees, as far as possible, to their status as bodies: bodies that would work productively, and in time merge with the existing population. The clash between the attitudes of the policy makers and the DPs' own sense of themselves – fiercely protective of their nationalities, and their sense of a homeland – could hardly have been greater. And in fact marriage between single female Europeans and English men proved to be quite rare. The DPs tended to marry each other. As one local journalist discovered as early as 1950, the new arrivals made their own worlds:

> The first home I visited belongs to a Polish married couple ... They spend virtually nothing on tobacco and liquor. They do not invest in football pools. They save pennies by always walking to work. They never go to dances, hardly ever to the cinema. They save on food by preparing large solid meals ... and refusing to be tempted to cakes and other British luxuries. The husband showed me a huge packet of bread sandwiches. 'This I eat at work,' he said. 'You English eat a bit of this, then a bit of that. In five minutes – pouf!': and he sucked in his cheeks to indicate gaunt hollowness and tapped his stomach with a

shake of the head. I visited another house, bought this time by a Czech couple ... She spends £4 10s a week on food. 'Food comes before everything,' she said. They smoke too – eighty cigarettes a week among three of them. 'If I buy twenty I smoke twenty,' said the husband. They walk to work, a fifteen minute journey, rarely go to the pictures, never dance, have had one bottle of schnapps – to celebrate the husband's birthday – in eighteen months. Both houses were neat and clean. Having bought them, these foreigners are now saving again to furnish them ... Oldham people look on, in uncomprehending amazement.[23]

But perhaps the single most important factor in allowing them to be absorbed into a background of respectability and conformity was that the tide of European refugees was finite. Once the camps were emptied and the Cold War borders secured, there would be no new arrivals from the Continent. Britain had fulfilled its promise to a selection of the refugees, and on its own terms.

3

Villagers

Every day he hears about the metropolis. The name of the city changes. It is all cities, overlaying one another and becoming a city that exists nowhere but which continually transmits promises. These promises are not transmitted by any single means. They are implicit in the accounts of those who have already been to a city. They are transmitted by machinery, by cars, tractors, tin-openers, electric drills, saws. By ready-made clothes. By the planes which fly across the sky. By the nearest main road. By tourist coaches. By a wrist watch. They are there on the radio. In the news. In the music. In the manufacture of the radio itself. Only by going to this city can the meaning of all the promises be realized.

John Berger, *A Seventh Man* (1973)[1]

The first migrants from any community have to create the place to which they will belong – one pitched precariously between the home they have left and the place of arrival. The immigrant is by definition an outsider, or at the very least a newcomer, not yet integrated into the 'host' community, perhaps never to be integrated. At the same time the immigrant is someone who has left somewhere. The most fundamental thing about him or her is that he or she is not-at-home. One of the striking things about this displacement is that the consciousness of loss doesn't appear to depend on distance. Irish migrants, for example, often left home on a whim. They could (and often did, to the consternation of their employers) return home whenever they felt like it. But neither the easy journey, nor the fact that friends and neighbours were all taking it, seems to have lessened the wrench at parting.

John B. Keane left Ireland in January 1952:

> When I boarded the train at Listowel that morning it seemed as if everyone was leaving. It was the same at every station along the way. Dun Laoghaire, for the first time, was a heartbreaking experience – the goodbyes to husbands going back after Christmas, chubby-faced boys and girls leaving home for the first time, bewilderment written all over them, hard-faced old-stagers who never let on but who felt it worst of all because they knew only too well what lay before them . . . All around us as we left Dun Laoghaire, there was drunkenness. The younger men were drunk – not violently so but tragically so, as I was, to forget the dreadful loneliness of having to leave home. Underneath it all was the heartbreaking, frightful anguish of separation . . .[2]

Stories of post-war migration from the West Indies stress hopes and expectations – hopes of a prosperous new life that for the most part were to be cruelly crushed. By contrast Irish emigration, if we are to believe the written accounts, took place in an atmosphere of dread, fear, or resignation. A few years later John Healy described much the same scene on the 'emigrant train' out of Mayo:

> The train would pull into Charlestown to a crowded platform. It had travelled about 30 miles from Sligo through Collooney, Coolaney, Tubbercurry and Curry and the young girls who had left these towns and villages were still crying as the train came to a stop . . . The Guard's door slamming shut was the breaking point: like the first clatter of stones and sand on a coffin, it signalled the finality of the old life. They clutched and clung and wept in a frenzy.[3]

The moment of departure signalled 'the finality of the old life', and no amount of repetition made it any easier to bear. From that moment onwards home would never again be part of everyday experience. It had become the past, and variations on nostalgia (or sometimes rejection) would become the only way to relate to it. From these accounts it is clear that ordinary migrants understood very well that they were entering a limbo between the community they left behind and a future of non-belonging. In fact it may have been precisely because the experience was so common that it was so painful. As the play-wright Tom Murphy put it, of another west-of-Ireland train station: 'I think the most important feature of my growing up was the emi-gration from the family. Somebody always seemed to be arriving or going away. A lot of emotion centred around the little railway station in my home town of Tuam.'[4]

For the DPs and other forced migrants the past was, quite literally, another country. The places they had left in Poland or the Ukraine became lost geographical territories, swept away by redrawn borders, no longer visible on any map. At the same time the idea of the national territory was central to their sense of themselves – they did not think of themselves as DPs but as Poles, or Ukrainians, or Latvians in Britain. Home was kept safe by being recreated in the imagination, and necessarily so. But something similar happened to the voluntary migrants, the large numbers of rural poor who travelled from Ire-land, India, Pakistan and Southern Europe to make good in the industrial north. The irony was that they left home in order to make enough money to send it back home and eventually to return them-selves. To capitalize, as John Berger put it, on the promises that the metropolis had to offer. They were investing in a future which, for the most part, they understood as an extension of the past, in the homestead, and village and small town back home. But in doing so they were to lose that intimate contact with the home they wanted to preserve.

The term 'economic migrant' implies a criticism, or a qualification. At the very least it places the migrant somewhere near the bottom of a hierarchy of deserving, some way below the asylum seeker and the refugee. Economic migrants, so the argument goes, have choices which those fleeing war and devastation do not; they are propelled by a desire to better themselves, and the very fact that concepts such as 'choice' and 'desire' form part of their stories appears to disqualify them in terms of 'need'. If a migrant wants more than life currently offers him, or her, then almost by default he needs it less than others, the really desperate, who are simply grateful to be given safety and the means of survival. Distinctions like these thread their way right through attitudes towards migrants and refugees who have made their way to Europe, from the Second World War to the present day. They are far from completely bogus. It obviously makes sense to acknowledge the difference between a person fleeing war or torture and a person fleeing poverty. Nonetheless the category of the economic migrant plays fast and loose with the concept of survival. To castigate the man who chooses to abandon his uneconomic smallholding (or, in the present day, his poorly paid seasonal job) in order to earn money abroad is to imply that bare survival is sufficient for some people, though not for others. In this view the economic migrant is someone who should accept his lot, and resist the small greedy voice inside his head which whispers that he could have what other people have if he only relocates to the thriving industrial economies of the north. Without denying the differences it should be possible to acknowledge that the person whose home offers no viable economic future, and the one whose home has been destroyed by war, are both bidding for survival. In the late 1940s the British government attempted to persuade a war-weary populace that the refugees from the Continental camps would be economically productive members of their new society – they were to be welcomed not as victims but as workers, and people who sought to make a living. And it is just as correct to think of those who arrived as workers, the economic migrants from Asia, Ireland and Southern Europe, as refugees from poverty.

The two groups were processed in much the same way, through a system of highly bureaucratic group employment schemes, involving the British government and industrial delegates who dispensed permits, carried out medical checks, and ran the transit camps and hostels. The bones of this bureaucracy had been created during the war, and with the Irish in mind. Ireland was officially regarded in Britain as a reservoir of labour for the British war effort. According to the formal MI5 report on Ireland, produced in 1945, 'So great was the need for this Irish labour before and during the Battle of Britain in 1940 that without it the aerodromes, so desperately needed, could not have been built, and great as the need for Irish labour was then, it increased throughout the war as the calls on our own manpower became greater.' Girls went into service in Grimsby, Chester and Swansea, joined the land army in Scotland, Lincolnshire, Warwickshire and Yorkshire, or found nursing or factory work in Liverpool,

Huddersfield and London through advertisements in Irish news-papers. Men went harvesting in Scotland, worked in arms factories in the Midlands, the Ford factory in Dagenham, and the construction works in East Anglia and Hampshire. MI5 estimated that there were up to 120,000 workers from 'Eire' in Britain and Northern Ireland during the war, including women. The Northern Irish government calculated in turn that about 65,000 of its workers had transferred to England during the war – 9,000 of them women. The writer Peadar O'Donnell, who spent some time in England between 1942 and 1944 investigating conditions for Irish workers as the Fianna Fáil govern-ment's Advisor on Migratory Labour, estimated in 1945 that there were a quarter of a million Irish workers on war contracts, in add-ition to seasonal migrants.[5]

Most of these workers were hired on group contracts, in a system of direct recruitment by British firms that continued right up until 1953. Stories of walking to Dublin from as far away as Kilkenny or Carlow, of selling a bicycle, or a shotgun, in order to afford the fare, of borrowing money for the journey on the promise of a return from first wages, all slowly faded as the traffic in Irish labour became cen-trally funded and managed during the war. One young farmer's son who left Kerry in 1946, recalled:

> Well I got fed up with home and I wanted to travel. I didn't see much of a future at home and everybody was coming to England, they were all going to the labour exchange, all signing on to come over here for jobs. So I decided to do it; and I came and I was sorry after!
>
> I went to the labour exchange at home and signed on. That was for a job in England, and you had to take the job they gave you . . . Your fare was paid; the only thing you had to get was a permit. Well, you'd get your photograph taken and went to the police station. You had to stay in your job for so long, you couldn't leave when you came over here and you had to report to the police station with your travel permit.[6]

Young men could be interviewed for a Civil Engineering Federation job in their local employment exchange. Once a job was secured and a travel permit arranged by the agent through the Permit Office (a process which took about six weeks), the fare to Dublin was forwarded to the prospective migrant. Men and women travelled by bus or train to Dublin to receive their papers, if necessary to lodge overnight in the city (paid for by the Ministry), and eventually to embark at Dun Laoghaire. The process was streamlined for minimum hassle.

At best this made for a trouble-free passage; at worst it could be dehumanizing. In 1944 H. L. Morrow – who had left London in the summer of 1940 – took a return trip on the mail boat:

> Steerage passengers still cattle-herded in tin-roofed quayside shed. Lumpy luggage in brown-paper parcels, cracked fibre suitcases. Shiny-faced pippin-cheeked girls and youths. One or two whey-faced middle-aged men. All – or nearly all – hatless. All with coat-collars upturned – like umbrellas blown out by the wind. Wretched-looking. The song knocked out of them. As they stumbled on board noticed why: Each wore a label – like stock cattle. 'British Factories,' it said, simply. As if on their way to be spam-canned.[7]

The experience of being treated as livestock, bid for at market, intensified as workers were hired in ignorance of their future jobs and destinations. In effect they were reduced to labour power, to their status as able bodies. The application process made a distinction between skilled and unskilled labour, but agreements struck in Ireland were often ignored once 'on the other side'. As one TD (Teachta Dála, a member of the Irish Dáil) protested, 'people find overseers going through the ranks of our people as they are landed at Holyhead and cutting them out in different classes according to their physical build. Men who appear to be strong and able to do difficult work have been packed off to do underground work in aerodromes and air-factories and things like that', despite the fact that they may have been hired for skilled work.[8]

Like the EVWs the physical health and stature of the labourers became a medical issue. Given the degree of poverty and malnutrition, and the slum living conditions of some of the workers, there were fears in Britain over the spread of infectious diseases. Alarmed by outbreaks of typhus and typhoid in Ireland in 1942, the British Ministry of Labour instituted medical examinations at Holyhead. Travellers who were found to be carrying infection were returned on the next boat to Dun Laoghaire. By the end of 1942 the health officials at Holyhead were carrying out two to three hundred examinations a day (and around a thousand at Christmas time) although they were only processing travellers from three infected counties – Galway, Sligo and Mayo. There was panic over the numbers; they needed more personnel, towels, nurses' uniforms, linen bags for storing possessions, floor coverings, and they faced particular difficulties in processing women, for whom they had no separate facilities and no female medical officers. Officials planned a full-scale hostel, stretching over two and a half acres, with a receiving and disposal hall, cleansing unit, dining hall and day room, dormitories and washrooms, administrative block, dispersal block, laundry block and staff quarters. In the end these elaborate plans were radically scaled down due to fears over 'what the Eire authorities will think':

> we have throughout made it clear that we do not mind how flimsy the construction is, provided the accommodation reaches a reasonable standard and the place does not look too much like a concentration camp. As you know, the incoming Irish workers represent a cross section of different classes of the population of varying industrial and social standards.

Class and the voluntary nature of Irish war work lay at the heart of the problem. It might be alright to hose down an Irish-speaker from the far West, or a lad from Dublin's north side, but what about people with higher 'social standards'? One excited health official recounted with glee the efficient manner in which 1,495 Italian prisoners of war had been deloused at Prince's Parade, Liverpool, on 29 June 1943. The vessel berthed at 11.15, with the first party of POWs landing at 13.00. They were stripped by 13.15 and thereafter delousing was kept up at a rate of 480 per hour: 'Amount of soap used: 25 lbs; amount of water used, 4000 gallons. Bathing complete at 18.00. Vessel left again 20.15.' Couldn't we deal with the Irish in the same way, he asked?[9]

But they could not. The Irish were not prisoners but volunteers, making a choice as individuals to work in Britain. In doing so they were becoming part of a highly regimented and bureaucratic state system in which choice – where to work, what to wear, what to eat, how to travel – had become less and less part of everyday experience.

So much was to be expected in wartime Britain, in which almost every aspect of everyday life was regulated and controlled, even if it was important that it didn't look like 'a concentration camp'. But as travel restrictions eased after the war people were increasingly unwilling to subject themselves to being 'processed' through the official channels, and especially wary of the medical checks they involved. They could instead answer any of the many thousands of advertisements in Irish papers: 'Opportunities for Girls to Work in London Factory and Canteen . . . Interviews and medical examination will be held in Dublin'; 'Convent Hospital, large English town – Domestic Assistant wanted. All Irish staff. Radio and Television. £4 weekly. Fare paid. Met at Boat.' Or they could simply travel over to try their luck on the building sites and in the factories on their own. The jobs they shunned, along with British workers, were partly filled by the refugees from the European camps, partly by Punjabi villagers, funnelled into the foundries and mills of the Midlands, Lancashire and Yorkshire, and partly by labourers from 'the defeated nations', including the countrymen and cousins of those lice-infested Italian POWs.[10]

It is true that the impact of Britain's wage economy was imagined in very different ways in Ireland, Italy and India. Throughout the 1950s Irish men and women left their villages and smallholdings for work in London and the Midlands in increasing numbers. Nearly a sixth of the total population of the Republic – and a vastly greater proportion of the working population – was living in Britain by 1961. Irish officialdom, particularly in its more clerical and conservative manifestations, was unsympathetic to the migrants, complaining that they were allowing themselves to be seduced by the 'lure' of modernity, and were turning their backs on the traditional rural, Catholic ideal which was meant to define the independent Irish state. From this perspective industrial England stood for moral and economic corruption, and capitalism was a form of godlessness. The fundamental reason for this hard line was panic over a population that was dwindling so fast that the future survival of the 'race' itself appeared to be in question. There was no comparable form of anxiety in either the Punjab or Southern Europe, both areas which were deemed to be suffering from too many rather than too few people. Indeed migration from Calabria was actively encouraged by the Italian government, which collaborated with the British Ministry of Labour's 'Official Italian Scheme', designed to transport labourers from Europe's rural south to the mines and factories of its industrial north. It was a way of offloading 'excess' population at no cost. It was only in Ireland that emigrants had to battle a romantic discourse of rural poverty, and their own confused feelings of guilt at leaving a country that failed to provide for them. But deep fears that the integrity of families and communities would be destroyed by migration were almost universal, and almost universally true. The cash which was to save the peasant smallholding might as easily sweep it away, along with the traditional moral and religious values on which it was built. Yet there was no future at all without it.

The Official Italian Scheme began in 1949, aimed at recruiting workers for foundries, textile mills and the rubber and pottery industries. The supply of Latvians, Lithuanians, Estonians and Ukrainians recruited from the German DP camps was running out, and the British Ministry of Labour decided to widen the net to members of the 'defeated nations' – Germans, Austrians and Italians – although at least some officials did not consider them equally viable as future Britons.

> I have been given to understand that the order of intake of foreign labour is approximately Poles, Balts, Ukrainians, other DPs, Volksdeutsche, Italians and finally Germans [ex-POWs]. I have never been at all happy about the proposal to take in male Italians in preference to Germans ... The Home Office experience suggests that Italian immigrants do not, generally speaking, make any valuable contribution to the economy of the country,

complained one Home Office official to his Ministry of Labour counterpart.[11] Such worries were easily overridden, given how keen the Italian government appeared to be to ship its rural poor out. Local labour exchanges were encouraged to advertise foreign jobs from the late 1940s onwards. The government built five 'Emigration Centres' across the country (in Milan, Genoa, Messina, Turin and Naples – most migrants heading for Britain were processed through a former military compound in Naples), dedicated, as the historian Michele Colucci puts it, to 'enabling the highest possible number of people to

leave Italy in the shortest possible time'. The centres offered administrative facilities to foreign delegates; officials from the British Ministry
of Labour were stationed in Naples until 1951, and long afterwards
individual companies were still using them to recruit and process
their foreign workers. By 1955, 92 per cent of male Italian immigrants
were recruited by the London Brick Company for its Bedfordshire
works from Apulia and Campania via the Naples centre.[12]

The journey started with a notice in the labour exchange:

> In 1955 I was working in my uncle's wood firm in the province of
> L'Aquila. Then the emigration adverts arrived. My stepmother told me
> that in England according to statistics there were seven women for
> each man. So me and my brother went to the job centre and applied.[13]

The next step was to borrow money, and take the long and unfamiliar journey to the nearest Emigration Centre, where many hopefuls
got stuck. The vetting process was nothing if not thorough. The task
of the doctors and nurses was to flush out people with poor health in
general, and TB in particular. As one woman interviewee remembered, 'we were all gathered there, you know, from the town . . . one
had not wanted to come . . . they were scared . . . and later in Milan
we passed all the examinations . . . and they told you, you have to
undress completely. I had never undressed, no, but you must do it!'
British businesses sent their own representatives to cherry-pick the
best, and especially to flush out Communists and Communist sympa-
thizers, although the rural areas of Calabria did not throw up many
trade unionists. British trade union officials were there to check that
foreign workers' contracts were not going to enable them to undercut indigenous labour; there were checks on reading ability, on age,
on passports and birth certificates, and even on the contents of the
migrants' suitcases. One English official, a Miss Rathbone, argued
that women migrants should not be allowed to travel on to work in
Manchester's textile mills without at least a full length coat, two
pairs of 'strong leather shoes', toiletries, towels, and several pairs of
thick stockings. It appeared that one might not only be too old, or
unfit or unskilled to migrate, but too poor.[14]

You could fall foul of even more dodgy standards. In 1952 the
Director of the Naples centre suggested that potential migrants like

A 1950s certificate of registration. Migrants from outside the British Empire and Commonwealth were governed by the 1920 Aliens Order, and were required to register with the police.

the village women who had never previously undressed were quite right to be scared. British delegations weren't basing their judgements on formal and established criteria 'like all other foreign missions, but they also follow certain other criteria, very difficult to define and that we would call "psychological".' In addition to medical examinations and skills tests the British were assessing psychological (and perhaps 'moral') 'type': 'the way the candidate presents him/herself, how s/he behaves and speaks during the interview, his/her general demeanour, clothes, how s/he reacts to certain questions: all this, however, very difficult to define and predict, because it is inspired by a certain subjectivity in the examiners' approach'.[15] The southern Italian type enjoyed less than wholehearted official approval.

The advantage of Germans and Italians was that as 'aliens' they had little power to protest against their terms of employment, and – unlike the Displaced Persons, who had no homes to go back to – they could be deported if they proved unsatisfactory. (And in fact a contingent of Italian miners was sent back, after a row over their work at the pit.) They were 'guest workers' in the technical sense of the term: they were employed for a period of three or four years and had no right to change their jobs; they had no right to bring family members with them; and no automatic right to stay beyond the terms of their contracts. All this endeared them to the Ministry of Labour. Their disadvantages were harder to pin down: they were socially suspect. In the case of Italians this had less to do with wartime Fascism than their supposedly 'Latin' traits. The Italians were apparently not like the Balts, hard workers, ideal material for assimilating to the British way of life, and 'of great benefit to our stock'. They were like the Cypriots, the Maltese, or the Polish peasantry. While newspapers like *The Times* were keen to support the government's recruitment drive, and found the Italians to be 'thrifty' and 'diligent', other reports were more predictably negative. In South Wales in 1952 the Italians were accused of having too much 'sex appeal', and causing disturbance to the miners' wives and daughters. Neighbours of the Italian brick-workers in Bedford made a similar complaint, tinged with class prejudice:

> We've got to remember they're peasants ... They are terribly noisy, blaring radios, shouting across the street, lounging around. One very nice family I knew here simply had to leave. Their daughters had just left school, the Italians ogled and whistled so life was unbearable![16]

'We've got to remember they're peasants.' Arguably it was impossible for the peasants themselves to forget. The fact that they came from rural poverty was the reason why they came. The work in mines and foundries, the time off in overcrowded lodging houses or government hostels and camps, everything which was part of the migrants' everyday and 'present' experience, was directed towards a future in which the past – the family home, the village – would be made viable again. And this condition was the same whether the peasants came from the peripheries of Europe or the heart of the Empire, from Ireland and Italy, or from the Punjab and Sylhet.

It was the colonial legacy that determined that British cities would function as the Punjab's metropolitan centres, but it was the uneven distribution of resources which drove Punjabis to live in them. The main promise which Britain held out to South Asian migrants was the promise of relief from the economic stagnation which afflicted rural life. In this respect Indian and Pakistani migrants had more in common with the peripheral European countrymen and women who moved, inexorably, to the cities of the industrial north during the 1950s and 1960s – the Portuguese who powered French industrial expansion, the Turks in Germany, the Greeks in Sweden, and the Irish, southern Italians, Cypriots and Maltese in Britain. Cities have always drawn their food, raw materials and manpower from their undeveloped, rural hinterlands of course, and those hinterlands were always expanding. Indeed Britain was one of the first industrial economies to draw on emigrant labour, when large crowds of the pre- and post-famine Irish built the canals and roads which would help power the industrial revolution. As Raymond Williams acknowledged in his classic 1973 study, *The Country and the City*, 'One of the last models of "city and country" is the system we now know as imperialism.' Punjabi villagers, like European peasants, were physically cut off from the benefits of industrial modernity – for the most part they earned no wages, and they bought no goods. They lived their lives outside the nexus of production and consumption which powered the Northern European post-war boom, in a traditional subsistence economy where the financial health of the family and even the tribal unit, rather than the individual, was the measure of progress. But if tin-openers and ready-made clothes may have seemed irrelevant to that economy (at least to male heads of household), tractors, drills and saws, not to mention wells and roads, were not. The money to pay for these things was only to be had in England. Subsistence farmers as far apart as Ireland, Calabria and the Punjab were propelled to post-war Britain by the same economic laws. Their only chance of altering their circumstances, indeed of imagining a future at all that was different from the present, lay abroad. 'The migrant wants to live. It is not poverty alone that forces him to emigrate. Through his own individual effort he tries to achieve the dynamism that is lacking in the situation into which he was born.'[17]

Nonetheless, although the villager from India and the villager from Ireland or Italy may have been subject to the same economic laws, they were poles apart when it came to the laws of geography, and nationality. 'Before I came here my mother told me not to cut my hair, but I told her frankly, "Ma, they take it off at Bumbay even before we start."' The straightforward acceptance by intending Sikh migrants that the symbols of their religion would have to go if they were to find work in British foundries and factories suggests a profoundly pragmatic attitude – they were not going to let faith get in the way of livelihood. The Partition of India in 1947 had proved particularly violent in the Punjab, where the boundary between the two new states was contested. Over 5 million Muslims fled or were forced to go, on trains, ox-carts and by foot, from India to West Punjab in Pakistan. Over 3 million Hindus and Sikhs escaped the other way, to settle in East Punjab. But the population transfer was carried out with terrible violence and slaughter, and with the rape and abduction of women, as communities took revenge on one another. Refugees flooded into Delhi; others tried to settle on newly divided parcels of land on both sides of the border. Incoming Sikhs, in general, were offered poorer land than they had farmed in West Punjab. But the influx of newcomers also meant that the landholdings of residents already settled in East Punjab had to be sliced up, with the new parcels averaging as little as two and a half acres in some places. Punjabis had been shaken loose from their land in ways not experienced by people in other parts of South Asia. For the displaced on both sides of the border who decided to move on from this precarious existence, England was the latest in a series of migrations.[18]

The ritual of cutting hair and shaving beards wasn't only about fitting in at the labour exchange in Southall or Wolverhampton. It was also part of the smuggling racket. Shanker to Jalandhar city in the Indian Punjab is less than 15 miles; Jalandhar to Delhi is nearly 340 miles, and Delhi to Bombay a little over 900 miles. From Bombay to Southampton by P&O ship took nearly eighteen days in the mid-1950s. A member of the servant class living in Shanker, Nathu Singh, unable to read, and knowing no English, had travelled as far as Jalandhar only a few times in his life. He got to Southall (careful not to go outside the train station in Delhi for fear of getting lost) by paying over 3,500 rupees to a travel agent, Mr Kapoor of Jalandhar, who arranged everything for him: passport, entry voucher, and bribes to avoid police investigations, clerical delays and official objections. Yet in 1954 the cost of the cheapest P&O fare from Bombay to Southampton was £60, less than 1,000 rupees.[19]

The 1948 British Nationality Act kept the door ajar to immigration from India and Pakistan by offering the same rights of abode to Commonwealth citizens as to citizens of 'the United Kingdom and the Colonies'. It was regarded as a way of keeping India in the fold. But just as in the Caribbean, it took some time for regular migration to get going. In South Asia, it wasn't so much a lack of ships to carry people to England as a series of unofficial controls, including pressure on the Indian government not to issue passports, or endorsements to travel to Britain, which created practical difficulties for would-be migrants. Between 1947 and 1950 very few passports were issued in Punjab, and, after the main passport office moved to Delhi, bureaucratic delays could take up to two years. Even then officials were likely to refuse a passport if they didn't consider the reason for going abroad valid. When bribery failed to work, travellers resorted to an increasingly well-organized system of forged documents. In 1958 Jawaharlal Nehru, the Indian prime minister, claimed that of the 17,300 Indians who had reached Britain between 1955 and 1957, fewer than 5,000 travelled on passports issued by his government.[20]

For many of the first migrants from rural Punjab the very notion of 'papers', whether that meant a national passport or a birth certificate, was fundamentally alien. Home, for this first generation of migrants, meant not the territorial entity, the Punjab, which had been so recently carved out on the map. It was not until much later, in the late 1970s and 1980s, that the idea of the Eastern Punjab as a Sikh homeland began to take hold, and gave rise to the Khalistan movement for political independence from India. But still less did home mean the political entity, India, as a whole. Indian citizenship seems to have been experienced as something remote and bureaucratic. Indeed it came into play only in the moment of deciding to leave, because leaving required official papers and, above all, a passport. Stories of migration from India often focus on the hassle, and expense, of having to apply for a 'pass', and the number of agents and middlemen who had to be paid off in order to get it. And in the end the passport was simply a necessary piece of paper, which bore little relation to any sense of national identity. Whether it was forged or real made little difference. For these men and women from villages in the Punjab identified with their families, and with larger networks of caste and tribe, but had little social imagination of being 'Indian'. It was the same for the Muslim Punjabis who left for Britain from just across the border in Pakistan. Much like islanders from Jamaica or Trinidad, who gained an awareness of being West Indian only when resident in Britain, or like forced migrants from Poland and the Ukraine, who created new senses of their geographical homeland in exile, the idea of Indian or Pakistani identity grew only slowly among migrants to Britain in the 1950s.

In the long run, entering the country on false papers was to make it harder for these immigrants to settle – if only because the fear of being 'illegal' in England pushed them further towards relying on middlemen for jobs and housing, and reinforced their dependence on a migrant network for favours and support. While these networks certainly worked to smooth the way, especially for men with no English, they also made it harder for the majority of migrants to make good on the promises England offered. There were a number of different scams involving forgery and counterfeit identities. Agents applied for passports on behalf of their clients which were initially endorsed for Singapore or Mauritius. From there the migrants could sail for Britain without endorsement. It could take up to two months to travel these routes. Alternatively, Indian immigrants were smuggled through Pakistan with forged Pakistani passports. These might be real passports bought off migrants who had already got to England and which were then doctored, or you could apply for a Pakistani passport as though you were resident there, under an assumed Muslim name. All this increased the cost of travel to three or four times the price of a simple sea voyage. And for Sikhs trying to pass themselves off as residents of Pakistan or Singapore it meant the absolute necessity of shaving and cutting their hair.

This pragmatic ritual vied with more traditional ceremonies. One Indian Punjabi, who left an account of leaving home for a future in Wolverhampton, described carrying out a series of rites to local deities and kindred spirits, including the Sufi Sakhi Sultan, the medieval saint Guru Ravidas, and Earth Goddess Mai. This syncretic form of religion, in which the gods of the Sufi, Sikh and Hindu faiths were worshipped on an equal footing, was typical of rural, lower caste Indians (and also of Punjabi Muslims before Partition). They prayed to the gods of their village, for it was their village they were leaving, rather than the Punjab, and still less India itself. The same was true of migrants from Sylhet in East Bengal – the other main source of South Asian manpower in 1950s Britain. Before a man left Sylhet he was encouraged to eat vast quantities of rice at a ritual meal, so that he could take with him the essence of his home on his long journey. It was like packing food for a voyage, a sensible precaution against

An immigrant from India at Victoria Station. He had made the
journey by sea and was detained at Dover in November 1959,
before being allowed to enter the country.

hunger, but also a way of keeping home near for as long as possible.
One of the most poignant moments in V. S. Naipaul's account of his
journey to Britain from Trinidad is the story of him transporting a
whole roast chicken, which had been cooked the day before by his
mother, on the plane from Port of Spain, via San Juan, to New York.
He eventually tore into it with his bare hands, crouched over the
wastepaper bin (to catch the dripping fat) in his Manhattan hotel
room. Food from home was a kind of talisman, a protective charm
that was rooted in family and community. Rice and roti were little
bits of the rural landscape brought into the urban metropolis, though
most travellers' supplies ran out long before they got there. The gifts
of food later sent by family members who stayed at home – butter
from Ireland, rice and spices from India and Pakistan, olive oil and
nuts from Cyprus – were all versions of those magical meals. They

were the nurturing fruits of home soil and so also, by default, messages from the past.[21]

Rituals like the rice meal had a long history, for Sylhetis were people who had traditionally worked as seamen for the British East India Company. The historic route by river south to Calcutta had been carved out by stokers working on the steamships bringing tea from Assam to the port. There they found work as 'lascars' on British ships – a tradition which held strong during the war, when significant numbers of Sylhetis were taken on as merchant seamen, working in the engine rooms and kitchens of merchant and troop ships. But from 1947 Sylhetis became foreigners in Calcutta, which was absorbed into West Bengal after Partition. From 1952 East Pakistanis (East Bengalis) needed visas and passports to enter West Bengal, which meant that the seamen were effectively cut off from their livelihood. Aftab Ali, leader of the Indian Seamen's Union, campaigned for passports which would allow the destitute seamen to emigrate. A passport office and travel agency, which he opened in Sylhet town in 1956, was mobbed by crowds clamouring for papers. One thousand passports were issued to Sylhetis in 1956. As in the Punjab, the cost of cutting through the bureaucracy in order to gather together 'admissions cards' sponsoring entry into Britain (many of which were bogus), 'labour vouchers', or the paperwork for medical passports (allowing travel for treatment unavailable in East Bengal) was far in excess of the cost of the P&O fare from Calcutta.

The majority of these pioneer migrants, or 'frontiersmen', had little education and, apart from those who had already worked as seamen, no skills suited to an industrial economy. Literacy levels were low in both East Pakistan and the Punjab – and for that reason much of the experience of these early migrants is recorded not in novels and manifestos but in epic oral poetry and song. But they did not come from the lowest rungs of society. Landless labourers could scarcely have hoped to afford the initial costs, not to mention all the 'money greasing middlemen's palms' along the way. The migrants were smallholders, whose families could gather the capital to invest in the down-payments for migration by selling parcels of land and livestock. Even more than the 'lunatic' West Indians, who arrived in Plymouth with nothing more than their fare to London and no idea of how or where they would find work, the grand ambition of the pioneer migrants from India and Pakistan seems the stuff of fantasy, of the heroic tale. Often illiterate, and with no knowledge of English, they were willing to stake everything on a future which was not simply unknown to them in Sylhet or the Punjab, but impossible for them to begin to imagine.[22]

That willingness stemmed from the way that industrial Britain took the place of 'opportunity' for people living in a subsistence economy half-way across the world. The villages of Sylhet and the Punjab were linked in an imagined geography not with Dhaka or Delhi, but with 'Londoni', Birmingham, Leicester and Bradford. The chance of economic and social advancement – at a basic level the chance of any kind of future, measured against the static nature of life on a rural smallholding – lay with abroad. The poems and songs put it with characteristic bluntness:

> When sitting at home, arose an ambition in my heart
> That I should also get a passport, like many who have emigrated.
> Those who have gone to England have sent loads of money.
> Why God willing and helping, I should also see that country of gold.

This was different from the idea of Britain as the 'mother country' – an attitude far more common in the Caribbean colonies, where people had been educated in the English system, and as Christians. Language, religion, culture, all stood in the way of Indians and Pakistanis identifying with their Commonwealth cousins. Like the very first Jamaican immigrants, many of whom had wartime experience of Britain, a good proportion of the earliest post-war Asian migrants to Britain had fathers and grandfathers who had fought in the British Indian Army during two world wars, or had themselves worked as stokers and boiler men on British merchant ships. War service certainly fostered familiarity with Britain, yet for the most part the links were regarded as purely economic, purely instrumental, the flip side of the instrumental manner in which South Asians had long been regarded by functionaries of the British East India Company and members of the British Raj.

Few of the post-war migrants from Ireland, India or Southern Europe initially imagined they would settle permanently in England.

Even if they were not technically hired as 'guest workers' they thought of themselves as temporary migrants, intent on making enough money, or gaining sufficient skills, to create a future for themselves back home. It was for this reason that this first generation, particularly the men, set so little store by integrating with their host communities in England. It was not just that they were considered alien – not only peasants, but Catholics, Sikhs and Muslims – but that their lives in England were lives lived in suspension. Memory became anticipation, as they looked forward to the future in which they would rejoin the world they had left behind in the past. Two developments were set to change this dynamic radically. For a start, the money sent back home swept the past away. The financial promise work in industrial Britain offered to a rural peasantry vastly sped up the modernization of those now distant traditional villages and their rural farm life. The remittances sent home ensured that that promise was kept, but also that the migrants had no past to go back to. There was no return ticket. And so, as a consequence, the migrants' life in the present – settled, however precariously, in Britain – had to become its own reward.

PART TWO

Presents

Whatever futures the immigrants imagined before they left their farms, villages or refugee camps, once they arrived in Britain they were going to have to live in the present. The bulk of this book is devoted to exploring their everyday, present-tense interactions with the strangers they encountered in Britain on the street, in lodging houses, in the workplace, in pubs and dancehalls, in the doctor's surgery and the hospital, in the labour exchange and the dole office, in the police station, with the social worker, across the garden fence, and in the bedroom. Undoubtedly things panned out differently for people according to their culture, language, religion and skin colour – quite apart from their personalities. But what the immigrants who arrived between 1945 and the mid-1960s shared was their encounter with a still largely ethnically homogeneous Britain, where previous waves of migrants such as the Irish and the Jews had either become ghettoized 'local colour' or seemed to have been absorbed into the English working class. First generation post-war migrants were pioneers in the sense that the lives they made in Britain were transformative not only for themselves but for the British people around them.

And wherever they came from they shared the experience of being news. They were talked about in Parliament, in the press, in trade union and local council meetings, on street corners and behind front doors across the country. The public, political discussion about immigration was initially framed in response to the government's decision to actively promote Britain as a destination for those in search of work. The schemes which brought European refugees to work in mills and mines, or Barbadian immigrants to work for London Transport, were worked out in long consultations with the trade unions; the impact of the camps which housed the new arrivals was debated openly, in the local and national papers. This was a highly managed migration and there was absolutely nothing silent about it. The people who came on the group schemes arrived into a country where everyone had an opinion about them. And although the British population's attitude towards the newcomers is not my primary focus, it naturally shaped their experience. Arguably, by the mid-1960s, it had begun to dominate it.

James Chuter Ede's 1948 insistence that the 'coloured races' of the Empire were the equals of people 'in this country' looks admirably colour-blind, and it might have stayed that way except that British subjects from the West Indies, Asia and Africa actually began turning up. As early as 1953, when the number of 'coloured immigrants' was still tiny, a Cabinet Committee was formed to look into the problems they caused, and the possibility of restricting immigration from parts of the former Empire. On the whole the Committee discovered that immigrants from the New Commonwealth caused very few problems. Yet the conviction that somehow they nonetheless caused a whole lot, took increasing hold.

Leaching off the welfare state, clogging up the NHS, putting pressure on primary school places, exacerbating the housing shortage, lowering wages – despite little evidence of these abuses, and often considerable evidence to the contrary, the popular image of the immigrant was a largely negative one. Long before the 1958 riots, the problems caused by immigration were put down not to xenophobia and racism but to the immigrants themselves. The riots, paradoxically, solidified this view. In the courts, in Parliament and in at least some of the national newspapers, it was accepted that West Indians had done little or nothing to cause the violence, which had been orchestrated by white youths, egged on by white neighbours. Black immigrants were the victims, though some of them defended themselves and were arrested and charged in their turn for doing so. Yet the response was not to argue for more funding for deprived areas, or better education, or support for race relations initiatives. It was to intensify calls for restrictions on immigration. Fourteen years after the inclusive form of citizenship enshrined in the British Nationality Act, the 1962 Commonwealth Immigrants Act tightened regulations governing the free movement of those holding Commonwealth passports, limiting entry to those who had work vouchers, which were graded A, B or C according to employment prospects. At a stroke, unskilled migration (Category C) from Asia and the West Indies was cut to a trickle, but not before urban centres saw a huge new rush of people arriving, particularly from India and Pakistan, in order to 'beat the ban'. Meanwhile, attempts by backbench MPs to bring in legislation against racial discrimination met with no success. The argument, which seems virtually impossible to credit now, was that legislation would draw attention to discrimination, and might therefore encourage it.

The Commonwealth Immigrants Act in effect legislated for, not against, racial discrimination, since it drew a distinction between black and Asian unskilled workers, who were no longer welcome, and Irish unskilled workers, who were, even though they were not members of the Commonwealth. The racist aspect of the Act was lost neither on Commonwealth immigrants, who campaigned vigorously against it, nor on the Labour opposition. The Labour leader, Hugh Gaitskell, denounced the Act as 'cruel and brutal anti-colour legislation'. Yet when Labour came to power in 1964 they did nothing to dismantle the restrictions, but actually increased them. In 1965 the total number of voucher holders was limited to 8,500, with 1,000 of these reserved for the Maltese, who thus appeared to have become the new Irish, the acceptable – and white – face of immigration. Category C vouchers were abolished altogether, in a move which *The Economist* condemned as 'pinching the Tory's white trousers'. And in 1968 restrictions were hurriedly reinforced again, limiting entry only to those with a parent or grandparent born in the United Kingdom. This was in order to stop up to 200,000 Kenyan Asians, who were fleeing the 'Africanization' of their country and who still held British passports, arriving in Britain.

By the end of the 1960s, the debate on immigration had polarized along racial lines. On one side was the Campaign Against Racial Discrimination and the Black Power movement, on the other Enoch Powell and the fledgling National Front. Powell's notorious 1968 speeches were motivated in part by the Wilson government's plan to extend the ineffectual 1965 legislation against racial discrimination through a new Race Relations Bill, which targeted discriminatory practices in employment and in housing. Powell argued that British citizens should not be disallowed the 'right to discriminate'; to circumscribe their freedom to employ or house whom they chose was to discriminate against the indigenous population, who would thereby be 'made strangers in their own country'. The Race Relations Bill would give the new, immigrant strangers 'the power to pillory them for their private actions'. He painted a picture of black immigrants united in their desire to dominate and bring down white culture. In this doom-laden scenario the traditional British way of life was on the way out.

In the short space of twenty years what it meant to be an immigrant had fundamentally altered. The Poles, the Irish, the Cypriots, Italians and Maltese had effectively disappeared from the dominant debate, if not from everyday life. But it is only by bringing them back that we can begin to understand the character of immigrant life in post-war Britain. The quotidian encounters between locals and migrants which I elaborate here – sexual intimacies, battles around housing, tensions in the workplace, dancing and dance music – all took place against the background of a political debate which, often wilfully, failed to acknowledge who the immigrants really were, how they lived, and the fact that they were far more like 'us' than not. The roles they played were complex and varied. The characters they inhabited were forged in the ongoing encounters between strangers, as stereotype and reality met and were confirmed, overturned, or modified according to circumstance. Those circumstances were closely tied to the growth and decline of Britain's industrial centres during the 1950s and 1960s. Commonwealth and European migrants moved from their rural villages to Britain's cities just at the point when the metropolis began to invade all social space through consumerism, car ownership, motorways, air travel and mass communications. The immigrants were threatening because they appeared to stand for all that was most disorientating about the new urban experience in post-war Britain. So that although Powell made his argument in explicitly racist terms, targeting the most visible of the new immigrants, one part rang true. In complaining about being made strangers in their own land, Powell and his allies were pointing to the avant-garde effect of immigration – that by living with and alongside others, the whole country was now a little bit elsewhere.

4

East Enders

It was a small hole in the wall catering almost exclusively for West Indians; on Saturday the place was full of 'coloured people' ordering zoot suits. There was a betting shop upstairs, and much of the profit from the old man's hard-earned calluses, produced over forty years of cutting with the huge shears, was frittered away on the nags, the dogs, and anything else from poker to bridge ... Dad mostly did tailoring for 'schwartzers' – Yiddish slang for black immigrants – who wanted the jackets to their fingertips and trousers that swelled out at the knee and tapered at the calf like a giant leaf. The pleats had to be reversed and the loops dropped so that the belt did not ride over the waist. The lining had to be satin and the jacket was invariably single-breasted with a long, narrow lapel that swept down to the hips and would be done up with one button.

Steven Berkoff, *Free Association* (1996)[1]

At the end of the 1940s, when the future actor and playwright Steven Berkoff was twelve, his family was rehoused by the London County Council. They moved from two-roomed lodgings in a condemned house in Anthony Street, off the East End's Commercial Road, to a flat in the brand new Woodberry Down estate at Manor House. The young Berkoff was sent to Hackney Downs Grammar School (where Harold Pinter was also a pupil), but he spent his leisure time back in the East End: swimming in the river down at Tower Hill, wandering through Petticoat Lane market, playing table tennis at the boys club at Berners Street synagogue, and hanging around his father's tailors shop in Whitechapel. His family's move north was part of a general 'upwardly mobile' shift – of Jewish residents, but also of their British, Irish and Italian neighbours – out of the East End and up the Hackney Road to Dalston, Stoke Newington, Stamford Hill and Golders Green (often Golders Green by way of Dalston and Stoke Newington), leaving the crumbling tenements and cottages to be taken over by a new wave of immigrants. The 'traditional' area of Jewish settlement, around Stepney and Whitechapel, was becoming the destination instead for Cypriot, Asian and West African migrants.

The East Enders were not particularly welcome further north, but for the most part they were unwelcome because they were poor and not because they were Jewish. The established residents of leafy Manor House objected to the '£1,000,000 slumdwellers' paradise' being built on their doorstep. But racial and ethnic differences were far from obvious. In 1939 around half Stepney's 200,000 residents were Jewish. When Tom Harrisson carried out a survey on anti-Semitism in the East End for Mass-Observation, the ambitious people's anthropological movement he had set up with surrealist poet Charles Madge, he noted down quite contradictory evidence. On the one hand he was able to acknowledge examples of easy accommodation between different groups. East European food, particularly bread, was common to the whole of the community, for example. But although he found 'Cockney and Jew living together in the same street and often in the same house', he insisted they were 'living in different social worlds'. Clannishness, lack of morals and flashiness were, he argued, more likely of Jews, who were also, apparently, less prone to whistling on the loo, had more dogs, and were less interested in dirty pictures. One contemporary commentator argued that Harrisson might as easily have been judging Cypriot or Italian behaviour as Jewish, since he didn't bother to actually talk to anyone. He conducted his survey mainly by standing at street corners and observing, for he believed you could tell the difference between a Jew and a non-Jew just by looking. Like many of the social commentators on race and migration in this period, Harrisson's outlook was anti-racist but irredeemably racialized. He was primed to see 'types', whether he designated them Cockney or Jew. But as the Jewish-American journalist William Zukerman had pointed out two years earlier: 'The truth is that what goes under the name of the East End Jew is in reality no specific Jewish type at all. It is but the general East End labour type with which the East End Jew has assimilated so thoroughly that it is difficult to differentiate the two.'[2]

The novelist Alexander Baron (who had also been a pupil at Hackney Downs School, though twenty years before Berkoff and Pinter) agreed. Sixty to seventy years after the large-scale settlement of Eastern European Jews in the East End, it was not possible to tell them apart from any other East Ender just by looking. His 1952 novel, *With Hope, Farewell*, features a Jewish grandfather named Jacob Strong:

> He was sixty-four years old, and until a few years ago he had worked as a fruit-porter in Spitalfields market, one of the many Jewish porters there who are only distinguished from their Gentile workmates by the fact that they are burlier, their Cockney accents more pronounced, their language more obscene and their capacity for beer greater.[3]

This looks like complete assimilation, even absorption. From Berkoff Senior's love of gambling, to the adoption of the drinking, swearing and even physical stature of the 'East End labour type', by the middle of the twentieth century East End Jews might worship differently, but in many other respects they had learned to do as their neighbours did. After all, many of those neighbours lived not just across the road, but across the hall.

The difficulty of distinguishing Jew from Gentile did not, however, discourage anti-Semites from whipping up racial tension in the immediate post-war years. Their job was made easier throughout 1947 and 1948 by newspaper coverage of Jewish violence against British troops deployed to keep the peace in the Palestine Mandate. There were riots in Hackney's Ridley Road, stirred up by Oswald Mosley's revamped Union Movement, and ugly incidents in Liverpool and Glasgow. The Hampstead branch of the Union Movement briefly gained new members in 1948. Between October 1948 and October 1949 nearly 7 per cent of violent attacks in London were against Jews (including, in March 1949, an attack on an eighteen-year-old Harold Pinter). As Baron described it, the grim post-war conditions of austerity, the news from Palestine, and the slow shift northwards of East End Jews created a perfect, if passing, storm:

> Now that there was a shortage of everything – of housing, of transport, of food and goods in the shops – Jew and Gentile saw each other as rivals. The Jews were still sick with the memory of their six million kin murdered by Gentiles in Europe. Their neighbours were inflamed by the knowledge that in Palestine, in the last year, Englishmen had been killed by Jews.[4]

Such open expression of anti-Semitism so soon after the end of the war may come as a surprise. British nationalism was intensely bound up with pride at having not only survived but won the war, but the idea of victory was not at that time closely bound to knowledge of the Holocaust. The notion that the war had been fought partly on behalf of the Jews did not settle into public consciousness until many years later. Jews (at any rate the ones you could tell just by looking) were seen as aliens, or at the very least outsiders. Even for the most sympathetic observers, they were a group apart, and they knew it.

On VE day in 1945 Verily Anderson, diarist and (later) children's author, had left the children with her mother in the country and travelled up to London to celebrate with her husband, who had been working for the Ministry of Information. They strained to see the King and Queen on the balcony of Buckingham Palace and then wandered past the pubs (with extended licensing hours), the bonfires, firework displays and street parties:

> We walked through Soho. There the celebrations had a pattern of their own. Traditional dances of central Europe were being performed with all the skill and seriousness of Highland Reels. Foreigners, as grateful for victory as any of us, if not more so, advanced and retired and turned and skipped to their own thin, mournful chants. Their old people stood around in the firelight clapping in time.[5]

The dancers they encountered in Soho Square were mostly members of the long-established Jewish settlement in London's West End. During the late nineteenth century a thriving Yiddish-speaking community had developed around the tailoring businesses, hat makers and dress shops of Berwick Street, where they lived cheek-by-jowl with the Greeks and the Italians. Their numbers had been swelled in the late 1930s by refugees from Germany but in fact the majority of these newcomers – more Westernized, German-speaking, more middle class and professional – had found homes further north and further east, in the leafier suburbs of Hackney, Hampstead and Golders Green.[6]

By the middle of 1945 the concentrations of pre-war Jewish refugees in newer (more 'genteel', less traditionally Jewish) areas of London had produced a depressingly familiar xenophobic backlash. S. H. Stanley, the Conservative parliamentary candidate for Kennington, blamed the arrival of the 'rag-tag and bobtail of the continent' for local housing shortages in his 1945 election bid. (He resoundingly lost the seat to Labour's Charles Gibson.) That same year Jeffrey Hamm directed his 'anti-alien petition', under cover of the pretext of securing homes for returning ex-servicemen, against the predominantly Jewish refugee population of Hampstead. Two Belsize Park residents, Margaret Crabtree and Sylvia Gosse, gathered 3,000 signatures for the cause, blaming housing shortages on the most recently arrived Europeans. The local paper, the *Ham and High*, carried articles insisting that 'Aliens should quit to make room for servicemen' and arguing for

> the prompt repatriation of the thousands of Austrian and German refugees who have taken up residence here and have turned so many of these houses and flats into factories and workshops, which same houses and flats are now sorely needed for our returning daughters and sons and for our evacuated daughters and their children.

Sylvia Gosse, a painter and printmaker associated with the Camden Town Group, was the daughter of the writer Edmund Gosse. Her upbringing had been cultured and cosmopolitan; she had rubbed shoulders with well-known authors such as Henry James, Thomas Hardy and Rudyard Kipling, alongside the bohemian pre-Raphaelite set of which her father was a part. Her mentor, the painter Walter Sickert, was himself a (Danish and Anglo-Irish) immigrant from Germany. There is something more than a little dispiriting about the fact that in her sixties she could only see the refugees from Nazi Germany as a nuisance and a drain. However, it would be mistaken to think that, even with the 3,000 signatures, this antipathy towards refugees was widely shared. A counter-petition by the 43 Group – a militant organization set up by demobbed Jewish servicemen to combat anti-Semitism (and which would later include Vidal Sassoon among its members) – gathered more support; and the pages of the *Ham and High* carried letters and articles denouncing the anti-aliens: 'To the Jews from Germany their former country is the graveyard of their families . . . they have no desire to return to the country where these atrocities were committed and be compelled to live amongst people who perpetrated the murder of the Jews or connived at these crimes.'[7]

Much of the emphasis on housing shortages was simply a way of attacking the new Labour administration. The anti-Semitic Face the Facts Organization attempted to harness people's disaffection over endless austerity by accusing the government of giving better housing and better rations to Jewish refugees. And the language of deportation and repatriation was in the air, in part borrowed from the minister for labour, Herbert Morrison, who was arguing for the need to repatriate the hundreds and thousands of refugees then languishing in the camps of the British Zone in Germany. Yet the danger of 'anti-alienism' had never lain very far below the surface of wartime and post-war Britain. Indeed, the fear of a rise in anti-Semitism had been one of the reasons given for the small number of Jewish refugees who had been admitted to Britain during the 1930s – as though the Jews themselves were to blame for the anti-Semites.

Populist anti-Semitism – at least the kind that was openly expressed in riots and petitions – faded away after the Palestinian mandate was handed over in 1948. The ultra-nationalism that fuelled it found more mileage in loud-voiced opposition to immigration from the Commonwealth in the early 1950s. The rash of 'crackpot Hitler cults' that flowered in the immediate post-war years sported indiscriminate dislikes, and were happy to hitch themselves to, and stoke, any popular resentments. The fact that the Union Movement was able to 'replace' one enemy with another without, apparently, much difficulty, suggests that anti-Semitism provided a model for colour prejudice. Interviewed in the early 1970s, elderly Jewish residents of Hackney were able to acknowledge parallels between contemporary resentment of black Britons and attitudes to Jews in the 1920s and 1930s. ('They are anti-*schwarze* now, but they are really fascists and anti-Semites.') But though xenophobia and prejudice might be general, the Jews themselves, as well as a host of 'expert' observers, were also keen to maintain distinctions. Some characteristics of Jewish immigrants, so the story went, were not so easily passed down to the next wave of post-war settlers: their sense of community, their capacity for hard work, their respectability – at root their assimilability.[8]

As Jews moved upwards and outwards from the East and West Ends they 'disappeared' ethnically, although this had as much to do with moving out of areas associated with Jewish communities as with social or financial upward mobility. The 'new Jews' – refugees from Europe – may have caused a wave of anti-immigration panic in the posher parts of London in the late 1940s. After all, they dressed, ate and spoke differently. They were visible as outsiders. But for the long-settled Jews, like the Berkoffs, who were rehoused in council flats in central Hackney or Manor House, or the better-off who were able to buy their own flats and houses in Dalston or Edgware, a principal marker of their Jewishness had been the fact that they lived in the East End. Now that these burly, drinking, betting, swearing Jews lived somewhere else, their Jewishness became more of a private matter – for sharing when and with whom they wanted.

That option was not going to be available to many of the new immigrants who replaced them in the 1940s. That was not only because of their skin colour but because of the nature of the East End, which had been so heavily bombed that it was largely destroyed during the war. What was left, particularly south of the Commercial Road, was slated for demolition, its remaining inhabitants soon to be the lucky recipients of London County Council flats in Hackney, or houses further afield in Woodford and Dagenham. It was no surprise that Willmott and Young's bestselling 1957 study, *Family and Kinship in East London*, sounded a nostalgic note for the lost community of the East End – how could the bombed-out streets and condemned houses support traditional neighbourhoods or the customs and mores of civil society any more?

The collapse of community is a common base note which runs through all the accounts of the new East End immigrants in the 1940s and early 1950s. It was as though the war damage had unleashed a terrifying new set of social and economic problems, which were embodied by the newcomers. Take this account by a (mostly sympathetic) local philanthropist, Edith Ramsay. Ramsay begins by repeating the popular notion that the East End constituted London's very own 'melting pot', an area that had welcomed and succoured waves of persecuted and desperate migrants in succession: the Huguenots, the Irish, the Jews. But the new migrants of the 1940s were different:

> Perhaps it is this tradition of welcoming the stranger, that has made possible the recent invasion of men who came not to work, nor to worship, but to make vast profits out of commercialised vice. Their technique was simple. They bought derelict shops, turned them into All-Night-Cafes (permissible on payment of £1 to the L.C.C.), encouraged wayward and homeless girls to come from the provinces, Scotland, Eire, Wales. They provided these girls with food, rented for them, often at fabulous cost, flats in privately owned buildings, and bought houses empty, because insanitary and scheduled for demolition.

Ramsay rued the crowds of 'pavement waitresses' lining the Commercial Road, the jukeboxes, the illegitimate children, the filth. Certainly the number of all-night haunts was impressive: 'Within three minutes' walk of St. Paul's Church, Dock Street, there are 32 Cafes and Clubs. In one spot, within 25 yards, there are six combined Cafes and Clubs, four of them adjoining.'[9]

This so-called degenerate 'invasion' was made possible by the disappearance of both people and homes during the war. Between 1939 and 1945 the population of Stepney reduced from 200,000 to 60,000. Men and women were mobilized, families were evacuated, and the heavy bombing of the area around the docks and railway lines meant that locals who moved out did not move back again. The derelict buildings and cheap lodgings acted as a magnet for many isolated men with nowhere better to go. These were men who arrived before the 1948 British Nationality Act, many of them deserters and former seamen – such as the lascar deckhands and engine crews who served on battleships and merchant vessels throughout the war – who jumped ship and attempted to disappear into the twilight community of the wartime East End, and those whose contracts ended after the war while they were in England. They joined the 'old-timers' – a mixed group of men who had arrived from various British colonies during the 1930s, as musicians, seamen and, sometimes, students, and had gravitated to an area where they were tolerated, if not accepted. In the summer of 1949 Derek Bamuta, an East African social science student, was living in the Bernhard Baron Settlement on Berners Street (where Steven Berkoff played table tennis), when the warden, Basil Henriques, suggested researching the welfare of 'the coloured population'. Bamuta encountered and befriended a number of men from East Africa, Pakistan and the Caribbean, but found none more desolate than the West Africans, of whom he had

> reason to suspect that a lot of them actually sleep in bombed houses; it would appear that they hang about the streets until 1–2 a.m. and then find a reasonably sheltered spot for a night's rest. Their main amusement is sitting in cafes, drinking tea and talking; later in the evening they go into pubs for a drink and to look for girls.[10]

If this was an extreme version of lost and lonely immigrant existence, there were plenty of studies of ostensibly more 'integrated' lives which also liked to stress atomization, social disorder, isolation and criminality. In 1944 Phyllis Young was employed by a committee of local clergy and social workers to survey new immigrants living around Cable Street. Despite the sympathetic tone of her report – she accepted they got the worst deal in terms of housing, for example – she could not get past the idea that the 'coloured man' was responsible for his situation because of his promiscuity:

> [Homes generally comprise] one or two poorly furnished rooms in dilapidated and overcrowded houses in one of the back streets ... A few are more fortunate in having flats in the older blocks of building in the area, but even if the family should want good housing accommodation they are unlikely to obtain it as most of the landlords of the better type of property do not want coloured men as tenants. This is chiefly due to the fact that the coloured man, in the minds of the landlords, is connected with promiscuous living in the neighbourhood; investigation has shown that a very large percentage of coloured men in the area are living promiscuous lives while some of the white women

with children consort with other men while their husbands or unmarried partners are away at sea.

She listed statistics such as that in 27 per cent of families headed by a black male the parents were unmarried; she counted twenty-three 'half-caste' children then in council care; she argued that children born to black fathers were more likely to live in domestic turmoil, and to be deserted by their mothers. The trouble was not so much that the new communities of Africans, Pakistanis and West Indians failed to conform to standards of respectability; it was that they failed to act as communities at all. They were problem people, who lived in a problem area.[11]

The cafés were the most obvious sign of corruption and social anarchy. They were regarded as centres of 'vice', as well as haunts for black-marketeers dealing in cigarettes, drink, nylons and drugs. In October 1947 local residents (those who were left) started a petition detailing the 'grave moral and physical danger' around Cable Street, due to the 'excessive number of cafes open at a late hour'. The story was taken up in lurid detail in the national papers, especially the *News of the World* and the *Daily Mail*. By the early 1950s Cable Street was the obvious choice for the young sociologist Michael Banton, keen to make his mark with a new study of the 'coloured quarter'. His description of the Aldgate end of the street is of an archetypal seedy underworld, a hinterland of dimly lit warehouses and bombsites which gives on to the lights of pubs and cafés, the sounds of men 'lounging' outside, and the occasional screams of furious or slighted women:

In this stretch of Cable Street there are also five Maltese cafés, each of which provides lodgings for six to twelve young males whose womanizing activities have given two of the cafes a particularly bad reputation. There is a Maltese-run fish and chip shop, an Italian restaurant which opens during the daytime for a white clientele, and a Greek café. Shops at the beginning of the street are of Jewish and English ownership and have a small retail trade in grocery, baking, second-hand clothes, bicycles, greengrocery, etc. A side turning leads down to a Somali café, a Greek café, and a Pakistani café-cum-lodging house. A little further up the street is a general store run by a French family, two hairdressers – one an Arab, the other from Trinidad – a dyers and cleaners run by a Guianese, and a Pakistani café with an African and West Indian clientele. Another side turning leads to the Somali lodging house and the premises of the club for coloured men run by the Anglican Mission . . . A large house just here is owned by an East African and rooms are let out to Africans and West Indians; a few other houses are occupied by West Africans and another by West Indians – for the two groups tend to keep separate.[12]

Ten years later, in his classic of East London Jewish 'low-life', Alexander Baron could count on his readers' familiarity with the new associations of Cable Street. Once the site of Jewish and Communist riot and resistance against Mosley's Black-shirted fascism, now it was home only to chaos and despair: 'I walked down Cable Street – this once respectable street of working people that is now a garbage heap of lost, ferocious schwartzers and the wretchedest of whores . . . This bomb crater, patches of diseased weeds, black puddles, rusty

A jukebox café in Spitalfields in the 1950s.

bedsteads, sodden newspapers, old prams, smashed packing-cases and the turds of tramps . . .'[13]

The fact that the black immigrants were 'lost' as well as 'ferocious' was central to the story that was being told, which was as much about weakness as about criminality. Reporters and sociologists were apt to blame the women who 'enticed' vulnerable young men and tricked them into looking after them, stole their money, and indiscriminately bore their children. One East End lodging house was owned by a part-Somali, part-Abyssinian woman named Kathleen, who had been brought up in council homes. She argued that 'the reason the men fall for the worst class women who take their money and give them disease is because they are so lonely and she is determined to give them a place where they will feel at home'. For Derek Bamuta, the men were certainly the victims of desperate but ruthless women ('Their whole intention is to live on the coloured man'), though his language suggests that something rather more complicated was going on:

> if the man has a room of his own and takes the woman back with him he is as good as married, because once the woman is sure of a place to live she will stick to him like a limpet; once you get one she will not leave until she has taken all you have, and no amount of beating will get rid of her.[14]

Lost and ferocious schwartzers were apparently rivalled by the equally ferocious and lost women with whom they consorted. It would be easy to fill these pages with similar descriptions from other surveys, and articles in local and national newspapers, all focusing on the broken world of the immigrant East End. And it is clear that there was a real issue with the Cable Street cafés. On one night in the late 1950s Edith Ramsay counted twenty-one clubs open for business on the streets south of Commercial Road: eight were run by Maltese, seven by Cypriots, four by Somalis, one by a Gambian and one by a man from Sierra Leone. Yet it was obviously not the case that immigrants, uniquely, peopled the criminal underworld. A far greater proportion of the sex trade was controlled by white racketeers, including East End gangs such as the Krays and their less successful imitators. Nor were immigrants the primary customers of the clubs, whether for prostitutes or drugs or black-market cigarettes. There were hardly enough of them to provide business for more than twenty clubs. Ramsay found that while the clientele in the less well-appointed clubs were mostly black, that was not the case in the more profitable joints. Of Abdulla Wsrama's club ('the Abdullah', 12 Ensign Street), she noted:

> The members were most mysterious – all well-dressed, some certainly well-educated, and with the exception of one man who claimed to be a member of the local R.C. Church, none of them local. For the most part, not Somalis nor coloured.
>
> One woman, drunk or drugged, but oozing money, told me she drove up every week-end from Norfolk, to this Club.[15]

Arguably the Somali owner of this café was not only financially successful but was making a go of it in terms of integration. He so effectively performed the role of East End gangster and drug baron – modelled for him by men like the Kray twins – that punters travelled from Norfolk to do business with him. This fact – that against all the odds Abdulla Wsrama, and others like him, fitted in – was almost impossible for contemporaries to acknowledge. But, in retrospect, it is by far the most obvious thing about them.

Moreover, the same was true of many of the other colonial migrants who lived in the East End in the late 1940s and early 1950s. They fitted in. For all the stereotype of work-shy colonials, the majority were in employment and had been for some time. Mothosir Ali, a Sylheti seaman who jumped ship before the war, recalled that:

> There were many Jewish owned tailoring shops in the East End of London, which employed Sylheti men to stick soap. The people who did this job were called 'soap boys' and were paid about seven or eight shillings a week for six days' work. They also employed Shop Boys to carry big loads in wheel barrows from place to place. This job paid a little better then [sic] a soap boy's job, but the work was much harder, as it required running around outside in all types of weather.[16]

Men like Steven Berkoff's father adapted to the needs of the fashion-conscious West Indian new arrivals, who gave a fillip to their customer base. And they relied on Asian new arrivals to provide the manpower they were losing as their former employees moved up and out to Manor House and Edgware. Mortuja Ali dated the beginnings of the Bangladeshi textile trade to as early as the middle of the war, when vacancies began to open up in the local tailoring concerns:

> In 1943 . . . there were altogether five or six hundred Sylhetis in London, all ex seamen, mostly working as caterers, cleaners, washers up and kitchen porters. Only a handful of them were cooks, and a few others worked in the East-End in the Jewish-owned tailoring shops. Their main job was fetching, carrying and pressing, but hardly any sewing.[17]

The wartime Sylheti migrants had been born in India. From 1947 the place they had left was the newly separate jurisdiction of East Pakistan (later to become independent Bangladesh), but many of the people who wrote about them still thought of them simply as Indian. In the crumbling houses off the Commercial Road they developed a bustling sub-letting economy, a sliding scale to suit all budgets, which brought enterprising tenants a healthy income. Derek Bamuta's report went into some detail:

> House containing one room and scullery in basement, one room on ground floor, two on first and two on second. The tenant is an Indian earning £10 per week and paying a rent of £1 10s. p.w., 5 rooms are sub-let to Indian lodgers, 2 of whom are co-habiting with white women; the rents vary from 4s. p.w. for the basement to 21s. p.w. for the first front room.
>
> Similar house where the tenant is a Negro married to a white woman, rent 25s. p.w., 4 rooms sub-let to couples at 20s., 20s., 18s., and 15s. rents.
>
> Similar house, tenant an Indian paying 30s. p.w. Nine sub-tenants paying 7s. to 20s. p.w.

By 1949, Bamuta argued, these men were mostly working 'as peddlers, running eating houses, ships' cooks, small shops, etc. . . . their form of entertainment seems to be sitting round talking and smoking for hours on end. A great deal of "hashish" smoking goes on.' His description of one group he got to know reveals them as canny rather than lost, content rather than desperate, and well able to figure out for themselves possible futures:

I became friendly with four Indian lads; they had come over as ships' cooks. They had come on shore for holiday, so they put it, i.e. they were spending their earnings and when exhausted intended to sign on again for another port, or if they could obtain employment preferred to stay. They were a very happy group and a nice bunch of chaps and seemed to enjoy life immensely, which was divided between attending cinema shows, walking about the streets looking for girls and smoking hashish – Indian hemp. They had rented a room from a fellow Indian who is resident in the area and had a dilapidated four-roomed house. He sub-let two of the rooms to others, and of these two rooms my four friends had one between them with two double beds. The rent was £2 per week. If one of them brought a woman the others had to sit on the door-step or stand at the street corner. They had an adapted gas ring on which they cooked all their meals. They used the Public Baths. The sanitary arrangements for the whole household were filthy. I felt somehow that the house was condemned as it was adjacent to a lot of bombed houses.[18]

Looking back from 1963, Hamza Alavi could describe these early migrants as 'de-tribalised by comparison with later comers; they were individualists who fitted in more easily to the local life and customs, including pub-going and drinking, and some married local women.' As migration to Britain increased in volume during the 1950s more men arrived whose move was sponsored by the family and village back home, and who were therefore bound by stricter religious and customary ties and tended to live together with men from the same neighbourhood. Perhaps it was too much to ask that the 'individualist' migrants who were happy to adapt themselves to the kinds of work and sociability East London offered should be praised for their ability to assimilate. But it was certainly unfair that instead they were targeted for being the cause of breakdown and civil disorder.[19]

The issue of fairness loomed large in the attitude of philanthropists and social workers towards the 1940s colonial migrants. Edith Ramsay, for example, saw her role with the Colonial Office Advisory Committee to be to dedicate as much time and as many resources as possible to helping those whom she felt were 'unfairly' caught up in the degenerate world of East End vice. She wrote letters home for

African and Asian men seeking news, asking for support to set up businesses or to raise the fare home. She stood up in court for men who had got mixed up in nefarious dealings but whom she felt were basically on the side of the good. She applied to charities for clothes and support for 'deserving' families, and tried to help parents deal with errant children.

She was particularly concerned to help a number of mixed-race couples who fell into an ambiguous category somewhere on the edge of respectability. In the late 1940s she was helping two different couples, both living at 24 Fenton Street, a street of small terraces leading south from Commercial Road (adjacent to the Berkoffs in Anthony Street). Azir Uddin's Indo-Caribbean wife Beatrice had become pregnant by a white friend of Azir's and Ramsay was asked to help smooth the situation. Across the hall lived 'Uncle Abdul' and his wife, Peggy. Just upstairs lived Molly Ullah, who was looking for a divorce from her violent husband who had returned to India, so that she could marry Mahomar Ali, with whom she was living and had a number of children. When Molly died Ramsay helped Mahomar claim her Post Office savings, for, as Molly's sister Lily put it to her, 'he is a very good man he may be dark but I do know he has a white heart'.[20]

A year later Ramsay was involved (as a character witness) in defending two women whose children had been taken into care. The court claimed that both Mrs Eden, married to an African man whom she had left, and Mrs Pereira, married to a Ceylonese man, Wilson Pereira, who was away at sea, were involved in prostitution. Ramsay insisted the women were respectable and good mothers, and that their children should be returned to them. It was important, she argued, to draw a distinction between those with 'elastic moral standards' and professional prostitutes. And although it was true that these mothers spent much of their time with women who were working as prostitutes, as Ramsay put it they had little option: 'both the [friends of the] women are prostitutes, but then that is the only female society that is open to women who marry coloured men, and by no means all those women are prostitutes'. Nonetheless, the general assumption among middle-class officialdom seems to have been that, on the contrary, no one except a prostitute would consort with a black immigrant. When Guyanese novelist E. R. Braithwaite, author of *To Sir, With Love*, arrived for his first day teaching in an East End secondary school he found the local charwomen happy to sit chatting with him on the bus crawling up the Commercial Road, but 'respectable' women preferred to stand. In the summer of 1947, Ramsay attempted to help in the defence of a man from Sierra Leone, Momo Kagbo, who was accused of living off the immoral earnings of his lover Violet. Despite both women's protestations of his innocence – they insisted they were just living together – he was sentenced to three months in prison.[21]

It is clear that these individuals, couples and families were all living rackety lives, on the edge of criminality, though so too were many white local men and women. And what comes across most strongly in all these accounts is not sensationalism but ordinariness. Insofar as it was possible to lead an everyday existence perched on the edge of bombsites and dereliction, that is what the immigrants did. Towards the end of the 1950s Edith Ramsay took a government official named Philippa on a tour of the East End clubs. Philippa wrote a long account of her impressions in a letter of thanks. She was depressed by 'those horrible bare cafes in Commercial Road with their one or two seedy looking men inside and groups of really evil looking youths outside', but mostly she found herself having to downgrade her expectations of scandal and melodrama. Talking to the girls waiting to be picked up in one of the cafés was 'just as though we were all standing in a bus queue'; she was 'amazed to think that I would have £10 put in my hand if I walked down Cable Street, is that the basic pay?'; she was charmed by the 'little bar' in the Barbados Café, though found that the jukeboxes made a 'ghastly noise'. And in the Somali Café:

> I don't think I have had a more interesting gin and orange in my life. The red-headed girl from Sunderland and her Somali husband explained some Somali grammar, showed me a photo of their (white) 8 week old baby, wanted to know what I did, told me about their café to be opened in three weeks and quite made me forget I was in the backroom at the end of Graces Alley. There seemed to be so much normality in both these cafes but was it just a blind? Can you be untainted with so much vice about. – Or was I just taken in here and in the Barbados Café? I noticed that the girls drank a lot of milk which seemed out of place, I don't know why.[22]

A Whitechapel night-club in the 1950s.

Milk, tea, sandwiches, fish and chips: the enterprising men who were making a profit on sub-letting rooms in condemned houses used their money to open shops and cafés, which catered for the local population as much as for immigrants. In time many of the cafés would rebrand themselves as curry houses, as their owners slowly introduced Sylheti-style dishes alongside the spam and chips. By the late 1960s Chaim Bermant found the transformation of the East End almost complete, with new languages and customs superimposed on the old.

The Samuels and Cohens have given way to the Selims and Khans, but each little shop displays a bewildering variety of goods, fruit pies and torch batteries, bananas and brilliantine, tea-bags and tights. One gentleman's outfitters is also a travel agent and some sort of notary public. The Hebrew lettering on the facias has given way to Bengali, though many of the *mezuzoth*, the little scrolls in a metal casing which most Jews have on their doorposts, still persist. Mosaic law has given way to Moslem law.[23]

5
Carers

My own belief is that there is nothing but good in the English
Health Service. Go into any doctor here. You find yourself in
a nice warm room awaiting your turn. When you get in to the
doctor, he treats you pleasantly even though he may be busy
enough. He'll give you to understand that you are a person
and not a beggar; and he'll give you a prescription to take to
the chemist where the best drugs and medicines are given to
you with a heart and a half.

At home, such as I saw of it, if you get a ticket to go to the
doctor, you have to wait in an old ruin of a house. Look
around you and all you see is poverty, despair and dirt both
on people themselves and on their clothes. The people go in
to the doctor as they used to go in to the aristocrats or the
landlords long ago – shaking with humility.

Dónall Mac Amhlaigh, *An Irish Navvy* (1964)[1]

In 1951 Dónall Mac Amhlaigh was twenty-two years old and getting
22 shillings and sixpence from the Irish Labour Exchange while living in Kilkenny with his parents. He had been unemployed for three
months after his discharge from the Irish army, when, 'The Mother
saw the ad in the paper: "Stokers wanted. Live in. Apply Matron,
Harborough Rd. Hospital, Northampton."' So Mac Amhlaigh wrote
away and when news of his acceptance came by letter a few weeks
later the family celebrated with a shop-bought cake. Arriving in
Northampton he found himself working alongside Ukrainians, Lithuanians and fellow Irish, first as a stoker, and then as a ward orderly.
Most of the nurses were Irish; most of the ward orderlies and

domestic staff, and some of the patients, were Displaced Persons from the camps nearby. Mac Amhlaigh didn't stick the job for long – there was more money to be made on the building sites, even if the living conditions were far worse. But he never recanted on his admiration for the NHS: 'I can't get over how nice the doctors and others like them are in this country – quite different from home. Of all that are here, there's only one that's anyway arrogant and she's an Irishwoman.'[2]

Right from the beginning the NHS was a source of national pride. Hence the catchphrases. Providing healthcare to everyone 'from cradle to grave', 'free at the point of use', and funded from a universally participatory social insurance scheme – it signalled democratic modernity, a mini medical state which looked after all its citizens, and even other people, as Mac Amhlaigh was pleased to find out. What impressed him about the NHS was not just that it provided for everyone, but that it treated them all as 'persons'. There were plenty of indigenous Britons who did indeed regard Irish immigrants as beggars, but Mac Amhlaigh's point may have had more to do with his experiences back home in Ireland, trying to get treatment from status-conscious, fee-driven, small-town doctors working in a health system still operating under conditions not far removed from the nineteenth-century Poor Law. Nonetheless, however much he liked the NHS, he didn't want to work in it, and in this he was just like his English neighbours.

Vesting Day, 5 July 1948: the new Regional Hospital Boards took over the management and running of the old voluntary foundations, many of which were near bankruptcy, as well as the municipal hospitals, run by local councils, together with TB hospitals, maternity wards and mental institutions. In effect the hospitals were nationalized. Institutional mergers had in fact been occurring quietly during the war as care was streamlined for maximum wartime efficiency. The really new thing about 1948 was the social insurance scheme that was supposed to pay for it all. National Insurance linked social reform with a rejuvenating national spirit, a kind of communal citizenship which was very different in design from post-war welfare systems in other countries. The ambition was 'to make a healthy nation'. In the United States, benefits were targeted towards the (increasingly stigmatized) poor, whereas in Britain they were extended, very deliberately, to everyone, including the middle classes. And everyone, including the middle classes, signed up. Within a month of Vesting Day, 97 per cent of the general public had their names on the freshly printed buff NHS cards. There were no new hospitals, no new treatments, no extra doctors, but a new financial and managerial framework, and lots of new patients. The manpower shortfall was catastrophic.

It was not only doctors and nurses who were in short supply. There was an acute shortage of men and women available and willing to work as porters, stokers and cleaners in hospitals, convalescent homes, nurseries and old people's homes. The problem was that the British Ministry of Labour could no longer compel people to work in undesirable jobs, and this left hospitals, like the textile industry, mining and agriculture, in a situation bordering on crisis. All the various types of hospitals suffered a crisis of manpower, and they turned to the vast pools of unemployed Irish to solve it. The Irish, after all, had filled the vacancies opened up in the hospitals by war service, even if, according to disgruntled former employees, they had not done it very well:

> When I resumed my work as a nurse in the hospital where I had been prior to the outbreak of War, I was sorely disappointed. Many Irish nurses had been recruited during the War and were given Sisters' and Charge Nurses' posts. The most irritating thing about this was that they were not very good nurses. They mainly came from the West of Ireland, had little education and only a limited understanding of the mentally ill. Those of us who returned found ourselves at the bottom of the pecking order and had to start all over again to build up years of experience before we got promoted.[3]

While it may be hard to imagine that mental health nursing had offered much of a career or particularly high levels of fulfilment during the 1940s, according to this nurse whatever status it once had was messed up by the Irish. Poorly educated, ill-informed, bad at their jobs, they were nonetheless given the top spots while everyone else was away at the war. Setting this nurse's pique and prejudice aside (presumably some of the Irish recruits were competent and some less so), it was certainly true that, like munitions factories and wartime construction sites, British hospitals had determinedly sought out Irish labour during the war.

Because passage between neutral Ireland and wartime Britain was restricted, an elaborate bureaucratic system developed to facilitate the Irish war workers. In 1943 the Ministry of Labour posted a UK 'liaison officer' in Dublin, whose job was to channel Irish labour to the most needed areas in Britain. There was some hope, too, that he would be able to control the type of recruit turning up at the hospital gates. As one civil servant complained:

> There is at the present time a very considerable volume of recruitment in Ireland for hospitals in this country. The great majority of the applicants are accepted on a written application and testimonials only, though doubtless in many cases the applicant is introduced by a present employee of the employer. We know that the better class of hospital, which is not in desperate straits for staff, declines to engage girls on this basis. We also know that girls who are accepted are quite often not suitable and that a fair amount of false pretences goes on.[4]

The job of the Liaison Office was to regulate the migrants, to match applicants to vacancies, to check the background of the women and girls for hospitals and factories, and the large numbers of men taken on to build airfields and camps. They organized permits, sorted out transport and hostel arrangements, helped out with tax allowances, and, in a good number of cases, paid both the fare and a subsistence grant to tide the workers over until their first wages came through. By 1944 Mr Toms, the chief liaison officer, had a small team working for him on hospital recruitment, including nursing officers stationed in Cork, Limerick, Athlone and Sligo, whose job it was to visit the girls who had applied 'for England', and decide how suitable they would be. They were loud in their complaints. The girls, they claimed, were more often than not dull-witted and unkempt, and in order to get about the country to interview them the nurses had to travel on trains that 'are most uncomfortable and in almost all cases verminous'.

Lice, as we have seen in relation to the delousing stations at Holy-head and Liverpool, featured rather heavily in discussions of wartime and post-war immigration.

It is worth considering exactly what was at stake in these argu-ments over cleanliness. On the surface it looks like a way of distinguishing between more and less 'suitable types', a euphemism for class. To some extent the Irish were privileged migrants in that it was allowed there might be different classes of them, unlike their New Commonwealth cousins who were all considered more or less indistinguishable from one another. Yet the categories of the Irish – more and less educated, rural and urban, nurses and factory workers, better and worse – had a disturbing habit of merging with one another. One wartime nursing recruitment officer on a visit to Dublin claimed that even among the 'better class' of applicant, the rate of women found to be 'verminous' was very high:

> I was very exercised in my mind about the advisability of requiring women coming over for nursing to undergo this ordeal, but when I saw the records and realised that 85 per cent of the women were dirty, I felt it was most essential that they should be examined, even if they are quite a different type from the women being submitted for work in factories.[5]

By 1948 the Dublin authorities were arguing that there was no further need for medical examinations, since most women left under their own steam, and therefore did not go through the Liaison Office procedures. Travellers crossed back and forth all the time, and – with DDT now distributed throughout the country – the threat of typhus was negligible. But the British Ministry of Labour was still con-cerned, fearing they would attract 'public odium' for billeting lousy Irish. A visit to the Dublin recruitment service in May 1948 suggested lice checks were still necessary:

> The need for cleansing treatment is very real: on the evening when the Service was inspected, 26 out of 55 men and 18 out of 22 women examined required treatment . . . It cannot be dispensed with, and it is better that it should be carried out by their own people who under-stand the conditions under which they have been living rather than

risk the girls being ostracized by their fellow workers or room mates in Great Britain.

And Irish doctors agreed. While maintaining that 'Poverty, as indicated by underclothing, is no guide as to the likelihood of infestation. I have seen silk clothing crawling with vermin, and girls in miserable rags scrupulously clean,' Dr Ethna MacCarthy implied in a 1948 report that rural customs and education militated against basic cleanliness. Many of the women she examined were wearing brand-new underclothes 'with the price label still attached':

> The standard of cleanliness among women emigrants is low. Although aware that they are presenting themselves for medical examination and have presumably come prepared, many appear engrained with dirt, while a vintage accumulation in the umbilicus is common even in otherwise clean people. A considerable number, in spite of brand new clothes, have made no attempt to wash their bodies at all. From enquiry 'washing' refers only to the face and hands; daily washing cannot be assumed. One girl boasted that she 'washed once a fortnight', a statement that was meant to impress.

With tales of unembarrassed girls so infested that the lice lay like sand in the bottom of the bath after washing, MacCarthy put the dirt down not to lack of running water but rural custom and old-wives' tales, such as that their rashes were caused by food or menstruation, or the belief that washing 'weakens' children.[6]

Ethna MacCarthy was the young woman whom Samuel Beckett had loved when they were both students at Trinity College in the mid-1920s. She appeared as 'Alba' in his early fiction and poetry, and was the most likely source of the dreamlike memory of lost fulfilment in his play *Krapp's Last Tape*. But she may well also have been the type of medical professional who would have given Dónall Mac Amhlaigh to understand he was not a person but a beggar. She certainly seems to have treated these young women from small, poorly equipped and unmodernized farms with disdain. Her condescension acts as a useful reminder that there are no national boundaries on snobbery. In fact many Irish doctors and dentists also migrated to the NHS, alongside their poorer cousins, and they presumably brought their assumptions of class superiority with them, if they had them. And the newly minted NHS hospitals proved fertile ground for their class-consciousness. For the early NHS was steeped in social hierarchies, so that prejudice, or simple concern, about 'lousy' Irish nurses seeped easily into opinions about their working capability. It was rare for Irish trainees to be taken on in the teaching hospitals, for example, which thought of themselves as a cut above the rest, a 'better class' of hospital. And added to the hierarchy of hospitals was a hierarchy of grades within the hospitals. Most large institutions still had separate dining rooms for domestics, orderlies and nurses, much like a caste system. One former ward orderly recalled that when she applied to train as a nurse, the matron was scandalized: 'What? and all your friends on the domestic staff!'

In 1951 a series of interviews with Irish nurses in England published in the *Irish Democrat* was titled 'They Treat Us Like Dirt': ' "When I came over here," one of the Irish girls was saying in her attractive Kerry accent, "Matron asked me would I be able to mix with the other nurses without having had a secondary education. She doubted if I would be tolerated at all." ' As the possibility opened up of employing nice clean Baltic women, not of the 'peasant type', instead of the Irish, hospitals apparently jumped at the chance: 'there is no doubt that matrons generally hope to obtain a satisfactory supply of labour from the women now under recruitment at the displaced persons camps on the Continent'. If they could manage without the Irish they would. Within a few years the role of 'undesirable' nurse had been expanded to include women from the West Indies. They were fine as cleaners, but not in caring roles. As a Ministry of Labour official explained in July 1953:

> Most employers to-day are reluctant to engage coloured workers . . . Because of the constant and unsatisfied demand in some areas for domestics in hospitals, institutions and private domestic employment, it is not unduly difficult to find openings for coloured females, but it was reported recently that a Jamaican girl anxious to become a nurse could not get accepted in Preston.

Recruits from the West Indies were discouraged from undertaking the longer State Registered Nurse training, and set on the State

Enrolled Nurse track instead, which meant they were kept in low-grade nursing jobs and could never make a career in the profession: 'A lot of us fell for that. If we were given a chance at the time to sit the test to do SRN a lot of us would have got through. We were sort of cheap labour really.'[7]

Perhaps the most striking aspect of the stereotype of the dirty, ill-educated and 'not very good' Irish nurse is how quickly it disappeared. By the late 1950s Irish nurses, particularly female ones, were associated with care, patience and natural good looks: the smiling, self-sacrificing country girl humanizing a vast, anonymous urban institution; the lively, fun-loving young woman extending a caring hand to people in ill-health, those who were at their most vulnerable. Part of the reason for this volte-face lay in the contradictions of the NHS itself. For all that the NHS stood for modernity, efficiency and organization, many of the hospitals were badly run, and housed in crumbling buildings with poor facilities for both staff and patients. British women had no intention of putting up with those conditions. Factory and secretarial work won hands down over nursing, and domestic work in hospitals was considered worse than a last resort. While middle-class girls continued to enter the teaching hospitals as nursing trainees, and Mills & Boon traded in stories of true romance with their handsome doctors, in the majority of institutions nursing simply meant hard physical work and long hours for indifferent pay. For TB and mental health nurses the job was barely a step above domestic service. Yet as increased professionalism, efficiency and trust in the NHS took hold, the Irish (and, later, Caribbean) nurses were able to take advantage of these contradictions. They became associated with all the virtues of the modern, caring state.

For despite the matrons' attempts to dispense with Irish labour, they could not manage without it. In August 1946, for example, Runwell Mental Hospital in Essex was recruiting in Limerick; this was a hospital that had only opened in 1937 and the staff were very proud of its modernity. Listed among its attractions was the fact that 70 per cent of the nurses were from Ireland, and that ten of the fourteen sisters and assistant matrons were Irish. The recruiting drive was so successful that they were back in October, signing up girls in Kilkenny, Donegal and places in between. In the same month, staff from

Nurses dancing at a benefit for the St John and St Elizabeth Hospice in
St John's Wood, 1960s.

Birmingham Infirmary were out looking for pupil assistant nurses, and a Miss Kerrigan from Yardley Green Sanatorium, in the east of the city, contacted the Liaison Office with plans 'not only to seek recruits but to address women's meetings and organisations with a view to breaking down the prejudice against tuberculosis nursing'. For the Irish government these recruiting drives proved too successful. They fed into the moral panic about the destruction of rural communities, and even the bedrock of the Catholic family, as Irish girls were lured to pagan and industrial Britain by the promise of high wages and good working conditions. In October 1946, *Reynolds News* reported that Éamon de Valera was considering banning ads offering jobs in Britain from appearing in the Irish press.[8]

The advertisements appealed to workless young women, of course, but also to their parents, who were having to support young men and women with no prospect of work on the meagre hand-outs from the dole. It was, after all, Dónall Mac Amhlaigh's mother who drew his attention to the job in Northampton hospital in 1951; within six years his three brothers and a sister – all the children of the family – were living and working in England. The Irish writer M. J. Molloy felt he was witnessing the destruction of rural life, and became incensed with what he termed the 'extermination through emigration campaign' run by British recruiting agents, and the 'infinitely more deadly' advertisements for employment in England 'which swamp every newspaper, especially the provincial newspapers, which are bought in every farmhouse'. As he bluntly reasoned: 'What farmer would give his daughter £150 of his hard-earned money [for a dowry] when he could get rid of her for nothing to a respectable job worth £4 or £5 a week?' Father Eamon Casey (later Bishop Casey, who became notorious for having had a long affair with and fathered a child by his housekeeper) worked with the Irish in London in the late 1950s. He argued it was not only the parents who might do well out of the exchange: 'I know of a factory where each member of the staff was paid £10 for every girl she succeeded in bringing over from Ireland.'[9]

Looked at squarely, it was a market in bodies being sold to England. In 1948 the new Irish government set up a commission to advise on the problem of depopulation; the phrase 'the vanishing Irish' was coined to describe the problem, and in truth it was acute.

Nearly a sixth of the total population recorded in 1951 had left Ireland by the end of the decade, and that meant a vastly higher proportion of the working-age population. But for British hospitals the recruitment did not go nearly far enough. A few years after Miss Kerrigan's attempts to lure Irish girls into TB nursing, questions were asked in the House of Commons about the shortage of nurses at Yardley Green, as one ward of fifty beds and another of fifty-six were under threat of closure, despite a long and growing waiting list for admission.

The decline of TB was one of the first post-war medical success stories, as mass X-ray screening, treatment with streptomycin and, finally, vaccination brought a disease associated with poverty and overcrowding under control. Nonetheless in 1949 (before the BCG vaccine was approved) the death rate from TB in England and Wales was an astounding four hundred per week. The sanatoria were still full to overflowing in the late 1940s, with waiting lists of three or four months, and they needed vast armies of workers – all separated according to a hierarchy of roles – in order to keep going. This diary kept by a private patient in the 'basins' category at Frimley Sanatorium in Surrey, in 1945, gives some idea of the labour-intensive nature of the regime:

> I am on 'basins'. Everyone is 'on' something. 'Absolute' is entirely in bed, 'basins' is getting up to wash in own room (mine is a basin and taps) and go along to the toilet, 'OTW' is out to wash, through 1 hour up, 2 hours up to 4, and then 'exercise', 1 round, 2 rounds up to 6, and then 'grades', which is work, graded upwards. All very interesting. Spoke to one other person in the weighing room – seemed pleasant and serious – only allowed to whisper or, as she puts it, 'I'm on whispers'. 9.30 pm lights out. Thank goodness windows wide open.
>
> Didn't sleep, of course, till early this morning but did get a bit between 5.30 am (when they take your temperature) and 7 am when night sister burst in on her round and woke me out of a lovely slumber to ask if I'd slept! 7.30 am they make your bed and you wash. 8.30 am breakfast – porridge, bacon and fried bread, butter and marmalade, but only one cup of tea. Then a constant stream of nurses, orderly

with a clean hankie (provided by the house), patient with newspapers,
maid to sweep the floor, nurse to dust, sister on her ward round etc.

By the end of the 1940s the maids, the orderlies and the dusting nurses
were as likely as not to be from the European refugee camps, or to be
Irish. Who else was willing to work upwards of a fifty-hour week
(some nurses were clocking up sixty-three hours in particularly
stretched hospitals) doing boring work, for indifferent pay, and to live
in isolated, institutional accommodation far away from towns and
cities?[10]

The situation was the same – if not worse – in the old asylums. In
1946, for example, all leave was cancelled at St Andrew's Hospital,
near Norwich, and staff were asked to work overtime for standard
pay. Three wards, catering for eighty-eight women patients each,
were operating with just three day nurses and one night nurse apiece.
Nurses customarily worked twelve- or thirteen-hour shifts. A study
by the University of Manchester in the early 1950s found that during
these long hours, as much as 50 per cent of the nurses' time was spent
on basic tasks – feeding, bathing, teeth-brushing, shaving, bed-
making, for example – and as little as 5 per cent on what was termed
'technical nursing', an activity which included accompanying medical staff on visits, but was mainly limited to dispensing drugs. The
survey team noted that even more of the nurses' time would have
been spent feeding patients and cleaning wards if it weren't for the
patients themselves, who did vast amounts of the work in the wards.
In fact the descriptions of the 'higher-grade' patients feeding and
clothing their fellows, sluicing, cleaning and setting the wards to
rights rendered them all but indistinguishable from the nurses.[11]

In the summer of 1948, as the NHS creaked into gear, my mother
left a small farm in West Cork and joined her older sister Mary at
Netherne psychiatric hospital in Surrey. She had just turned eighteen
and was to spend the next several years learning the work of the
'mental nurse' in a large hospital which enjoyed a reputation for
up-to-the-minute care. In the early years of the NHS two rival con-
ceptions of psychiatric care competed for dominance. On one side,
psychiatrists argued for the benefits of occupational and talking therapy, and many hospitals unlocked their wards in an effort to restore

dignity and agency to the long-term ill who had become dependent and institutionalized. On the other, they lauded the therapeutic effects of new, and often under-researched, treatments such as electro-convulsive therapy (ECT), insulin comas, psycho-surgery and the new anti-psychotic drugs (such as Largactil). Staff shortages impacted on the use of these therapies in more or less predictable ways. It was no wonder that anti-psychotic drugs were swiftly taken up by the hospital doctors: they released both patients and nurses from the horrors of straitjackets, padded cells and force feeding; the wards became noticeably calmer, though nurses complained that their role was now limited to handing out pills. Other therapies, such as insulin treatment and ECT, were manpower intensive, requiring trained nurses to administer, observe and aid patients for several hours. One survey in the late 1950s discovered hospitals that had, for the sake of expediency, instituted 'mass production' ECT sessions, with patients herded together witnessing their peers in various states of shock and unconsciousness.[12]

What both approaches shared was an assumption that the nurses were there primarily to observe and to act as custodians, but not to get involved in treatment. The training offered to the 'mental nurse' was minimal, and much of it was devoted to general and low-grade skills such as bed-making. In the early years of the NHS as many as 80 per cent of trainees left before completing their course. Yet the Ministries of Labour and Health argued that rather than improve training and increase pay in order to attract more nurses, the answer to the employment shortfall was to expand the number of untrained assistant nurses, or even to leave the work to the patients themselves. It was an open admission of disdain for mental health nursing – anyone could do it, and they could do it without any training.

The Ministry of Labour wanted a continuous supply of unskilled foreign workers to fill the unattractive jobs in lower-grade hospitals, and the Health Ministry wanted the cheapest solution to maintaining the asylums and TB hospitals, even if that meant manning them with patients. The logical extension of these policies was a kind of closed circle, in which migrants cared for and lived with patients in institutions cut off from the towns and cities. In fact this was exactly the situation in the Polish hospitals. These were institutions initially run by the Polish Resettlement Corps until they were taken over by the NHS, where the patients, medical, nursing and domestic staff were all compatriots, and all lived in the same terrible conditions – hutted camps without ceilings or indoor sanitation, heated by free-standing stoves. Administrators objected to the 'very lax and promiscuous' way that TB patients and staff mixed: 'Patients are continually going in and out of Nurses' quarters, and we have one patient who is married to a Sister. I had a request from one of my domestics yesterday to be given a married quarter, as she had married a patient.' Setting aside the inconvenient fact that ten out of the eight hundred Polish nurses in Britain got pregnant each month throughout 1948, the Poles created a nicely self-supporting system which the Ministry of Health might have been pleased to replicate with other immigrant populations, except that they needed their labour power in the NHS. But a version of this closed circle was evident in hundreds of hospitals throughout the country. Dónall Mac Amhlaigh's Northampton hospital was far from unusual in the mix of migrant workers who manned the wards, stoked the boilers, cleaned and sluiced, tended the gardens, and married each other. At Netherne my mother found herself working on the wards alongside many Irish, as well as those she termed DPs (Displaced Persons), and demobbed Poles. But she also found herself treating them. Disturbed patients who had found their way to England after years of abuse and terror in concentration and refugee camps were treated with the latest in psychiatric therapies: insulin comas, leucotomies, ECT and (if they were lucky) the talking cure.[13]

The migrants were in the strange position of providing the manpower to combat TB and to care for those afflicted by 'mental infirmity', but at the same time being targeted as the carriers of disease, not only louse-born typhus but – ironically enough – TB, and even mental infirmity. Throughout the 1950s the Ministry of Labour remained keen to bring working immigrants into the country, and so ended up tangling with medical professionals who were keen to keep them out, or at least to screen them effectively at the port of entry. Migrants from the European camps were supposed to be screened for TB in their transit camps on the Continent, but – like the pregnancy checks – the X-rays were often less than accurate or rigorous. Nevertheless, despite public pressure for more border checks, the Home

Office insisted that additional hurdles on arrival in Britain might put off prospective migrants, and thus could put the country's post-war recovery into question. This fear ran directly counter to the public perception, then as now, of hordes of hopefuls who would stop at nothing to get across the border.[14]

As the problem of lice-carrying migrants faded – with the spread of the use of DDT, and with improved access to running water in rural areas – so the type of contagion associated with immigrants shifted into new areas: first TB, then smallpox, and even excessive fertility. It was true that the incidence of TB among immigrant populations, and particularly the Irish, was far higher than in the general population. Following the results of a 1953 survey of all hospital beds, which revealed the gap between resident and immigrant populations, there was a flurry of popular anxiety that TB was being 'imported' by foreigners, and that all the advances in prevention were being set at naught: 'TB Aliens fill our clinics' claimed the *Daily Herald* in February 1953. In fact, of course, aliens such as the EVWs were screened for infectious diseases before they left the European camps, even if imperfectly. But Commonwealth, colonial and Irish citizens all had the right of free travel – all were invisible to border controls under the 1948 British Nationality Act. Nothing could be done about it if they were carrying disease. The following year, in 1954, a study of tuberculosis beds in north-west London found that one in nine infected people were Irish immigrants, compared with one in seven who were Londoners, although of course the vast majority of local residents were London- rather than Irish-born. The problem with the Irish, it was acknowledged, was not that they brought TB with them, but that they caught it so easily when they arrived. 'The susceptible country-dweller', the authors of the report claimed, was 'the weak point in our defences where the invader pours through unmolested'. The Irish had poor immunity to the disease, and lived in the worst housing after they arrived in British cities. And the fact that they were so susceptible to disease meant that they could go on to infect everyone else.

We have been told: 'They bring it over with them; you will find whole families over in Ireland who are rotten with it.' A tuberculosis officer said with obvious sincerity, 'It's the Irish who are our biggest problem; if it weren't for them; things would be much easier.' On the other hand, we came across, time and again, among Irish patients the bewildered and pathetic plea: 'How did I get it, doctor? None of my family ever had it. I was always perfectly well *until I came to England*.' It was their genuine and sincere conviction that England was responsible for giving them tuberculosis.

In this scenario immigrants were the victims of the slums in which they lived, and, indeed, of the hospitals in which they worked. TB was rife in mental hospitals, in part because of the chronic overcrowding on undermanned wards.[15]

The Ministry of Health produced leaflets designed to warn the intending Irish migrant of the dangers across the water. 'A Ticket to the Future' flagged up the danger of infection (by a disease which could certainly compromise your future) and tried to instil in travellers the need to be X-rayed once a year. For there was no legal way to insist on health checks.

> What about those who have been born and brought up in rural parts? It's the best life, true – but not always an easy preparation for those who have to work in cities, in overcrowded conditions. In the countryside they may not have met the germ of tuberculosis, and when they step into a city environment, they will be totally unprepared.

Similar leaflets were designed for other migrant groups. 'A Warm Welcome to a Cold Climate' advised Commonwealth migrants on how to avoid getting TB. 'Eat more than at home, stay away from crowded places as much as possible.' 'Stay away from people with a chronic cough; avoid sleeping in a room with lots of other people and keep the window open.' The leaflet was distributed in the West Indies, Ghana and Nigeria, and translated into Cypriot, Urdu and Punjabi.[16]

In the end it was vaccination with the BCG that turned the tide against TB, though no doubt telling immigrants to stay away from people coughing helped a bit. By the early 1960s mass vaccination had begun to reap rewards, though fears of migrant contagion merely moved on to other areas and other populations. The TB hospitals closed, and the psychiatric institutions slowly began to fold up as patients were moved into the community, leaving only chronic and geriatric cases in the old wards. So the least desirable nursing jobs disappeared, and with them went those deemed the least desirable nurses. But the problem of immigrant contagion simply moved on, and by the late 1950s it was located securely in the sexual health and fertility of 'problem' migrants. And as so often, stories of immigrants abusing the services of the NHS provided a figleaf for other, more broadly Social Darwinian, concerns.

Take the rise in cases of venereal disease in Caribbean migrants, for example. One early 1960s study pointed out that gonorrhea was a fast-growing problem among West Indian men, but also (to a lesser extent) West Indian women. It seemed clear that the disease was primarily being contracted after arrival in Britain, and mainly from local prostitutes. The conclusion was that it would be better to allow immigrants in in family groups. Of 25,942 male gonorrhea patients in 1963, 46.3 per cent were UK born, 25.2 per cent were West Indian, and 28.5 per cent other immigrants. The West Indian figure was certainly high, given the tiny proportion they formed of the overall population. But so too was the 'other immigrant' category. Perhaps the most interesting thing about these statistics was that the other immigrants were not broken down into their different nationalities. There was an assumption of a West Indian problem.[17]

Then there was family planning. It may have been concern for Caribbean women's health and desire for control over their own bodies, or it may have been concern over the rising black population which encouraged the British Family Planning Association to distribute leaflets to clinics across the Caribbean, specially targeted towards intending migrants:

> When you arrive in Great Britain, everything will be new and strange, and you will certainly want a little time to settle down before you think of starting a family or adding to the one you have.
>
> The Family Planning Association, however, with headquarters in London, wants to help you to have your babies when you want them, so they will be born when you are well and have a home and are able to take care of them.

Babies are best born about two years apart, so until you are ready for the next one, go to one of our clinics where the woman doctor will show you what to do.[18]

In fact the wisdom of handing out family planning advice to Caribbean women was contested, given the fact that many of them in long-standing unions were not married. In March 1958 a member of the Family Planning Association (FPA) called at the office of the 'Liaison Officer for coloured people in Birmingham', a Mr Gibbs. Gibbs was a former probation officer (elsewhere he is called an 'ex-policeman') and the FPA reporter outlines his quite decided views (as well as her own) on the women with whom he dealt in his role as Liaison Officer:

He says he knows that some of the girls who have been to us are prostitutes, or have formed temporary attachments with men, often as the only way of getting a room to live in. He agrees that it is impossible for us to sift them out in the course of one short interview but says that if we will refer doubtful cases back to his office he can easily find out the circumstances and either refer them back to us or discourage them from coming. He says that a great many more women are coming here from the West Indies. Some are wives or girls sent for by their men over here. Others are girls coming on their own and they often tell him they come because it's easy to get a job, 'or if they can't get a job, you can live with a man'. What it boils down to is that he feels, and I agree with him, that we ought to face the fact that at present we are undoubtedly giving B.C. [birth control] advice to a great many coloured girls who are thus encouraged to live promiscuously. We ought to have a definite policy about coloured people. Either we should definitely draw the line somewhere, or we must admit that we think it more important to keep down illegitimate births than to stick to our 'married only' line. He thinks that very few of the so-called common law marriages among West Indians are permanent arrangements.

Plenty of voices were raised against this pathologization of Caribbean unions, and the official policy of the FPA itself was to take the woman's word for it. In August 1959 the Birmingham FPA wrote to a local doctor to explain why its policy was not to ask for proof of marriage. The general practice was to treat 'Jamaican' patients as they did all others, and to regard those in 'stable partnerships (who are what is known as "common law wives") in the same way as any Housing Authority would deal with them, namely as married people'. They offered a short history lesson: 'The historic reason, as you know, for so few Jamaicans marrying is that in the old days we would not permit slaves to marry. Hence the pattern of life that is common among colonial people throughout the West Indies.'

Nonetheless, behaviours around sexual health and reproduction became tied to the issue of scarce resources. As the anti-immigration lobby gained ground in the wake of the 1962 Commonwealth Immigrants Act it was common enough to find concerns over the ability of the NHS to handle all-comers mixed with broadly racist stereotyping of the 'foreigners' turning up to use the services. Writing in support of the Conservative MP Cyril Osborne, who had argued in the Commons that 70 per cent of maternity beds in Willesden were occupied by immigrants, the chief medical social worker in Willesden, Mary Park, and the pathologist at the Central Middlesex Hospital, George Discombe, wrote a joint letter to *The Times* outlining their concerns, along with their prejudices. They noted that of 400 expectant mothers attending antenatal clinics in the area, 45 per cent were born in the United Kingdom, 35 per cent in 'Eire', 16 per cent in the West Indies, and 4 per cent elsewhere:

> Many of the immigrants from Eire are indistinguishable from our indigenous population save by accent and religion, but there is a considerable minority of stupid, self-neglectful unmarried Irish girls who appear to come to England to obtain maternity care and to have the baby adopted.
>
> Such immigrants often refuse antenatal care and arrive in hospital only when labour is established. When they do arrive they need urgent treatment, and have to be detained longer than usual; and before discharge they impose a considerable load on the hospital's social workers because they are usually homeless and without means of support.
>
> A minority which is very troublesome consists of those who cannot speak English. In our hospital we can usually manage the more widely used European tongues and often, but not always, Greek, Arabic, Ibo,

Yoruba, Persian, Urdu and Hindi; but we cannot be expected to provide at a moment's notice a midwife who speaks fluent Pushtu or even Greek. Patients who cannot communicate with their nurses are usually terrified of their surroundings and cannot co-operate. Such patients are more likely to come from Cyprus, Pakistan or India than from elsewhere.[19]

West Indian mothers actually came quite well out of their survey. Nonetheless the medics argued that the country should 'be much more selective in admitting immigrants and much more ready to deport them if they prove unsatisfactory citizens. A minimum standard of education is desirable. We suggest that no immigrant be accepted who is not literate in English or some European language which uses the Latin alphabet.' It was an imaginative way of trying to distinguish desirable from undesirable immigrants, though it would have proved useless against all those unmarried pregnant Irish girls, who when they weren't having babies were as likely as not working in hospitals.

6

Troublemakers

The news of any attempt to reduce the numbers of Jamaicans at Causeway Green Hostel suddenly, other than by gradual running down, would spread rapidly from hostel to hostel with most unfortunate results . . . At present my information is that the atmosphere in the hostel is subdued even if smouldering, and dances, etc., are in abeyance. Incidentally, I understand that the Rector of Birmingham had a Pole and a Jamaican together in his pulpit at Sunday Evensong pleading for harmony between the races. It will be noted from the Press Extracts attached that the writers seem, in general, to favour the Jamaicans against the Poles . . . To take action which would have the effect of these men losing their jobs because of feuds with foreigners would merely kindle the colour bar issue again . . . At present attempts to disperse them during repairs to damage to their sleeping blocks are handicapped by their fear of being placed amongst blocks of hostile Poles. There is no doubt that the mixing of coloured and white races in the same hostels, using the same dining and recreational space is a daring experiment which might well have been deemed impossible if it had not been tried. To have some measure of success in such an experiment despite a series of 'incidents' is no mean achievement . . . The presence of coloured workers in our factories, etc., is now losing its novelty and the population is becoming used to their presence. There are signs that the freely expressed fears of vendettas between rival races of EVWs, e.g. Serbs and Croatians, have been remarkably falsified by our adherence to the policy of non-segregation. Any deviation from this policy especially in

the case of coloured <u>British</u> subjects as against white EVWs . . .
would be most unfortunate.

'Disturbances in National Service Corporation
Hostels . . .' Ministry of Labour Memo (1949)[1]

How to keep the peace? Harassed officials, such as this one at the
Ministry of Labour, had organized the European work schemes
bringing labourers from Ireland and the Continental camps. They
had dealt painstakingly with the trade unions. They had requisitioned
accommodation for the workers, revamped some of the facilities, and
employed cooks and cleaners. They had liaised with local councils.
They had set up the Barbados scheme, targeting vacancies in London
Transport. They had found work for individual West Indian migrants,
and billeted men of all nationalities in National Service Corporation
Hostels around the country – only to find that they refused to get on
with one another nicely. Fights kept breaking out in the camps and
hostels, where men were crowded together with little to do after work
but annoy one another. After a particularly vicious set of battles in a
camp at Castle Donington, they decided to restrict the number of
West Indian immigrants in any one camp to a maximum of twelve.
'We must be realistic,' argued one civil servant, 'and face the fact that
however charming they may be individually these West Indians do
tend to get across, and then to start fighting with, other residents, in
particular the Irish and the Poles.' Whitehall wrung its sensible English hands. The Irish and the Poles in particular 'intensely resent
seeing black men dancing with white girls, whereas white girls all too
frequently seem to prefer dancing with the black men'. One Yugoslav
in Bradford in the early 1950s recalled the fighting at dances: 'the
trouble we had was again different nationalities and because of girls.
And we used to fight, you know, because, you know, when foreigners
fight they really fight, they don't just, you know, take off the coat and
punch up, you know.' Although there was no evidence to suggest that
the Jamaicans were the aggressors at Castle Donington, 'the practical
needs of the situation made it necessary to appease the foreigners and
to remove the minority'.

The situation was tricky because the West Indians were British subjects, while those who were being appeased were technically 'aliens'. But what was striking was how each of the 'races' involved came out badly in comparison with the rational and reasonable English. Officials in charge of the hostels regretted that, because of a shortage of beds, it was 'impossible to reallocate West Indians to avoid contact with Poles or Irish or other combustible white material'. They commended their own broadmindedness in recognizing 'that there is a degree of prejudice against coloured men and that the Irish and certain foreign elements have this prejudice strongly developed'. European immigrants were racist and Jamaicans caused the trouble apparently merely by being there. Nobody seemed to think that the overcrowded conditions of the camps, with hundreds of single men living on top of one another, were bound to cause trouble, wherever their inmates came from.

We have surprisingly detailed information on the types of trouble immigrants were in in the early 1950s. In January 1953 a Home Office committee was tasked with examining the social and economic impact of recent immigration, with a view to advising on whether or not the government should introduce restrictions on the right to settle and work in Britain. The investigation was couched in explicitly racial terms: 'to examine the possibilities of preventing any further increase in coloured people seeking employment in the United Kingdom'.[2] As this suggests, at least some of the members of the Working Party were already – in 1953 – convinced that the impact of the colonial and Commonwealth migrants was plainly detrimental, and should be stopped. And although information was requested from the Ministry of Labour and National Assistance, most of the evidence for the 1953 report was derived not from those who could comment on employment and economics, but from the police, who were hardly likely to offer a value-free account. The police had to do with immigrants insofar as they were trouble, and it was as troublemakers that the chief constables of urban constabularies throughout the country were asked to 'grade' them.

What can be said of the conduct of these coloured people? Is it true, for instance, that the coloured community as a whole, or particular sections of it, are generally idle or poor workmen, have low standards of living, live under bad conditions either from choice or necessity, or are addicted to drug-trafficking or other types of crime?[3]

In effect the chief constables were asked to evaluate immigrants' moral as well as their criminal conduct – were they idle and bad at their jobs? Did they like living in slums? It was a sign of the heavily paternalistic structure of the police force, and indeed civil society as a whole, that none of the respondents seemed to think the task beyond them.

The police chiefs were asked about 'coloured' immigrants, but in their replies most of them broke their local migrants down by nationality, and they often compared them to European migrants, especially the Irish and the Poles. In Bristol 'the standard of life of the coloured people . . . is just as high as that of many of the Irish labourers who have come here in large numbers to take up work, and who, despite good wages, are often content to live in conditions of squalor'. In Birmingham the Irish were particularly prone to fighting, even by comparison with other immigrants. 'The incidence of crime among West Africans is not great. The trouble they cause is mainly by engaging in drunken brawls, particularly with Irishmen after the closing of licensed hours, usually at weekends.' In contrast in Coventry, although 'the Indian is also addicted to drink, and when under the influence, is inclined to become quarrelsome and violent . . . the tendency is to quarrel amongst themselves, and it is seldom that any other nationality is involved'.[4]

The reports did their best to suggest national patterns of criminality. In Glasgow, Indians were inclined to deal in forged clothing coupons, as well as theft, assault and robbery. In Coventry and Birmingham, Pakistanis were apparently addicted to gambling, and crowds of them would happily play cards and dice for up to forty-eight hours at a stretch, for large sums of money. In Tynemouth, Birmingham and Cardiff, West Africans had been prosecuted for possession of 'Indian hemp', but in South Shields drug-trafficking was the domain of the Indians. And all over the country all kinds of 'coloured' people consorted with prostitutes – in Glasgow, Liverpool, Leeds and Birmingham, Indians, Pakistanis (sometimes described as Punjabis and Bengalis), West Africans and West Indians were to be found in the company of 'women of low repute', in 'poor class licensed premises'. Some police chiefs put this down to a lack of other options for intimacy, but there was often an edge of something like moral turpitude in the accounts. In Birmingham, for example, we learn of West Africans that:

> A fair proportion are of the 'spiv' type and spend much of their time in public houses, pin table saloons and low class cafes with women of the prostitute class. In their gaudy and flamboyant style of dress they are to be seen lounging about in groups, and not a few are ready to pick a quarrel at the slightest provocation, real or imagined.

Just occasionally the police homed in on political rather than social troublemaking. In March 1953, Kingston upon Hull police officers kept watch on African students protesting that British troops had fired on 'fleeing native villagers' in areas of rural Kenya in which the Mau Mau had been active. The report argued that 'elements of the Communist Party' were exploiting the situation for their own gain, just as later the activities of the Indian Workers' Association, campaigning for equal pay and equal trade union rights, would be blamed on disaffected Communists.

However, the really striking thing about the police reports is just how little trouble Commonwealth immigrants appeared to be causing – especially in comparison to the Irish, and to home-grown criminals and rabble-rousers. In Edinburgh and Fife, for example, the 'coloured' population was comprised mostly of Indian and Pakistani men who made their living as peddlers and 'behaved exceptionally well'; in Coventry they were 'not less law abiding' than the locals. In Sheffield, where 'new men are found almost daily', the police admitted that 'there seems to be little serious crime amongst the coloured population'. In 1955, when the chief constables were asked for an update, the situation had not changed. Most reports from around the country acknowledged that the immigrants in the main were 'well behaved' when it came to illegal goings on. In Birmingham '[c]oloured people do commit offences and are dealt with from time to time, but their behaviour gives no more cause for concern than that of white residents.' In Bradford, while the chief constable argued there was no chance of assimilation, there was not much crime either, apart from gambling. The only group for whom this was not broadly true was not a national group at all, but a social one: the stowaways and deserters.

Everyone agreed that while fare-paying passengers were mostly law-abiding, the stowaways were not. They lived in fear of deportation and so attempted to live their lives under the radar. In Leeds, for example, 'They have no documents and change their names as often as they change addresses. There is no power to detain them pending enquiries, even if it were known that a man was a deserter.'⁵ Stowaways and seamen who had jumped ship were at risk of repatriation until they had lived out a period of residence. But without documents they could not get work, and it was nigh impossible to repatriate them – where should they be sent? During the war undocumented seamen had to report to local police stations in order to access rations, but once rationing finally came to an end in 1954 the police had no control over, or access to, these men at all. Ironically, the chief constables considered that what had amounted to the 'huge problem' of displaced and indigent seamen at the end of the war was alleviated by the Korean War, when stokers and boiler men and ship's cooks were again needed in large numbers. In reality the problem presented by stowaways and deserters would soon be dwarfed by the numbers of bona fide fare-paying passengers arriving from Asia and the Caribbean.

For despite the difficulty in laying crime or 'bad behaviour' at the immigrants' door, the police were in no doubt that they were trouble. They were obsessed with the newcomers' apparent sins of idleness, and lack of industry and ambition. This was one way of signalling the cost of immigration. If the immigrants were to be welcomed insofar as they would set their shoulders to the wheel of post-war recovery, any evidence that they either did not work, or did not work hard enough, would count against them. In fact the Ministry of Labour insisted that they were not work-shy, and the National Assistance Board that they were not unduly burdensome. But in 1953 the newspapers were full of stories of scrounging immigrants following a series of parliamentary questions by Labour MP Thomas Reid. The figures belied the fears, since a mere £150,000 to £200,000 a year went to 'coloured' immigrants, out of a National Assistance budget of £8 million. In one week in May, 1,870 men received assistance, but 500 of these claims were for small supplements to low wages, in order to support wives and children. But these fairly straightforward numbers made little impact on the Home Office Working Party, when set against the vague observations of policemen.

> In the London area, the Chelsea, Hammersmith and Paddington divisions have the impression that on the whole coloured people are work-shy and content to live on national assistance, and the Chelsea, Paddington and Kentish Town divisions mention that their officers have been called to Employment Exchanges and Assistant Board Offices to deal with coloured claimants who cause trouble.[6]

It appeared self-evident to these observers that work-shyness went along with being content to live in squalid conditions. The Arabs in Swansea were 'inclined to a low standard of living, rather from choice than necessity'; in Staffordshire Indians and Pakistanis lived in 'the most primitive and squalid conditions', 'of their own choosing'. In South Shields Indians and Africans 'have a low standard of living by choice, and will not hesitate to gamble all their earnings'. In Newcastle-upon-Tyne the chief constable had to admit that the immigrants worked hard, but noted that they were not engaged in really 'productive' industrial labour. He even had them selling luxury silks to miners, so they were not only 'spivs' but exotic spivs, who went one further than the traditional wideboy trade in stockings: 'The Indians and Pakistanis cannot be said to be idle, as in many cases they travel long distances on foot round mining villages in Northumberland and Durham, carrying suitcases of silks and draperies. On the other hand it cannot be said that they engage in any useful or productive work.' By contrast the Indians in Coventry, who undoubtedly did work hard in factories and foundries, were blamed for being content with such 'low-grade' work. This was taken as proof, not that many jobs were barred to them by virtue of their colour and difficulties with the English language, but that they had no wish to better themselves. All they wanted was a job and they did not care what kind: 'It has been found that by far the greater percentage of these persons desire to enter the United Kingdom merely with a view to obtaining remunerative employment, without thought for personal advancement, and in the main, they are only suitable for employment in the most menial types of work.'

Indians and Pakistanis were, in effect, being accused of being out of step with the upwardly mobile drive of British society as a whole. All they wanted was a job, any job. West Africans and West Indians 'prefer to dress in flashy colours than better their home conditions'. Africans didn't appear to know how to behave. In Sheffield they not only wasted their money, but acted as though they were the equals of their neighbours:

> They have the least respect for authority, and within a short time of arriving in this country are demanding their rights as British subjects. They seldom show the quiet respect found in the Arab and Pakistan men. Their object in coming to the United Kingdom is in some cases obscure. Good wages, which are the rule rather than the exception, are perhaps the attraction, but as most of the men from Africa spend all they earn, they make no provision for the future, either for themselves or for the families they have left behind.[7]

It would be easy to fill these pages with more or less prejudiced comments detailing the failure of immigrants to live up to British expectations of work and social propriety. In fact all the careful 'ranking' of different nationalities was a waste of time. What the Working Party wanted was evidence that would allow them to mount a campaign arguing for the need to restrict entry of 'coloured' people in general. The trouble with such legislation was that unless particular problems could be laid at the coloured immigrants' door, legislating against them alone would look like – in fact it would be – racial discrimination. In the early 1950s, the vast majority of colonial and Commonwealth immigrants to Britain came from Canada, Australia and New Zealand. How could the government enact legislation which excluded Jamaicans but not New Zealanders, without appearing to discriminate on racial terms?

The Ministry of Labour was adamantly against discriminatory legislation. This was not only because it was a period of full employment and the country desperately needed all the workers it could get. The ministry was also worried about antagonizing the trade unions. The unions had no objection to individual companies refusing to employ 'coloured' labour, but they baulked at a national policy on race – although they were to change their minds about this before the decade was out. Officials argued that rather than new legislation, it would be better to use existing measures to encourage the right type of immigrants and discourage the wrong type. Colonial and ex-colonial territories should be urged to restrict passports; stowaways and other undesirables should be rounded up and deported; and dis-heartening propaganda about the perils of life in England should be circulated, particularly in the West Indies.

The Working Party's emphasis on West Indians was perverse, given how few of the reports from across the country commented adversely on Caribbean migrants. It was one sign, if sign were needed, that the moves towards legislation had nothing to do with actual immigrant behaviour but were led by public concern (fanned by the newspapers) over the newcomers. In November 1955 the Working Party acknowl-edged that the increased number of West Indian arrivals was the trigger for controls. Although so far 'the better types' had travelled to Britain, there was bound to be more trouble to come, especially given the pressure on housing. And since migration from the Indian sub-continent was growing and 'these people are not assimilable', it was wise to include them in any new legislation.[8] In fact the Common-wealth Relations Office tried to argue for new laws targeting only people from the Caribbean. Since Indians and Pakistanis had not been causing much adverse public comment, they reasoned, they shouldn't get lumped in with West Indians.

The trouble caused by immigrants was, as often as not, located in other people rather than in the immigrants themselves. But police officers, like employers (and landladies), often appeared to have diffi-culty in disentangling cause and effect. In Stafford, for example, in 1953, the immigrants were fine as long as they did not try to drink in certain pubs, or work in certain jobs:

> In one or two instances licensees of public houses have refused to serve coloured people in the best rooms and in February this year a strike occurred amongst the drivers and conductors of the Corporation Bus Service in protest against the employment of Indian conductors.

However, in general the coloured population are well behaved and cause the police little trouble.

In Sheffield the confusion was even more stark – men from West Africa were citizens of the United Kingdom and they knew it. However, if they acted as citizens, they caused trouble, and the Sheffield police force were quite clear that the fault lay with them, and not with the locals who were prejudiced against them:

When the influx of coloured men first became apparent in the City, there was considerable trouble caused when they demanded equal facilities in public houses and dance halls. They were made the object of cheap jokes by the more ignorant type of persons who normally frequent these premises, which by their locality and patronage, have always been considered low class and violence was often the result. No doubt the young West Africans who were the only race involved, had come to this Country with the idea that they could have a free rein, and their arrogance was most pronounced. They were in the habit of visiting a particular dance hall in considerable force, and they did not hesitate to use violence towards anyone who cared to oppose them. This resulted in strong police action in 1952, when mass arrests were made and many coloured men were charged. Since that time there has been no further trouble, but police vigilance has not been relaxed. The coloured men have become more educated to the local way of life and have come to realise that equal partnership is not theirs by right but must be worked for.[9]

The idea that Commonwealth migrants had to earn their 'equal partnership' with indigenous Britons was hard-wired into attitudes in the early 1950s, when both employers and trade unions attempted to treat 'coloured workers' on a par with imported foreign labour, despite the fact that they enjoyed British citizenship. From 1954 labour exchanges began to ask employers to accept 'coloured' labour instead of European Voluntary Workers, but their attempts were met with protests and strikes. In February 1955, for example, TGWU members in the West Midlands, fearful of the loss of overtime, objected to the employment of an Indian bus conductor (who had previously worked as a conductor for Bombay Tramways). They called a number of Saturday strikes, which were supported by bus crews from Birmingham, Wolverhampton and Walsall, calling for a maximum 5 per cent 'coloured quota'. This was trouble, but certainly not of the Indian conductor's making.[10]

The 1950s immigrants themselves have left few accounts of their own criminal or anti-social tendencies. What group of people ever willingly sat down to write the story of their failings? It is true that Irish migrant writers cast a cold eye on their drinking and fighting companions; 1960s memoirs by men such as Michael de Freitas (Michael X) described pimping and rack-renting in the Caribbean community; and Punjabi stories in the early 1960s outline tax evasion and passport fiddles. But for the most part, in order to gain an alternative perspective on the troublemaking migrant, we have to read between the lines of the official accounts. What can they tell us not of English prejudices, but of immigrant life? Take the experience – universally described by the experts as a problem – of living with women of 'low repute'. By the end of the decade, as we will see, the relationship between immigration and prostitution was almost exclusively a problem associated with West Indians. But in the early 1950s Sikhs, Muslims and Hindus across the country were apparently living with people the police identified as prostitutes or 'of low moral character'. In Leeds it was the Indians; in Bradford in 1955 the *majority* of Indians and Pakistanis then living in the city were reported to 'have white women living with them, although not always the same woman'.[11] Oddly, the Bradford chief constable insisted that living with English (or European) women was not necessarily an aid to assimilation, and much of the co-habitation was temporary, until either the man returned home, or his wife and children joined him in England. Nonetheless, these unions must have functioned domestically on a day-to-day basis and some of them were permanent. It is a picture that belies the frequent accusations that Asian migrants in particular had little or nothing to do with people outside their own circles.

One of the most frequently cited immigrant offences was that of running illegal betting houses – hardly a crime unknown to the home-grown English, Irish or European populations. Other financially motivated crimes included breaches of Board of Trade regulations (in other words, black-marketeering), and income tax and insurance fiddles. The Asian habit of stashing large amounts of money in their homes (reputedly in £1 notes) in order to avoid paying tax was credited with creating a new crime wave, of house breaking and entering in the poorest parts of town.

The piles of £1 notes may have been linked not to tax evasion but to a quite different series of crimes and misdemeanours. Throughout 1954 police forces in Newcastle, Sheffield and London put considerable effort into trying to crack open a forged-passport racket, which they discovered was linked to a larger smuggling operation. They lost interest when it dawned on them that the nature of the scam only made it illegal in Pakistan, and not in England. But the racket itself tells us a good deal about day-to-day life among a certain stratum of Pakistani society in Britain.

Applications by Pakistanis for passports endorsed for travel to Britain were supposed to go through the Aliens Registration Office in Karachi, where a check could be made on the employment sponsor in Britain before the passport was issued. However, the Karachi officials were open to bribery and forged passports were the norm in the early 1950s. In 1954 Ali Hussein Shah, who lived in some style in a semi-detached house in Neasden in north-west London, and drove a new car, admitted bringing over 170 men from Karachi in the single month of May. Working with a contact on the Pakistani side he would furnish the men with bogus offers of employment in Sheffield. They paid between 2,000 and 3,000 rupees for the stamped passport. Shah conceded bribery but 'said that conditions in his country were such that nothing could be obtained from official sources without paying the official concerned'. And in fact it turned out that the passport business was a small link in a chain of irregular transactions. As part of the passport deal, each man was given £145 in travellers' cheques, and £5 in cash, to bring with him to England. Once the men had safely arrived in Britain with their £150 pounds on them, Shah met up with them. He went with them to a branch of Thomas Cook where they cashed their cheques, and then he collected the money from them. In effect the men were mules, carrying foreign currency like contraband.[12]

Pakistani regulations prohibited taking more than the equivalent of £150 sterling out of the country. The poorest migrants – those with no money of their own to bring with them – proved immensely valuable to the growing ranks of Pakistani businessmen like Ali Shah, who needed sterling not just in and of itself, but in order to smuggle foreign goods back into Pakistan and sell them on the black market. There was a cap on the amount of goods traders could import into Pakistan, and many goods (classed as 'luxuries') were entirely prohibited. In order to import over the amount, traders needed to be able to pay for goods 'silently'. Fridges, agricultural machinery, wells, tractors, fans, toilets, baths, washing machines, all had to be bought with laundered money. This was also how immigrants sent money back to their relatives at home – not directly, in an envelope, or through postal orders, but by giving their sterling savings to a middleman who used them to buy goods for smuggling back to Pakistan. The relatives at home were paid out in rupees. The piles of £1 notes were probably being readied for just such transactions.

Exactly the same racket was discovered in Newcastle. A man named Noor Ahmed supplied migrants with passports – for a hefty fee – and then sent travellers' cheques worth £150 out of the country with each traveller:

> The emigrant was told to contact Kufait Ali [of 18 Wentworth Place, Newcastle] on reaching this country. As these men were usually illiterate, Kufait Ali would go with the man to a branch of Thomas Cook and Sons Limited in this country and receive the money which had been transferred from Karachi on behalf of that man. However, the money would never be handled by the man but would be remitted by Ali to Noor Ahmed by post, and the man would be given work to do by one of the Pakistani nationals already in this country. The idea behind the transfer of money from Pakistan to this country I was informed, was to make a profit on the exchange of Rupees to Sterling and also on changing the Sterling to Rupees.

Kufait Ali was apparently making £300 a month just on the exchange rate. In May 1954 (the police operations in Newcastle and Sheffield appear to have been co-ordinated), Ali was arrested with another man, in a branch of Thomas Cook. He had just helped his companion hand over the travellers' cheques and sign the receipt with a thumb print. He then pocketed the money his companion had received. Ali had on him seven passports belonging to different men. One of these men, Bagh Ali, gave this account of the mechanics of his journey when he was interviewed by the police:

> I applied in early December, 1953, for my passport for UK. I tried about one month at Karachi for my passport which I got on 25th January, 1954 . . . After that I could not get the boat, therefore I went back to my home . . . Again in April I came . . . and tried for the boat, but it was difficult to get the boat for eight or ten months. Therefore I travelled by air and paid the fare about 1,141/- rupees and exchanged about 1350/- rupees from the Eastern bank at Karachi. From all that money two thousand rupees were at my home and for over two thousand I had to sell my horse, cart and a few other cattles. I took the aeroplane 5th May from Karachi. Mr Munshi and Mr Dil Mohammad were travelling with me. I did not know them before. I reached at my brother Mr Alf Din's home at 18 Wentworth Place, Newcastle, but I found that he left for Bradford for few days and about that I did not know. I met Mr Kufait Ali there who also told me about my brother. I gave him my passport so that he could help me to get the money. I do not know Mr Kufait Ali and Mr Noor Ahmed before. That money which I brought, that was my own money. I shall try to get any job in any factory somewhere. If I could not get any job then may be I start as a pedlar.

Most of the men gave similar accounts, and as the police acknowledged, most of it was probably true – all except that the money they had brought in travellers' cheques was their own. Rural migrants, even those who had a horse and cart and cattle to sell, could not manage without middlemen like Shah and Kufait Ali to arrange their passports and travel. They were Commonwealth citizens, so they had no need of a visa, and there were no extra hurdles for them to jump at Heathrow or Southampton. But without the promise of a job, they had little hope of getting that far. How were these peasants, often illiterate, and knowing no English, supposed to secure a job in a British city? Even if they had relatives already living in Britain, unless their brothers and uncles spoke good English and had good contacts, they were not likely to be able to arrange sponsorship from an employer. And employers had steady streams of men turning up at their gates anyway, without having to bring people direct from Pakistan and India. The forged passports were vital because they got round the problem of needing a sponsor or guarantor. And the migrants in turn were vital to the middlemen. Not only did they pay hefty fees for their papers, but they could be turned into a useful source of revenue through currency-exchange scams, which in turn fuelled the business of smuggling luxury goods back into their countries. Shah and Ali were probably not traders themselves – their business was getting sterling for traders or factors who wanted to be able to buy foreign goods, and who would pay over the odds for it.

None of this could be proved, as the police ruefully acknowledged, without evidence from India and Pakistan 'which was unlikely to be forthcoming'. And anyway, none of these men had broken any English laws, except those travelling under false papers. This was where the real trouble lay. As a Sikh man living in Gravesend explained to one researcher, 'if you are smuggled into England, you are never a free man again'.[13] It meant a lifetime of looking over your shoulder, paying off loans from people back home who had helped finance the operation, and paying bribes to people in England for work and overtime, and to guard against getting shopped. The smuggled, like the stowaways, found it very hard to become legitimate. This was certainly trouble, but it was not the kind the British constabulary cared about.

Ten years later a study of immigrants and crime in the Birmingham area found the situation much the same. It was true that centres of high immigration such as Calthorpe Park, Balsall Heath, Anderton Park and Sparkbrook had high crime rates. Houses were overcrowded and often lacked basic amenities. The population of these areas was unusually mobile. But even so, it was white people who committed most of the crime. The researcher John Lambert calculated that of all the indictable offences recorded (and solved) in 1966, 74 per cent were committed by white UK-born citizens (and 50 per cent were Birmingham locals); 20 per cent by the Irish; 3 per cent by West Indians; 1 per cent by Pakistani nationals; and none at all by immigrants from India. Non-indictable offences played out slightly differently. Here the Irish were significantly over-represented. They were responsible for 36 per cent of lesser crimes, including 60 per cent of all drunkenness offences, 42 per cent of drink-driving and 17.5 per cent of convictions for prostitution. Birmingham-born men and women accounted for 34 per cent of the convictions for non-indictable offences, with 23.5 per cent attributed to white people from elsewhere in the United Kingdom. The numbers for the West Indies, India, Pakistan and other jurisdictions were so small as to be insignificant.

What was distinctive about the Irish crime profile was that it was not being hiked up by the presence of lots of young, hot-headed and out-of-control Irishmen. It was older, single working men in poorly paid and insecure jobs who were committing petty offences – those who, as Lambert put it, 'have assimilated to, rather than risen above, the conditions in the areas in which they live'.[14] There was nothing (apart perhaps from a tendency to drink) particularly ethnic about the high crime rate, except that the Irish were over-represented among the urban poor and so over-represented among the ranks of offenders. But if that was so then the low crime rate for other immigrant groups was even more remarkable. They too were over-represented among the urban poor. In 1966 Lambert counted fourteen indictable offences which ended up with the conviction of West Indians – primarily theft, possessing offensive weapons and violent offences (though they were also found guilty of more minor offences such as possession of cannabis, disorder and prostitution). This was 3 per cent of recorded crime, but West Indians comprised 6.4 per cent of the population, and a much larger proportion of working-age men, so their crime rate was significantly below the norm. Either that or they were very good, and Asian immigrants even better, at not getting caught.

7

Drinkers

One of the greatest temptations for an Irishman, and for an Irish girl away from home, is that of drink. The home-sickness you will feel at times can make your lodgings seem very lonely indeed and, if you do not know a good Catholic family on whom you can call, you will be tempted to spend your leisure time in public houses ... There have been far too many cases of drunkenness among Irish people in England and these have so often ended up in street fights which have been fully reported in the English newspapers.

Drink is created by God and is therefore good when it is used properly – but it can be the cause of repeated mortal sin. The same is true of dance halls; dancing is good in itself as a recreation but have nothing to do with halls which permit or encourage sin. Remember that the full marriage act is not the only thing to be avoided by the unmarried. The Sixth Commandment forbids whatever is contrary to holy purity in looks, words or actions. It is here that the Irish girl has a great responsibility. She it is who will dictate whether sin is to be committed or not. She is failing in her solemn duty if she allows a man to be impure with her by word or action. She has little chance of avoiding such sins if she takes to drinking in public houses. For both boys and girls, the great safeguard is to have a deep devotion to Our Lady.

A Catholic Handbook for Irish Men and Women Going to
England (1953)[1]

The 1953 *Handbook for Irish Men and Women Going to England* – published by the Catholic Truth Society of Ireland and specially pocket sized so it could be carried at all times and consulted anywhere – was full of such sage advice. That the 'average Englishman'

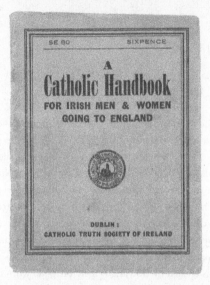

may be even-tempered but for that very reason cannot understand strong beliefs; that some Protestant churches look dangerously similar to Catholic ones; that the English are caught up by a 'craze for money' which can corrupt Irish people who then spend all their cash on drinking and gambling; and, as here, that drinking and dancing inevitably lead to sex. The obsession with sin, the danger of drink, the unique role of women as the guardians of their own and everyone else's purity – all this would have been familiar to young emigrants from all over the country. They heard it, and similar messages, given out from the altar week after week. What was new was the sense of opportunity.

The idea that emigration meant licence seemed obvious to everyone, whether or not they were pleased about it. The patronizing tone favoured by the Catholic Truth Society was not limited to it by any means. A few years later, Father Gaynor's *Shamrock Express* took a similar line: 'You are leaving a country where the Christian way of life shines clearly and are entering the darkness and confusions of twentieth-century materialism.' The dangers of life in such a country could only be staved off by regular attendance at Sunday mass, daily prayer and penance. Priests in Ireland repeatedly warned of the perils of lapsing into sin and immorality. To add to the rather general problem of 'materialism', there was the threat of Communism – apparently rife among British workers and, especially, Tenants' Associations – and of course the mortal sin of fornication. Reports from Birmingham published in the *Irish Digest* implied that once released from the bonds of family and community, young people were immediately lost to hedonism and immorality: 'Irish girls found living with coloured men and Poles!'; 'Irish boys living in illicit association with their landladies and divorced women'; 'coloured landlords' had offered sums of £20 for Irish girls to be brought over as 'housekeepers'; girls were being trapped by advertisements in Irish papers into 'working in houses little better than brothels'.[2]

The hysterical tone of these reports echoed the Irish government's line that anything was better than the 'hell' of emigration. In 1951 there had been huge publicity over a speech by Éamon de Valera claiming that fifty workers were living in one house in Birmingham, fifteen to a room, and men and women on shift work slept in the same beds by turns. The mayors of Midlands cities were reportedly 'up in arms' over the slur on their neighbourhoods, and some Irish immigrants complained that following newspaper coverage of the speech they were relentlessly teased by their workmates over the fourteen others with whom they must naturally be sharing a room.[3] But the hysteria gradually subsided. After all, these morally compromised emigrants kept coming home for their holidays and behaved much as usual. Many of them married fellow emigrants, attended mass and brought their children up as Catholics. It became harder and harder to maintain the line that England meant diabolical lawlessness and excess. Yes, it was true, according to a 1958 report by Oliver Reilly, that England offered a varied landscape of licence and dissipation, but the Irish weaved their way through it with everyday sense and tact. A layman from the ironically named town of Prosperous in County Kildare, Reilly had gone to work as a labourer in order to report 'undercover' on conditions of the Irish in Birmingham. He found Irish men and women living in the same lodging houses while waiting to get married, and was told he was 'old-fashioned' for raising an eyebrow; in the pubs and clubs he found 'Wine, women and song. The people talk sex with a candour that would truly shock our toughest egg at home. Nothing is sacred and it is considered broadminded. Young men and girls in their teens fraternise freely in the many Youth Hostels throughout the city. Prostitutes by the dozen roam the streets, and hundreds of unmarried live together for years.' And at the same time he found that huge numbers of Irish emigrants kept going to mass:

> Big crowd at the Mass is unmistakably Irish. Churches are overcrowded, and overflow went to school nearby and had Mass there. A young priest robed and disrobed at side of the altar. Great fervour by women, but not so many receiving Holy Communion. Not many children present. Men noisy in the back benches. The Irish go to Mass in vast numbers, and it is the last act of Faith they cling to. I stand outside and try to place the accents: Cork, Kerry, Donegal. I give up, they were all there.

Why did they keep going? As well as the act of Faith, the churches offered a regular meeting place and reminders of home; but as Reilly kept hearing from the emigrants, they were also manned by a different breed of priests. At home in Ireland the priests were 'snobs'; there was 'bitterness at the neglect of clergy at home, who do not use their power to help'; 'All the emigrants I have met and they were many seemed to have the notion that Church and State combined against them at home, and that the opposite prevails in England.'[4]

Was this a kind of reverse emigrant nostalgia, or was it true that priests were more human across the water? Why should the clergy have behaved differently in England? No doubt part of the answer lay in the fact that lonely and isolated emigrants did need the kinds of help the priests could offer – finding lodgings, or getting the children into schools. The liberal priest Eamon Casey was well liked among his parishioners for his support of young Irish emigrants, and in particular the mortgage-loan scheme he started up, partly modelled on Caribbean savings plans, which helped get young families out of lodgings. The chaplains who worked among the labourers building the M1 wrote letters home for them, and assisted them with forms and taxes, as well as saying mass in huts along the route of the motorway. But it was also the case that many of the young priests and chaplains who were sent by various Orders to work among the Irish in England were men from poorer homes, at the bottom of the church hierarchy's pecking order. They came from similar backgrounds to the rural poor to whom they now ministered. And anyway, living in England as they did they were all – to a certain extent – in it together.[5]

The warnings and exhortations from clerics based in England were just as doom-laden as those coming from Ireland, but the tone tended to be more understanding. Writing in support of an Irish Centre to help orient new arrivals, one group of priests pointed out that a large part of the problem was that Irish people did not feel comfortable among English parishioners, where they were 'not always welcomed wholeheartedly'. Those parishes which ran special dances for the Irish were hugely popular:

> They are very anxious to be among their own sort, who understand them. After marriage they more easily fit into ordinary parish life, especially if there are children. There is no club or centre of any description for Irish Catholic workers in the whole of London. No library, reading room, or Irish canteen.

The lack of Irish facilities mattered because in their absence emigrants frequented 'the commercial dance halls'. For commercial, read immoral. The priests counted eighteen commercial halls in London, each of which held six hundred to a thousand dancers and opened on at least three nights a week. These were venues which, they argued, the 'better type of Irish avoids after the first visit'. They were the haunts of 'spivs and barrow boys'. But, they concluded, 'perhaps they are better than nothing and do supply a need. Many are forced into them or else walk the streets or attend worse types of entertainment.'[6]

It was optimistic, to say the least, to argue that if the Irish had a reading room or canteen to call their own they would avoid the dancehalls. Long after the Irish Centre was opened in Camden in 1955 – where new arrivals could find cheap accommodation, support in looking for jobs and lodgings, and legal advice – the dancehalls were still packed. Dónall Mac Amhlaigh was living in Northampton in the mid-1950s when he came down to London for a Gaelic football match, and afterwards went drinking and dancing:

> We moved off to dance in the Garryowen [in Hammersmith] when the pub closed. Big as the hall was, it was full and I met as many there that I knew as I had met in Mitcham. The Irish in London, I'd say, have a

great life, plenty of their own people all around them, galore Irish
dances and somewhere to go every night of the week.

There was no more and no less company-keeping than at home, he
suggested. On the bus back to Northampton, 'Most of the men had
their own woman going back with them, all but myself and one or
two others. Now if we were back in Connemara or in Spiddal, you
can be sure I wouldn't be without a nice little girl to see home at the
end of a night!'[7]

Many of the dancehalls were owned and run by Irishmen: the Buf-
falo Ballroom in Camden (later the Electric Ballroom), the Gresham
on the Holloway Road, the Galtymore on Cricklewood Broadway.
The Shamrock at the Elephant and Castle was owned by Caseys (the
wrestlers) and had built up a reputation as a Connemara dancehall
where you could meet people from home.

> Joe Green (Joe Paddy Pats) from Mweenish was there, his sister Mag-
> gie and Maire Molloy from Ardmore as well. As well as them, I met
> Peter Naughton from the same town and we spent some time remin-
> iscing about the old days when we were in the First Battalion in
> Galway. Colm was there too and he half-plastered.[8]

Mac Amhlaigh's published diary reads like an attempt to recreate
west-of-Ireland village life in London, a local communication written
to be read by the neighbours and friends of the people he named. It
was a more ambitious version of the tape-recorded greetings gatherings of immigrants would send home via band-members in the early
1960s. When local bands from home came to play in the dancehalls
it was an opportunity for people to get together and shout a hello to
family and friends into the cassette-recorder.

There were dances to cater for all sorts of tastes. In a single month
in 1964 the Camden Irish Centre held a ceilidh, a Corkmen's Social, a
Mayomen's Bacon and Cabbage Supper and Dance, the Roscommon
Association Dance, the Galway Association Bacon and Cabbage
Supper, as well as Derry and Waterford events and a meeting of the
Gramophone and Recording Club (which, admittedly, probably didn't
involve much dancing). These were respectable, non-commercial,
occasions. The publicity for a (free) Corkmen's Social in the Gresham

in Holloway boasted that it would be attended by the Bishop of Cloyne and Canon Ronayne, parish priest of Inniscarra, who were 'hoping to meet Cork people'. The Corkmen's Annual Dinner in 1965 was held at the Piccadilly Hotel, with special guests George Brown, then secretary of state for the Labour government, Jack Lynch, then minister for finance for Fianna Fáil and soon to be Taoiseach, and the Irish ambassador. Church-run dances were not shy about engaging popular stars such as Bridie Gallagher and later the Dubliners. A fund-raising Marian Agency dance in Kilburn featured not only the Dubliners, the Tinkers and Maeve Mulvany but Father Michael Cleary as the compère, the TV personality who, like Eamon Casey (it was later discovered), had had a long-term relationship and fathered children with his housekeeper. But these were special occasions. For dancing every night of the week there were the commercial dancehalls, which mostly featured ceilidh bands and, from the early 1960s, the Irish showbands – local groups that toured the hundreds of small Irish ballrooms and specialized in covers of pop and country songs. During one week in September 1964, the All-Ireland Dance Club in Camden featured the Conchords (twice), Martin Codd and the Herdsmen (a showband from Wexford), Noel Pender and the Peep O'Day Boys, and the Royal Showband from Waterford. Five nights of dancing, in a hall which easily catered for six hundred dancers. And there were four or five other dancehalls within a radius of a few miles.[9]

The struggle between church-run and commercial dancehalls was all about propriety. Nuns in the convent schools warned prospective migrants (a large proportion of any class of fifteen-year-old girls) to avoid the men in the dancehalls as 'they can't keep their trousers up'. One member of a Galway ceilidh band that toured England in the early 1960s remembered the boundary between the stage and the dancefloor at the Galtymore in Kilburn as 'a wall of sex'. People were there to make contact. Churchmen were obsessed with the fact that dancehalls encouraged 'sin', but their worries seem almost comically misplaced. They offered an opportunity for men and women to meet each other and considerable numbers of emigrants did first encounter their future partners on the English dance floors. Some married couples returned home to Ireland, some settled in Britain, but as the priests acknowledged, 'after marriage they fit more easily into ordinary parish life, especially if there are children'. The dancehalls were in fact the secret weapon of the priesthood, if only they had been able to see it.[10]

The idea that Irish immigrants were pumped up with uncontrollable sexual desire is not one that passed over from Irish Catholic to British rhetoric. The Irish Don Juan, like the Irish pimp, was a character sketched only in outline, at least in comparison to the more sexually dangerous immigrants, the West Indians and the Maltese. This may have been because the Irish wanted to have sex with each other. What was unacceptable about the West Indians was that they wanted, and could get, relationships with 'our' British girls. The Irish were far less of a threat. Newly immigrant Irish men in post-war Britain tended to court Irish women, or they didn't court at all. And it is also the case that an Irish lover would in practically all cases have been more acceptable to British parents than a 'colonial' one. Nonetheless, it is striking that of the concerns about Irish immigrant behaviour in Britain – drinking, fighting and sex – sex dropped out of the picture for the British. Drinking and fighting, however, did not. 'Everyone dances, everyone drinks, and from time to time everyone fights, and I do mean both sexes, but the fights are not vicious or prolonged.' Despite Oliver Reilly's admirably gender-blind perspective, mostly it was single Irish men who fought, and according to both British and Irish commentators they fought bitterly and often.

Risteard de Paor, or Richard Power, was a Trinity College Dublin graduate who spent a year living on the Aran Islands in the mid-1950s, perfecting his Irish. He became so acclimatized to the culture that when his friends left Aran for labouring jobs in Birmingham he decided to go with them. There followed a season of hard labour – he may well have run in to Oliver Reilly, who was investigating conditions at much the same time – working with a shovel, living in 'relentless proximity' with fellow navvies, dancing, drinking and, inevitably, fighting.

I suppose the English are constantly surprised at the fighting instinct of the Irish on social occasions and the number of times they have to employ 'Paddy's taxi' to transport them home via the police station.

The English themselves are not blameless, either. In the district where I was working, I got to know young Englishmen who'd go to the parochial dances each Saturday night in order to get in some pugilistic practice. They weren't Teddyboys by any manner of means. They were simply indulging in some kind of contemporary *joie de vivre*.

The Irish troublemakers were not quite the same, however. They were not adolescents. They were not contestants in a jousting tournament, nor did they get much pleasure out of fisticuffs. It was easy to observe the venom in any strife in which they were involved. It was some unspoken pact between the members of each clan, a tribal loyalty that was responsible for it. That and the restless, unsettling way of life that they engaged in, without any definite goal, without household, without authority, without having to answer to their family, to the state, to anyone at all.[11]

Power suggested that there was a hierarchy to the violence. At the bottom (or the top, depending on how you looked at it) were ordinary English lads, out for a bit of fun 'jousting', harmlessly expressing their '*joie de vivre*'. At the other end were the Teds, whose aggression had a dangerous undercurrent, a vicious edge closer to gang violence. Several seemingly random knife murders – one on Clapham Common in 1954, another in Holloway a few years later – had increased public concern about Teddy boys to a kind of low-level hysteria. In the middle were the Irish. Their violence may have been 'tribal', but it was also undirected, Power suggested; a consequence not of knowing they belonged more than the Cypriots and the Maltese, but of knowing they did not. If this was true, however, it was true only of the newly arrived, restless and unsettled, post-war Irish. Writing in the *Irish Press* in 1954 of a late-night encounter in Waterloo with a group of Teddy boys hanging around a jellied eel stall, Brendan Behan recorded his nervousness on being accosted by one of the group with the question, 'Yew Ahrish?' He admitted, uneasily, that he was:

He turned to his friends, and said: 'Vere. Woh eye sye?'

He smiled at me, and said: 'These geezers contradicted me, I knew you was Ahrish w'en I 'eard your browgue. We're all Ahrish 'ere.'

Proudly he pointed out his friends: "'e's Mac Carfy, en 'e's O'Leary, en 'Ealy, en 'Ogan, en Kelly, en my name is – give a guess.'

'Murphy.'[12]

Which turned out to be right. Behan had spent much of the war in a British borstal. In 1939 he was arrested just off the Liverpool boat, in possession of explosives which he was carrying for an IRA 'mainland' campaign. Part of the joke in 1954 is his lily-livered fear of the new-look rebels. Decked out in 'velvety' suits, Behan imagines them ready to pull a knife at the slightest provocation, or even just because they don't like the Irish. But the joke is on him as he discovers that the children of Irish immigrants have become indistinguishable from the English working class, except that they love their Irish heritage.

In comparison with the Teds, whether Irish or English, Behan favoured an old-style version of Irish troublemaking – though he was only in his early thirties himself. His public profile – unshakeable after he appeared drunk and swearing in a live television interview with Malcolm Muggeridge in 1956, to publicize his play *The Quare Fellow* – was a caricature of the drinking, fighting Irishman. (Behan was being watched by MI5, because of his IRA and Communist activities. A report dated 11 June 1956 concludes that 'as an individual he is too unstable and too drunken to be particularly dangerous'.[13]) But there were plenty of people, including the men themselves, who thought the caricature was all too true of Irish migrants in general.

Dónall Mac Amhlaigh's memoir of labouring in the 1950s is punctuated with stories of pitched, 'tribal' battles. He spent much of 1952 living in a camp at Stanford in the Vale, while working on the airfield at Brize Norton. Fights started out of nothing. 'As I went to sleep tonight, the silence was broken with shouting and screaming, dreadful cursing and the noise of heavy blows. It was the Connemara men and the people from Dublin. They've been fighting this many a day.' On one occasion Mac Amhlaigh got into trouble for speaking to an Englishman in the van transporting them from the camp to the site: ' "Why the hell are you getting great with that bowsie from Dublin?" "Yerra, Bartley, he's not from Dublin," I answered [in Irish]. "He's from Grimsby." "They're all the same, all them devils ... You shouldn't be talking to them at all if you're from Connemara." ' Later, laying rails in a railway tunnel near Northampton, fights started easily from an unguarded word or a look, either in the pubs after work or on site. A small amount of spilt tea ended with two men 'lamming away at each other in anger and hate; and what matter but there was so little reason for the whole thing'. Richard Power found the Birmingham pubs divided on tribal or 'County' lines. The Lion was a west-of-Ireland pub, where some 'wore bus drivers' uniforms and others had on rubber boots with the clay stuck to them', while the Angel's Head was frequented by Dubliners, 'a fierce, wild treacherous crowd' where the young men dressed like 'teddiers' and rural emigrants feared to enter.[14]

In a series of interviews conducted in the early 1960s by Charles Parker, a producer at BBC Pebble Mill in Birmingham, Irish labourers were disarmingly open about the violence which lay just beneath the surface of Irish emigrant life. Tony Crumlin, who had left Dublin aged fourteen to work on the construction sites and who described himself as 'a delinquent' in his youth, acknowledged his own prejudice against the English and the Culchies – men from the country. 'Dublin people think they are superior', they wear Teddy boy suits, and at the slightest provocation 'there would be a row'. He recalled his digs in Manchester in the mid-1950s: ' . . . a smell of dampness. Three beds in the one room, 10 by 8. A little box to put your clothes in, and your suitcase you kept locked all the time.' The men were only allowed in the house to sleep, and to eat their evening meal:

> A dozen blokes round the table. At least twice a week there was a row, a punch-up in the dinner room . . . They were like condemned to take the lower things that were dished out in life, such as the women they got to choose from, apart from the one, or two, at that time who was courting, going decently, and not just out for the one thing . . . Always proving that each one was better than the other, mostly with women, then with drink.

Crumlin spent six years working in England, and returned home in 1960, where he found he could not settle: 'I left Dublin for the second time to drink. I was drinking every night of the week. Friday night I wouldn't even bother to go home, I'd be stinking . . . going straight to the pub – out from Saturday to Monday night.' Several of Parker's interviewees pointed out that they had been pioneers (they had pledged not to drink alcohol) before they left home, but had given up because they were lonely, and pubs were the only places to meet. 'I started with a shandy.' They were drowning their sorrows.[15]

The violence between rival groups was a common theme in the Irish churches. Soon after Dónall Mac Amhlaigh arrived in Camden:

> Murphy and I went off to Mass together. I was astonished at the sermon that was preached – all about the lads fighting in the pubs and dance halls. The priest came out very strongly against them, saying they were nothing but ignorant beasts that let down their country and their Faith. There's no denying that this sort of thing is necessary for the devil has seized hold of enough Irishmen here in London.

For all the fuss about sex, Mac Amhlaigh argued of Irish Club dances that the lads were more interested in playing pitch and toss (with big bets) or in the fight after the dance than they were in women:

> I'd estimate that a third, or maybe half, of the crowd that comes here never gets out on the floor at all. They hang around the door chatting or up at the tea counter and they're usually the finest looking men in the place whatever is the cause of it. Some lovely women attend the club, and strangely enough, most of them go home after the dance unaccompanied.

He came across one priest in Northampton who made a habit of organizing fights every Saturday night after the local dance was over, as a way of keeping the peace during the dance itself: 'there's many a good fight takes place there under the priest's auspices'.[16]

To their English neighbours, the Irish habit of fighting looked like a racial characteristic, rather than one that was caused by circumstances. They just liked to fight. Concerned Irish commentators attempted to diagnose the causes of the violence – too much freedom, too much money, too much drink; too little space in the digs and lodging houses, too little privacy. But there were also arguments that the violence was rooted in something deeper, even more existential. Tony Crumlin insisted that the men drank and fought 'for the sake of doing it'; they had no sense of responsibility, but a feeling of wanting to rebel. This wasn't so far from the general line on the violence of the Teddy boys – they had found new freedom, with good wages and leisure time, and had no idea what to do with it. Irish fighting was a form of misdirected rebellion which mirrored English anomie, according to a priest writing in 1958:

> I think it is true to say that a fair percentage of Irish emigrants leave Ireland not because of economic compulsion but out of a sense of frustration. They do not realize that this frustration is experienced just as much in Britain or in any other country as in Ireland. In Britain, it manifests itself in juvenile delinquency, the teddy-boy craze, the rock-'n'-roll craze, the 'angry young men' movement. Emigration will not cure what is really a form of growing pains.[17]

If Irish frustration was simply a version of growing up, it could only be deepened by emigration, or so the argument went. Too much money and too much drink could only spell disaster, in the absence of any checks by family and community. This was the argument Richard Power made when he claimed that the problem for the Irish labourer was that he was 'without household, without authority, without having to answer to their family, to the state, to anyone at all'. A labour contractor interviewed in the early 1960s agreed, explaining the violence as a consequence of the sudden licence offered by being away from home: 'They're over here. Their father and mother aren't here and they can do what they blooming well like, more or less. Nobody can say a word to them.' As Mac Amhlaigh put it, 'Drink, squabbling and big pay – that's all they want and the devil take anything else.'[18]

All these explanations were at root the same. Irish immigrants were unable to cope with freedom as they had never experienced it; once liberated from the constraints of home they did everything, especially drinking and fighting, to excess; their living conditions did nothing to encourage stability; they drank and fought because they did not belong. In fact these were not explanations at all, but observations. Some comments went further. When a labourer told the filmmaker Philip Donnellan, 'We're dependent on nobody. We have to fight to exist,' he was acknowledging the flip side of freedom and independence. It might mean no one had authority over you, but it also meant you had no protection. You had to protect yourself. Or the playwright Tom Murphy argued that the real issue was not too much freedom but too much guilt. Like Richard Power and Oliver Reilly, Murphy spent several summers in the late 1950s labouring in Birmingham, living in 'predominantly Irish ghettos' where he found 'an extraordinary cult of violence'.

> Some of the reasons for the violence were that the men had money for perhaps the first time in their lives, and they did drink too; but much more importantly perhaps, they had a sense of being betrayed by the country of their origin here, and they also felt that they had betrayed that country. They were carrying a most curious guilt that they were much inferior to the people they had left behind, and they were people who didn't belong in England. When they came back for the summer sojourn, they found they didn't quite belong here either. Strange dichotomies had grown up in them, and they didn't know what to do with themselves, with their freedom, with their money, with this fragmented, fractured identity. All that I observed, or absorbed rather than observed. A brother of mine had told me a very cruel and awful story about a family that operated around Birmingham, in which one of them carried half of another man's ear in a match box.

When Murphy's play *A Whistle in the Dark* – about a group of Irish brothers who believe they have to fight to exist – was staged in London in 1961, the reviewers found it hard to distinguish the playwright from his material: 'The only thing that separates his characters from a bunch of wild gorillas is their ability to speak with an Irish accent.' Kenneth Tynan warned that 'Thomas Murphy is the kind of playwright one would hate to meet in a dark theatre.' Like Brendan Behan, indeed perhaps because of Behan, he was regarded as an 'anthropoidal' ape man, as one reviewer put it, a savage thrilling the London theatre.[19]

No doubt all these factors played a part. But so too did the often brutalizing conditions in which the men worked. This was something that was rarely mentioned in contemporary accounts of Irish violence. In fact, although several of Charles Parker's interviewees attempted to explain the effect of daily rough treatment on the worksites, their comments were not included in the film he made with

Philip Donnellan about the day-to-day life of Irish labourers in 1965. It amounted to a form of censorship. This was despite the fact that most of the complaints were about Irish companies, and Irish gangers, not about the English.

The men living, like Tony Crumlin, three to a box room (one worker claimed that when he arrived in Birmingham in the early 1950s there were forty men living in the one house), were working in a cut-throat industry. Many of them earned cash in hand, and were taken on on a weekly, or sometimes daily, basis. They queued for work on street corners, hoping to be given 'the start' by gangers (foremen) who loaded up their vans with men willing to dig trenches, lay cables, shovel ballast and pour concrete for ten- to twelve-hour shifts. It was here that the County prejudice had real effects on earning power. Gangers liked to employ their own men. 'The first thing they'll ask you is what county you come from and if it's not their county you're out.' Richard Power tried convincing a Galway ganger he was a local but he was let down by his accent. (He also shared a bed for some months with a man from Connemara who never spoke to him because he distrusted men from Aran. If he had known Power was a college student who had simply adopted Aran as his home, no doubt he would have distrusted him even more.) Where you came from dictated how easily you could find work, and how much you were paid. Dublin men were apparently paid less by the Murphy brothers, who were from Kerry, as were many of their men. You would need to 'be able to shout' if you work for Murphy's. 'If you talk about trade unions on Murphy's you're sacked straight away.'[20]

John Murphy (the green vans) and Joe Murphy (the grey ones), Lowery, Coleman, R. S. Kennedy – these small and medium-sized contractors thrived during the 1950s and early 1960s in part because of a lack of regulation in the building industry. Gangers in charge of teams of ten or twelve men made their money by agreeing a price for a job, calculated on a number of hours' labour, and an amount of equipment. If they could get the job done quicker (reduce the number of paid hours) and skimp on materials, that was money in the pocket. This meant driving the men hard, sacking any who were unable to keep up the pace, and often refusing to provide cover in wet weather, wellington boots, or even sufficient timber to create safe working

A man digs a trench in Philip Donnellan's 1965 documentary, *The Irishmen*.

conditions. Richard Power found himself working in leaking welling-
tons because the subcontractor had sold off the supply he had been
given for the men. One man interviewed by Parker argued that even
simple digging jobs – like digging trenches to lay cables and pipes –
became hazardous under these conditions:

> Men are dying in trenches – you might be down 12 maybe 13 feet, no
> timber there and anything can happen, I often saw a crack maybe four
> feet back. You say to the ganger man is there any timber here he'll just
> laugh at you. If you don't put your jack to it you're not wanted. There's
> twenty maybe thirty contractors who won't buy timber, looking for
> big profits.

The brutal terms on which men were required to work for many
(though not all) contractors, and the physical toll which it took on
them, created a permanent need for 'raw men' coming across from
Ireland, who could not refuse the work. 'Man lands here he might only
have a pound, he might have nothing . . . he has no option, if he doesn't
get down in that trench he has no food, he has no digs, he's lost.'[21]

Even the larger civil engineering projects, such as power stations and oil refineries, operated with an informal economy of bribes and kickbacks. Many of the larger, unionized contractors sold off parts of the job to smaller businesses, subcontractors or 'subbies', who then had to cut corners to make the work pay. 'The way the Isle of Grain was getting run, it was worse than the Yukon.' The Isle of Grain on the Kent estuary was a huge project, including a power station and oil refinery, which employed nearly 5,000 men at any one time from 1950 until 1962. The major employers were McAlpine, Wimpey and Costain, but access to the best jobs, to regular work and to overtime was controlled by 'bouncers', who determined who was in and who was out: 'Bouncers were there and in a big job like that everybody sides with the bouncer, whether they are right or wrong.' The subbies and the bouncers made extra money by taking bribes, and pocketing 'dead men's wages' – agreeing a price for a job based on a number of men working a number of hours, but then employing fewer men, who then had to work harder.

Many foremen and subcontractors were of course reasonable men, who had no intention of systematically exploiting their own country-men. Many of the labourers themselves preferred working for cash rather than paying tax, insurance and union fees. They liked the free-dom that a nomadic lifestyle brought them. But they were also being

Laying cables, from *The Irishmen*.

exploited and they knew it. The men at the bottom of this heap knew they were 'condemned to take the lower things that were dished out in life'. They worked long hours in poor conditions, and the worst off lived in lodging houses that were little better than slums. The pub became their refuge. Several contractors who had made money and invested it in lodging houses and pubs were notorious for paying the men in their own pubs on a Friday night – so that almost before they had got their pay they gave it back to their employers in the price of drink. The men were restless and unsettled, but it was not so much freedom as the lack of it that was the cause of all the drinking and fighting.

8

Broadcasters

So, the BBC, with its adjoining pubs . . . each section of the
BBC had a peculiar topography at the time. There was the
third programme, and those people drank in one place, and
the home service people drank in some other place. And then
there was the overseas service . . . on Oxford Street. 200
Oxford Street is really what Bush House became and 200
Oxford Street had its own pub. This is where the connection
began, because off 200 Oxford Street, leading down into
Soho, there would also be the famous Magdala Club, where
one would run into MacNeice, who was a producer, R. D.
Smith . . . George Barker . . . They talked money, or rather
the lack of money. It was rare to find poets and so on actually
talking about literature. They may quarrel about somebody
getting too favourable a review or something, but there was
no literary discussion.

George Lamming (1997)[1]

For aspiring immigrant writers in 1950s London, the central character in almost all accounts of day-to-day life was the BBC. Not quite
a human personality perhaps, and certainly not the proverbial
'auntie', the corporation nonetheless figured as far more than an average employer, providing publishing contacts, drinking companions,
the opportunity for love affairs and an all-important artistic aura, as
well as a necessary source of income. The producers, writers and critics associated with the Third Programme, above all, stamped their
personalities on the institution and the social circles which came to
dominate its 'adjoining pubs'. BBC cafés, clubs and pubs, like the

George, on Great Portland Street, and the Stag's Head, on New Cavendish Street, helped shape the geography of bohemian Soho and Fitzrovia in the 1940s and 1950s. But in the eyes of the pre-war generation they also changed the area's character, tainting it for ever with the suspicion that what was on offer was bargain-basement culture, subsidized by the arts division of the welfare state bureaucracy. The BBC, the Arts Council and the new universities were all run by and, worse, encouraged characters like the plodding corduroy-clad critic in Graham Greene's *The End of the Affair*.[2]

Golden ages only ever thrive in the past of course, if sometimes the very recent past. Anthony Cronin was in his early twenties when he arrived in London from Dublin, a recent graduate keen to make his literary mark. He had met Lucian Freud in Dublin through the Irish artist Patrick Swift, and Cronin's Soho acquaintances included Freud and Francis Bacon, fellow Irish 'exiles' – Patrick Kavanagh, Brendan Behan – 'locals' such as the artists Robert MacBryde and Robert Colquhoun, and poets Elizabeth Smart and George Barker. But – perhaps conscious of his own ambiguous status as a 'hanger-on' – Cronin distinguished between real and wannabe bohemians on the basis of age:

> Soho was largely inhabited by failures, the ruined men of the forties, whom the war had somehow confirmed in a natural dislike for the mere struggle for circumstantial success . . . In North Soho, during the war years, a true bohemia had flourished and, in a measure, a true anarchy prevailed. The sort of artist who emerged from it was apt to be a higher type than the success-oriented younger poets or painters of the fifties, but he was also apt to be a more than usually highly developed misfit . . . None of these people made a virtue or a life-style out of rejection or bohemianism, as, very shortly, another generation were to do, and as do the hangers-on, the amateurs and the free-loaders in any such milieu. They knew that artists as well as many other people had been poor and that some people must accept poverty as preferable to the waste of time and corruptions inherent in the struggle to avoid it.

The 'true' artists – people like Dylan Thomas, Constant Lambert, Julian MacLaren-Ross and Patrick Hamilton – were men ruined by drink and ill-health and unspoiled by worldly success. They were followed by a generation for whom art had become institutionalized, a matter of getting the right sinecure on the radio, the next Arts Council gig, or a set of good reviews in the *TLS* and the *Listener*. It was about getting the right publicity. Cronin's distinction was relatively crude, between real and cut-price risk-takers. But it had the merit of acknowledging the impact of the financial safety net provided by the government-funded arts institutions. As George Lamming remembered, the writers he encountered in Soho in the 1950s talked not about writing but about money, and that was because now there was money to be had.[3]

The majority of West Indian writers who emerged in Britain in the 1950s benefited from institutional funding, in the form of university scholarships and grants. V. S. Naipaul, Andrew Salkey, Edward Kamau Brathwaite, Jan Carew, Stuart Hall, Sylvia Wynter, Barry Reckord – all arrived in the early 1950s to take up university places, though not all of them stayed the course. By 1950 over a thousand students were arriving in Britain each year from the British Caribbean alone, funded either by colonial government scholarships, or British funds made available under the Colonial Development and Welfare Acts. They were from mainly middle-class and occasionally wealthy backgrounds, and as Sheila Patterson argued in 1963, they tended to live apart from West Indian migrant workers:

> Most coloured students lodge north of the river. A minority however live in South London, either because it is cheap or because they are attending one of the South London hospitals or technical colleges. As might be expected, most of these students avoid the working-class migrant settlements and congregate in areas with greater social pretensions such as Streatham and parts of Norwood.[4]

They were also far more politically active than most of their compatriots, partly through the West Indian Students Union, which was founded in 1945 and provided a meeting place for those interested in independence and federation in the islands, and through campaigns against racial discrimination in Britain. By the late 1960s the students' centre was being used as a base by the Caribbean Artists Movement and the West Indian Standing Conference.[5]

For those without student funding, London still stood for the dream of ambition fulfilled. Sam Selvon and Lamming were unusual in simply borrowing the fare and taking a chance on London as the place where they could 'make it' as writers, but travelling to the centre of art and writing was not so different from migrating like any other worker – England held the promise of work, money and recognition. And London was the 'literary Mecca' for West Indians in no small part because of the BBC. Since 1942 the Overseas Service had been putting out a programme dedicated to Caribbean writing, edited first by the Jamaican Una Marson (under the title *Calling the West Indies*, when it primarily served as a recruitment tool for the Forces, broadcasting messages from serving men and women to their family and friends in the islands, and showcasing stories about Barbadian nurses, or mechanics from Trinidad and Jamaica), and later by Irishman Henry Swanzy. Broadcast on Sunday evenings, the programme also featured West Indian fiction and poetry, and everyone who wanted to be a writer sent material to London hoping to be broadcast. As Lamming remembered:

> we had already been in touch with England through *Caribbean Voices* … So, there was a man called Henry Swanzy who was a very important figure as a contributor to the evolution, really, of the literature of the Caribbean, who edited *Caribbean Voices*. And he would have been expecting us. That is, we would have written to Swanzy. Everybody who had seen themselves as writers in Trinidad or Jamaica, whoever was going to England, would have written to Swanzy. And Swanzy would have been expecting you. So what happened was that the first kind of real, personal, and official call you made was to Swanzy.

In fact many of the letters, weighed down with hopeful manuscripts, which were directed to Swanzy in London never left the Caribbean but were instead rerouted to Jamaica. When he took over the job in 1946 Swanzy had no experience of West Indian writing, and he relied on a Jamaican couple, Gladys and Cedric Lindo, to screen submissions, forward possible scripts, and send feedback on how the programmes were received. The young Trinidadian Michael Anthony recalled scrutinizing the stamps on his returned work: 'I knew, when you sent material up, it got as far as Jamaica, and it came back to you

George Lamming broadcasting for the BBC in the early 1950s.

from Jamaica, because we had Mr Lindo there who was sorting these things out. It seemed a very hard task.'[6]

If access to the quasi-mythical Swanzy was difficult to negotiate from afar, once in London he proved approachable. He welcomed writers to the studio offices, set them up with contacts, tried to get them funding, and organized bi-weekly social evenings in his house in Lyncroft Gardens, Hampstead, fostering links between writers newly arrived in London and building up his stable of BBC talent. And he paid well. As nearly all the 1950s writers remembered gratefully, the BBC offered not only recognition but very good money. Sam Selvon earned seven guineas for his short story 'And Then There Were None', which was broadcast in 1948, and a windfall twenty guineas for the longer 'Behind the Hummingbird'. According to George Lamming, the BBC 'helped to confirm the status of writing as a serious activity by paying for the work it received', though the money also had the opposite effect. Jan Carew recalled that the

Corporation 'paid by the word and so some of us wrote some very long poems, or submitted quite a few'. But the programme paid its readers well too, and Swanzy had a reputation for going out of his way to help young writers whom he thought might be struggling:

> If you looked a little thin in the face, he would assume that there might have been a minor famine on, and without in any way offending your pride, he would make some arrangement for you to earn. Since he would not promise to 'use' anything you had written, he would arrange for you to earn by employing you to read.[7]

In 1954 Naipaul was living in 'dirt and discomfort' with a cousin in West Kilburn, and washing in the public baths, when he got work reading stories on *Caribbean Voices*. The first story, 'Bogart', in his first collection *Miguel Street* was written on a typewriter in a spare office at the Overseas Service, which had by this time moved to Langham Place:

> The Caribbean Service was on the second floor of what had been the Langham Hotel, opposite Broadcasting House. On this floor the BBC had set aside a room for people like me, 'freelances' . . . People were in and out of the freelances' room while I typed. Some would have dropped by at the BBC that afternoon for the company and the chat, and the off-chance of a commission by a producer for some little script . . . The freelances' room was like a club . . .[8]

When Swanzy was seconded to Accra (to a new post as head of programmes in what was then the Gold Coast), Naipaul took over the job of producer for a time, at the very healthy salary of eight guineas a week. He described the atmosphere in a later novel:

> He loved the drama of the studio, the red light and the green light, the producer and the studio manager in their sound-proof cubicle. His script was part of a longer magazine programme. It was being recorded on disc, and he and the other contributors had to sit through the whole thing twice. The producer was fussy and full of advice for everybody . . . Don't listen to your own voice; try to see what you are talking about; speak from the back of the throat, don't let your voice fall away at the end of a sentence . . .

He got to know producers, studio managers, contributors. Some of the contributors were professionals. They lived in the suburbs and came in by train with big briefcases that held many little scripts for other programmes and outlines for other little scripts. They were busy people, planning little scripts for weeks and months ahead, and they didn't like sitting through a half-hour magazine programme twice. They looked bored by other people's pieces, and Willie learned to look bored by theirs.[9]

While the suburban professionals remained the principal beneficiaries of the BBC's largesse, for a short time in the 1950s they shared their quarters with a growing circle of Caribbean interlopers. *Caribbean Voices* had created a virtual community of listeners in the West Indies, linking the islands through the ritual of the Sunday night audience, as Jamaicans overheard poems from Barbados, and Trinidadians listened in to Guyanese stories. And in the early 1950s it helped establish a pan-Caribbean circle in London. The freelances' room and its adjoining clubs became a forum for cultural and political discussion as much as a source of income, though practical contacts were important too: 'That was where West Indian writers and peripatetic journalists, escapees from boring nine-to-five jobs, university dropouts, graduates seduced by life in London and reluctant to return home, ex-servicemen . . . and, of course, poets, artists, hangers-on and aspirants to literary fame . . . They all met at 200 Oxford Street . . .' It was another of the freelances, the Jamaican Andrew Salkey, who brought Naipaul's stories to the attention of an English publisher. When he wasn't reading his stories on the radio Salkey was working at the Golden Slipper night-club in Piccadilly (an experience he fictionalized in his 1960 novel *Escape to an Autumn Pavement*), where he got to know Diana Athill, second-in-command at André Deutsch, who would remain Naipaul's publisher for more than twenty years.[10]

But none of this came free. Even as they did their best to make the programmes their own, Caribbean writers were having to buy in to the idea of London as the arbiter of West Indian literary culture. *Caribbean Voices* offered them opportunity but it also trapped them in a kind of racial cul-de-sac, safely isolated from the main thoroughfare of British culture. When Naipaul applied for work on the General Overseas Service he was fobbed off with the excuse that 'you are not a European'. He managed to engineer a meeting with the head of Features, Laurence Gilliam, and other producers, in which 'I said I wanted to do some features and they roared with laughter, as though I had said I wanted to write the Bible'. These were unsympathetic, or at the very least unimaginative, individuals but the problem was at root a structural one. London was the centre and 'the colonies' could not hope to compete, let alone set their own agenda. The mother country 'had made us pupils to its language and its institutions', said Lamming. And for all Swanzy's support of West Indian writers, he did – at least initially – treat them like pupils. He had taken on the job reluctantly in 1946, confiding to his diary, 'I do not feel greatly enthused; it seems the literary counterpart of youth centres', and 'a kind of do-gooding parish tea (almost kindergarten) affair'.[11]

Swanzy appears to have thought better of his opinion that West Indians were all children who needed encouragement and looking after, but he remained convinced that what was valuable in their writing was that it expressed another age, an earlier stage in the development of culture. The islands were 'full of oral life, combining the traditions and folk lore of every great racial unit of the world'. In the Caribbean, he explained to readers of the *Caribbean Quarterly* in 1949,

> the racial stock of a potential writer is one of the richest in the world, providing wonderful chances of cross-fertilisation: European, African and Asiatic strains mingle, as with the Greeks of old; as amongst Aegeans and Dorians of Greece, the Teutonic and Latin are contrasted. So far as the subject-matter is concerned, the self-realisation of a people through the acceptance and sublimation of the facts of slavery and the colour-bar are the grand theme for tragedy and eventual triumph. There is all the colour, there are the capes and promontories of a rich peasant life. And, linked with this, there is reverence for the word, preserved in a society still largely illiterate, unspecialised, given to open air gatherings. In the view of someone writing in contemporary Europe, this is perhaps the most important

of all the factors that should encourage the development of a really significant regional literature within the Caribbean, the first stage towards the establishment of standards recognised in the wider English-speaking world.

The idea that West Indian writers channelled the spirit of a vigorous and illiterate peasantry triumphing over the colour-bar must have grated on the highly literate, mostly urban intellectuals who gathered in London. Their artistic formation owed rather more to T. S. Eliot, Thomas Hardy and Albert Camus than to Harriet Beecher Stowe, to Frantz Fanon and Aimé Césaire than to Caribbean folklore. Their political interests ranged from international Marxism to anti-colonialism, the complexities of West Indian Federation and the politics of contemporary immigrant experience. Swanzy's emphasis on a rich 'oral life' did answer the demands of the radio medium – he favoured stories and poems which made a virtue of local colour, and showcased dialect and native speech patterns. But what was odd about the Caribbean voices was that they weren't humanizing the sounds of the radio for a British audience, since the programme only aired in the West Indies. The colourful capes and promontories of a rich peasant life were being sent up to London to be selected and shaped, only to be returned to the islands as examples of best practice. 'It was not only the politics of sugar which was organized from London. It was language, too.'[12]

The idea of London as the centre of post-war Caribbean art and writing was hopelessly contradictory, and it didn't take long before it began to unravel. Writers like Lamming and Kamau Brathwaite thought of themselves as modernist exiles rather than immigrant hacks. Brathwaite argued that it was listening to Eliot's poetry being read on the BBC Overseas Service that spurred his ambition to be a writer – his ambition was modern and metropolitan. There was nothing folksy about it. When Lamming first arrived in London in 1950 he was writing poems rather than novels. He sought out the survivors of English poetic modernism:

I used to spend most of my time at a place called the Mandrake Club. This was really where all sorts of writers and people around the BBC hung out. I met Dylan Thomas a few times talking his head off. Barker,

John Heath-Stubbs, David Wright – these were the sort of people, the poets of the time.

This was a modernist and European-oriented group. By the end of the 1950s Wright was editing *X* magazine, publishing, for example, Beckett's work in progress and reflections on painting by Frank Auerbach. It was precisely the sort of circle Lamming might have imagined for himself from the distance of Barbados and Trinidad. But it existed in some tension with the requirements of Swanzy's *Caribbean Voices*, where the emphasis was on authenticity, and the language and rhythms of a pre-modern age.[13]

It would take time for these contradictions to be ironed out, and it would take an acknowledgement that the politics of blackness lay at the heart of Caribbean writing. In the summer of 1958, during the build up to the Nottingham and Notting Hill riots, Lamming was living in Parliament Hill and working on editing six weeks of *Caribbean Voices*. He chose not to showcase new work but to produce a series of retrospectives charting the story of West Indian poetry, fiction and comic writing, and offering 'Third Programme' type literary and philosophical discussion. He invited Stuart Hall to join the resident critics Roy Fuller and Arthur Calder-Marshall. Hall had left Jamaica in 1951 to take up a Rhodes Scholarship at Oxford. By 1958 he had set aside his Ph.D. thesis on Henry James to edit the *Universities and Left Review* along with the young Marxist historian Raphael Samuel and the poet and critic Gabriel Pearson. Hall was teaching English in a South London secondary school, and helping to run the Partisan Café in Soho in the evenings. His cultural Marxist perspective could not have been more different from Swanzy's benignly patrician view of Caribbean culture. But Lamming went further and sketched the final programme in his series as an opportunity to take advantage of a visit to London by Aimé Césaire, Jean Price-Mars (from Haiti) and the Sengalese Alioune Diop. They were to discuss the concept of negritude and the 'présence Africaine' in the West Indies with C. L. R. James.[14]

Swanzy sometimes suggested that his Anglo-Irish background – he was from Glanmire in County Cork – gave him a particular sympathy for peasant and downtrodden cultures, and there were certainly parallels between the ways in which the BBC promoted both West Indian and Irish sounds. Caribbean accents, like Celtic voices and Hibernian dialect, offered a form of time-off from the real business of broadcasting, which was always done through the formal and clipped tones of Received Pronunciation, except when it came to 'ethnic' pursuits and cultural tourism. Cricket had to be acknowledged as belonging to the West Indies as much as to Britain after they won the Test series in 1950. The gentle Barbadian accent of Tony Cozier, commentating on *Test Match Special*, levelled the broadcasting playing field just a little. Cozier offered an alternative to the usual manner in which 'negro' voices were associated with 'negro' song, most benignly in Cy Grant's nightly calypso on the BBC's current affairs programme *Tonight*, and most notoriously in the long-running *Black and White Minstrel Show*, which was first broadcast in 1958 and by 1964 was regularly drawing audiences of over 20 million on a Saturday night. As Dominican journalist Edward Scobie put it in his Afro-Caribbean magazine *Flamingo*, the show 'has provided audiences with a neat bit of escapism for there on the screen are the dancing, singing Nigger Minstrels, all dressed up in "massah's clothes" and making massah laugh'. One reader took this article to show his white colleagues at work and explained: 'they could not understand why we should feel so badly about the programme. They kept telling me it was good fun and full of entertainment. I think you are right. Most English people see us like black and white minstrels.'[15]

Caricatures of garrulous Irish songsters never reached the depths of 'Celtic-face', but BBC programming did like to showcase Ireland wearing tourist dress: traditional Irish music and song, traveller holidays, folklore and folk-life. Irish writers and performers, like the West Indians, were paid for their exotic speech patterns and verbal charm, but according to Anthony Cronin, unlike the West Indians they didn't mind. Cronin published his satire of a failed Irish writer in 1950s London, *The Life of Riley*, in 1964. He had himself been living hand-to-mouth, struggling to make ends meet as literary editor of the journal *Time and Tide* and trying to get work through the Irish clique at the BBC – the producers and poets W. R. Rodgers and Louis MacNeice, and one of Naipaul's professional contributors, Harry Craig. Everywhere Cronin saw talent ruined by the performance of

Irishness, the only thing for which it appeared people reliably got paid. Writers and producers exaggerated the Celtic note, but to make their productions 'authentic' they needed to perform Irishness outside work too. 'In the circle in which I moved an unmistakeable Celticism of word and spirit was demanded. One was required to subscribe to the tweedy view, at least in theory, as an aesthetic and a way of life.' Cronin's portrait of W. R. Rodgers in the novel (in the character of Billy Boddells), is of a man destroyed by his relentless performance of Irishry:

> He was the most extreme. He spoke in gnomic pseudo-proverbs, inde-
> cipherable to the rational mind, indeed probably meaningless. What
> he intended to convey I imagine was a sort of dark peasant wisdom,
> something from the deep and mysterious consciousness of the race,
> the knowledge of centuries gnarled and knotted and knuckled, knob-
> bly and knotted as the hands of an old knaught man . . . But I am
> talking like Boddells himself.[16]

MacNeice had recruited Northern Irishmen Sam Hanna Bell and Rodgers as BBC producers and, while both worked on the Third Programme, Rodgers came to be known specifically as a Third Programme producer since much of his work was broadcast on the network. The listings of 'Irish-themed' cultural programmes on the BBC during the 1950s do suggest a narrow 'Emerald Isle'-type inter-est, suggesting that despite the high-brow aims of the Third Programme (and some noticeable Irish successes, such as Beckett's 1957 play *All That Fall*), in order to make money – in other words, to ensure fees from repeats – feature writers needed to buy into tourism, folklore and traditional culture. The first programme in Rodgers's series *The Irish Storyteller*, for example, was subtitled 'Picture of a vanishing world':

> On the western fringe of Europe are fast vanishing evidences of a civili-
> sation that once covered the whole Atlantic area. Its literature was oral;
> and the storyteller with his sagas and wonder-tales was the book, the
> newspaper, and the film of his society. This programme presents the
> fading picture of storytelling today. The Gaelic recordings were made
> by a BBC recording unit in the course of a recent Irish journey.[17]

As one of the Irish storytellers featured in the series, Bryan McMahon, acknowledged, the world was vanishing in part because of the radio itself. Youth, emigration, the radio, cinema and the printed page were all at fault for bringing to an end 'an ancient world'.

The playwright and balladeer Dominic Behan (brother of Brendan) also wrote for the Third Programme, from 1955 onwards, but the folk imperatives stretched beyond the Third. Between 1952 and 1958 the musician and song collector Séamus Ennis curated a long-running folk-music programme on the BBC Home Service, *As I Roved Out*, which featured Irish traditional music alongside English folk. The filmmaker Philip Donnellan worked with Ennis on his 1965 BBC documentary on Irish labourers, and he recalled meeting him first in the George in Great Portland Street (the 'Gluepot'):

> We had first met in the Gluepot near Broadcasting House in 1949. Seamus and big Brian George, the Dubliner, just back from the ould sod recording singers. MacNeice was there, Dylan Thomas in the other corner of the bar and David Thomson in his thick glasses putting down the Bass. After that there were lots more times when amidst the beery uproar Seamus would suddenly murmur 'Ach now that puts me in mind . . .' push his faded trilby back on his head, reach into an inside pocket for a fistful of penny whistles and choosing one, silence the bar with an instant rattling jig or delicately command consent with an exquisite slow air in which the notes would seem to hang upon the smoke.[18]

It is perhaps not surprising that this cast of characters was responsible for peddling the caricature of Ireland as home to a romantic, mythical and fading civilization. So in Cronin's satire the aspiring writer Riley is assured by Coosins (the real life Harry Craig):

> 'Ashtowk Paddy it is not trash you'll be writing for the Home Service or any other service. It is for the third programme that you'll be making the randy words tumble each other like rabbitts in the morning sun. Ay', he concluded in a voice genuinely hoarse with emotion, 'and if there was a fourth programme aself, it is you that would be on it.'[19]

Not all Irish writers were prepared to put up with this level of stage Irishry – what the poet Patrick Kavanagh denounced as 'bucklepping' – as the price of employment. The value of the 'buck-lep' lay not only in the reproduction of 'peasant' quality but in the reproduction of an Irish sound. What men like Cronin and Kavanagh objected to was the tendency for sound to overwhelm meaning – Irish people could say almost anything so long as it sounded authentic. As Brendan Behan discovered after his drunken appearance on *Panorama*, incoherence was no barrier to popularity. What English audiences found themselves warming to in Behan's performance were the same qualities to which they objected in Irish immigrant labourers en masse: drunkenness, irreverence, lack of inhibition (he sang a song from his play on air), the refusal to be tamed by the expectations of civil society. But plenty of other Irish performers found a way to smuggle intelligent commentary and satire in under cover of the gift of the gab. The 1950s saw the beginning of the long heyday of Irish entertainers on British popular radio and TV, including Eamonn Andrews and, slightly later, Terry Wogan, Dave Allen and Val Doonican, all of whom offered caustic, witty, kitsch and sentimental, but most of all soft-voiced and articulate versions of Irishness.[20]

The caricature of emotional, truth-telling, spiritual, rooted Irishness, the type Cronin suggests was being peddled on the Third Programme, had just as long a history as the violent, cunning, drunken type. Running right through attitudes towards Irish migrants as stupid, dirty, feckless, unreliable and dangerous lay 'more natural', untamed, sociable qualities. It was not that they were positive and negative sides of the one coin. Rather they were the same side of the coin – Irishness as code for forms of pre-modern conviviality that were both desired and feared by the 'ordinary' English. It was much the same for West Indian artists – their musicality and their rich oral culture were the acceptable face of their primitivism, which otherwise needed to be educated out of them to bring them up to the 'civilized' standards that would eventually enable them to enter into 'equal partnership' with white Britons. Naipaul's fury over being treated as a peasant writer (it was 'as though I had said I wanted to write the Bible') was the fury of a man who knew he was being patronized.

Part of the problem was that the BBC saw its role as educating the immigrants, not being educated by them. Soon after the Labour government under Harold Wilson came to power in 1964 this role was formalized through the Immigrant Programmes Unit (IPU), an explicit attempt to use the national broadcaster to teach immigrants English (even those who knew it already, because they could always learn to speak it better), and to school them in British culture. In effect the IPU's job was to encourage new arrivals to fit in, to persuade them to leave their traditions behind and translate themselves into their new surroundings. In 1965 BBC Director-General Hugh Greene held a series of conferences that aimed to involve Asian and West Indian organizations in programming for and about the immigrants, and heard requests for black actors to feature in programmes 'simply as people in their own right and in their own jobs', rather than as representatives of the immigrant 'problem' or the black problem. But this would be a long time coming.

Wilson appointed Maurice Foley, Labour MP for West Bromwich and the son of Irish immigrants, to a Cabinet position with special responsibility for the welfare of immigrants. He was an ardent advocate of assimilation, and believed it was possible to use the broadcast media as a tool for social cohesion and integration. One of the first fruits of his policy was a programme designed for Asian immigrants and put out on both radio and TV (radio ownership had bypassed most Indian and Pakistani migrants but they were enthusiastic purchasers of television sets – and by 1965 91 per cent of the United Kingdom population had TVs in the corner of their living rooms). *Apni Hi Ghar Samajhiye* ('Make Yourself at Home') was first broadcast in October 1965, at 9 o'clock on Sunday morning, and it would run for fourteen years. Many Asian children remember being shaken out of bed early on a Sunday in order to watch 'their' programme. It was broadcast in Hindustani although the Commonwealth Relations Office complained this would alienate Pakistan, so it was also billed as 'basic Urdu' – they stuck to the Hindi–Urdu mix despite the fact that a majority of South Asian migrants at the time spoke Punjabi. The two co-presenters, Mahendra Kaul from India and Saleem Shahed from Pakistan, provided national balance. (One producer recalled that no one in the BBC studio understood what was being said except the presenters, but it was assumed they would keep a check on one another.) The programme mixed musical segments with interviews and sections in which the presenters explained scenarios such as how to vote (with a mocked-up voting booth in the studio), how to use a gas cooker, or how to register for an NHS doctor. Mahendra Kaul was clear about the purpose of the programme: 'our job was to make our kind of people more acceptable to the general population' by teaching them how to manage and fit in to everyday life in England.[21]

The radio version included answers to listeners' questions about life in Britain, music from Indian and Pakistani films, and an English lesson, designed by the English-by-Radio Unit and built around the fortunes of two new immigrants, Mr and Mrs Chaudhury, 'making their first attempts at speaking English in shops, in buses, at railway stations, or in telephone kiosks'. One of the attractions of using the radio and television for English teaching was that it was possible to reach Asian women, who were far more likely to be isolated at home and unable to access classes run by local councils. But so were women of other nationalities, who were not considered a priority in the same way as Commonwealth immigrants. The Greek Cypriot community lobbied for its own dedicated programming, including language teaching, but were ignored, presumably because Cypriot immigrants caused insufficient racial conflict to warrant it. The focus of both the government and the BBC was on easing racial tensions by offering lessons to black and Asian immigrants on how to integrate, so much so that by 1970 BBC Radio London began producing a radio comedy soap designed to help West Indians learn to speak 'proper' English. *The University of Brixton* was a twenty-six-part serial dedicated to teaching British Caribbeans the importance of speaking 'standard English' in order to be understood and accepted. Set inside the Plummer family household in Brixton, the principal drama played out between the Plummers' lodger, Bertie Johnson, who speaks Jamaican Creole and gets caught out by all sorts of comic misunderstandings, and their neighbour, Mr Reasoning Pinnock, who tries to persuade Bertie to give up dialect and accept the norms of the English people he encounters at work, in the doctor's waiting room, at the local beauty contest and in the police station:

BERTIE: All right, all right, Mr Reasoning. Why you so particular about your English?

REASONING: Because we're living among English people, in
England. When you're at home it's perfectly in order to speak
your own language, and when you're among your own there's
nothing wrong either. But you have to know how to speak
English for English people to understand you, because most of
them don't speak your language.

Reasoning was played by the writer of the series, Louis Marriott, a
member of the Caribbean Artists Movement. Marriott's involvement
in producing such an anodyne version of West Indian culture in London was further proof, if proof were needed, of the difficulty of
getting mainstream British cultural institutions to look beyond the
figure of the immigrant as a colourful, and sometimes troublesome,
character. 'Race Relations' programming explored white people's
anxieties about mixed-race relationships, or immigrant pressure on
housing and employment; and it offered tips to black and Asian people (exclusively) on how to fit in. But it did nothing to represent the
immigrants themselves. As a West Indian man in the audience for a
speech by civil rights and Black Power activist Stokely Carmichael at
London's Roundhouse in July 1967 complained, black immigrants in
Britain were invisible as people:

We're not even noticed till we're moving in next door, or going out
with a white chick or something like that. Then people look at you
and say 'look at that black man.' Otherwise, they don't even know
we're here. You know, I mean, we realise your situation in America,
man, but we got an even bigger problem here cos we ain't even noticed.
You are . . . I would like to see a Negro on television doing a part as a
lawyer, or a doctor, something I respect, you know.[22]

9

Strangers

I am walking up the street, and three men are walking towards me. I do not think they are the enemy from Notting Hill; nor do I think they are not. I simply do not know, for there is no way of telling. It is my particular way of seeing which creates this doubt, in spite of all I have read about what was happening. And it is in this moment of doubt that my life is endangered, for while I wonder and watch and wait, the men and I are actually getting nearer. I begin with the grave disadvantage that if they actually are the enemy, then they have seen their target long ago. While I am working out the possibilities, they have already chosen unanimously the result. There it is. I am completely in their power by the fact that experience has not trained me to strike without the certainty of the enemy's presence. I am completely immobilised by all my social and racial education as a West Indian.

George Lamming, *The Pleasures of Exile* (1984)[1]

How was the black man to judge the intentions of the white strangers all around him? The enemy from Notting Hill looked different depending on who was doing the looking. For the mostly young white men who orchestrated the street violence in West London in August and September 1958, the enemy was easy to spot. They were out to 'get rid of these niggers', and according to the police reports of incidents and arrests, they were not in the least shy about saying so. For the large crowds of 'sightseers' who came to watch the violence the identity of the enemy was a little more complicated. Many spectators were in sympathy with the attackers, and objected when the police attempted to arrest them. But they were not keen on having their streets turned into battlefields, on being unable to walk freely at night, or having to pick their way through broken glass during the day. The throngs of reporters and cameramen crowding the streets also began to lose their lustre, especially as the first days' excitement at being 'in the news' wore off. For the reporters themselves, and their public, the real enemy were the Teddy boys – delinquent white youths who, so the argument went, were responsible for this un-English and intolerant behaviour – and the grubby fascist fringe groups, such as Oswald Mosley's Union Movement, which incited them.[2]

For the targets of the violence, the ordinary black citizens of Britain, the question of who exactly was the enemy was not so easily answered. It was true that the principal agents of the violence were local youths, and that the Union Movement and the – possibly even more bigoted – 'Keep Britain White' and White Defence League factions had been organizing in Notting Hill for some months before the riots began. But black residents had no way of gauging the depth and breadth of the hinterland of racial hatred which lay behind the attacks on them. Unlike the experience of black people in the United States, where racial antagonism was openly acknowledged and a matter of historical record, the rhetoric of liberal tolerance in Britain made the new situation almost impossible to read. George Lamming had been living in England for eight years when the spark was lit in Notting Hill. His principal reaction was, as he put it, 'a feeling of stupefaction'. He couldn't believe that this was happening in England. In his account of the riots in his 1959 novel *Absolute Beginners*, Colin MacInnes insisted on the 'moment of complete surprise' visible on the faces of those who were attacked – surprise which was expressed as hesitation when it came to fighting back.[3] And along with stupefaction came fear and uncertainty. In an England where some degree (but how much?) of violent racial hatred had now to be accepted as given, the black person was at an obvious disadvantage. The immigrants were not ready to assume they were under attack, and in hesitating made themselves more vulnerable. But doubt was also a strategy for mental survival, for once the fundamental aggression of the white man was accepted, how could day-to-day life continue normally? The black immigrant needed to cultivate a sort of double consciousness, one in which he might both know and not-know of the hatred directed against him.

The series of confrontations in the summer of 1958 which so profoundly altered black people's perspective on their place in British society were brutal and aggressive rather than tragic. No one was killed until a separate incident the following May, in which a thirty-two-year-old carpenter from Antigua, Kelso Cochrane, was murdered (a single stab wound to the chest) by a gang of white youths in Golborne Road, while walking home late one night. But the riots proved a watershed, and laid the ground for Cochrane's murder, because of the fact that colour was explicitly invoked as a mark of English identity. The riots were by white people against black, and no amount of fudging could disguise that fact. The battle lines were clear – they were meant to be – and they were racial.

The summer of 1958 was unusually hot and, though it would be foolish to blame the weather, it did mean that people spent more time out on the streets. In July and early August there were repeated raids on a black-owned café, and on a 'coloured house', in Shepherd's Bush, followed by the arrests of six young men from Shepherd's Bush, Fulham and Notting Hill, all of them aged between eighteen and twenty-three. On Saturday 23 August, after the pubs closed in Nottingham, a pitched battle developed between black and white residents of the St Ann's district in which 'dozens of men and women were injured by knives, razors, palings and bottles'. Nottingham's Assistant Chief Constable argued that the violence was a response to a series of attacks on black people which had been increasing over the previous weeks: 'The attacks made by "teddy boys" in the past fourteen days were responsible for Saturday night's outbursts. The coloured community, he said, apart from a few isolated cases, was "very well behaved".[4] Meanwhile in London on 23 August, a gang of nine white men aged between seventeen and twenty, and 'armed with iron bars, torn from street railings, starting handles, table legs, pieces of wood and a knife' toured the areas around Shepherd's Bush and Latimer Road (known then as Notting Dale) in cars, stopping to attack black men whenever they saw them. Five of the assaulted men were hospitalized, with broken limbs and chest wounds. The following Saturday night the rioting in Nottingham was worse, but the Chief Constable continued to insist that, 'This was not a racial riot. The coloured people behaved in an exemplary way by keeping out of the way. Indeed, they were an example to some of our rougher elements. The people primarily concerned were irresponsible teddy boys and persons who had had a lot to drink.'⁵ Over the following weeks officials clung to this line – that badly brought up kids were to blame rather than their parents and neighbours – despite considerable evidence to the contrary.

Nottingham quietened down after that but not so North Kensington in London. On Saturday 30 August there were attacks on 'coloured' houses in Bramley Road. Windows were smashed with bricks and bottles, one house was set on fire, and a crowd began fighting in the streets. By 31 August the police were expecting further trouble and reinforcements were called in. Inspector Sydney Vass, of 'F' Division, described the events he witnessed in the early hours of the morning near Latimer Road tube station:

> Hundreds of people, probably about 800 had gathered in groups on Bramley Road etc., and were lining the pavement and roadway. From the remarks I overheard, it seemed that by far the greater majority of the people were assembled to watch, what they called 'nigger baiting'. Most of these people would not themselves have taken any active part in the violence but appeared to be willing to enjoy [observing it].

MacInnes described a crowd which 'didn't shout, or bawl, or cheer; they just stood by, these English people did, and *watched*. Just like at home at evening, with their Ovaltine and slippers, at the telly.' The press and their cameras were there to watch too, and by the following evening, 1 September, the sensational coverage in the papers had drawn more people out into the streets. Inspector Vincent Coventry was in Bramley Road that evening, where he found a crowd 'of both sexes and varying ages', all determined that something should happen. Coventry was convinced that most of them were 'sightseeing following previous press publicity given to that area'.

Clashes between police and white youths in Notting Hill, 1958.

On many occasions, a few young men in the crowd would shout slogans such as 'Let's us find another nigger' or 'I know where one lives, let's do him.' They would then run in one direction and the crowd would follow to see what happened. Persons in the vicinity of where any disturbance or fight took place, however, would run away in order to ensure their own safety. Bottles would be thrown, usually by persons at the rear of the crowd and in consequence could not be detected by police. The sound of breaking glass added to the excitement and some of the more violent of the crowd began to show signs of fear at the possibility of sustaining injury to themselves. I had many remarks made to me by residents such as 'Where is all this going to end officer?' or 'We'll all be frightened to go out soon.'

Dramatic eyewitness accounts appeared in all the newspapers. The *Manchester Guardian* correspondent saw a West African student, later named as Seymour Manning, run from a 'lynch mob' down Bramley Road and take shelter in a greengrocers; *The Times* reported crowds of youths smashing the windows of houses of black residents in Oxford Gardens, and cruising carloads of 'nigger-hunting' young men stirring up violence. The police appealed for people to curb their morbid curiosity and stay away; they hoped for rain to 'damp the trouble' down, and on the 3rd the climate briefly obliged, providing thundery showers just as the pubs closed.[6]

The police made 140 arrests in that first week of September. One quarter of those arrested were black, and 60 per cent of the whole group were under twenty years old. This fact, and the detail that very many of them were carrying weapons such as flick knives, stilettos and razors, encouraged the Teddy boy thesis. Both sides, naturally, insisted that their weapons were carried in self-defence. When Cellie Kamara, a twenty-nine-year-old Jamaican, was arrested for possessing a knife, he argued that 'I only got it in case of being attacked . . . I was attacked last Saturday and I got the knife for my own protection.' The self-defence claim was part of the ritual of arrest: 'I'm only carrying it for protection. You want to get those white bastards'; 'They kill if we didn't help our selves'; 'if they come for me, I will get them'. The fact that everybody said it didn't necessarily make it

A confrontation in Notting Hill, *circa* 1958.

untrue, of course. But the knives and razors did not help the men appear innocent when they came up before a magistrate. Kamara, it turned out, already had convictions for theft and living off immoral earnings. It certainly suited the police to drag up as much dirt as possible on the men they brought in, not only to secure convictions but to prove the thesis that what they were dealing with on the streets was a form of gang warfare, rioting between groups of ruffians, rather than unprovoked attacks on a racial minority.[7]

Take the case of Denton Boyd. A forty-year-old Trinidadian who had been employed as a merchant seaman during the war, Boyd was arrested with Kamara and several others on 1 September 1958. He was caught with a 'chopper' and a razor in his pocket. Unlike most of the convicted black men he was not fined but given a twelve-month prison sentence, undoubtedly because of his previous record, which included a spell in prison after a shooting incident in 1945, and another in 1957 for possessing offensive weapons (razors and a knuckle-duster). The police made a great deal of the fact that he was unemployed and that they suspected, but could not prove, that he was acting as a pimp: 'Frequents East end of London in low class cafes, and associates with prostitutes', read the report. But Boyd appealed against his sentence, arguing that his character had been smeared. When asked by the judge how he had lived for the past years, the police implied they had no record of his employment since 1951.

> The Judge quite naturally said, 'How has this man lived, not on fresh air?'
>
> There was an audible mention of immoral earnings. I am a coloured man, and as the case was concerned with race rioting, in which the worse elements who live on vice are usually involved, and was of influence to the Judge in sentencing me, this was of course the picture of me the Police wanted to present to the Judge. I started as a cabinet maker in 1950 with the firm of Wenlaw furniture. The firm sold out to Henry Ronson, but I was kept on in 1951. I worked 8-years with these firms as a foreman for Ronson's, my wages were £20 per week. I have paid over £2,000 in Income Tax to 1958. The Police to the best of my knowledge were fully aware of this . . .

Whatever the police knew or did not know, Boyd lost his appeal.

Many of the witness statements provided by the police emphasize accusations by white residents that they sympathized with the immigrants. On 1 September Constable Edward Cooke encountered a crowd of three or four hundred white people while chasing a (white) suspect down Lancaster Road: 'the crowd appeared to be very hostile, and when the arrest was affected, gathered around whilst various people were shouting "You nigger loving bastards", and "Let him go", and "We'll get you copper."' But there is plenty of evidence that the opposite was the case. Indeed the police were apt to condemn themselves out of their own mouths. So Constable Dennis Clifford described the way his arrest of Michael de Freitas unfolded:

> On Tuesday 2nd September 1958 at 10:35pm, in St Luke's Road, Notting Hill, I saw Miguel DE FREITAS of 10 Kensal Road W.10, with other coloured men, surrounded by a large hostile crowd.
>
> I said to the accused 'Get out of the area quickly.' He replied 'I don't need you to fucking protect me.' He walked slowly up the road, and stopped to talk to a white woman. I again asked him to keep moving, and he said 'I'll go when I'm ready.' The crowd became menacing, so I arrested him, where he was charged, when cautioned he said, 'I suppose I'm to blame.'

De Freitas's laconic assumption of the law's bias proved correct. He was fined £2 by the magistrate, presumably for being lippy.[8]

The police lens focused on violence – it was, after all, what they were trained to look for. They were unwilling, and certainly untrained, to see racism as its primary cause. But they were not the only ones. Michael de Freitas, who was a keen jazz fan, was in contact with Stuart Hall and Raphael Samuel through the Partisan Café, the club associated with their broadly Marxist journal, *Universities and Left Review*. Hall recalled that through de Freitas and others the club 'got involved in the Notting Hill riots and their aftermath'. Hall's job as a supply teacher in a secondary school in Kennington brought him up close to what he described in the journal as:

> the aimless kicking of dustbins, the scraps and 'giggles', the 'bashing' and 'doing' (including the more organised 'doing' of Irish or West Indians) which is so much an integral part of working-class adolescent activity. I think the teenagers who explain all this in terms of boredom

and bottled up energy, rather than consciously thought out violence directed against any one group, are close to the truth. Particular prejudices about 'niggers' or 'paddies' or 'yids' are inspired: they develop *out of* a deeper level of social frustration against the society and the adult world. They are not, in themselves, the source of violence.

When youngsters, who have been on a giggle to Notting Hill, talk about it afterwards, they are perfectly aware that it is a pointless, and degrading, kind of self-indulgence. But, at the moment, the urge to commit violence is quite clearly overpowering. 'There's nothing to do, see, and you're tired of sitting around. They don't want to argue, and if you start an argument they just start swearing to shut you up. And then along comes someone, and there's something about him you don't like, see, he's a coloured man or an Irish or something, and one of the boys gets a thing about him. Let's rush him, he says, and before you know what's going on . . .'

For Hall, the secondary-modern kids of the late 1950s were 'really the alienated generation'; their training for semi-skilled jobs was all but over by the age of thirteen, and the 'aimless frenzy of their leisure life is a displacement of the energies and aspirations which have been trained or drained out of them by school and work'. They suffered from cultural rather than economic deprivation. In fact he first became aware that something was going on in Notting Hill some time before the riots began, after encountering a group of his pupils on the train, out for a 'giggle':

So when we got back to school I said, 'What are you doing up there?' 'Oh, you know.' I said, 'Why are you shouting at them?' 'Well, they're taking our women.' I said, 'What do you mean? If only you had any women!' [Laughter] 'They're taking our things' etc. So I said, 'Do you mean these?' And I pointed to several black kids in the class and they looked at them as if they'd never seen them. 'No sir.' 'He's one of us.' 'They're one of us.' So I said, 'What about me?' 'No sir. Not you. Them.'

The kids' aimless frenzy was born of having been let down by the adult world, but it also channelled adult prejudices. When Hall went to Notting Hill to see for himself he found the kids 'were on the street corners and the adults were in the pubs behind them shouting through the doors; and they were harassing black women who were walking home from work, going in to the multi-occupation flats in Powys Terrace and the terraces behind.'⁹

This line was in sympathy with that of the chief constable who claimed that the riots were not 'racial riots', although Hall was clear that race proved the excuse for them. Urban problems were expressed as racial problems. But for the most part (beyond the small circles of the New Left) laying the blame at the feet of disaffected young men, both white and black, was a means of sealing off the disturbances from the public at large. It wasn't the English, still less the British, who were racially prejudiced – it was just the kids. This was one way of marking the difference between tolerant Britain and the United States. Exactly a year earlier, at the start of the 1957 school year, the scandal of racial segregation at Little Rock High School in Arkansas had filled the newspapers. Nine African American students were registered at a formerly white school, Little Rock Central, as part of the vanguard which was to lead to desegregation across the board. But the students were boycotted and segregationist protests were officially supported by the state governor, Orval Faubus, who deployed the Arkansas National Guard to block the black students from entering the school. The belief in England was, as Lamming put it, that such a thing could never happen here. Hence the insistence that the riots were orchestrated by out-of-control youths, and a fascist fringe which lacked popular support.

In mid-September the case of the nine young men who had toured the area beating up black men in August came up in court. Sentencing each of them to four years' imprisonment, Mr Justice Salmon's judgment on the 'brutal and debased' youths focused on racial hatred, and on their gang mentality: 'Your quarry was any man, providing there was not more than two of them together, whose skin happened to be a different colour from your own.' His outrage was clearly heartfelt, but his belief that they were 'a minute and insignificant section of the population' was perhaps more questionable. There were calls for the sentences to be reduced from both ends of the political spectrum. 'These youths were as much the victims of the hysteria which swept over Notting Hill as the West Indians', claimed Fenner

Brockway, Labour MP for Eton and Slough, and champion of legislation to end racial discrimination; others argued the youths had found themselves in a 'trouble cauldron' and should not be singled out; that they should be punished for the violence only, and not for the fact that it was directed against black people. George Rogers, Labour MP for Kensington North, went further, and argued not only that the boys were not wholly responsible, but that they were not wholly at fault: 'It was wrong to say this trouble had been started by hooligans. It was the reaction of people, very sorely tried by some sections of the coloured population.'[10]

Along with blaming the kids went blaming the area, and, by association, the 'coloured population' that lived there. As the sociologist Ruth Glass argued at the time, calling them the Notting Hill riots contained and minimized them. Notting Hill then meant slums, and a criminal underworld where the 'worst types' lived. In reality the violence was spread over an area that stretched from Paddington to Kensal Rise, and there were isolated incidents in North London, in Liverpool Street and Southall throughout September. As Glass pointed out, the epicentre of the violence – Bramley Road – was not even a strongly 'coloured' area, while those places which were densely populated with Caribbean migrants, such as Colville Terrace, stayed quiet during the riots. And it was perfectly obvious to the black targets of the violence that the problem was not just one of an unruly mob in a small area of West London: 'We were not resident in Notting Hill; but we were not so foolish to think that locality was a matter of importance.'[11]

It was no wonder that black migrants felt suddenly at sea, awash in a tide of white strangers whose attitudes and intentions they could not easily fathom. It was impossible to know how deep the racial hatred went, and some people in the liberal establishment appeared not to want to know. Writing some months after the murder of Kelso Cochrane, George Lamming argued that popular revulsion over the behaviour of the hooligans of White City and Shepherd's Bush should never have been confused with racial tolerance. The same people could disapprove of the violence and still hate black immigrants:

One of the paradoxes of Notting Hill was that the vast majority of the people in this country felt a deep sense of outrage. They genuinely felt that it was wrong and beastly that such a thing should happen. It's one reason why those English kids were so severely sentenced (a decision which I thought at the time, and still do now, was not altogether sound). It was not altogether sound because it was done as a way of informing the world how this country felt about Notting Hill. But a large number of the people who felt so bitterly about the events in Notting Hill feel no less bitterly about the presence of these black men in this overcrowded country.[12]

Lamming wasn't the only immigrant to feel that the 'English kids' had been wrongly singled out. The Trinidadian Communist and civil rights activist Claudia Jones had arrived in Britain in 1955, having been imprisoned in and then expelled from the United States for 'un-American activities'. In the spring of 1958 she launched the newspaper the *West Indian Gazette*, which served as a voice of the Caribbean community in London for the next six years. But her principal legacy is the first 'Caribbean Carnival', a celebration of West Indian music and culture which was designed in part to 'wash the taste of Notting Hill and Nottingham out of our mouths'. The prototype Notting Hill carnival was held in January 1959 in St Pancras Town Hall and was televised by the BBC. Part of the proceeds from the sale of the souvenir brochure was earmarked to 'assist the payment of fines of coloured and white youths involved in the Notting Hill events'.[13]

After all, where had the kids got their attitudes from? In the months that followed the riots, as right-wing and openly 'anti-coloured' groups stepped up their activities in North Kensington, they were blamed for 'fanning the flames' of violence and race hatred. The newssheet of the White Defence League appeared more frequently than before, its headlines 'full of colour': 'Blacks Invade Britain'; 'Reds Count on Blacks'; 'Blacks Seek White Women'. Oswald Mosley's Union Movement began holding a weekly meeting outside Notting Hill Gate tube station, in addition to their regular street-corner hustings. In the spring of 1959 the Movement opened an office and a bookshop on Kensington Park Road, and Mosley announced he would stand as a candidate for North Kensington in the forthcoming general election. Ruth Glass described an atmosphere of growing 'apprehension and animosity' throughout the months leading up to Kelso Cochrane's murder:

> There was a routine of minor rows and incidents: 'Keep Britain White' notices stuck up on walls and lamp posts, and pushed through letter boxes; street corner agitation; Mosley meetings; rumours; occasional fights – no big explosion, but a lot of rumbling, sparks and flickers, in an environment of physical decay and social discontent. Altogether, there was a smell of tension in the air.[14]

We get some sense of Mosley's contribution to the tension from a series of notebook jottings written by an undercover 'spy' named Rachel, who sent her secret reports on Union gatherings to the social activist and politician Donald Chesworth. She first encountered a vulpine Mosley in September 1959, speaking to a crowd of three or four hundred on Golborne Road (near the site of Cochrane's murder):

> Impression v. sleek. Must be 63 but doesn't quite look it. Hair still good. Macmillan smile with lip drawn back over teeth – predatory air . . . Plushy voice with calculated use of 'chap like you' but no attempt to adopt working class noises. Occasional talking down – 'going round your houses, canvassing it's called.' 'I will explain to you how your problems are connected with world politics.' 'I will tell Europe about your troubles when I go there because I speak their languages – .'
>
> Several key phrases – go into Europe – black colonies – blacks round our necks – black sweat shops – black brothels – their coloured friends – one law for the blacks & another for the whites – forcing the blacks on us – capitalist exploitation with aid of cheap black labour – five more blacks on your streets – multiplied by five – financiers – etc.

Despite the inclusion of 'financiers' in Mosley's list of bogeymen, by the late 1950s the group had radically toned down its anti-Semitic rhetoric. This was a long way from the attacks on Jews in Ridley Road in 1947 and 1948. The Union Movement, and its little flotilla of extremist organizations, was both jumping on and driving the new racist bandwagon. The demands were not simply for an end to immigration but for forced repatriation, on the grounds that black migrants were aliens, who proved it by their criminality, their sexual deviance and their domestic habits. It was all too much for Rachel, who punctuated her reports of his speeches with sardonic asides:

> Who knows about the life here since the coloured people came? When I am elected I shall make everyone realise your sufferings . . .
>
> Housing – all houses will be repaired (app. immediately.) overcrowding alleviated by deportation of all coloured people, housing made cheaper by lowering interest on housing loans . . . Building for rich will have higher interest so that rich will pay for your kind of building – yours will be cheap.
>
> Deportation. All good blacks want to go back to Jamaica – (app. They all come from Jamaica) and the racketeers & vice gangs will be swept away anyway. We have the right. We shall pay passages.

The cost of ridding the country of black migrants he estimated at £11 million – arguing that any man earning under £12 a week would contribute a mere three shillings. 'And I have never heard anyone in Notting Hill say that he wouldn't pay that to be rid of them & be glad of it.' In the end Mosley garnered 8.1 per cent of the popular vote, a figure which may seem disturbingly high, but which Mosley himself – still harbouring fantasies of being a future prime minister – experienced as a humiliation. It was a figure which would have given George Lamming pause: one in twelve of the white strangers in North Kensington had voted to get rid of him and his compatriots. It was not just a humiliation for Mosley.[15]

The Union Movement and its fascist fringe attempted to capitalize on the riots at a local level. But the most lasting consequence of the violence in Nottingham and Notting Hill was to transform immigration from a local, or regional, issue to a national one. Sporadic eruptions of racial tension and interracial violence in the dock areas of Liverpool, Cardiff or East London had been contained as 'local' problems. But the press coverage of the Notting Hill riots placed Commonwealth immigration centre stage in a debate about contemporary Britain. The debate was built on the assumption that the inner cities were in crisis, and although the youngsters with too much money and too much freedom were at fault, their patience was being sorely tried by an influx of outsiders who brought with them alien attitudes and alien ways of life. Some journalists, MPs, lawyers and parents might be sympathetic to the rioters and some less so, but all broadly accepted the basic argument that a threshold of tolerance had been reached. The riots formed the crucible for the assumption that good race relations depends on tight control of immigration. At the same time the violence made restrictive legislation trickier to introduce, since politicians were wary of appearing to be motivated by racist sentiment. When Cyril Osborne, Conservative MP for Louth in Lincolnshire, argued in an October 1958 Queen's Speech debate that there was an 'urgent need for a restriction upon immigration into this country, particularly of coloured immigrants', and introduced the spectre of 6 million New Commonwealth migrants within two decades, he was roundly condemned by fellow MPs for racist scaremongering. And apart from the problem of looking like a racist there was the uncomfortable fact that it was going to be far from easy to restrict 'coloured' migration from the Commonwealth at a time when the majority of Commonwealth migrants were white – travellers from Australia, Canada, New Zealand and South Africa, as well as people 'of United Kingdom descent' who had been living in India, Pakistan and elsewhere.

Nonetheless, the basic tenets of the debate on immigration were laid down, and they cut across party lines. Few people suggested that the problem of racial tension should be tackled with measures such as improved housing and education, or legislation against racial discrimination. (Arguing against introducing anti-discrimination legislation, one Conservative suggested that 'The Act would run a risk of recognising the existence of discrimination in a way which might draw attention to it and would tend rather to foster it than do away with it.') It appeared to be common sense that racism increased in proportion to the quantity, and even quality, of immigrants, and over the next four years this credo, despite its flawed logic, would come to dominate the immigration debate. It would result in the 1962 Commonwealth Immigrants Act, in which legislators managed to pull off the trick of restricting New Commonwealth migrants while allowing other – white – immigrants (notably the Irish) freedom of movement. In the long run the rhetoric surrounding the riots would lend credibility to Enoch Powell's anti-immigration agenda.[16]

Those were the warnings, and challenges, as the white strangers saw them. For the black strangers the lessons were rather different. For beyond the political frame the riots had a more everyday, and deeper, effect. It is not an exaggeration to say that for British citizens from the Caribbean and Asia, the meaning of personal experience – their way of seeing – had changed. What had been doubt about their welcome was now crystallized into knowledge of underlying hostility towards them. 'Suddenly the coloured people no longer walk singly.' It was clear that the purpose of the riots had been in part to get West Indians to strike back (hence the term 'nigger-baiting' used by people involved). As Lamming put it, 'We must accept that racial antagonism in Great Britain, is, after Notting Hill, an atmosphere and a background against which my life and yours are being lived . . .' And beyond this new knowledge about the neighbours lay a further realization, about the police: that it would be foolish to count on prompt protection from them in the event of another attack. Now-familiar terms, such as 'institutional racism', were still years in the future, but, as talk of restricting immigration gathered pace and efforts to combat discrimination foundered, it was no longer possible to argue that racial antagonism was limited to a number of disaffected individuals. It ran as an undercurrent through society at large. 'The Devil was at work in Notting Hill; and there is no point trying to say it was the Teddy Boys.'[17]

10

Lovers

My love affair was with Sybil, a sweet person, intelligent,
easy to get along with and who oozed sincerity. She was
immensely warm and at times unable to control her passion,
in that it was not always channelled in my direction, but
nonetheless her sincerity for me was stout and unshakeable,
and transcended her otherwise immense fault. Marriage
seemed an inevitable outcome of the usual predicament, and
though I knew her fault I was prepared to comply with con-
vention and surrender myself to the good soul that she was.

Wallace Collins, *Jamaican Migrant* (1965)[1]

In February 1954 Wallace Collins, a trained carpenter, paid three
pounds – and handed over his watch – to a man who promised to get
him a working passage on a banana boat to Britain. He had been out
of work for a year, and since his father's death had been the main
breadwinner for his family. 'The only straw I could clutch on to, was
a ship to Great Britain.' He travelled from the Jamaican hills to Port
Antonio where he found he had paid to become a 'common stowaway', bundled into the coal store until he was discovered by an irate
captain far out to sea; when the ship docked Collins was rewarded
with three weeks' imprisonment. His memoir of his eight years in
England tells a mainly upbeat story – he overcomes poverty and prejudice to prove his worth as a skilled carpenter, he goes to night school
where he learns to write, his mother eventually moves to England
to live near him, and he meets and marries a fellow Jamaican with

whom he eventually re-emigrates to Canada. Collins clearly thought of his marriage to a girl from home as a step up from an earlier relationship with a young white woman called Sybil, aged seventeen and a trainee nurse – a relationship which was swiftly brought to an end when she became pregnant by him.

Collins's account of his interracial romantic adventure is disarmingly honest. Because Sybil is sweet and passionate (and, he claims, undiscriminating) the pregnancy appears to be entirely her fault. He gallantly offers to marry her, but a single conversation with her irate parents in their lower-middle-class North London home (if you love her, why did you get her into this mess?) is enough to dissuade him. He leaves Sybil, desperate in her 'ruin', and though he acknowledges that 'somehow I felt guilty', he does not appear to give her another thought. She has eased the way for him socially and solved the problem of lonely nights, but she was never going to form part of his long-term plan. Respectability for him means a good job where he is the equal of white workmen, and a stable marriage and family with one of his own. He accepts without much question that a marriage cannot work across colour lines, not least because, almost by definition, Sybil is not quite decent.[2]

Collins's stance towards his own lover was a mirror-image of the attitudes common in respectable white society too: that women who got involved with black men were either bad or foolish. Sybil's whiteness put her in a double bind with regard to the 'respectable' black man, who could not value a white woman who wanted to be with him. By virtue of the very fact of loving him, and loving him passionately, she could not deserve him.

Sybil faced a particularly cruel version of the sexual double-standard. As Colin MacInnes put it in his 1957 novel *City of Spades*, the problem with mixed-race relationships was that the children gave the game away: 'An arrival of white babies they can somehow explain away. But if their daughter has a brown one, then neighbourhood fingers all start pointing.'[3] And it was certainly true that mixed-race children born in the 1950s were rarely straightforwardly accepted as the fruit of loving unions between equals. Rather, they tended to be regarded as the signs of failure and dysfunction, of gullible young white girls being caught out by unscrupulous foreigners, or, worse, of the grubby world of 'vice' which must surely lie behind any relationship between black and white. Interracial love was, for a large section of British public opinion, impossible to fathom.

Take the following couple of short vignettes, both from 1958. The first comes from a report of an Irish missionary priest, asked by the family back home in Ireland to check up on a young emigrant woman who seemed to have gone astray. The priest found the address, left his bicycle a little way down the road – priests' bikes being, apparently, instantly recognizable – rang the doorbell and then flattened himself against the wall of the house so those inside wouldn't see who was calling:

> The stratagem succeeded, for the door was opened by a lovely young Irish girl. Beside her stood a little mite of perhaps three years, with a ribbon in her hair. The girl admitted that she was married in the registry.
>
> 'Is that little girl yours?'
> 'Yes.'
> 'What's her name?'
> 'Fatima.'
> 'That's a nice Catholic name.'
> 'Not at all; it's the name of the Prophet's daughter.'[4]

The second comes from a BBC radio programme, broadcast a few weeks after the Notting Hill riots. Much of the debate following the 1958 riots focused on anger among local white youths over West Indian men taking their jobs, their unemployment benefits and their women. The BBC interviewer records the conversation of a group of young Teds from a nearby estate in White City, home to seven of the nine rioters convicted by Justice Salmon of racially aggravated violence. The conversation certainly reveals a good deal of insecurity among the youths, as it keeps circling around the belief that black migrants got more money and better treatment at the dole office, of foreigners taking their jobs, of working for less pay, and, perhaps above all, of black men going with white girls:

> '. . . Just that a lot of ponces [pimps] live round here. I mean, it's not very nice to see a coloured bloke with a white girl out in the streets, is it? I don't mind white people doing it but not black . . . Well, it's not

them it's the children – they're half-castes. You want to know about the kids – the half-castes. Well, we don't want a lot of half-castes running around, do we?'

'I'll tell you how they get them [i.e. cars and houses] off the backs of white girls, and black girls now. You go up Bayswater Road you'll see black girls out on the game now.'

Of the several hundred thousand black migrants in Britain in 1958, one young man insisted that 'ninety-five per cent' were sending girls out on the game. The group interview is full of openly racist comment: the men admit that some of them were involved in the Notting Hill attacks, and that given the opportunity they would get involved again. The following passage leads on from a discussion of the need to stop West Indians from entering the country:

2ND VOICE: Who is a British subject? Is a darkie a British subject, correct, an Irishman isn't, right? Now who would you sooner have in your country an Irishman or a darkie?

VOICES: An Irishman definitely.

INTERVIEWER: An Irishman definitely, why?

VOICE: Me old man's Irish isn't he?

2ND VOICE: Well, OK, why would you prefer an Irishman in your country, because, not because your old man's Irish, but why would you prefer an Irishman in your country to a darkie?

VOICE: Why because they're not so much scandal are they?

2ND VOICE: Not so much scandal? Well, I'll contradict you there, an Irishman can be the worst man out . . . He can drink (yes), fight (yes), he can run brothels, same as the darkie (yes). He can do anything.

VOICE: But they're not so bad as the darkies are they? Are you running your own country down?

2ND VOICE: No I'm not running my own country down, no no, but I've seen myself in Shepherd's Bush, in Acton, in Camden Town, in numerous parts of London, I've seen Irishmen in trouble.

VOICE: So you condemn all the blacks.

2ND VOICE: No, no, I'm not condemning the Irish or the black men. But I do believe this, I've met Englishmen that condemned

the Irishmen. My name is Danny and they condemn me
because I am Irish. They know my name is Danny but they
won't call me Danny, they call me Pat, but when they meet a
darkie they call him by his name.[5]

The passage is fascinating because of the way the young, second-generation Irish man gives voice to more than he can clearly understand. His main point seems to be, it's not fair that the Irish are treated badly since we are better than West Indians, as everybody knows. But he argues this by claiming that the Irish are really just as 'bad' – 'the worst man out'. They can run brothels too. Then there's that slippage between the Irish who cause trouble, and the Irish who are in trouble. The young man's confusion about where to place himself isn't edifying: what he wants is to be the same as his white mates, including in their racism, but what he articulates is his own uncertain racial designation, neither one thing nor the other.

Perhaps these two stories just tell us that people are different; that some Irish in Britain identified with other others, and some didn't, or couldn't. And there is a difference in migrant generations, of course. The young woman who married a Muslim may have been a similar age to angry, confounded Danny, but she was a fairly new arrival. Like several others in the group of Teds, while Danny's old man was Irish, he was born and bred in London and he felt that England was, or should have been, 'my own country'. He lived in Local Authority housing in White City; he felt himself to be a rightful beneficiary of the Welfare State; houses, jobs, benefits and even women were the wages of belonging. Fatima's mother, on the other hand, had arrived in London in the 1950s. Not quite an alien but not an insider either, she staked her claim on the wrong side of the battle for resources. In this she was at one with the other immigrants of the 1950s, whether from the Caribbean, Cyprus, India or Pakistan, and her marriage to a Muslim migrant suggests that it was an affinity she recognized.

Fatima's mother appears to have found happiness and security in her relationship, and in her adopted religion. She was certainly not in need of saving, and the next time the priest came to call the door stayed resolutely shut against him. It was obvious that she had nothing at all in common with the girls out on the game in the Bayswater

Road, but majority public opinion in the 1950s appeared blind to distinctions between women who had relationships with black men. After all, to people who believed that 95 per cent of black migrants sent their women out onto the streets, there could be no distinctions. It was a matter of arithmetic. The very fact that women could accustom themselves to, not to mention desire, their partners from the Caribbean and South Asia appeared to place them on the side of indecency. The accommodations required for love and sex and marriage were, in themselves, a problem for outsiders.

The idea that mixed relationships, liked mixed lodgings, may have performed an important function in fostering mutual understanding between immigrants and their hosts was an oddly contested one during the 1950s and 1960s. The assumption seems to have been that white women in relationships with Asian and Caribbean men were 'social misfits' rather than the vanguard of the future, that mixed lodgings were harbingers of disorder rather than crucibles of knowledge and experience about other people. It was at work, so the argument went, that migrants learned to get on with the English, and vice versa. Once they left the factory, the foundry, the mill, the office or even the school, they separated again into ethnic silos. It goes without saying that this theory could only be sustained if love and sex were discounted.

One reason why the tag of social misfit may have stuck so easily was that historically (before the post-war migration boom) white women who had forged liaisons with black men had mainly lived with seamen and ex-seamen in the dock areas of cities such as Cardiff, Liverpool and London, areas where 'respectable' white women did not venture. Michael de Freitas, who worked as a deck hand with the Norwegian merchant navy and spent some time between jobs in Cardiff's seamen's hostels, described the Tiger Bay area in the early 1950s as entirely apart from the everyday experiences of the majority of working-class Cardiffians:

> The Bay was a world of its own, cut off from the rest of the city. A black world. It swarmed with West Indians, Arabs, Somalis, Pakistanis and a legion of half-caste children. In its food stores you could buy cassavas and red peppers and in the restaurants you could eat curries and rice dishes just like those in the West Indies.[6]

By the mid-1950s pockets of Notting Hill and Brixton appeared to have taken on the flavour of the dockside areas, largely because of the ready availability of slum housing, providing homes for the underclass of London's apparent post-war boom. Several 'social problem' documentaries made towards the end of the decade focus on the burgeoning, informal red-light district around Bayswater Road and Paddington. In one highly coloured film by an Irish Catholic social action group, the camera lingers pruriently over the ads for sex posted in telephone boxes around Paddington ('Cutie-Doll, For Sale, Ring Bay 1503'), while the voice-over laments the difficulty of keeping young Irish girls in check, with 'results more or less unfortunate'.[7]

Girls falling prey to unscrupulous men in an atmosphere of seedy urban misrule – it was a Victorian trope, but one which could be easily updated to fit the new 'coloured' underworld. No doubt some of it was true. And it sometimes suited the girls themselves to reinforce tales of their own ruin at the hands of immoral foreigners. Take the case of Majbritt Morrison, a Swedish woman married to a Jamaican who in 1958 was living in Bramley Road, North Kensington. Her verbal defence of her husband against the threats of youths like the young men from the White City estate was one of the flash points of the Notting Hill riots. Insisting that her husband was not a pimp, and that they were simply a mixed-race couple out for the evening, she was abused by the crowd and taken to the local police station 'for protection'. Yet in her ghost-written memoir published a few years later (complete with 'authentic' misspellings) – after she had left her husband and struggled with alcoholism – she blamed the 'mostly West Indian' ponces of Kensington and Notting Hill for dragging her into a 'school of vice'. She began by frequenting 'a couppel of clubs where vice was written over every ones face. A hole for prostitutes and drug-salers, full of smoke and loud-playing jukeboxes.' She got used to sharing her husband, Raymond, with another woman, and eventually – with Raymond in prison – earned money for herself and her child through prostitution. 'Shattered' by the 'savagery' of the 'twilight jungle' of West Indian prostitution she had finally 'succumbed'.[8]

By contrast, there were others who argued that West Indian men were not the ones at fault. 'It is the girls who make the ponces,' argued the sociologist Cecil Rolph in 1955. Colin MacInnes agreed, putting this argument in the mouth of the teenage narrator in *Absolute Beginners* in 1959: 'Say what you like, in that set-up it's the female party who controls the situation . . . the simple reason being that her own activity, whatever you may think of it, is legal, and the boy's is not.' Rolph maintained that the insecurity was worse for migrant than for home-grown pimps:

> These men, often uneducated and unable to recognise the good from the bad white girl, arrive in a new and bewildering culture, find that they are not wanted by white people and are often forced to form associations with the class who will associate with them . . . Many of these girls already have the habit of going out to solicit and continue to do so, some-times against the wishes of the man. The suggestion that the coloured man drives the girl out and beats her if she will not go is dramatic but, so far as I know, unfounded.[9]

In the same year Michael Banton, a sociologist of race, blamed loose women and their 'unmistakeable temperament' for the problems in mixed marriages. The women themselves, as Wallace Collins's girl-friend Sybil found, were caught in a vicious circle – even if they were married to their partners, by definition they could not be 'respect-able'. One young woman married to a Jamaican and living in Lancaster Road was asked in 1958 if she had problems with her neighbours. Yes, she did: 'She has often been addressed as the "Nig-ger Lover". Furthermore, she mentioned that the behaviour of the police in the district is ["]downright disgusting", and that they were always ready to "pick you up" for prostitution.'[10]

The idea that the naïve and rejected black man was the natural vic-tim of a white underworld was hardly majority opinion. It is safe to say that most people thought the problem – such as it was – was the fault of foreign men. As one of the White City youths declared about pon-cing: 'I don't mind white people doing it but not black.' In the wake of the Notting Hill riots school children in West London were asked their opinions of the causes of racial tension, and, like Stuart Hall's Ken-nington pupils, nearly all of them mentioned the way black men behaved around women: 'When they come over from their own coun-tries they pinch our houses and the work, that's if they go to work but most of them are just too lazy and live on National Assistance. Then with the money, they take out our White girls and start up brothels and other vice rackets'; 'And they drug our girls and take them into broth-els. That's how the riot began because a house occupied by the blacks was nothing but a brothel and the boys didn't like to see our white girls being mucked around by the Blacks.' One local detective claimed the system was hard-wired into 'foreign' cultures. 'Ninety per cent of pimps are foreign, either coloureds from the West Indies or Cypriots or Maltese . . . This is significant. The pimps are not only foreigners in a land whose morals do not accord with their own, but they all come from countries in which women are under-privileged and servile.'[11]

The Maltese connection cropped up right through the 1950s, fall-out from the Messina Brothers scandal. The Messinas were a Maltese family involved in trafficking women for prostitution, appar-ently with the collusion of the Metropolitan Police. Their activities were initially exposed by a series of articles in the *People*. The broth-ers were said by journalist Duncan Webb to be behind 'the most complicated and certainly the most powerfully organized gang of vice this nation has ever known', and the long-drawn-out series of trials ensured that the activities, and lifestyles, of the brothers were kept on the front pages through much of the decade. And for the White City youths, the problems were caused equally by the Jamaicans and the Maltese: 'the Maltese, they're the same thing. They won't work at all. So if they find our girls . . .' In the late 1950s the left-wing journalist and campaigner Tosco Fyvel spent some time trailing groups of Teds in North London for his study *The Insecure Offenders*: 'I remember one boy in a beautiful Italian suit who carried not merely a knife but actually a gun. When I asked him why, he said: "There's all sorts of Cypriots and Maltese walking about round here . . . you've got to put your hand on something."' The permeable racial barrier between colonial citizens from Europe, Africa, Asia and the Caribbean was a feature too of more 'official' statements. In his parliamentary speech urging the need for immigration restrictions following the Notting Hill riots, Cyril Osborne targeted as ripe for repatriation all those 'loosely termed coloured people, including Maltese and Cypriots'. Oswald Mosley took a similarly inclusive view of certain ethnicities. The undercover reporter Rachel found him arguing in the spring of 1959 for a pan-European white alliance:

If we join Europe we shall gain in civilisation. We shall let the civilised European stay here – & the Irish – I'm very fond of their people – because they have been here a long time – but we shan't keep the Maltese & Cypriots, the vice mongers. They aren't European.

Undoubtedly part of the reason for the focus on Caribbean and African pimps in the newspapers was their shock value. They were 'doubly black sheep', Colin MacInnes argued, enjoying 'from the Sunday press, a generous publicity withheld from the deeds of the less exciting native entrepreneurs'. And there were obvious advantages to stretching the category of black to include anyone you didn't like. Not least it made those tricky distinctions between good and bad peoples far easier to make.[12]

There was no proof, of course, that the main agents behind the gambling and prostitution rackets were only, or even mainly, black migrants, however broadly conceived. As Ruth Glass pointed out in 1960, the idea that either Notting Hill or Brixton had the character of a 'coloured quarter' comparable to the ghettos of some US cities was wildly inaccurate. Caribbean migrants – far more than those from India and Pakistan – were scattered throughout London, rather than confined to a few areas.

> The West area, for example, contains here and there some streets in which several, or quite a number of, migrants live, often in adjacent houses; but there are many other streets in which only one or two West Indian addresses can be found ... Only a small proportion of West Indians in London live in these particular places, and in most parts of these districts it is not the coloured people but the white people who are predominant.[13]

As a *Times* article insisted in May 1959, the behaviour of even the most badly behaved section of the migrant population was not sufficient reason for the racial tension:

> It is often said that working class white people resent an influx of coloured neighbours because they 'lower' the district with their crowded houses, ignorant behaviour, and rowdy habits. This is emphatically not a satisfactory explanation of the interracial resentment in North Kensington at the present. The great majority of the coloured inhabitants are semi-skilled West Indian workers, with respectable habits, a

strong ambition to do well for themselves, and at least as much education as their white neighbours. There are a few West Indians in the area who are either prostitutes or who live off the earnings of prostitutes; but they are an insignificant minority. Certainly the proportion of criminal or immoral elements in the coloured people in this area is smaller than among its white population.[14]

Nonetheless the area's reputation as a harder-edged and blacker Soho flourished in the press, particularly following the riots. A police raid on Holland Park Avenue in the autumn of 1958 counted seventy-three prostitutes in the half hour between 10 and 10.30 p.m. And the coupling of blackness and permissive sex became a mainstay of London memoirs, fiction and film of the period, much of it written by the immigrants themselves. In 1956 Sam Selvon painted a portrait of West Indian male sexual power centred on Hyde Park ('the things that does happen in this London people wouldn't believe'); in Colin MacInnes's 1957 novel *City of Spades* the principal black character, Johnny Fortune (a Nigerian), impregnates not one but two white lovers, and behaves with equal insouciance towards both of them.[15]

There were also less experimental portraits of the black sexual underworld. In 1954 Wallace Collins got his first job as an underpresser in Aldgate East (for £6 a week), and after work he would go to a pub on Cable Street

> frequented by Jamaicans and the odd Maltese with a few 'wooden faced whores' . . . They would greet each other with 'Wa' happen sa?' and the other would answer, 'Boy ah tek it easy no?' while their women would greet each other with 'Hello darling, how's business?', 'Hi ducks', and inhale strongly and take a wicked puff on their cigarettes.
>
> Some of these characters had names like Horse Mouth, Chow-Chow-Mouth, Shine, Blues, The Wizard, Arnor, Razor, and what they talked about was anybody's business, from who is living by vice to who's got how many Judys on the road hustling for them, to who's got a pound weight of the 'weed' (called 'shit') selling, or who's screwing who's Miss Anne.[16]

Michael de Freitas clearly relished producing his own gritty portrait of the atmosphere of the streets of West London – which was in part designed as a way of excusing his own activities as a pimp a couple of years later:

> At night the ghetto takes on a different hue, a sexual quality. The daughters of all these families issue from their poky rooms all dressed up and start to ply their bodies for hire. They make a lot of money.
>
> In the next room to ours lived a Trinidadian friend of mine named Nick, whose Italian girl friend also earned money by going out on the streets. It was the order of the day. Nobody was shocked by it.[17]

Undoubtedly some people *were* shocked, however. Even if, as *The Times* pointed out, the prostitutes and pimps formed 'an insignificant minority' of the inhabitants of Notting Hill, it was large enough to stain the reputation of the area as a whole. From 1956 onwards, aspiring new arrivals from the islands avoided the area if they possibly could: 'Room wanted,' said the small ads, 'but not in Notting Hill.' They tended to choose Brixton instead, so that by 1958 18 per cent of Caribbean migrants in London were housed in Lambeth, compared to Kensington's 12 per cent or Paddington's 10 per cent. Or they found lodgings as far as possible from either of the immigrant centres. By the time of the riots only two metropolitan boroughs (Marylebone and Bermondsey) were without a Caribbean presence.[18]

It was true, then, that a number of Caribbean hustlers were making their money by pimping off their English girlfriends. But the level of public outrage over 'black men going with white girls' clearly could not be put down simply to that. For a start it was far from clear that the women would not just as readily be handing over their earnings to white boyfriends, if they had happened to have them, instead. The indignation over immorality masked deeper concerns. Part of the issue focused on the hustlers' financial success. It was galling to see men who had only recently arrived in the country wearing flashy suits and driving flashy cars. But underlying the jealousy lay more disturbing attitudes, rooted in biological racism. Take the slippage in the comment by one of the White City rioters, from complaining about the 'lot of ponces' to complaining about the children: 'Well, it's not them it's the children – they're half-castes.'

Mixed-race relationships were presented as problematic because they encouraged illegality (paying for sex), promiscuity, disease and social disorder. This all hung on the assumption – insistence rather – that the women involved with black men were 'the worst type'. But the real issue was more fundamental. It was about control over the families – and hence the English nation – of the future. 'Would you let your daughter marry a negro?' asked one *Picture Post* article in 1954. It was just one of a spate of 'social concern' features that dominated the immigration debate of the 1950s and early 1960s. The ITV series *People in Trouble* ran a feature on 'Mixed Marriages' in 1958, which focused first on the problems that young John, the three-year-old child of Mr Jackson (a Jamaican) and his English wife Olive, was bound to encounter; and then on the disastrous and seemingly inevitable breakdown of the relationship between 'Helen' and her Nigerian husband. 'Because one must remember,' explained the presenter, Daniel Farson, to a weary-looking Helen, who has just described her husband's physical abuse, 'the different country and background that the coloured man comes from. And in your case, Nigeria has only been civilised in the last few years, really, hasn't it?'[19]

By 1961 Roy Ward Baker could cast Brenda de Banzie as the hysterical mother in his 'love across the racial divide' film *Flame in the Streets* and know that her tirade against her daughter marrying a black teacher would be instantly recognized, if not necessarily condoned. The film was based on Ted Willis's 1958 play *Hot Summer Night*, which was broadcast on ITV's *Armchair Theatre* in January 1959. An estimated TV audience of at least 5 million watched the bitter row between Kathie Palmer (played by Andreé Melly) and her on-screen mother (Ruth Dunning). Kathie accuses her mother of prejudice ('All you can see is black, black, everything else you're blind to') and fear of what the neighbours will say. But her mother's racism goes far deeper than that:

> I'm ashamed of you, ashamed. When I think of you and that man sharing the same bed, it's filthy, it's disgusting, my stomach turns over and I want to be sick. You're no better than the women who wait for them on the high street. You can't wait to be with him, that's the truth. All you want is one thing . . . Well don't just stand there, go to your nigger, go to your nigger . . .[20]

The amount of sound and fury the issue generated (compared, for example, to the sober accounts of workplace integration) suggested that interracial sex was the front line in a battle over the future of England, and thus necessarily also the vanguard. The real problem was not prostitution but marriage, not sex but love. That is one explanation of why the overwhelming focus of public anxiety was on white women's relationships with Caribbean men. There was plenty of evidence that Punjabi and Mirpuri migrants were just as likely as their Caribbean counterparts to get involved with local women. The chief constables' reports of the mid 1950s had often homed in on Arab and Pakistani mixed-race relationships. In Bradford, Hull, South Shields, Nottingham and Birmingham, Asian men lived with white women, those who it was assumed could not do any better. In December 1957 the *Yorkshire Evening Post* reported that:

> A social worker in Bradford, Miss Anderson, believes that the solution to Bradford's colour problem might be that coloured men should bring their womenfolk with them. The presence of many coloured men in the town has attracted a number of girls and women of an undesirable type, who have come from all over the country.

This was the world explored in Abdullah Hussein's extraordinary novella 'The Journey Back', written in the 1970s but recalling the experience of living a subterranean life in Birmingham during the 1960s. Hussein was already an acclaimed writer (and trained engineer) when he moved from Pakistan to England in the mid-1960s, where, over the next nine years, he tried to find time for writing while working as a dishwasher, petrol-station attendant and eventually as an apprentice chemist for the London Coalgas Board. His story – later filmed as *Brothers in Trouble* and set in Leeds – focuses on a mixed group of Pakistani Punjabis, Pathans, Mirpuris, Hafizabadis and Bengalis who have been smuggled into England and who live mainly confined to their overcrowded lodging house, for fear of being picked up by the authorities. The weekly routine of work, food and sleep is broken only on a Sunday, first by the communal outing to the cinema to watch – and weep with longing for home – Urdu and Punjabi films ('At precisely three o'clock, the thirteen of us filed out in our well-pressed, clean clothes and shining boots and marched off to the movies'); next by the visits of the agents, to collect their fees and bribes; and finally by the ritual of weekly paid sex:

I heard that before I came people went to them on their own and paid individually. Then everyone got together and decided it was a waste of money. Husain Shah came up with the alternative which everyone liked: the prostitutes were to be hired for a fixed time and rate. And they were to come to our house ... Every Sunday, at eight o'clock sharp, one of the prostitutes would appear at our house, all spruced up. We would all be sitting inside waiting. She would trot in calling, 'Come on boys, feeding time!' and go up to the second floor. There was a Hafizabadi room up there set aside for this particular event. All of us would crowd outside talking softly amongst ourselves. But as the action picked up, the laughing and joking got louder and louder.

For the *namazi*, the devout who pray five times a day, the weekly ceremony is followed by a long and elaborate cleansing ritual. But the routine of the house is disrupted when Husain Shah forms a long-term relationship with Mary, who is 'that class of woman', but who befriends the men in the house, giving them the confidence to speak to shopkeepers, call the doctor, challenge the agents, and even go to the pub (with admittedly tragic consequences). 'From our relationships with women we learn about ourselves,' says the narrator. By contrast, police and social workers alike seemed to find it impossible to acknowledge that Asian immigrants might have complex and fulfilling relationships with local women. No doubt there were many Marys, but, primarily because of the perceived barriers of language and religion, those concerned about prostitution in Bradford or Birmingham, stopped short of the conclusion that Asian men were 'taking our women'. Relationships between white women and Caribbean men were more threatening precisely because they appeared more likely to be permanent, and not because they were transitory and financially motivated.[21]

The problem of the dangerous Caribbean lover existed in interesting tension with the simultaneous belief (held by a number of British civil servants as well as many West Indians themselves) that Caribbean migrants were a 'better' type than Indians and Pakistanis because of their British education, and the fact that they spoke English. According to officials from the Colonial Office, writing before the Notting

Hill riots, immigrants from the Indian subcontinent were 'hardly fit to compare with the West Indians either socially or as industrial workers'; the Indians and Pakistanis then beginning to enter Britain in larger numbers were 'nearly all of them feckless individuals, who have neither the "British" backgrounds of the West Indians, nor their abilities'.[22] One of the ironies of the situation was that British and strict Muslim attitudes to mixed relationships were remarkably close. Islamic mores condoned male polygamy, and marriage to monotheists (i.e. Christians and Jews) was acceptable only so long as any children were raised as Muslims. By contrast, there was no toleration for women marrying 'out'. The patrilineal prohibition on Muslim women marrying non-Muslim men was not so very different from the British fear of the dilution of 'white Englishness' through miscegenation.

The danger of mixed-race relationships was that they would produce mixed-race children and thus increase the 'coloured' population. The prejudices of biological racism were seldom openly articulated in official documents – except for the products of the far-right fringe groups such as the White Defence League and Oswald Mosley's Union Movement, whose public profiles depended on claiming they were expressing the thoughts that ordinary people were too scared to voice openly. These groups bolstered their arguments by appealing to pseudo-scientific theories purporting to be derived from genetic science. Characters such as Colin Bertram, secretary to the Eugenics Society, argued for example that geographical distance had enabled the 'genetic specialisation' of different races, but that now 'modern transport' was contributing to their 'mongrelisation' because of the 'lowering of proper standards' of segregation.[23]

It is important to acknowledge that these kinds of arguments were never considered politically or socially acceptable, and they were strongly countered by invocations of equality and the brotherhood of man: as one West Indian BBC interviewee put it, 'if God didn't want us to mix he'd of put us on one of them planets, and put you down this side. But he want us to mix so he put us all here.' Neither main political party pandered to eugenicist racial theories, though certain politicians, such as Cyril Osborne, got pretty close in his increasingly vociferous arguments for restrictions on immigration from 1952 onwards. And the true extent of popular prejudice is notoriously hard to gauge. What is clear is that it was strongest when it came to sex, marriage and children. A nation-wide Gallup poll investigating the extent of British 'tolerance' of immigrants in the aftermath of the Notting Hill riots found that while just over half of the respondents thought that black immigrants should have equal access to employment in Britain, and a third felt the same way about council housing, 71 per cent of them said they disapproved of interracial marriage. In another survey of attitudes towards 'the colour problem', eighty-four out of one hundred female Oxbridge students said they would be unwilling to marry an African, though the majority put this down not to scientific theories but to what the researcher called 'the misery of half-caste babies'.[24]

People in mixed marriages themselves argued that the problem was other people. As a young white woman interviewed for the television show 'Black Marries White' in 1964 put it, 'The only difference that I can see with going out with English boys and coloured boys is the difference that other people can make against you, you know, the distinction they make.' Those other people could be both black and white. Of coloured boys, she recalled, 'the majority thought I was like even a prostitute on the street', and white people in mixed-race partnerships often commented on black prejudice, those who 'don't like the idea of their own colour marrying a different colour'.[25] But their principal difficulties were with the white majority, difficulties which ranged from being cast out by their families, to being unable to find decent accommodation, to being shunned by 'normal' society. Several television documentaries focused on the new social circles which developed out of necessity, comprised entirely of people in mixed-race relationships. 'The majority of white women they look at us rather disdainfully,' explained one woman who had been disowned by her family after marrying a Jamaican man,

> just believing you're something bad because you're married to coloured. But most of my friends are married to coloured men, and we all congregate together, we all more or less try to stick in a group, even if we walk to school with children, we walk together, we come home together, and people will pass remarks when they see about 12, 14 coloured, half-caste children, you know.[26]

The focus on the 'problem' of the children was in part a way of masking prejudice as concern. It appeared reasonable to want to save the younger generation from 'the misery' of being neither one thing nor the other. The BBC aired a discussion among traders at Ridley Road market in Hackney that gave loud voice to such attitudes: 'what about the kids when they grow up? . . . They won't know if they're coming or going or if they been'; 'It's the children that suffer, nobody else'; 'Let them get married if they want. If a coloured man loves a white woman, let them get married by all means. Don't have no children. Don't on any account have any children. Either you get yourself sterilised or paralysed, but don't have no children.'

It was no wonder, with views like this openly professed, that people in mixed marriages stuck to themselves. And in some cases it was simply easier to adopt a new colour. In 1948 Betty Cox married a Muslim in Birmingham, becoming Betty Ali. Twenty years later, a devout Muslim herself, she had made her choice. She insisted, 'We are coloured people, you know. We are. It's a mixed marriage, but he's coloured, I'm coloured too. That's all there is to it. He's my husband, and that's it.'[27]

Mrs Ali chose to define herself according to the standards set by her husband's culture – her ambitions were to make the journey to Mecca and eventually to retire to Pakistan. But for the majority of people involved in mixed-race relationships that was neither a viable nor a desirable option. The association between race and illicit or permissive sex was partly a consequence of the fact that migrants, and their partners and lovers, ended up in the seedier areas, zones which appeared to mark the boundaries of respectable Englishness. Their much longer-term seediness now simply took on a new 'coloured' complexion. One solution for middle-class black migrants was to exaggerate their 'respectability', in order to distance themselves from caricatures of low-life migrant culture. Being accepted, said one couple to the BBC in 1958, was about 'proper breeding'; ten years later the key for many middle-class black migrants was to look middle class: 'it counts quite a long way when you're moving about in London, if you look reasonably respectable it's easier'; 'if you go out with rags and looking very unkempt and very dirty and ask somebody for something then there might be a sort of revulsion'.[28] There was a kernel of truth in this line; it had the merit of acknowledging, albeit implicitly, that the problem of West Indian pimps, such as it was, was an economic and not a moral one, and that the hassle and abuse thrown at white women married to black men in the 1950s was acceptable because they were poor. But the 'just look respectable' line of argument did nothing to help the men and women trying to bring up their families in the lodging houses and slums of Notting Hill or East London's Commercial Road.

It is not surprising that sex and the family should have been the fault line around which so much of the debate about immigration coalesced in the 1950s. Love and sex went to the heart of concerns about population and the question of who was truly British. The 1948 British Nationality Act had offered a version of Britishness to one in four of the global population. Now that colonial and Commonwealth citizens had started arriving in some numbers, the fact of 'colour' (including discriminations such as 'coffee-coloured', or 'rather dark', for example) could no longer be confined only to others but threatened, so the anti-immigration argument went, to alter the fabric of the 'host' population itself. It was probably the case that a good proportion of parents asked in 1954 whether they would allow their daughters to marry 'out' would have answered no. But – as the rise in mixed marriages proved – it was also clear that many of their daughters, and their sons, were beginning to give a different answer.

11

Bachelors

In the early days, we were all bachelors together. We worked
very hard and we lived very rough, but when we enjoyed ourselves we really had a good time. We had plenty of beer and
girls too ... Now our families have arrived, everyone has
turned very strict. Many people have put their turbans on
again and some won't even drink now.

Ballard and Ballard, 'The Sikhs' (1977)[1]

In 1958 Madho Ram Mahimi said goodbye to his mother and to the
wife he had only just met, left his village, Bhardwaj in Jalandhar, and
travelled to Wolverhampton in search of employment. After a year
out of work (for the British economy was just pulling itself out of
recession) he landed a job in one of the foundries and settled down to
a number of years hard living: hard manual labour in the foundry,
hard drinking in the evenings, and a relationship with a local woman
who moved in with him. We know this because he wrote a long epic
poem about it, and about the events which unfolded when his wife
caught up with him.

The poem is a version of a traditional Punjabi *qissa* – a classic tale
of love set to a number of rousing poetic metres, with an elaborate
rhyming and repeating structure, customarily performed at traditional fairs in rural Punjab. Madho Ram was most likely of Dalit
caste, traditionally people of low status in the rural villages due to the
fact that historically, as cobblers, leatherworkers and butchers, they
worked with animal remains and were therefore deemed 'unclean'.
Yet he certainly appears to have been more highly educated than
the majority of 1950s migrants from the Indian Punjab. These were

principally Sikh Jats – peasant landowners – who had far higher social status, but often rather basic skills in literacy. His poem, composed over twelve years from 1958 to 1970, fuses a conventional story of love with a bitter and funny commentary on the moral dilemmas and tragic consequences of migration.[2]

Like all adult migrants from the Punjab in the 1950s Madho Ram (who was born in 1918) lived the majority of his life in India in the pre-Partition state, and therefore in a mixed community made up of Sikhs, Hindus and Muslims. Urdu and English were the official languages and Punjabi – the local language – was the shared vernacular. It was the language of private life, community ritual and folk culture. The Partition of India and Pakistan in 1947 was a catastrophe for the populations of the Punjab, which were violently 'unmixed' in a manner similar to the massive displacement of peoples in Europe in 1945. There were 18 million Partition migrants in the Punjab alone – Sikhs and Hindus who moved east to lands evacuated by Muslim refugees, who in turn moved west to abandoned holdings in Pakistan. Many of these Partition refugees found it hard to settle in closed village communities, which were often suspicious of outsiders, and they would be among the first to move on as routes to Britain began to open up. As they did so they left the newly mono-cultural communities of South Asia – Sikhs and Hindus on one side of the border, Muslims on the other – and became part of a community of migrants. Sikh and Muslim were lumped together as 'Asians' by the British. They worked in the same factories, shared the same digs, and many of them spoke the same language – Punjabi. And to a surprising extent these early migrants also shared the same religious practices. The historic mixing of religious communities in the tribal lands of rural Punjab had led to a situation in which people of different faiths tended to be tolerant of a range of deities – when Madho Ram prepares to leave his village he prays to Sufi, Hindu and Sikh gods. Later, as turban wars, debates about halal meat and wearing the veil became firmly associated with ethnic-religious identity, this form of syncretic practice would become hard to credit. Though the everyday adaptations between Sikh and Muslim Punjabis had been destroyed by the violent shock of Partition, once in Britain migrants of different faiths, as well as different castes, were forced by circumstances to rub along together.

For a start they worked side by side in the same foundries. Many of the 1950s migrants found their first jobs as general labourers in the factories and furnaces which punctuated the industrial landscape of the West Midlands until the late 1970s. The Midlands foundries grew fast in response to the consumer boom of the 1950s, and particularly the race to keep up with the growing demand for family cars: by the mid-1950s a quarter of all manufacturing in the West Midlands was car related. The shift in production from heavy engineering and shipbuilding – making large one-off castings – to the mass production of consumer goods meant a rapid shift in the centre of production from Scotland to the Midlands towns. This in turn was to put pressure on the small foundries, where metal casting was still regarded as a craft but where conditions for unskilled workers were tough, to say the least.

When Dónall Mac Amhlaigh found work in a Northampton foundry in the early 1950s he found himself in an environment not much changed from the beginning of the century.

> The first thing I got to do in the foundry was to take a sledge-hammer out into the yard and start breaking up some old iron that was to be smelted. Heaps of this stuff was scattered here and there about the place . . . I was put to working indoors, hauling huge casks of molten iron around and pouring them into the moulds. On overhead rails, there are wheels that carry around the casks (or skips, as they are called) with the skips hanging by chains from the wheels.

Mac Amhlaigh couldn't stand the heat and the dirt and he jacked the job in after a few days – but the reason he had got the job in the first place was that no one else wanted it either. 'You can't get white people to do the menial tasks that have to be done in any foundry, not even the floating workers like the Irish.'[3]

Like work in out-of-date mines, or unmodernized textile mills, school-leavers had no interest in such jobs when they could get work in the newer, cleaner, manufacturing and light-engineering industries. And until the recession of 1956–58 workers could take their pick of jobs – there was simply no need to go into dirty foundry work. Several managers interviewed at the end of the decade recalled the difficulty of hiring anybody at all:

The big influx of immigrant labour began in 1954. At this time you couldn't get an armless, legless man, let alone an able-bodied one. Any worker could leave the works and get a job literally within three or four minutes simply by going to the factory next door. We tried recruiting Irish labour but this didn't come off. The Manager went over to Ireland himself and recruited 36 men. Of these, only 8 actually turned up at the works, and only one stayed for any length of time.

The first foreign labour we employed were German and Italian prisoners of war. When these men were repatriated, the firm found itself short of labour. Poles were employed and a number still work here. They were very good workers, but we couldn't get enough to make up for the labour shortage. The Ministry of Labour had coloured people. We wouldn't look at them at first, but eventually we succumbed. It was a case of necessity: there was no-one else. Well, there was the Irish, but they were dreadful. Only about one in twenty was any good.[4]

It was this kind of foundry – an unmodernized one – which Peter Wright spent six weeks observing for the Institute of Race Relations in 1961, in order to write a report on racial integration in the workplace. The status of foundry work had steadily declined since the high point of the hungry 1930s when, 'it was almost impossible to get a job here; you practically had to wait for someone to die before you could get in.' In 1953 the 'newcomer' element in the workforce amounted to one Italian (an ex-prisoner-of-war) and one Pakistani. But by 1962, 75 per cent of the workforce were from Asia and the Caribbean, and they were mainly doing unskilled, physically demanding jobs. Knocking out and quenching of castings, for example: 'Neither job is relished by the white workers. Knocking out is a sledge-hammer job. It's outside work, so it's cold in winter and in summer the bits of sand stick to you when you're sweating.' Or electrode cleaning: 'This is the sort of job that if a white man took it, he doesn't really want a job at all. The West Indians are mainly employed on scrap-crushing. A sledge-hammer job. They also do the loading and unloading of pitch. The highest job done by any coloured worker is fork-lift truck operator.'[5]

It was clear to this manager that there was a hierarchy of labour, and it was coloured. It was a hierarchy structured around job security ('Whenever I have to put off staff,' explained one manager of a non-unionized engineering works, 'I sack the coloured ones first. I must. There would be a riot if I did anything else. The trouble is that whenever you dismiss West Indians they make such a fuss. They say you have done it because of colour prejudice, and that makes you feel a rotter'), as well as through assigning tasks and duties. There were jobs that were so demeaning that for a white person to do them meant he didn't 'really want a job at all'. Or he wasn't really white. It may be worth pointing out that these comments offer a gloss on the ubiquitous complaints against the Irish for their unreliability. It suggests that the Irish were 'dreadful' insofar as they insisted they were 'white' – insofar as they were not prepared to take the jobs that other white workers felt were beneath them. Men like Mac Amhlaigh walked away from such work, and they were not offered the jobs that the white English (as opposed to Germans, Italians and Poles) thought were theirs. Irish fecklessness and unreliability, then, were partly the flip-side of Irish pride.

Here is Wright's description of the first break of the day:

At about 9.45 a.m. . . . . the pace slackens somewhat and preparations begin to be made for the morning tea-break. An Indian places a saucepan (later seen to contain curry) on a red-hot casting on the moving conveyor belt, and then carries on working. Another Indian is heating a saucepan on a similar casting on the shop floor. A West Indian woman is toasting bread in front of a stove in another part of the factory. Chapattis are being heated over a brazier in yet another part of the factory. An Indian working next to the track leaves his track, goes further up the conveyor system, places a billy can of water on one of the freshly filled moulds and goes back to work again. The mould, containing red-hot metal, continues to move along the track. Five minutes later, it has almost reached the Indian's work position.

At ten o'clock an electric bell is rung. The conveyor-belts are brought to a halt, the moulding, grinding and drilling machines are switched off, the casters lay down their ladles and the workers begin to congregate in groups. The Indian casters and Indians from other parts of the foundry gather round the brazier next to the casting platform. On the brazier billy cans of water are boiled, chapattis are heated and saucepans full of curry are cooked. One of the Indians leaves the group to heat a chapatti in a casting ladle which has recently held red-hot metal, then rejoins the group. Tea and sugar, measured out by the handful, are added to the freshly boiled water and the Indians squat or stand around drinking tea and eating pieces of chapatti dipped into the curry. The group around the brazier is quite lively and boisterous, with much talking and shouting back and forth.

One Indian who does not join this group is the man who has been working next to the track. By the time the tea-break bell was rung, his can of boiling water was within a foot or so of his place of work. Having made his tea, he then heats a saucepan of curry on the now stationary mould. Usually he eats alone, but occasionally he is joined by one or two other Indians. He is somewhat older than the Indians who congregate round the brazier and spends his lunch time in a much more quiet and leisurely manner.

The Pakistanis squat together in a group on the opposite side of the casting platform from the Indians. The Italians sit in a group at the end of the line of moulding machines drinking tea and eating sandwiches. Although the two groups are quite close together, there is no social interaction between them.[6]

Wright was interested in the outward lack of friction between the various groups of workers, which appeared to be matched by a lack of friendliness – although perhaps what strikes us now most forcibly is the lack of fuss about health and safety, and the rather relaxed, even individualist atmosphere of the shop floor.

This kind of foundry was on the way out in the late 1950s. As the industry adapted to the consumer boom, the smaller, craft-based concerns closed in favour of amalgamated companies, kitted out with new semi-automated machines and a much faster through-put system. At the height of the boom in ownership of British-made cars the foundries were turning out castings so fast they were still warm when they arrived at the vehicle assembly lines at Longbridge. For this scale and speed of turnover what was needed was not a group of skilled craft-workers, aided by a small team of knockers-out, scrap-crushers and electrode-cleaners. The new factories were machine-driven, but they were not yet fully automated. Teams of machine operators needed the support of a large pool of unskilled labourers who were tasked to work the conveyor belts, clean the machines, stack the cast-ings, and so on. It was in these new labouring jobs, in the quickly expanding amalgamated foundries, that many of the first-generation migrants from the Punjab found work. One of the less obvious con-sequences of foundry modernization was a stricter division between skilled and unskilled jobs, just at the point when the distinction was becoming meaningless (since operating the machines actually required very little skill). The men operating the machines were classed as skilled or semi-skilled, and paid piece-work rates, in order to encourage greater output; by contrast the (mostly immigrant) labourers were time-paid, and the only way for them to increase their earnings was to put in overtime. This would become an issue not only for their wives and children – the disaster for family and sex-life spelled out in hundreds of knowing Punjabi folk songs: 'My husband is an overtime man/No better than Woolworth's goods' sings one young bride to her lover – but also for the anti-immigration lobby, for whom it seemed self-evident that the immigrants were driving down wages. The causal link between cheap, non-unionized and seemingly unlimited immigrant labour, with men working endless amounts of overtime, and lower wages for British workers must have seemed like common sense. In reality the immigrant workers were the victims as much as the beneficiaries of the system.

The speed with which the West Midlands foundries became associ-ated with Asian labour is striking. In 1947 Midland Motor Cylinder, part of Birmid Industries, was the biggest private employer of Indian labour, with 20 per cent of the workforce Indian – this amounted to a couple of hundred men. By 1950 a survey of thirty iron-foundries employing 'foreign' labour found that 54 per cent of the newcomers were 'Asiatic', 33 per cent Irish, 10 per cent European (mainly Poles) and 3 per cent Jamaican. (In later years the overwhelming concentra-tion of immigrant labour in unskilled work would mean that labourers on wildcat strikes could paralyse large sections of the workforce with relative ease.) And by 1967 70 per cent of Coneygre's 500-strong workforce were Asian, and in the newer plants the percentages were higher still. Nearly all the 'Asiatics' were employed as labourers, and they were concentrated in the newer, semi-automated and poorly unionized concerns. In several foundries there were so many Sikh employees the members of the workforce were identified by number rather than name: '181 Singh', '42 Singh', and so on.[7]

One theory about the large concentrations of Asian workers was that it suited the managers. For a start they did not have to provide accommodation for them, as they had done for previous waves of 'foreign' labour. Workers recruited in the European camps or from Calabria had had to be housed and sometimes even clothed. And it was undoubtedly convenient that Indian workers had their own methods of recruitment, bypassing the labour exchanges and passing on notice of vacancies by word of mouth, so that managers could count on a steady stream of applicants without having to go to the trouble of advertising. In the initial years of migration from the Caribbean, the Ministry of Labour had taken care to limit the number of black workers in each concern (with the exception of transport), in order, as they saw it, to reduce the possibility of racial tension. But this was far harder to police in the largely non-unionized foundries which were swiftly modernizing in response to the consumer boom.

By the early 1960s a pattern was emerging in the foundries of a segregated labour force, with white workers on piece-work and Asians in labouring and ancillary jobs, where they were heavily dependent on (and invested in) overtime. As we will see, key to this process were the Asian intermediaries, English-speaking foremen who became the unofficial managers of Punjabi- and Urdu-speaking labourers. ('Often the Pakistanis cannot speak English, and orders have to be given through the few who can. Usually there is one Pakistani per shop who can speak English and he is used as a "go-between".[8]) None of this did the reputation of Asian immigrants any good. The sight of large groups of non-English-speaking men, living together in poor housing, and appearing to accept the very worst working conditions, fed into prejudice against them as socially 'retrograde', and appeared to confirm the belief that their way of life was rooted in poverty and backwardness. The fact that they were willing to accept bad employment conditions was taken as a sign that they were used to them. Their apparent reluctance to join unions and their docility in deferring to middlemen who took bribes, in order to secure jobs and overtime, was interpreted as a throwback to rural village systems of power and corrupt authority. They were submissive in the foundries (and, elsewhere, in the mills and factories) because they had been submissive back home, or so the argument went.

It is worth pausing here to unravel the levels of misrecognition and misunderstanding on both sides of the immigrant–local divide. What was incontestable was that large groups of Indian and Pakistani men were engaged in working-class jobs, at the heart of Britain's industrial recovery. Yet they did not behave like the white working-class men alongside whom they worked. They tended (at this stage) not to join unions, to work unbelievably long hours, to sacrifice family life for higher wages, to spend nothing on leisure, and to refuse to integrate into the communities in which they lived. And not only did they fail to understand working-class solidarity, their reliance on the bribery and 'pull' of middlemen appeared to confirm the suspicion that they did not understand democracy either.

Leaving aside the fact that Asian labourers were in practice offered no encouragement at all to integrate with their white co-workers, we can still understand the fear that their 'clannish' and 'tribal' conduct was only going to result in a levelling down of pay and conditions: 'These blokes here, cheap labour that's all it is. They have a low standard of living in their own country ... The boss would like to bring us down to their level if he could.' It was possible to find Punjabi workers who broadly agreed with their co-workers that they were a threat to English workers. One man told the Gujarati researcher G. S. Aurora in the late 1950s, 'The fact is that the white people do not like to see us working hard, because then the management expects them to work hard also.' But most were clear-eyed about the bargain they had struck on coming to Britain. They could work hard and earn well, but they could not progress: 'they keep us bottom ladder'.[9]

In effect Asian men were being asked to fill jobs that fell below the standard the British industrial worker would now accept (jobs that 'if a white person took it, he doesn't really want a job at all'), and then they were criticized for not conforming to the behaviour expected of and by their British workmates. They were accused of 'backwardness', and of transplanting an almost feudal system of power, deference and authority from rural Punjab to the West Midlands factories. But the paradox was that their failure to conform to working-class and trade-union expectations was not rooted in tribal or feudal backwardness, but had far more to do with social aspiration and entrepreneurial ambition. It was true that many of the early migrants from the Punjab lived in extraordinarily overcrowded and uncomfortable conditions, often bed-sharing and bed-rotating with up to sixteen or eighteen other men in small two- or three-bedroomed houses. Yet they were not serfs, but minor capitalists.

The bachelor household was the most efficient way for the migrants to save money to send back home. Initially these funds went to pay off the costs of their travel, which had often been borrowed against the surety of land. Further remittances went to settle family debts, then to buy machinery and more land, and to build modern brick 'pukka' houses in the villages at home. Buying a house in Britain was, at least initially, conceived of not as putting down roots but as a way of increasing the financial investment back in the Punjab, through sending rent money home. For as with the migration from Sylhet it was not the poorest who left the Punjab, but those with capital to spare: principally young men from small landowning families who needed to supplement their incomes in order to improve their holdings. Going to work in Britain was not the last hope of a reluctant and desperate peasantry (as it was for some migrants from as near as Ireland in the early 1950s), but an investment in the future. 'Migration fever' took hold first among the landowning Jats, but quickly spread in the late 1950s and early 1960s to other 'status-conscious' members of Punjabi society, as Madho Ram wryly points out in his *qissa*. He has just arrived in Wolverhampton, and been taken immediately to the pub, where he discovers his countrymen spend a good deal of their time. As they get more and more drunk they obsess over their rank and importance back home, ironically the very thing they have lost in seeking to improve it by earning money in England. They moan in Punjabi, but a Punjabi punctuated with English loanwords, such as 'pass' for passport, and of course 'pub', and even 'time':

When *Sachurda* [Saturday] came, I was in the *pub*. I saw countless Indian men,
Drinking full glasses there, drinking and drinking as if there's no tomorrow.

When they had all become drunk, they each began to sing their own
    praises.
All of them spoke of their own merits, each one thinking himself
    better than the others.
Some said: 'I had a thousand *bighas* of land, and people called us
        Sardar [Chief].'
Some said: 'There, we were warriors. No one stood against us.'
Some said: 'We had stacks of wood. We were great traders.'
Some said: 'The shop in the bazaar was ours. They called us great
        merchants.'
Some said: 'We worked in fabrics, clothing. We were doing a great
        deal of business.'
Some said: 'My work was as a watchmaker, we made a great
        business.'
Some said: 'We traded in leather, we made lots of money.'
Some said: 'We worked as *bhattis*. They called us contractors.'
Some said: 'We worked as jewellers, we made lakhs of rupees.'
Some said: 'We were the district scribes, we oversaw everything.'
Some said: 'I was the police superintendent, I swaggered and ordered
        everyone about.'
Some said: 'I was a village accountant there – getting sugar cane and
        rice free.'
As one, they were all in England and were just fools who were full of
    pride.
When *pub* closing *time* came they all got up and went home.
They would all spend a comfortable night and tomorrow they would
    get up in the morning and go to work.
Oh, Madho Ram, they all forgot their troubles, those that had made
    their own troubles with the *pass*.

This shared drinking culture was the public face of the bachelor
houses – as for the Irish men living in digs who found they had nowhere
to go in the evenings and at weekends, the pubs were a refuge. But they
were also places where 'back home' could be recreated, through remin-
iscence, jokes, storytelling and songs – the very existence of Madho
Ram's poem is testament to this. The poem, and many others like it,
was recited regularly over the years in shared gatherings, growing and

altering as events took place and were incorporated into it: the hardships of bachelor life, the arrival of wives from India, buying a house, the birth of children. Poems and songs like this were shared performances, with the audience thumping out the rhythm with their feet, joining in on repeated phrases and dancing or shouting the refrains. The atmosphere was closest to one we might now associate with karaoke. For these were entirely traditional and familiar oral forms – the *boliyan* were harvest songs customarily performed to the measure of frenetic dancing, the forerunner of later bhangra styles; the rather more sedate *qissa* had an even longer history, in oral tales of romantic love stretching back to the eighteenth century. While the subjects of these songs had traditionally been life and love in the Punjab, now they focused on the challenges of the new world of the migrant. And if the songs themselves are anything to go by, chief among these challenges for Punjabi men was the new power and forthrightness of their womenfolk, which forms the basis of literally hundreds of witty *boliyan* composed in England in the 1960s. By translating the new world of work and relationships into old styles, the songs, and the shared performance of them in the pubs, acted as forms of socialization, ways of bringing the new situation home. Like the world of traditional Irish music, which was opened up and expanded when previously isolated rural migrants met together in the pubs of London and Birmingham, Punjabi cultural expression was given a fillip by the economic conditions in which the migrants lived – in men-only digs, working long shifts, moving from foundry and factory to the pub, and back again. And like Irish music, traditional Punjabi culture was entirely vernacular. Punjabis knew Urdu and a little English, but it was Punjabi that was spoken at home, and the language of community rituals, fairs, and so on. Paradoxically this rural, oral tradition was given new life by industrial settlement.[10]

The poems and songs celebrated, and poked fun at, shared experiences across tribal and caste lines: getting your first job in England, managing the heavy work and long hours, having your wife find out about your affair, your wife's delight at the décor of her English terraced house ('flowers on the floor, flowers on the walls'), the extraordinary generosity of the welfare state (where children get 'money, milk, and a lot of attention'), the joy of two opening times in the pubs, the dread of having your in-laws descend on you when you had got used to having them safely back in India, the shock of British-born children on their first visit 'home' to India or Pakistan, horrified by everything from endemic bribery to the state of the lavatories and public transport ('there's no end to the flies and mosquitos there, the ants and insects torment us . . . the unemployed get shamed and shovelled around . . . there are a lot of people squashed into trains and lorries . . .'). These were the levelling experiences of all Asian migrants in England, regardless of what caste they belonged to, and what their status had been at home. All those scribes and accountants and landowners listed in Madho Ram's poem were now in the same boat – and more than that, they were in the same pub. In this first phase of migration distinctions of rank really did go by the board, at work, in the shared bachelor houses, and in the pub. The pub above all functioned as a place where caste could be ignored – everyone paid his own way and drinkers were served by the barman, avoiding the risk of offering food and drink to someone who, because of rules over purity and pollution, could not or should not take it from you.

This situation was to change as the years passed and the migrants from the Punjab began to settle down and assume the status of immigrants. The intensification of divisions based on caste and religion has often been ascribed to the arrival of wives and families from India, which began in earnest in the early to mid-1960s. And it is true that as the men set up homes with their families, the shared Sikh and Muslim areas of the cities became increasingly distinct. Smethwick, in the 1950s a centre of mixed bachelor housing, servicing the foundries, became 'Sikhified', while Muslim families tended to move to areas such as Sparkhill and Sparkbrook. As children grew and marriage alliances were forged in the later 1960s families retrenched too in terms of caste, setting up rival gurdwaras to cater for their own, homogeneous, social groups. Though distinctions of rank and status were to develop in subtly different ways in the context of British industrial cities (so that in time levels of education, for example, began to figure in and even outweigh traditional markers of caste), they certainly did not disappear, and even became strengthened as the migrants consolidated their lives in England.

But it would be wrong to put the onus for all this on Punjabi women, as somehow more conservative and religion-minded than their menfolk, whether Sikh, Muslim or Hindu. It also had to do with 'pull', with the system in which family, village and caste-based contacts were the way to get access to everything from jobs and houses to school places, electricity, and licences and permits of all kinds. To the extent that, like all groups trying to establish a hold in a new society, Punjabis fell back on an informal network of contacts, critical views of their tendency towards 'undemocratic' and corrupt practices were not misplaced. Settlement in Britain did not automatically weaken the hold of the village system, rather it added new dimensions to it – particularly offering a new authority to people who could speak English. Most of the migrants had no choice but to rely on those who could translate and negotiate for them. It was common for illiterate workers to have to pay 'entry' money to secure a job, and further rake-offs went along with getting overtime, at least until the mid-1960s. The most successful of these entrepreneurs bought houses where the workers boarded, so that the men's earnings were funnelled back to them either through kick-backs or through rent. It was these practices that their white co-workers could only understand as 'backwardness' and evidence of their 'natural' predisposition to feudal and corrupt ways.

There was some truth in the claim that Asian brokers were a symptom of Asian corruption, but it was mainly the problem of false papers, rather than any natural racial tendency, which was to blame. Lack of English was a huge difficulty for all Asian migrants, whether from India or Pakistan, but so too was the fact that so many of them had travelled on forged passports – a point which did nothing to ease the nervous relationship with British officialdom. Men would rather pay one of their own to get them a job than submit their paperwork to a recruiting office. And no doubt they had a fair idea of how they would be received by the men behind the desks anyway. Between 1955 and 1957 70 per cent of Indian migrants travelled on invalid documents, a fact which said as much about the nature of Indian bureaucracy as any inherent bent towards bending the rules among individual Asian migrants – though many rules were bent.

Papers were forged for a number of reasons. First, there was little likelihood that rural villagers would ever have been issued with a birth certificate. This was to prove useful as Britain tightened restrictions on entry, as inconvenient facts such as age and marital status could be altered. Added to that, Indian government restrictions on the issue of passports meant that forgery was often the only way to get the necessary papers. It was hard enough in the early 1950s, but things only became trickier, and more expensive, when the passport offices were moved out of the regions to New Delhi. The already healthy trade in forged passports took off, with officials selling off stamped passport forms to racketeers. Papers, and the men you had to bribe to get them, prove an endless headache in Madho Ram's poem. After a wait of nearly two years his wife entirely loses her cool with the agent to whom she has paid five hundred rupees to smooth the way for her passport:

> I know nothing about you! You make a lot of false promises!
> I had everything sorted out by the police station and the district office.
> And again and again I have sent the papers to Delhi.
> I have done everything.
> If my *pass* isn't made, then I'll set you to rights.
> I'll die myself but I'll kill you right now
> If you don't give me my *pass* now! You make a lot of false promises!

The threats work and the agent promises finally to hand over the passport, though he squeezes a bit more cash out of her all the same: 'Give me another forty rupees and go the vaccination people.' Even the language of officialdom was alien, so that the process could only be described through English loanwords:

> > It's difficult work with all the *enquiries* for a *pass*
> > It's a question of the *officers* who want a lot of bribery.

The problem of how to repay the debt incurred for the passport, and the cost of travel, was only the start. On top of that there were fees to be paid for getting a job. Overtime was a necessity, especially if anything was to be sent back home. Migration needed to be made to pay. But this too played into the hands of the middlemen as they could control access to overtime. In the early 1950s a study in Birmingham found foundry workers handing over a weekly payment of £2 for the privilege of working overtime, and the situation only became more acute in the late 1950s as the recession squeezed employment opportunities. So for example one manager, exasperated by the flagrant bribery at work among Asians on the shop floor, argued that although it was deplorable it was also 'natural':

> We had trouble with ten-percenters – people who take a cut from their work mates. One man brought in eleven men and took £1 a week from them. We had to stop him. We couldn't reason with him: he thought it was natural. We had to threaten him with the sack, but he didn't see why. He seemed to think I was a lucky fellow because I was getting a pound a week from 625 men.[11]

Yet the reality was that the middleman system was both more home-grown, and more contested, than this implied. Despite the shadowy presence of caste, the power of the Asian middleman was not so different from that of the Irish foreman, or subcontractor, to whom labourers became indebted, both financially and psychologically – it was easier to rely for help on someone from 'home' than to blaze a trail alone. It was true that the Asian labour brokers wielded a great deal of power among the earliest migrants, whose stay was often temporary and who were continually being replaced by fresh innocents who had little English and even less knowledge of the mechanics of industrial wage labour. But it was not necessarily true that this power was ceded willingly. The English factory manager imagined his employee assumed that he must be taking bribes from his workers because he was so used to bribery in India. Maybe so, but it is also possible that he had become well used to bribery among English foremen and managers too. In 1966–67 an American sociologist, DeWitt John, carried out a study of Indian workers' associations in Britain that focused, in part, on attitudes towards the trades unions. In factories where the entire workforce was made up of Asian immigrants (such as Woolf's rubber factory in Southall), he found white foremen exacting bribes through informal immigrant 'leaders', who took their own cut for hiring a man or giving him overtime. ('British workers generally disapprove of bribery,' he generously explained, 'so the system works best in all-immigrant shops.') Gurbachan Singh Gill, a former soldier (and Japanese prisoner of war) with the Hong Kong Singapore Royal Artillery, arrived in London in 1951. After a number of factory jobs he applied to Woolf's: 'In order to get this job, we met its personnel officer, Mr Dunn, near Christmas time, and offered him two bottles of Whisky and other gifts.' DeWitt John's Punjabi informants argued that by the mid-1960s the practice was dying out, but that was down to the efforts of the immigrants themselves and had been resisted by English foremen and middle-managers, who stood to lose a lot of money.[12]

We get a sense of the cost (both mental and financial) of owing your livelihood to agents and fixers from Abdullah Hussein's story 'The Journey Back', which was set in the mid-1960s. The thirteen men stuffed into the Birmingham lodging house live like shadows, afraid of being picked up without papers when out shopping, and in fear of the agents who have smuggled them across.

> The illegals moved on the street in a peculiar sort of manner. Even now, when I see a band of them on a sidewalk, I can tell. They have a certain way of hanging close together, acting totally absorbed in the conversation, and every once in a while dropping their heads to sneak a glance around, as if they were peering around the edge of a wall; they'll never look you square in the face.

It was only in the factories that the men could relax:

> The management knew all about our illegal status in the country and that we were working for them on fake permits. But as I said, they stood to gain a lot from us: so they looked the other way. Some of them even pocketed our insurance money instead of giving it to the government. Rumour had it that our names didn't even exist on the factory payroll – in other words, we didn't exist. But our anonymity turned out to be a blessing in disguise. It may sound odd but we felt relatively well protected in that house of fraud. In fact we felt more secure there than at home.[13]

Right up to the early 1960s Asian workers in Britain tended to explain the difficulties they faced in practical terms – the problems of finding work, of living in overcrowded accommodation, of impenetrable forms, of overtime and tax, of being separated from their families. They continually expressed a kind of puzzlement about their encounters with English culture. The problem of colour appears only tangentially in their memoirs and recollections. The fact that they were operating within a relatively well-sealed Asian subculture, and subject to the authority of their fellow migrants, may be one reason why 'race' and racism were such muted concerns, especially compared with the experience of West Indian migrants. This situation was to change radically as the government moved to restrict Commonwealth immigration, and the labourers from India and Pakistan realized they were here to stay.

12

Dancers

These parties were indeed noisy, robust with a tantalising touch of eroticism as bodies touched in a slow grinding mento. In the beginning drinks were free. The parties were smaller then, and everybody was known to the host, and the following weekend he would be at one of his guests' party. By the end of the fifties, it no longer made economic sense to adequately provide drinks for nearly a hundred people. Most of these 'guests' would prefer a more personal choice by buying their own drinks. The temptation was great! Drinks were sold and the parties became illegal. Police raids were intensified as more and more neighbours complained about the noise next door. It seemed that if you were enjoying yourself after midnight, you were beating your wife, up to no good, indulging in illicit pleasure and generally beyond the law. The neighbour was always worried about the soul of the people next door.

Donald Hinds, 'The Island of Brixton' (1980)[1]

Donald Hinds' portrait of 'the island of Brixton' follows a familiar arc. From expressing the sound and feel of life inside the Caribbean home, he moves quickly, and inevitably, to what the neighbours say. An overwhelming sense of being watched, and judged, by the white community marks nearly all West Indian memoirs from the 1950s and 1960s – far more so than Asian migrant writing of the same period, which tends to focus on debates and tensions internal to the new community. For new arrivals from the West Indies the feeling of being on trial, or on stage, was paramount, and it helped to produce a kind of doubled consciousness. Everyday life was what you lived, every day, but it was also the background for your performance of that life for others – the well intentioned, the curious, the resistant and the plain hostile audiences of English people who were waiting and watching to see how you would make out. And after all, if you had been sent up on stage without warning, why not give the punters what they wanted? Wallace Collins, the Jamaican stowaway who arrived in Britain in 1954, described his fellow islanders as 'acting a part'. The time and distance that separated them from home gave them licence to remake themselves, 'to improvise and exhibit an individuality both to attract and confuse the society they lived in'. He describes his cousin Gerald exaggerating his pride and freedom from constraint, performing his rejection of 'a slave mentality' in his very bearing:

> He was a real cowboy both in gait and in manner. He was always rooting, tooting, shooting his weight around and floating his fists indiscriminately free of cost. He walked as if he expected to draw a gun any moment; squaring his shoulders, elbows open, toes in, chipping the asphalt; swinging his arm from the shoulders and glaring at anyone he suspected.

Or this is Collins's friend Ken, the Jamaican cat, trying his luck at picking up a girl:

> The left side of his body was taut his right hand caressed his chin, raising his eyebrow, his right foot shuffling forward as he jerked his right knee to vibrate his body, while in the same movement he did a quarter pirouette and swung his left arm from his shoulders like a rooster fencing in a hen; we called this movement towards the female, 'Constackling'.[2]

If this approach was ever likely to work, the fact that Ken tried it in Hammersmith tube station, on two girls waiting for their English boyfriends, ensured that on this occasion it ended in a fight. The bravura peacock performances by West Indian men were made possible, as Collins suggested, by the fact that they were far from home, with no elders to pull them into line and no younger siblings to puncture their coxcomb-ery. But he also maintained that all the strutting about wasn't simply performance: 'in fact they are "wild", for their monumental faith in their virility would incite them to move any mountain just to raise a skirt and claim its contents'. It was a kind of sexual one-upmanship, the stereotype of the sexually unruly black male reflected in a fairground mirror, 'internalized' and lived as one of a repertoire of roles. And it was certainly a more enjoyable role than work-shy layabout, or submissive lackey. But impersonating the figure of the sexually confident, physically assertive and loud Jamaican was also a form of protection, as inhabiting a stereotype so often can be. It was a type of armour, intended to 'confuse the society', and the need for a physical shield was not limited to the men. A Grenadian woman interviewed for one of the BBC's mixed-marriage investigations explained:

> So I never relax. I feel I am alone. John knows this because whenever I'm invited to a party, a staff party, a social occasion, he knows that I will make an entrance, because this is my armour. If I knew that I had a hair out of place I wouldn't dream of saying it doesn't matter. I'd say 'why didn't you tell me!'[3]

Nonetheless the habit among Caribbean men of making an entrance was one which riled their English male peers. From the smartly tailored suits, the trousers high-waisted, wide-legged and cuffed, the braces, the two-tone shoes and the pork pie hats, to their confident insistence on jive and swing rhythms on the ballroom dance floor, they were bound to enrage their rivals. They were out looking for partners and as a group they were wildly successful, though obviously not with everyone. A Mecca dancehall in Wolverhampton became notorious in 1955 when the management refused entry to a Bengali migrant who was accompanied by his white landlady. The management was unrepentant, explaining that 'A woman would not want a coloured person to tap her on the shoulder during an "excuse me" dance.' This 'open operation of the colour bar' continued until later in the year when the there was a change of management. And there were hundreds of small-scale versions. A dancehall in Manchester had a policy of keeping 'negroes' in 'the vault' and out of the main space; the Locarno Dance Hall in Streatham operated what was called a 'semi-colour bar' during 1963. West Indian men were banned from entering without a partner on a Monday night – R&B night, so the night they were most likely to turn up – after a disagreement over a woman ended in a full-scale fight. It would be too much to imply that West Indians were banned for being more desirable partners. And some of the women themselves claimed to be less than impressed with the swagger and parading. One even wrote in to the middle-class Caribbean lifestyle magazine *Checkers* to complain about the behaviour of black dancers:

> As a white girl who patronizes a certain London dance hall, I would like to protest at the number of coloured men who are allowed admittance. Personally I wouldn't dance with a coloured man if he asked me; I consider their behaviour disgusting. They fling themselves about the dance floor, and it's just too bad for anyone who happens to get in their way.[4]

The 'certain London dance hall' may well have been the Lyceum, the theatre off the Strand which was converted to a huge ballroom by Mecca in 1951, and which showcased big-band music throughout the 1950s and early 1960s. This was ballroom and Latin for the English dancer, though it might well have been played by West Indian musicians: Trinidadian Al Jennings's All-Star Caribbean Orchestra, and solo artists such as Rudolph Dunbar, Cyril Blake, Joe Appleton and Leslie Thompson. Caribbean bands playing swing and rhumba were popular in London in the 1930s and 1940s, partly because of Ministry of Labour restrictions on American performers. And, particularly during the war, there was a thriving black dance-music scene, with bands playing jitterbug and jive for American servicemen, merchant seamen and African students at the Hammersmith Palais or the Paramount Ballroom on the Tottenham Court Road, which was actually owned by a Jamaican immigrant. Lord Kitchener, the calypso singer who travelled to England on the *Windrush*, recalled that when the ship neared Tilbury a group of stowaways all flung themselves off the deck and into the water to swim ashore; a few days later he found them holed up in the Paramount, 'jiving and dancing around'. The Paramount was introduced by Colin MacInnes as 'the Cosmopolitan' in his 1957 novel *City of Spades*, where Johnny Fortune, recently arrived from Nigeria, finds 'a sight to make me glad! Everywhere us, with silly little white girls, hopping and skipping fit to die! Africans, West Indians, and coloured GIs all boxed up together with the cream of this London female rubbish!' The main attraction was not so much the white girls as the opportunity to relax among other black people: 'everywhere us'!⁵

In 1949 *Checkers* ran a piece on the Metropolitan Bopera House, then newly opened on New Compton Street, and catering equally for jazz music-lovers and dancers:

> The 'Met' holds 90 couples, and has a refreshment bar attached. Many coloured and white stars of the stage and radio have appeared there, accompanied by Ronny Scott's Quartet, which plays with spirit and sensibility pieces which contain nothing hackneyed, and nothing dull.
>
> As I paced near the walls, moved by the exuberance on the part of the dancers present, I was told – 'There is no better place on a Sunday afternoon.' At one corner I saw an African student jiving breathtakingly; at another, a Malayan graduate giving a display of the South American Rhumba with an 18-year-old lass from Dublin.⁶

This sounds like good, clean, Sunday afternoon fun, but by the mid-1950s the reputation of West Indian dancehalls and clubs – including the Bopera House – had become so closely associated with 'vice' (not only prostitution but also 'the dope racket') that MacInnes could rely on readers' recognition for his technicolour stereotyped Soho dive, the 'Moonbeam club'. Alongside the 'weed peddlers' (and the 'little packs of weed . . . falling like leaves on the floor', during a police raid), the club was a place to buy and sell sex: 'That GI's rendezvous is loaded up with chicks. Chicks of all activities and descriptions, some trading, and other voluntary companions full of hope.' The clubs were altogether more sleazy affairs than the dancehalls. MacInnes describes one in *Absolute Beginners* as 'about as glamorous as an all-night urinal'. The Moonbeam is located two floors below ground, in the entrails of a bombed-out building, the entry indicated by 'a queue of trollops and GIs':

> It was a long, low room like the hold of a ship, no windows and only walls. At one end, in front of a huge portrait of the rising moon, was a seven-piece orchestra, only whose eyes, teeth and shirt fronts were

visible at this distance. At the other, just behind us, was a soft-drink bar, with Coca-Cola advertisements and packets of assorted nuts, where teas and coffees were also being served. Among the square columns that held up the low roof were tables, some set in sombre alcoves. And between them a small floor where couples jived gently, turning continually like water-beetles making changing patterns on a pond.[7]

These were immigrant haunts; the large mixed dancehalls were more properly a feature of the mid-1950s, and accommodating different music and dance styles took some time. Sterling Betancourt, a steel pan musician who came over from Trinidad to play at the Festival of Britain and stayed, remembered that by the mid-1950s British dancers still had little idea how to dance to swing rhythms:

> I remember in the very early days when our steel band was playing in the Lyceum, we were playing a kind of jazz calypso thing, and they were moving so stiffly around the floor, holding on to each other and foxtrotting around the floor! Eventually they saw how the West Indians would dance to it and were shaking, and they soon follow.[8]

Two of those West Indians were Wallace Collins and Ken, for whom the Lyceum became a 'stamping ground', and where 'it was not long before we were womanising quite a few chicks' – those who were presumably not put off by the constackling.

The jazz calypso was already, in fact, an attempt to accommodate Trinidadian rhythms to the European dance floor. When the calypso singers Lord Kitchener and Lord Beginner – already celebrated artists in the Caribbean – arrived in 1948, they wanted to break into a growing international market for their music. Kitch's apparently impromptu performance of 'London is the Place for Me' in front of the cameras while disembarking at Tilbury was carefully prepared for the occasion – he wasn't going to waste the opportunity of a nationwide stage. Calypso was already popular in the US, having gained a following among American servicemen stationed in Trinidad, and American singers such as Harry Belafonte were to develop hugely successful careers with an 'Americanized' version of calypso. Throughout the late 1940s calypso

Dancing at St Pancras Town Hall, January 1959, at a carnival organized by Claudia Jones and the *West Indian Gazette* to raise funds 'to assist in the payment of fines of coloured and white youths involved in the Notting Hill events'.

singers were featured in dancehalls, and as a turn between orchestra sets on the ballroom circuit in London. But calypso rhythms also made their mark on the big-band sound; as an alternative to the more cerebral accents of bebop and modern jazz, calypso was simply a lot easier to dance to. By mixing jazz and calypso the sound

> moved it to where it began to appeal to English people because they knew how to dance to it. Up until then, unless it was some dance band playing Latin or something with a bit of a calypso beat, they didn't know what to do. After this, they figured out how to dance to it.[9]

And meanwhile the locals were learning. Steven Berkoff was still at Hackney Downs School when he caught the jive bug, spending Saturday nights at the Royal in Tottenham (owned by Mecca) where he danced to Ray Ellington alongside the 'tribes' from Stamford Hill and Tottenham. Style was everything.

> Anything could and would and did happen, since the Mecca played into your hands: it was the greatest money-spinner of all time because it restated and restored the tribe and tore away the constraints of the civilized world of work and buses and factories. Here you could be who you thought you were. You created yourself. You were the master of your destiny. You entered quiffed and perfumed in the most expensive aftershave Boots had to offer. You entered and already the smell of the hall had a particular aroma of velvet and hairspray, Brylcreem and Silvikrin, lacquer, cigs, floor polish . . .

Tuesday nights were spent learning to jive at Greys Dance Hall in Finsbury Park, and Sundays, showing off his new skills at the Lyceum, where sharp dressing was one way of rivalling the charm of the Caribbean dancers. 'The chaps at the Lyceum became fops and Beau Brummels and the suit was more than ever your calling card or your place of esteem. You had to be immaculate.' And then there were the small clubs like Studio 51, again frequented by West Indians like Wallace Collins, for whom 'the fun was good and clean', and Londoners like Berkoff, for whom:

> It was my sanctuary. A small dark room with some of the best dancing to be seen in the West End. I would come home some nights soaked to

the skin and it was even better than sex. I evolved a style that was ultra cool. By this time the Johnnie Ray era had been replaced by Teddy Boys and you wore four-button suits, shirts with stiff collars and double cuffs. My collars were sent each week to 'Collars Ltd' for starching and laundering, and woe betide if the collars came back soft or not stiff enough. I would go bananas. The style of dance was affected by the suit you wore and so you had to lift your arm, keeping your elbow fairly well in to your side or your jacket would be pulled up and you would appear ungainly. No, you had to dance cool so as to keep the form intact.[10]

This was very far from the counter-cultural modern jazz scene of the Soho clubs, where the audience was made up of Caribbean and African students, along with beat-generation radicals and aficionados of the folk revival, though many of the musicians played both types of venue. While for the foxtrotting clientele of the Lyceum and other dancehalls the Caribbean musical accents brought a new energy to the dancing (which was not always welcome), for the West Indian migrants Trinidadian and Jamaican sounds meant something entirely different. They were messages from home. Nearly all calypso was heard live in London in the immediate post-war period. Kitch and Beginner quickly began recording for Hummingbird Records, but their output was primarily for export back to Trinidad. For the first-generation migrants, songs heard between dancehall sets, or occasionally in pub sessions at places such as the Queens Hotel in Brixton and the Coleherne in Earls Court, were a way of connecting with the islands, even if the island they came from wasn't Trinidad. The music spoke of the islands, but the lyrics embraced the West Indians' new situation and brought it home to them in familiar style: the West Indian Test match victory at Lord's in 1950, nosy English landladies, Lyons Corner Houses, devaluation ('we got the best things off the ration, now is the money competition') or travelling on the tube:

> Never me again, to get back on the underground train
> I jump in the train, sit down on a seat relaxing mi brain
> I started to admire a young lady's face
> Through the admiration I passed the place

To tell you the truth I was in a mush
When I find myself at Shepherds Bush[11]

The listening, in the dancehalls and saloon bars, was social, an activity replicated in a hundred Irish pubs, where ballads and traditional fiddle and box tunes did similar work, or the Midlands locals where men sang Punjabi folk songs after escaping from the foundries on a Friday and Saturday night. The music both fed and assuaged nostalgia for home. It made the past present even as it reminded the group of everything they were missing.

And – like Irish folk revival bands, such as the Clancy Brothers and the Dubliners – calypso was commercial. In 1950 and 1951 EMI's Parlophone label gave plenty of work to Beginner and Kitchener, backed by Cyril Blake's Calypso Serenaders, with songs like 'Housewives' (queuing for the ration), 'Rum, More Rum', 'The Dollar and the Pound', and 'General Election': 'Socialist was glad, Communist was sad, and so it is they cheer, waiting to hear the results in Trafalgar Square.' But it was not until later in the decade that the market for Caribbean sounds really got going. In 1953 Emil Shalit, a refugee from Europe via New York (of indeterminate lineage – Lloyd Bradley describes him as 'a character so colourful he deserves his own paintbox'), employed Trinidadian pianist Robert Nurse to produce calypsos on his independent Melodisc label. These were songs designed specifically to appeal to the growing West Indian community. And some, such as Kitchener's 'The Ashes', celebrating England's 1955 win against Australia, were clearly meant to appeal more broadly: 'Good Captaincy from Len Hutton,/But the honours must go to Typhoon Tyson.' Likewise Colin MacInnes's spoof 'Lord Alexander' makes it to the big time in *City of Spades* by singing, 'Toad-in-hole and Guinness stout' and 'Please Mr Attlee, don't steal my majority'.[12]

The advantage of calypsos about cricket was that you got two-for-one of the most popular West Indian pastimes. 'Cricket, lovely cricket', sang Beginner after the West Indies won the 1950 Test match at Lord's: 'Yardley did his best/but Godard won the Test/with those little pals of mine/Ramadhin and Valentine.' Kitchener was at the match and recalled that afterwards,

I took my guitar and I call a few West Indians, and I went around the cricket field, singing. And I had an answering chorus behind me, and we went around the field singing and dancing ... So I took the crowd with me, singing and dancing, from Lord's, into Piccadilly in the heart of London ... So we went a couple of rounds of Eros. And from there we went to the Paramount, a place where they always had a lot of dancing.[13]

But as Donald Hinds recalled, by the mid-1950s cricket appeared to be losing out to the record collection as a way of staking out an immigrant identity:

The Saturday night party was the universal form of immigrant entertainment. The radiogramme had become a standard piece of furniture in every room. Indeed room-mates parted because the one could not find enough space for their 'Blue Spot' radiogramme, or because the other boys were always playing his radiogramme. Young men who a few months before limited the hero-worshipping to George Headley, Ken 'Bam-Bam' Weekes and the Three W's, now talked with intimate authority about Sarah (Vaughan), Ella (Fitzgerald), Billie (Holiday), Patty Page, The Singing Rage, and Jo 'Suddenly There Is a Valley' Stafford. Nationally, it was the time when the gramophone record became the disc, about the same time as the phenomenon of the teenager was born, and the Teddyboy in his Edwardian garb walked the streets. It would be interesting to know the West Indian contribution to the national sale of records. It was estimated that in the year 1956 about 67 million discs were sold at a total cost of some 18 million pounds. Of course, the Saturday night disc jockeys were not partial to Tommy Steele and Marty Wilde, but favoured Shirley and Lee, Lloyd Price and Fats Domino, none of whom might have ever featured in the British Charts.[14]

It was this growing market for Rhythm and Blues that Melodisc, and its later – more famous – subsidiary, Blue Beat Records, was trying to exploit, by offering a Caribbean (and West African) sound to rival the black American singers such as Shirley and Lee, Lena Horne and Billy Eckstine. Shalit distributed the discs through informal outlets rather than record shops – Caribbean barbers and grocers, for example – a practice which did nothing to dent the West Indians' feeling of ownership of the music. It was true that mildly satirical calypso had become a popular 'turn' on BBC programmes such as Friday night's live variety show *Kaleidoscope*, or on *Tonight*, with Cliff Michelmore, which featured the actor Cy Grant nightly singing a round-up of the news, written jointly by Grant and – an unlikely Caribbean – the liberal Jewish journalist Bernard Levin. 'We bring you the news you ought to know, with *Tonight*'s topical calypso.' (Later – and more bitingly – there were even more Anglicized versions, such as Lance Percival's regular news satires on *That Was the Week That Was*.) But Melodisc's jazz calypsos offered something different; they gave West Indian immigrants their own sounds back to them, and so endorsed them. The label put out recordings made by visiting musicians from Trinidad, Jamaica and Guyana alongside 'London calypsos' newly minted by London-based musicians, which gave listeners, uniquely, their own accents singing of something like their own experiences. The Blue Spot radiogram – hymned by Donald Hinds – has achieved almost iconic status in recollections of West Indian domestic life in the 1950s and 1960s. It was a highly prized symbol of status in the new society, and a focal point of social life for the new families who began to put down roots in Lambeth, Handsworth and Moss Side from the late 1950s onwards. But the Blue Spot would have meant far less without the records to play on it.

And so we come back to parties and, inevitably, the neighbours. In 1958 John Fraser, Lambeth's Commonwealth Liaison Officer, was invited to Wandsworth Town Hall to interpret the Caribbean way of life for their long-suffering fellow citizens. Having outlined the impact of slavery on West Indian marriage patterns, he turned his attention to their way of socializing: 'In the West Indies pubs are only for social outcasts,' he explained. 'The home is always the centre for social contact and that is where the West Indian does his drinking. Parties from 9 p.m. to 5 a.m., which upset the neighbours so much in Brixton, are normal behaviour for him. So are the juke boxes and calypsos.'[15]

Jukeboxes may have been stretching it, since they were hardly domestic furniture for even the most dedicated music lover, although one case which came up before the Milner Holland Committee inquiring into the state of London's housing was of a local tenant (a cobbler) whose new Jamaican landlords lived on the premises. In addition to apparently cutting the electricity of the tenants over

Dancing at home. West London in the 1960s.

Christmas, they had 'an American type Juke Box, which plays some-times until 4am very loudly'.[16] But in the absence of a jukebox the radiogram was essential, almost a sacred object. According to Mike Phillips, 'If you didn't have one in your front room you weren't any-body.' The Blue Spot came in a range of more and less upmarket versions. The Monte Carlo, for example, was fitted with an integral drinks cabinet, as was the rather neater Barcelona model – though one disadvantage was the persistent glass rattle that might go with it. Another was the hiss made by the valves as they warmed up. The short wave radio could pick up transmissions from the Caribbean, though it is unclear how often people tuned in, especially since the BBC's Caribbean programmes could be accessed so much more sim-ply on the World Service broadcast from London. The main purpose of the radiograms was to play records – the children of migrants recall their mothers' passion for Jim Reeves on a Sunday, and the stacked-up 45s on a Saturday night naturally featured everyone from

Elvis to the Jamaican Millie Small's 'My Boy Lollipop'. But the neighbours, apparently, heard only West Indian music. By the late 1950s, as West Indian families increasingly bought their own flats and houses and began to socialize at home, complaints about parties filled the local newspapers. It was true that Caribbean couples and families preferred to make their own entertainment, on their own terms, rather than gather in the pub, and parties to celebrate send-offs, homecomings, birthdays, christenings, or simply to have an occasion to dance, were frequent or – as the neighbours might put it – incessant.

Throughout 1960 the *Brixton Advertiser* ran a campaign against Caribbean partying, giving column inches to tales of neighbourly tension and disagreements over noise. The paper carried even the smallest story – the tenants of Southwell Road, Lambeth, who complained to a rent tribunal of the 'Hot jazz, calypso, and Dixieland music on records at one a.m. every night', for example. (Not only that but the named perpetrators – Horace Worrell, a bus driver, and his wife – also 'used a noisy sewing machine every weekend'.)[17] This was an obvious attempt to appeal to the growing resentment of Brixton's older residents, but it gained traction from the local campaign against illegal drinking clubs. The Worrells were just noisy neighbours, but there was a fine line between the private party and the pay-to-enter social, one that was exploited on both sides. As Donald Hinds suggested, people started charging for drinks when it got too expensive to cater for the numbers turning up at the front door. Rather than 'bring a bottle', the custom was to provide a range of drinks for which party-goers would pay. This turned them into customers, and further muddied the distinction between the party, the illegal club and – according to the neighbours – the clip joint.

Early in 1960 the Labour MP for Brixton, Marcus Lipton, condemned the fact that, as he put it, 'Any scallywag can start a club if he has five shillings in his pocket.' Lipton himself was, by any measure, not sympathetic to popular music. In 1954 he had asked a parliamentary question designed to draw attention to the indecency of several calypsos, including Marie Bryant's slightly risqué hit 'Don't Touch My Nylon'. If he was out of sympathy with the popular mood on that occasion, on the illegal clubs he had a following. As the

Brixton Advertiser reported, 'in a growing number of cases, these clubs are started in residential areas and the noise and inconvenience to neighbours is a serious matter'. Later that year the paper found residents of the Medora Road area of Brixton 'just about at the end of their tether'. They were furious over:

> 'disgusting incidents' and 'wild parties' at two houses in the road – a club and a private house run by coloured people ... They claim the coloured men and white girls arrive early every evening about 10 p.m. and are still there singing and shouting at four in the morning. A local elderly lady said: 'This used to be a nice quiet road before these people came. They call these places clubs but we have our own ideas.'[18]

This was a very different kind of culture clash from the one going on in Notting Hill. Brixton had never been an area of slum housing, but prided itself on being nice and quiet, a haven for the respectable aspiring middle class. The sociologist Sheila Patterson argued that the problems were as much about class expectations as about race:

> No immigrant group has in the mass so signally failed to conform to these expectations as have the West Indians ... Southern Irish migrants are often said to be 'as bad as the darkies'; but they are not so easily identifiable, and the criticisms are therefore not so sharply focused. In the case of the Southern Irish and the West Indians, of course, the differences and frictions are intensified by the fact that these are lower-class migrants moving into a highly status-conscious, upper-lower or lower-middle-class local society.[19]

Noise, 'vice', intimidation of the neighbours, fights ('And if they have to fight,' said Mrs Newton, 'I wish they would do so in their own rooms. It is getting so bad that you don't know what is likely to come through your window') all contributed to the bad press. The club in question on this occasion was called the Tropicana and was run by a Mrs Burrell, who insisted that the 'quiet, social club' was run on a membership basis only, and invited the *Advertiser* to call in. The reporter found a basement which 'consisted of two small rooms with a bar at one end serving beer and spirits. There was a juke-box in one corner and tables and chairs scattered about the room.' But the basement clubs were denounced – by Marcus Lipton again in the

Commons – as 'breeding grounds for vice and corruption'. Lambeth Council routinely denied licences to applications on residential properties but lamented that refusals 'may be ignored by the proprietor of the club'. Attitudes to the clubs were certainly not split simply along lines of colour. For the middle-class Caribbean and West African residents of Lambeth, the illegal clubs were just as unwelcome. As a 'coloured club owner' told the *Advertiser*: 'It is the activities at these unlicensed clubs and at private parties that cast a slur on all of us.' But unlike the neighbours he could acknowledge the real need for people to have somewhere to go, arguing that licensed clubs did 'a good job in providing somewhere for coloured people to get together other than in pubs where they run up against prejudice'. This was the main ground for appeal against the refusal of licences, that 'Jamaicans were not popular in public houses' and if they had no authorized clubs they would be forced to gather in illegal drinking dens.[20]

By the spring of 1961 Lambeth Council had found an ingenious, if expensive solution to the problem. Announcing a clean-up of the 'vice-dens' the council bought up the freehold of the Victorian houses lining Somerleyton and Geneva Roads. This meant they could refuse the renewal of leases, most of which had only a few years left to run, and eventually the houses were demolished to make way for the estates as we know them today. As Councillor Carr explained from Lambeth Town Hall, 'It may take a little time, but we are determined to solve the problem. Then all of Brixton will once again be a decent place in which people will be proud to live.' One trouble with this approach was that with fewer clubs there were more private parties. As a self-confessed 'dark stranger' put it in an undercover report on the club scene for the *Advertiser*:

> It is true that since the closure of the very many clubs in Brixton, life has been very dull for some of the immigrant residents who will not be readily accepted at 'whites only' social functions, there still goes on in some of these premises a number of week-end parties, where you can go in and have a drink and dance, the guest will of course contribute towards the cost of his own drink and meals.[21]

What appeared to be a battle over noise – the sound of the hot jazz and calypso, but also of the comings and goings, and people gathered on the street after the clubs had closed – was in reality a struggle over the legitimacy of expressing Caribbean culture in a British city. After all, white people played music and had parties and sometimes got into fights too. But when they did so they annoyed their neighbours as individuals, not as a culture. Paradoxically it was precisely because Brixton was becoming a centre for 'respectable' families, who wanted to socialize with one another, rather than a hub of vice dens, that the question of how the neighbours lived appeared to become more pressing.

13

Brothers

It was between 1960 and 1961 that approximately 90 men came from our village [in Rawalpindi] ... Up to 1962 there was no hatred against the immigrants in Bradford but after that it started slowly.

I did not do anything, my relative ... arranged my ticket through agents in Pakistan. He arranged my accommodation, food and job in the mill where he had worked for three years. Later my brother came to join us along with other relatives. We live like a Biraderi, as an extension of our Biraderi in Pakistan. This is the only way to be safe, successful and happy in this strange country.

Muhammad Anwar, *The Myth of Return* (1979)[1]

The shock of arrival occurs in migrant stories and memoirs with the force of a primal scene – the greyness and grime; for the Irish, the sheer size of towns and cities, and even train stations; for Caribbean migrants, the jolt of seeing white people engaged in menial jobs, sweeping and cleaning; for Sikhs and Hindus, the distress at seeing their own countrymen doing the same. It was not simply that the scenes of urban and industrial life were unfamiliar but – because they were unfamiliar – they proved to the immigrants they did not belong. And not only were they locked out of the community they saw in front of them, but they had also lost their own communities, sealed back in the past in Sligo or Trinidad, Mirpur or Jalandhar.

For post-war European migrants – the forced labourers who ended up in camps in Germany, the Poles and the Jews – the loss of home was absolute. They took up their new lives in England in the knowledge that they could never return; the German Jewish community had been entirely destroyed, and the population transfers along the new borders of Poland and the Ukraine meant that for many migrants the places they had left no longer existed. Yet the fear that home was now irretrievably lost was real too for many voluntary migrants, who could theoretically have returned whenever they wanted. For what they had lost was their involvement in the everyday, present-tense encounters of their communities. We can understand this most clearly in relation to Irish workers, who needed only £5 and a long weekend to plant themselves back in their home villages and farms, and many of whom went home regularly at Christmas and in the summers. Yet they returned always as outsiders to the life they had left, tainted by their experiences in England and marked out as people who had turned their backs on the ones who stayed. As countless descriptions of early post-war migrants attest, they inhabited a limbo between a world left behind and another yet to be created. They had lost their place in the unremarkable daily life of the farm, village or town, and for many people the only option was to recreate a nostalgic version of it, a kind of badge of home.

Another way of handling departure was to ignore it, to attempt to establish an existence in Britain that was a living extension of the world back home. Nostalgic recreation of the sounds and stories of the past, and the drive to keep up familial and commercial contacts, were not mutually exclusive strategies by any means. Nonetheless there was a vast difference between the Ukrainian and Polish households visited by John Tannahill in the mid-1950s – the rooms hung with national symbols and mementos of a home which seemed lost for ever, the children decked out for special occasions in hand-embroidered traditional dress – and the manner in which South Asian migrants understood their living connection with the families and villages they had left. For a start, the early post-war migrants from the Punjab and Azad Kashmir had no intention of making their new lives in England permanent. In particular the mainly Muslim men from Mirpur who were courted as workers for the mills of Bradford proved markedly reluctant to bring their families to England to settle.

They held out far longer than most, living as migrants rather than immigrants.[2]

Nearly 70 per cent of Asian migrants to Bradford came from Mirpur, and a majority of them from just a handful of Mirpuri villages. The pattern was similar in Oldham, Rochdale, Blackburn and the smaller mill towns of Yorkshire and Lancashire. On the face of it, it would be hard to imagine travelling a greater cultural distance than from a poor, isolated, rural village in northern Pakistan to the heart of industrial Britain. An area bordering north-west Punjab – Mirpuris spoke a dialect of Punjabi – Mirpuri society appeared in many ways to be the antithesis of modern Britain. Cut off from the major centres of population by poor transport and communications, Mirpuri villagers eked out a rather precarious living as small landowners (farming mostly rocky and infertile land), as landless tenants, labourers, craftsmen and artisans. Although Islamic society rejects the caste system, the villages were organized on almost tribal, occupational lines, a system kept loosely in place by broad, traditional guidelines over purity and pollution, such as who might eat with whom, and, especially, who might marry whom.[3]

Yet what appeared to be a highly traditional, closed, rural society was in many ways already thoroughly 'open'. For a start thousands of Partition refugees (known as Muhajirs) had been billeted in Mirpuri villages since 1947. The movement of populations was, tragically, nothing new. And the villages had long been connected with urban Pakistan through rural–urban migration. It was common for young men from all layers of village society – landowners' sons, labourers, artisans – to take up wage labour on building sites and in the factories of Rawalpindi and Lahore, and later in Islamabad. The remittances they sent home, along with their experiences of city life, were enabling forms of modernization (such as wells and irrigation systems) in their villages and farms. In fact, this social habit of young men earning money in urban Pakistan before returning to their villages to settle down set a pattern in which migration for work could be a way of welcoming modernization while remaining suspicious of Westernization. This pattern was, in turn, to shape the villagers' encounter with Britain.

In the late 1960s a Pakistani sociologist, Muhammad Anwar,

found that more than 90 per cent of the workers on the night shift in three Rochdale mills had come from Pakistan. The only white staff were the supervisors and the mechanics. On each shift one or two English-speaking Pakistanis were employed to act as intermediaries with the bulk of the Punjabi-speaking workforce. It was the same in mills throughout Lancashire and Yorkshire. And the workers didn't just come from roughly the same areas in Pakistan. They were for the most part actual 'family'. In one mill, thirty-six people on one night shift were related to each other, and a further fifteen of them had come from the same villages:

> We work together. It is a good thing because we do not feel lonely. We talk about our relatives, villages back home and other topics of common interest. We feel that we work in our own factory as there is no pressure from the management at night, although we work hard because our overlooker should not be let down. Another advantage of working together is that we can travel together in cars and save time and reduce the expense, although in our case the firm provides transportation, but it gets inconvenient sometimes to go to a pick-up point.

There were certainly benefits to the night shift. Chief among these was that there were 'no management and white people present' at night. The English-speaking Pakistani charge-hands acted as a buffer between the men and the mill, indeed, as we will see, between the men and British industrial society in general. And of course they could also earn more money at night.[4]

The arrangement suited the management too. The night shift could function almost autonomously as long as pay and overtime were guaranteed. Mirpuris could be relied on to find relatives and friends to fill any vacancies, without the mill having to advertise; they could instruct their co-workers on the job, obviating the need for periods of training too. Several mills produced Punjabi-language leaflets offering a £10 bonus to anyone who would bring in more of their countrymen for the night shift. One manager of a Bradford mill explained the benefits of immigrant night-shift workers:

> Why [white?] people ... English people I should say didn't want to work at night due to the unsocial hours aspect of it, but we then had a

A Pakistani worker in a spinning mill in Bradford, 1960s.

large immigrant population coming in who were quite happy to work at night and . . . er . . . the case that I put was that if we trained one or two as a nucleus, were confident that they knew the job, we could then bring in numbers gradually and we could use them to train their own countrymen, and that worked very well and we started to run at night in 1961 and we explained the move to Pakistani and Indian labour to the rest of the workforce to pre-empt any difficulties in that direction by saying that it was essential for survival for us to run three shifts, that they would be on from nine o'clock at night to eight o'clock in the morning, that the practical aspects of the situation were they would scarcely ever see them but they were an essential part of the firm for their survival and by explaining it to small groups of people we got this point of view across and we never had the slightest resistance to them coming in.

Luckily for this manager, in the late 1950s and early 1960s there appeared to be an almost inexhaustible supply of immigrants who could be hidden on the night shift.[5]

Before 1962 Pakistanis, like Indians and people from the Caribbean islands, were Commonwealth citizens and could enter Britain without restriction. A cap was kept on the numbers travelling partly because India and Pakistan restricted access to papers, including passports, and required proof of sponsorship by someone already based in Britain. But on the British side there was no limit to those who could be sponsored by relatives and friends. For people with sufficient funds to bribe the various officials, arranging the trip could be time-consuming and expensive but it was fundamentally straightforward. Or at any rate, any difficulties were encountered at home in Pakistan, rather than at Heathrow. In the early 1950s, as the supply of European Voluntary Workers dried up, mills in Yorkshire had begun sending recruitment officers to the Punjab. These early recruits became the first links in a migration chain reinforced by the sponsorship rules. Boosted by the extra payments they were offered by the mills for bringing in more workers, and keen to surround themselves with brothers, uncles, cousins and friends, it was not uncommon for men to sponsor up to ten or twelve new migrants each year. Anyone sponsoring fewer than one or two appeared to lack community spirit. One man interviewed by Anwar in the late 1960s had worked as a labourer in a Bradford woollen mill for ten years from 1954. During that time he had brought over two brothers, one brother-in-law and six cousins to work with him. Another had been born in Jalandhar in 1923 but migrated to Pakistan in 1947, along with most of his village. He arrived in Britain 1961 to work at Royton mill in Lancashire, alongside five other relatives on the same night shift. As he pointed out, he worked under a Pakistani charge-hand so he encountered no language problems, and he lived with his relatives so in effect he did not have to engage with 'ordinary' life in Britain at all.[6]

A thriving set of mini-institutions grew up to facilitate this trade in bodies – travel agents, banks, airlines and an array of middlemen and racketeers all made their money off migration. By the early 1960s, when preparations for the construction of the Mangla Dam required the resettlement of over 280 villages in northern Pakistan and the displacement of more than 100,000 people, the Pakistani government withdrew its restrictions on emigration and instead began to promote it, issuing work permits and opening up passport offices in Mirpur and Rawalpindi for the displaced people. The travel agents and their proxies and go-betweens were ready and waiting.[7]

It was at this time – in November 1961 – that Harold Macmillan's Conservative government introduced a Bill aimed at restricting immigration from the New Commonwealth. The Commonwealth Immigrants Bill was a direct result of the increased hysteria over immigration following the Nottingham and Notting Hill riots, but the wisdom and feasibility of denying entry to some immigrants had been discussed at Cabinet level (including by the Working Party on Coloured People seeking Employment in the United Kingdom) since the early 1950s. Macmillan nodded politely in the direction of India and Pakistan when he acknowledged that some immigrants had been finding it rather hard to come to Britain, despite their right to do so: 'knowing our difficulties, some Commonwealth countries have taken steps to limit the number of people coming here by various methods, and we are grateful to them. Several of them have used methods to discourage this mass movement.' But at the current level, he continued, 'the influx ... can hardly continue uncontrolled'. The 1961 Bill proposed a voucher system instead of an open door. Entry to Britain would be possible for people with employment vouchers issued by the Ministry of Labour, for students, for members of the armed forces, and for people with sufficient wealth to support themselves and their dependants without working. Category A vouchers were designed for people who had obtained a specific job in advance (i.e. professionals); B vouchers were for those with specific skills or training in short supply; and there were a small number of C vouchers for those with no specific skills at all. (In 1965 the category C quota was abandoned altogether.) It was obvious that most of the migrants from Asia and the Caribbean who arrived in Britain in the years before the Bill was drafted had fallen under category C – economic migrants who, as the bonuses offered by the Yorkshire mills proved, were determinedly courted by British industry. The Bill in effect broke the connection between the level of immigration and the needs of the economy – the laws of supply and demand no longer applied. Immigrants were to be regulated according to rough measures of desirability which were obviously racist in intent. The Labour leader, Hugh Gaitskell, denounced the Bill in the Commons:

> It is no part of our case to pretend that any amount of immigration of people of different colour and social customs and language does not

present problems, though I urge that we should beware of exaggeration here. Do the Government seek to deal with it by enforcing laws against overcrowding, by using every educational means at their disposal to create tolerance and mutual understanding, and by emphasising to our own people the value of these immigrants and setting their face firmly against all forms of racial discrimination? ... There is no shred of evidence that the Government have even seriously tried to go along this course and make a proper inquiry into the nature of the problem. They have yielded to the crudest clamour, 'Keep them out'.

The controversy over the Bill – the Commonwealth newspapers were full of it – and fear of the effect of new restrictions provoked (from the Bill's framers' point of view) an almost absurdly counterproductive rush to 'beat the ban' among Caribbean and Asian migrants alike: 21,550 New Commonwealth migrants arrived in 1959; 58,300 in 1960; and 125,400 in 1961. In the eighteen months up to July 1962, when the Commonwealth Immigrants Act came into force, 98,000 came from the Caribbean alone. Particularly for migrants from Pakistan, the loosening of restrictions because of the Mangla Dam and fear of the Commonwealth Immigrants Bill created a perfect storm, and the migration machine went into overdrive.[8]

The ninety men who arrived from one Pakistani village between 1960 and 1961 found work and lived in all-male households which mirrored those of the Punjabi Sikhs. Here is a description of one in Oxford, recalled in the early 1980s:

We lived in a two-bedroomed house. There were seventeen of us living there, including myself, my cousin Yunis from our village ... and also Anwar from a village near ours. The rest were strangers to me. It was terrible living there. We slept two or three men to a bed and each bedroom had two or three double beds in it. People also slept on the stairs and even outside, in the garden, like we do in Pakistan in the hot season. The British Government should not have called us over here for work without telling us how to live and providing some facilities. I was alright because I had been in the army and had learnt some of the English ways, but the others did not even know how to use English bathrooms or toilets. No wonder our English neighbours disliked us.[9]

Across the country the complaints of the English neighbours were the same: the houses were overcrowded and dirty; the yards were used as toilets; rubbish was piled in the gardens front and back, rather than properly disposed of; and while complaints about the smell of curry were mostly to come later, when the wives who made the curry had arrived, there were violent objections to the occasional butchering of chickens in the back gardens (not a cultic ritual as some thought, but the only way of getting hold of halal meat before dedicated butchers opened up). And there were other, less openly articulated, suspicions. Jeremy Seabrook noted this fragment of conversation while writing his study of Blackburn in the late 1960s:

> A bus stop on the fringe of town. Late evening. A lad of about eighteen has just been playing football in the park. He plays four or five evenings a week, would like to turn professional. We get on the bus. Pakistani conductor. 'Fuckin' Packies.' 'Don't you like them?' 'Like them? Biggest load of homos in the world. Living fifteen, sixteen, seventeen of them all in one house. What are they doing all them men in one house if they're not shagging each other?'[10]

What they were doing was saving. (This is not to suggest that some of them were not shagging as well, of course, though it may have been hard to find the privacy for that.) Men could put in up to seventy-five hours a week by taking any overtime that was offered, and it made sense for them to live a dormitory lifestyle when there was so little time when they were neither working nor sleeping. By earning up to £12 or £18 a week, and spending only £2 on food and accommodation, they could save as much as £500 in a year. (In 1959 in Southall, G. S. Aurora came across Punjabis who were saving and sending money home even out of their unemployment benefit.) In the mid-1950s, travel agents charged £250–£300 for passport and fares from Pakistan to Britain. By the early 1960s, the fees had gone up to approximately £800, while the average income of a Mirpuri villager was about £30 a year. Above all, migration needed to be made to pay back home. It was not principally, at this stage, about making a better life in England.[11]

Saving was also a source of status which could be accessed by anyone, regardless of caste. In time this was to have a major effect on the social structure of village society back home in Pakistan, as men of the artisan classes were increasingly able to send money home to buy land, build modern houses, and pay for an education for the younger members of the family. It was not so different from the way that the regular £5 notes sent home by young Irish labourers enabled their mothers to 'hold their heads up' in the status-conscious society of the west of Ireland towns. Although there was a substantial difference in scale. It was not just the differential standard of living in Ireland and Pakistan which meant that money saved went further in Asia. There was also far more suspicion of saving, and a far higher premium placed on conspicuous generosity in the pub, for example, among Irish workers. If Irish labourers saved, they did so furtively; there are plenty of stories which reveal the derision heaped on anyone trying to avoid the camaraderie linked to bingeing and excess, anyone trying to raise themselves higher than their mates. The opposite was true for Pakistani men, among whom the moral pressure was to save rather than to spend. Ironically, both groups of men lived frugally, in over-crowded and often unspeakably grim conditions. For both groups of men the trappings of comfort (a room of their own, a television, a car – all the markers of success for young English men of the time) were rejected. The trap for Irish men was that if they had money they had to be seen to be spending it, often recklessly; and for Asian men they had to be seen to be saving it. It was this that gave rise to another misreading of their behaviour among their English neighbours – the idea that they liked living in slums. The primacy given to frugality, and to saving money to send home, meant that it was far more sensible for them to buy cheap houses in poor areas, rather than 'waste' money on better stock. To onlookers it appeared that they were choosing deprivation and poverty – that they were simply unable to make good.

Asian migrants, like the Poles and Ukrainians before them, and unlike the majority of the Irish and the Caribbeans, moved early into property ownership. But they did so for entirely different reasons. House buying was not about settling but about accumulating wealth. They tended to buy cheap houses for cash, rather than take out mort-gages, and to rent out rooms in order to generate more income to send back home. This remained true even after the men began to bring their wives and families to Britain.

In the mid-1960s you could buy a back-to-back cottage in Bradford for £80, and the Pakistani sociologist Badr Dahya found some going for between £45 and £60. The system of rental purchase was common. 'The most that is required of the purchaser is a deposit of £10–12 and a weekly instalment of 15s (75p) to £1 to be paid to the vendor or his solicitor.' By 1964, 1,265 houses in Bradford were owned by Asian migrants. This was despite the fact that there was no difficulty in getting council houses in Bradford (in her 1967 study *Housing on Trial*, Elizabeth Burney found council houses in the town were 'going begging'). As one man explained to Dahya: 'Why pay rent for property which can never be yours? Better to save money and buy a house, so that you can live in it and also make more money.' But they also had no interest in buying houses in 'nice' areas. They avoided the suburbs:

> They refused these offers on the ground that immigrant-tenants could not be expected to pay more than 75p per week in rent; that there would be a problem of getting transport to work and of visiting their fellows in the city and that the houses in question were a long distance away from the immigrant areas and, therefore, getting provisions from Pakistani grocers and butchers would be a further problem.

'What is the use of spending so much money on a house in this country? We are not going to live here for ever.' 'Will the English people think better of me if I buy a modern house? Better to build a pakka house in the village where there are people who know you and respect you. They are the people who matter.'[12]

Most of the consequences of the 1962 Commonwealth Immigrants Act appear to have been unintended. This is perhaps not surprising when we consider that the majority of complaints about immigrants focused on social tensions and housing problems, which had been placed firmly in the public consciousness during the Notting Hill riots. Yet the Act failed to address these issues at all. Instead it offered a solution centred on employment, with a system of quotas limiting numbers of workers, despite the fact that unemployment was highest in areas where the immigrant population was low. The idea that immigrants were 'taking our jobs' not only wasn't true, but it wasn't

even the main source of popular anxiety. The response of the commonwealth immigrants themselves – to rush to beat the ban – could
only increase suspicion and resentment in the absence of any social
programme of integration and education. The numbers arriving from
Asia and the Caribbean in 1960 and 1961 outnumbered those for
the previous five years combined. And immigrant numbers were no
longer correlated with job vacancies, as they broadly had been in the
past. It was just about getting in before the door was closed.

The Act also encouraged those who were already in Britain to stay
put. In the years before 1962, Asian migrants in particular had tended
to return home after earning well for three or four years, perhaps
returning to Britain again for a further stint of industrial work when
the money ran out back at home. Under the new rules that strategy
now seemed too risky – who knew if they would be allowed back into
the country again? The more permanent status of Indian and Pakistani workers was of course to have a huge impact on the structure of
the immigrant communities themselves. For a start, the power of the
labour brokers, or middlemen, in the mills and foundries could be far
more effectively challenged once the labourers themselves were settled, instead of consisting of a constantly renewing stream of rookie
recruits who knew no English. By the late 1960s the new confidence
and political organization of settled Asian workers, both men and
women, was to result in a series of high-profile strikes, putting paid
to the idea that they were simply docile and 'backward' providers of
cheap labour. But undoubtedly the most far-reaching consequence
of the Act – and probably the least foreseen – was the reunification of
Asian families in Britain.

Some men began to call their families from Pakistan and India in
the run up to the passing of the Act. The fear was that wives and
children would not be allowed to join men already living in England,
although this was not in fact part of the terms of the Bill. But it was
immediately after the Act passed into law that the effect on families
became obvious. It was now hard to sponsor further unskilled men,
for they were not eligible for the government's employment vouchers,
but wives – and therefore also sons, who would be able to earn when
they were old enough – were still welcome. Over 90 per cent of

all Commonwealth immigrants between 1962 and 1965 were the dependants of men already living in Britain.

There is a telling discrepancy between the reasons given by both Sikh and Muslim men and women for the decision to bring women and children to Britain. Interviews with the first generation of Asian men tend to emphasize the new sense that life in England was now going to be long term, and the pragmatic realization that if you could no longer bring over a brother or an uncle, at least you could still bring a son to work alongside you.

> The 1962 controls were supposed to stop us coming in, but they left loopholes because you could still bring in your son or a brother's son and say he was yours. The Government soon realized that this was a loophole and stopped it by saying that children had to come with their mothers. That is why we brought our wives over.[13]

On the other hand, many of the recollections by the wives themselves suggest that they came partly in order to keep the men in check. There are stories of messages sent back by worried relatives, warning of young men going astray and spending money on drink and women, of women borrowing the fare in order not to lose their husbands to new English wives, of parents hastily arranging marriages in order to head off the danger of rogue liaisons with English girls. One Pakistani woman outlined to Alison Shaw the various levels of trickery and dissimulation which formed part of her own story of migration:

> You want to know how I came to be living here? Well, you might not think so now, but when Ijaz was first here, he got into bad company and his uncle was not much better. It is not surprising really, men here on their own. And he was only 19 at the time. But soon his parents got to hear that he had an English girlfriend: at least, that's what some people from his village were saying. His parents were very worried. They had started to build a new house with the money he had been sending back. Other people got to know too, and his parents thought that because of it they would have trouble finding a girl for him to marry. A man's family loses respect that way you know. So his parents came from their village in Jhelum to our city and spoke to my parents. Our families are the same caste – Pathans – but are not relatives. My

father had known his father for some time. They said their son was returning for the marriage. You know what they did? It was his mother's idea. They sent a telegram saying an uncle had died. It wasn't true, but it brought him home straight away. Before the marriage, women in our neighbourhood used to talk to me about what England was like. They said there was no control. Men drank alcohol and went with women and no one bothered. They also made remarks, not directly, but I knew, about my husband's behaviour, hinting at what sort of man he was . . . Perhaps they were jealous that I was going to England. Anyway, it made me very frightened about the marriage and I could hardly eat for weeks before it. But I couldn't refuse this marriage. My parents had decided and were so proud to have a daughter going to England. I couldn't shatter their hopes. But since I've been here, as far as I know, my husband has been a good husband to me.[14]

The 'problem of the English girlfriend' actually looms quite large in reminiscences from this period, and not only in stories by mothers and wives. In April 1959, G. S. Aurora found five or six houses in Southall in which Indian men and European women were living in 'common law union'. He was convinced this number would grow, but the opposite happened when Indian wives began to turn up. Men recalled with a complicated mixture of pride and shame the dalliances of their 'bachelor' years (including those who were married, and took second wives in England). As one man explained to Muhammad Anwar in the late 1960s, in the isolated atmosphere of the early 1950s it was hard to maintain a sense of religious and moral duty: 'Since I came to this country in 1954 I forgot how to recite prayers.' It was when he was working on the buses in Manchester that he met his Irish girlfriend:

I was on duty one day on the bus when I met her in Manchester. I offered her a drink. She left her address with me and I went to see her the same weekend. None of my relatives know about my affair because she never comes to Rochdale. If somebody came to know, there could be some trouble.

This man maintained that having a girlfriend was OK, so long as you took care not to get too involved. He kept his wife and children in his village in Pakistan, partly to shield them from Western influences, and partly, no doubt, to be able to take advantage of a Western lifestyle when he wanted. And he cannot have been alone in this. In 1961 there were 3,457 Pakistanis registered as living in Bradford, of whom a mere 81 were women, and this proportion was higher than in nearby towns.[15]

Undoubtedly it was handy to be able to divide your family from your sexual life, by keeping your wife back home and your girlfriend in England. Aurora's interviewees were open about their double sexual standards, arguing, for example, that European women could not possibly be faithful or respectable because of the way they dressed – not covering their heads and letting their legs show. It was almost axiomatic that women were to blame for male lapses in sexual morality, particularly those who came knocking at the doors of Indian houses: 'They are responsible for spoiling the morals of our boys, who are attracted by their white skin.'

> They might be richer than us but they are a decaying race ... Now look at their morals! Sometimes these people in the house bring women and they ask me why I do not also have a go. But I do not like these white women. I cannot even think of kissing one. When I see all these impressive buildings or escalators in the tube stations and glittering stores I don't first exclaim 'how wonderful!' Instead I think of the poverty of my countrymen and say to myself, 'Our people have paid for all these with their life and blood.'[16]

In all the warnings that England might bring material wealth but was sure to bring moral poverty along with it, the problem was not so much the immorality of the English, but the licence offered to the men away from home to be immoral in their turn. In Madho Ram's *qissa*, for example, it's drink that gets the better of him, making him 'forgetful of the first wife at home'. He makes it sound very easy:

> Having finished work and come to the pub, with a full glass before me
> And a box of cigarettes, *Players* ones, with a *lighter* to light them
> I was sitting looking at the white girl: '*Hello!*' I said and I called her –
> 'What'll you have? My beloved!' instantly getting her a drink.
> Having taken her hand, I'm kissing her and she's agreeing to go with me.

Meanwhile back in India, his wife bears the brunt of both her mother's and her mother-in-law's irritation, because he has stopped sending money home. 'Your husband never sends us any money! . . . Oh, Madho Ram has got entangled with a *gori*!' His wife is beside herself:

No one asks about what I have to say. I am a slave at home, tied to
the house.
Because of remembering you, I cry. Hai Hai ve crazy about England.
You haven't sent me a letter since you went. Having gone off, you
have forgotten me in your heart.
Your elder Uncle upbraids me, Hai Hai ve crazy about England.
We have not a grain in the house and you, in England, enjoy
pleasures.
Send some money for God's sake. Hai Hai ve crazy about England.
You went off, making some excuses. Your mother mocks, she is
sarcastic to me.
Send for me on any pretext. Hai Hai ve crazy about England.
Now you agree to whatever the *gori* says. Here, people who are owed
money are asking for it.
You have also got a house on a mortgage. Hai Hai ve crazy about
England.
Such anxiety has arisen, so it's impossible to sleep.
You are drinking alcohol with the *goris*.
You have broken the swing [burnt your boat]. Hai Hai ve crazy
about England.
Every day, I await your letter. I am yours and you are mine.
Call me there, and finish the dispute. Hai Hai ve crazy about
England.

As much as moral laxity, the problem with these new liaisons was the money they wasted – the whole point of a man going to England was to earn money to send back home. Once he began to spend it instead, or to spend it in the wrong place, the deal was broken. For families back in India and Pakistan it became impossible to keep up payments on land purchases and building work, and all the pride of having a son or a brother in England turned to shame that he had forgotten his duty to his family. The moral economy of village society was intimately linked to its financial structure and, now, to industrial employment in Britain.

The suspicion of British culture and mores felt by the first wave of

Mirpuri migrants was an issue for both men and women. There were plenty of tale-tellers who let it be known back home which of the men were straying from the straight and narrow path, and getting involved with drink and women. But, undoubtedly, fear of Western morals had their greatest effect on the lives of immigrant women. Again an Irish comparison may be instructive here. The fear of the loss of female 'virtue' associated with the pagan society across the Irish Sea formed a major plank of conservative Catholic rhetoric during the 1940s and 1950s. The anxiety was couched in moral (and sexual) terms but was as much as anything a fear of the effects of women's greater financial security – their access to jobs, money and independence – on a traditional, and frugal, subsistence farming culture. Women's economic independence was a threat, but it was far easier to target their sexual independence. The anxiety over English loose morals was similar in kind for all religious immigrant cultures, whether Catholic, Orthodox, Sikh, Hindu or Muslim. Where they differed was in the degree to which they felt that anything could be done about it. Irish priests might rail against the immorality in England, but there was not much they could do except exhort their followers to remember their religious duty. The structure of the traditional Punjabi Muslim family, with a relatively clear separation between male and female roles, meant not only that the immigrant Muslim community had more to lose in the encounter with British culture, but more ways of defending itself against it.

The term 'purdah', referring to the physical separation of men and women in different areas of the home, is little used now in Britain, since the concept of veiling has taken its place. Yet the first migrants from Pakistan faced real challenges in adapting household and village customs to the demands of everyday life in an industrial city. Traditions developed in the context of the communal life of the village had to be modified for life in a terraced home or an urban street; the customary ways in which women could work and eat and often sleep together had to be revised as families lived lives closer to the nuclear English norm. And for many women the move to Britain therefore meant an intensification of the customs of purdah, rather than their relaxation. Certainly many of them became more isolated than they had ever been at home. In the village environment, where most people were related in an extended family network, very strict rules around the separation of the sexes were unnecessary. Even when outside, a woman was unlikely to meet a stranger unannounced. Moreover, in poorer villages, where people worked together in the fields, the separation of men and women was difficult to maintain anyway. Strict purdah requires a decent standard of living – not least it requires a house large enough to maintain two distinct living areas, one for the men of the household and their male visitors, and the other for women. It requires servants (or children) to maintain contact between the two worlds, passing messages, and carrying food and gifts. It is a system which can only function properly if the womenfolk of the family do not have to work outside the home. This was the household system associated with wealthier city dwellers and the landlords of the village, and it was adopted by people who aspired to raise their social status, particularly in the cities. For most people living in rural Pakistan, emulating such a world of social niceties was out of the question.[17]

For Mirpuris in Bradford, Rochdale, Oldham and Blackburn it was obviously impossible to recreate the communal life of their villages. Where women of several generations had cooked, looked after children, sewed, and washed clothes together in the courtyards of their homes, and often worked together in the fields, they now found themselves cut off from female company inside their new houses. Even if it had seemed reasonable to suggest that they find jobs in the mills and factories (and overwhelmingly it did not, since this would entail encountering male strangers), they did not have sufficient English to make work viable, and there were no female intermediaries to help them. As at home in Pakistan, husbands (and children) took care of the shopping, so that most wives were reduced to spending the majority of their time cooking and childrearing within the home. As late as the early 1980s Alison Shaw found that while televisions and videos, telephones and central heating had become luxuries no Mirpuri home in Britain could be without, labour-saving devices such as washing machines were not thought essential. Kitchens were basically equipped, spices were ground and curries made freshly for each meal, washing was done by hand. Women themselves insisted it was only right that they should not spend unnecessarily on comforts. As the bachelor houses gave way to family homes the premium put on frugality seems to have become associated, in part at least, with women's hard work, even drudgery. As though that proved that Western ways were being kept at bay.

14

Homeowners

To give Adah a rent-book would have put him in trouble because, being a council tenant, he had pretended to the authorities that Adah was a relative and only a guest. He had begged Adah to withdraw her application for a flat from the Council but it was too late. There were, however, still lots of things he could do to make her life miserable. He would thunder at her kids for any of the slightest childish noises; this was so frequent that one of her boys would run at the sight of any black man, and she dared not leave them alone in the flat for fear of what might happen to them. She could not leave any piece of food or drink in the filthy shared-kitchen for fear of it being poisoned. All their food had to be kept under the bed, so it was hardly surprising that the number of rats had increased. The man was desperate and would stop at nothing. He had switched off the electricity so that she had to keep a candle burning all night, conscious of the terrible fire risk to the children, but even more afraid of what accidents could happen in utter darkness. But now there was something new: he was trying Magic.

Buchi Emecheta, *In the Ditch* (1972)[1]

'Which do you prefer, snakes or shrunken heads?' asked Sir Edward Milner Holland at the press conference to launch his Report on London Housing in 1965. The inquiry had been set up in the wake of the Profumo scandal, and the associated public outrage over rack-renting and the intimidation of tenants by the suddenly notorious Peter Rachman, who had been involved in liaisons with both Christine Keeler and Mandy Rice-Davies. In fact the link between Rachman and John Profumo was arbitrary and accidental, and certainly not linked to passing political secrets to the Russians. They moved in some of the same louche, newly moneyed circles in West London, and they slept with some of the same women, though they had never met. But when the Profumo scandal broke the Rachman scandal broke with it, highlighting the behaviour of unscrupulous landlords in the crisis-ridden and dog-eat-dog world of inner London housing. Stories of snakes in the bath and shrunken heads hung on doors – both methods of scaring sitting tenants out of their homes that were cited in the Milner Holland report – were not-so-subtle ways of signalling the unscrupulousness of *foreign* landlords, those who at the very least might have access to snakes and shrunken heads. In fact the report was relatively neutral on the question of whether 'coloured' landlords, and 'coloured' tenants, were better or worse than their white counterparts. The evidence pointed to deeper structural problems stemming from 'shortage of sites, multiple occupation, high prices for land, and ageing housing stock and homelessness', as well as the pernicious effect on the rental market of the liberalization of rent control in 1957. But it was a lot easier to blame migrants from the New Commonwealth. Though this might be claimed as a victory for the forces of reason against latent British anti-Semitism – since Rachman was a Jew – it was far from a victory for reason overall. The housing crisis coincided with the years of 'open door' immigration, and the migrants themselves tended towards areas of low quality housing, exacerbating overcrowding and appearing to 'cause' shortages. When they began to move into home ownership, and took advantage of legal loopholes to improve their finances, the anti-migrant lobby thought it had all the ammunition it needed.[2]

Peter, or Perec, Rachman – his name has become shorthand for ruthless and exploitative landlords – was a Polish Jew from Lvov (now Lviv, in the Ukraine). He had joined the 2nd Polish Corps when Germany declared war on the Soviet Union in 1941 and arrived in Britain in 1946, part of the large contingent of Polish soldiers who had seen out the last stages of the war encamped near Naples. Until 1948 Rachman was billeted in holding camps with members of the newly styled Polish Resettlement Corps. He then took a job in Cohen's

Veneer Factory in Stepney, entering the by-now traditional Eastern European Jewish working-class neighbourhood of the East End. This was a step down, as Rachman was middle class and Polish- not Yiddish-speaking. Before the war he had been training to be a dentist. A couple of years later he had moved from the veneer factory to a tailor in Wardour St, and was living in Golders Green. Too middle class for the East End, and 'not posh enough' for Hampstead's Polish-Jewish Ex-Servicemen's Association, he appears to have made his way through the twilight areas of the city, getting involved initially in black-market clothing and then the housing racket.[3]

Housing was a gift to the slightly dodgy post-war entrepreneur. The combination of bomb damage and the moratorium on building during the war caused a crisis of supply and demand. The value of houses with vacant possession rose by 62 per cent in 1946, 93 per cent in 1947, and 127 per cent in 1948. People with capital could make a killing. As one tycoon, Herbert Mortiboy, recalled:

> I came in, like most property millionaires, after the war when the markets were wide open and prices at the bottom ... I bought two houses in Porlock Road for £1. I bought many houses in Southam Street for £50 and any number for £200 or £300. Then later, of course, you could buy a house for £250 to £300 and you could find a Pole, not necessarily a Pole – but there were a large number of Poles, ex-servicemen, and I think they had plenty of grants with a view to buying houses in the twilight areas of London.
>
> And I specialised, as you know, in Notting Hill. There's more money to be made in the dust-hole than there is in Piccadilly. Find a Pole who has £300 or £400 to put down on a house. You could multiply the price probably by about three by decorating it, not spending more than about £150 on it ... It was a bargain to him, which to you was a substantial profit.[4]

Rachman began getting into property around 1954, and by the late 1950s he owned close to 150 houses in north-west London. It was at this point that the tactics of intimidation came into play. Secured tenancies were common, and rents had been held down to 1939 levels through a series of controls. Landlords who wanted to make a quick profit had to get rid of sitting tenants in order either to sell the house on with vacant possession, or to install new tenants, paying higher rents. And 'rack-renting' in this way suddenly became much more profitable after the Conservative government liberalized the rent-control system in 1957.

Landlords had been collecting pre-war rents, failing to realize a profit, and neglecting their properties. Getting rid of rent control was meant to encourage them to invest, and to pay for upkeep and improvements. All unfurnished accommodation rated at more than £40 was taken out of control, with rent increases limited to twice the gross annual value of the property – unless the tenancy changed. Landlords could fix any rent they chose when letting to a new tenant. On average, they tripled the rent (or doubled it for an existing tenant). And with the stock of places to rent already way below the number of households looking for accommodation, there was nothing that the tenants could do about it. It was a landlord's market.[5]

Although the overall population of London fell during these years, the number of households rose. Single people – some of them immigrants from the New Commonwealth but by no means all of them – flocked to the new employment opportunities in the cities. London, and the Midlands conurbations, were still the main places to go for work in industry, but London in particular saw a huge expansion in service-sector jobs in the late 1950s. People were moving into the city, but most new building was taking place in the suburbs. And slum clearance cut down the available housing stock in city centres even further. Council waiting lists grew exponentially. One member of the Milner Holland Housing Committee calculated that a family joining Willesden's housing list and enjoying average luck would be rehoused in 205 years' time.[6] There was no option but renting from private landlords, many of whom took the opportunity to stuff their properties full to overflowing.

The evidence gathered by the Housing Committee was compelling. In one Paddington ward, 497 households were crammed into 26 dwellings. Shocked members of both Houses of Parliament picked out what they considered the worst excesses, and the papers were full of it. Over a million families in London were forced into sharing a house, often without basic facilities, living in overcrowded conditions and paying very high rents. In 1961, 31 per cent of houses in London had no bath. There were stories of tenants too scared to complain about broken toilets and baths in case they were evicted, and having to use public lavatories instead. Robert Stopford, the Bishop of London, decried the 'half a million households without the use of a bath at all, and only a shared w.c.; 155,000 households living in one room, 40 per cent. of them without their own sink and stove.' That was if families got a place to live at all. One desperate tenant pointed out to the Committee that 'you might as well have smallpox as children' when looking for accommodation. Bishop Stopford drew the obvious conclusion from the figures that, 'the fact that you are going to have a baby is almost the surest way of ensuring that you do not have a home in which to bring up the baby'. As the medical officer of health assigned to the Committee insisted:

> The herding together of people, often incompatible, the inconveniences, the lack of space especially for such things as play or pram storage, the inadequate and inconvenient washing, sanitary and food handling facilities, stairs, noise, fetching and carrying distances, and the dirt, dilapidation and depressing appearance consequent upon the neglect of parts used in common, all have their effects.[7]

None of these long-standing problems – 'the paradox of squalor in the midst of progress' – could be laid at the feet of the immigrants. But it was hard to argue that the flow of migrants into already overcrowded areas was not making things worse. 'If the growth of housing does not match the growth of employment there will be trouble of *some* kind.'[8] Arguably, there had already been quite a bit of trouble, including the 1958 riots in Notting Hill, which many people argued were caused in part by the housing situation, even if the trigger lay elsewhere.

The 'dust-hole' of Notting Hill, and the area north and west of Paddington Station, had long had a reputation as the worst of slums. 'Up on Rotting Hill, beamed on by Negroes, shadowed by Afrikanders, displaced in queues by displaced persons, ignored by Brahmins, run over by hasty "fiddlers" of various extraction, we are foreign,' gloomed Wyndham Lewis in his anti-welfare state polemic *Rotting Hill*, in 1951. 'The houses are camps, towering brick camps, with gouged out clammy basements, packed with transients.' The 1951 census in fact

A man on his doorstep in Westbourne Grove, London, in the late 1950s.

showed that Notting Dale had the highest level of overcrowding in London. By the time that Trinidadian Michael de Freitas moved there in the later 1950s the area's reputation as a dumping ground for social outcasts of every colour was well established:

> ... every second house deserted, with doors nailed up and rusty, corrugated iron across the window spaces, a legion of filthy white children swarming everywhere and people lying drunk across the pavement so we had to walk around them.
>
> We came to the house which was to be our home and the African owner led us up the decrepit stairway to a room practically filled with ugly furniture and the noise of trains passing on the adjacent railway tracks. The floor was covered with worn linoleum, the single gas ring for cooking was outside on the dismal landing, there was no bath in the house – and he wanted £2 15s a week. We were desperate and we moved straight in.[9]

It was in this quarter that Rachman (and, according to Herbert Mortiboy, a number of other Poles) had built his mini property empire. By 1956 he had bought sixteen houses in Powis Terrace. Taking advantage of the removal of rent controls, and apparently intimidating existing tenants out of their homes, he established a 75 per cent black tenancy before selling blocks to 'black henchmen', who, in turn, sold them on.[10] A Home Office committee following up on the racial tensions after the riots in Notting Hill, explained that,

> Rachman has little direct contact with the premises he owns, but delegates rent collecting and other matters to two other Poles Paplinski and Szyman, who are assisted by two coloured men, Edwards and Hunte. Many of Rachman's properties are known to be used as brothels, and he is clearly an unscrupulous landlord and the worst type of racketeer, but so far the police have been unable to obtain sufficient evidence to prosecute him on any count, though they are leaving no stone unturned.

One rather optimistic Home Office suggestion was that the whole situation in Notting Hill would improve if long-distance lorry drivers could be dissuaded from 'giving young girls free lifts to London', since they inevitably formed new recruits to the prostitution racket.[11] De Freitas later rented a basement flat in Powis Square, a welcome step up from the single room he had shared with his wife and her child in the African-owned property. His description is of a lawless, frontier town:

> Outside there were brothels all the way down the street and opposite was the Blues Club which blasted on into the small hours. Adjacent Powis Terrace was immensely overcrowded with coloured families who spent a lot of time in the street and at night there were lots of fights and a great amount of police activity. If you stepped outside your door it was like being in Piccadilly Circus on a day when something riotous was happening there.
>
> There were hang-ups inside, too, due to the vast Irish family living on the top floor. They were really more like a colony: something like eighteen children and ten adults living in four rooms. I never could succeed in counting them all as they came and went about their

business. They were rather dirty people, which was inevitable with the overcrowding, and they made their bare living, appropriately enough, by dealing in junk.[12]

De Freitas painted both Rachman and his African landlord as exploiters. But he was tight-lipped about the general reputation of black landlords as ruthless and given to intimidation. Perhaps this was inevitable since he later became personally renowned for his own rough tactics as a landlord. But there was clear evidence that – whatever the reality – both white and black tenants thought immigrant landlords were the worst. 'Coloured vultures prey harder and get fatter in their pockets than their white counterparts'; as far as rent hikes went it was almost axiomatic that, as one tenant put it, 'coloured landlords are worse than white ones in that respect . . . They are all out to make a quick profit, and charge extortionate rents to do so.'[13]

Why should people have believed that was the case? In part it was simply the effect of the Rachman scandal, and the rumours about the property empires being amassed by his 'black henchmen'. Ivy Harrison, the welfare officer appointed by Paddington Borough Council after the Notting Hill riots, noted ruefully that following the Profumo affair she was inundated with requests for help from tenants, 'all of them quite convinced that Rachman must be their landlord'.[14] This was despite the fact that Rachman never amassed a particularly large housing portfolio – and, moreover, he had died a year earlier, in 1962. The scandal brought simmering tensions around shared housing and the deep insecurity of many tenants – 40 per cent of the London population – to the surface. Newspapers were full of stories of exploitation and activities bordering on criminality.

The scandal quickly spilled over into fiction and film, in a spate of lodging-house stories which hit the presses in the early 1960s. Roy Ward Baker's 1961 film *Flame in the Streets*, which features a mini Notting Hill-style riot set off by disaffected Teddy boys, takes pains to establish that the grim conditions in which the immigrants live are largely the responsibility of their Jamaican landlord. The audience follows Sylvia Sims on her visit to the crumbling tenement where her black lover lives. We look into each one-room dwelling in turn: the Caribbean couple with two children, eating, washing, cooking and sleeping all in the same room; the free and easy black couple enjoying sex in the daytime; the mixed-race couple trying to pull themselves out of the slum but without anywhere else to go; the room shared by two working men, paying over the odds for anywhere at all to live. And we meet the landlord, a Jamaican wideboy: new car, smart camel-hair coat, sharp suit and tie, hat at a stylish angle. He wants the rent but turns a deaf ear to the pleas of his tenants to fix the plumbing.

One other example is Alexander Baron's bittersweet novel *The Lowlife*, about a Jewish East-End gambler, which was written in 1963 in the shadow of the crisis. The gambler-narrator, Harryboy Boas, is badly down on his luck, and toys with the possibility of making money by becoming a rack-renting landlord. Baron's character is a kind of inverse shadow of Rachman – he is friendly with a high-class prostitute, Marcia, but she ends up employing him (rather than the other way round) to collect money from the tenants of her string of slum lodging houses. There is a subplot with underworld heavies, who end up laying into the narrator when he gambles away the rent money. Harryboy keeps flirting with the idea of buying up condemned houses, however, and making money off migrant tenants.[15]

Sex, money and housing: it should come as no surprise that novelists should mix up the housing crisis with their more staple fare in the wake of the Rachman scandal. Yet the fictional character of the exploitative immigrant landlord pre-dates the Profumo affair. The nature of the London housing market handed opportunities to ruthless landlords, of whom Rachman was only one. In Andrew Salkey's 1960 novel *Escape to an Autumn Pavement*, the Caribbean wannabe hustlers discuss the merits of the housing lark as a way of breaking into the big time:

> You know anything about the house business in Britain? What I driving at is this: Real-estate investment, man! I going in for it, but with a syndicate of fellers behind me. I want to buy up all sort of house and fix them up and rent only to coloured people who come up on all these extravagant excursions ... Look now in a place like Brixton! You'll find the Jew man, the few clever Gentile ones, one or two Englishfied Orientals, and even the odd African! All of them doing one thing, and

doing that thing well. They catching the coloured people like flies on flypaper.[16]

And it was true that the housing market was wide open for anyone willing to rent to black migrants in the years before the 1968 Race Relations Act, which finally made discrimination in housing illegal. Black immigrants often had no option but to pay way over the odds for poor accommodation, and black landlords were just as ready as any other kind to take advantage of them. When Rachman's deputy, Edwards, who had first arrived in London to study law, was interviewed by the *News Chronicle* in 1960 he confirmed that he was about to become the owner of numbers 1–16 Powys Terrace, but suggested that the houses were a financial drain rather than an investment:

> Mr Edwards, who lives at number 9, where he once paid £6 a week for a three room flat, now owns a new coffee-coloured Cresta. He seems to regard himself as public spirited. 'I know the accommodation problems facing coloured people in England,' he said. 'That is what brought me into this business. I have a very big programme for these houses – decorating, improvements and so on – but my greatest problem is finance. I have made inquiries about home improvement grants but have been told it will be difficult to get them.' The income from the 16 houses – said by Councillor Baldwin to be £400 a week – does not exceed £230, said Mr Edwards, with mortgage repayments of over £600 a month . . . in one basement a coloured housewife with a husband and a baby told me she paid £2 6s. for one room. The other two basement rooms were let for £2 10s. and £2.[17]

'A two and ten room' entered the folklore, but people often paid more than £3 a week for one room, and it was not unusual to find a number of single men paying £1 a head to share a room, and often a bed. Andrew Salkey implied that the fault lay with the grasping, hustler mentality of the Jew, the Oriental, the African and his own Caribbean compatriots. But there were also structural reasons why immigrant landlords might have deserved their poor reputation.

Urban sociologists of the 1950s and 1960s liked to talk about 'zones of transition', inner-city areas of poor or condemned houses which were being abandoned as locals moved to new estates. New Commonwealth migrants, turned away as lodgers and tenants by many private landlords, ineligible for the council waiting lists and refused loans by reputable mortgage companies, could buy large houses for cash and pay back their loans by letting lodgings at exorbitant rents to other newcomers, people with nowhere better to go.

Ruth Glass analysed advertisements for furnished accommodation in North Kensington in late 1958: just over 1 in 8 had what she called an ' "anti-coloured" tag' (No Coloured, Europeans Only, White People only, English only), while a small portion actively encouraged applications from 'all nationalities', or even specified 'coloured only'. A year later the proportion of anti-coloured ads had gone up to 1 in 6. And a telephone sample of neutral ads brought only 1 in 6 willing to consider West Indian tenants: 'the other residents in the house are all white and they wouldn't like it'; 'It's really against the conditions but I have taken one or two Indian people. You know, they're not so dark. I mean, well I could get away with it if they were sort of not too obvious – well, if they are coffee-coloured, for example, or lighter'; 'how dark is he? I mean, some are jet black and some are more coffee-coloured. But if he's very dark we couldn't consider it'; 'they would be Negroes then? I don't think we'd like that. Also, they wouldn't be the same class. My tenants are middle class people.' This was politely referred to as a 'colour bar', rather than racism, and it offered a niche to men like the public-spirited Mr Edwards. Black landlords welcomed black tenants in many cases because they were desperate, and would pay over the odds for a room.[18]

For black landlords had themselves had to pay a premium for their properties and were always repaying loans. Deposits for house purchases could be financed on the 'sou-sou', or 'pardner' system – where a number of people paid into a kitty each month and each member of the group took the proceeds in turn. But most people still needed a loan for the principal amount, and without credit or backing they often ended up with very bad deals. Interest rates of 15 per cent were not uncommon, though the bank base rate was 4–6 per cent in the early 1960s. They paid the highest prices for some of the worst housing in the country, slum properties reaching the end of their leases, in need of major repair work, and often with tenants *in situ*. For the position of white and black landlords vis-à-vis their tenants was asymmetrical. White owners could – and very often did – refuse black tenants. Black owners who bought into the bottom of the market often found they had acquired white sitting tenants along with the bricks and mortar. Moreover, they were more likely to be owner-occupiers, so that the very fact of house purchase created an involuntary mixed-race community, one that was foisted on both sides.

The snakes and shrunken heads do not appear to have been merely the stuff of fantasy. In the first of a series of articles published in *New Society* in the mid-1960s, Nigerian writer Buchi Emecheta recounted how she – and her five children – were hounded out of their one-room dwelling by her Ghanaian live-in landlord and his wife, who performed 'magic' dances at night. The articles were later published as a book titled *In the Ditch*, though tellingly the ditch refers not to the gruesome hovel from which she escaped (populated by cockroaches and rats, with just the one bed for all six of them), but the cycle of poverty and dependency into which she subsequently fell when housed on a nearby council estate with its own full-time social worker. Voodoo practices as a way of getting rid of unwanted tenants were uncommon, however. Both immigrant and indigenous landlords had access to a range of simpler harassment techniques: playing loud music, removing light fittings, changing locks, removing doors, emptying buckets of excrement, blocking gutters with cement, and evicting tenants who had gone into hospital to give birth, were all among the examples cited by the Milner Holland Committee. The Committee estimated that 25 per cent of moves from unfurnished lodgings were not voluntary but forced on tenants by their landlord. The figure was 21 per cent for those in slightly more protected furnished accommodation.

Even without deliberate intimidation, there was plenty of room for tension between families squeezed into cramped conditions with inadequate facilities for washing or cooking, and sometimes no facilities at all. Shared toilets were a particular source of conflict. Smoking and dealing in weed, holding all-night parties, playing music – none of these activities were necessarily intended deliberately to annoy. Alexander Baron's fictional lodging house in Dalston features a young Caribbean couple who have absolutely no clue that making their bedsitter on the

Buying dried fish in Brixton Market, 1960s.

first floor open house for their friends might be a problem for the aspirant young white family on the ground floor. Nor, probably, was the behaviour of the 'vast Irish family' who lived above de Freitas in Powis Square calculated to cause him 'hang-ups'. Nonetheless, it did.

The public image of black landlords was riddled with contradictions. On the one hand they were doing what everyone was supposed to be doing in the never-had-it-so-good years: improving their lot, investing, capitalizing, pulling themselves up (and by their boot straps!) out of the submerged layer to which the working-class immigrant inevitably belonged. In this sense they were, or should have been, a force for good within the immigrant community, as far as the ideals of integration and assimilation went. In her study of Brixton, Sheila Patterson described the immigrant landlords as 'virtually the only source of social control within the West Indian group'. A. G. Bennett, a middle-class Jamaican correspondent writing to the *South London Press*, wondered why 'the same people who object to West

Indians collecting doles are also against West Indians buying homes to make themselves prosperous'. When a Mr Gladden wrote in asking how come West Indians could afford to buy houses when in Jamaica a labourer could earn only 2s. 6d. for loading five tons of bananas, Mr Bennett's rage was palpable:

> For Mr. Gladden's information, I am suggesting that Jamaicans get the money to buy houses in the following ways:
>
> 1. They starve themselves and save; 2. They pool their resources; 3. Some brought money which they either earned in America as farm workers or realised from property sold in Jamaica; 4. They work hard and long, denying themselves of all forms of pleasures and unnecessary expense; 5. One or two have been lucky at gambling and have had sizeable dividends from the pools; 6. Some have robbed their fellow men in various ways.
>
> With regard to the low pay which the banana-loader is said to receive, I hardly expect Mr. G. to gloat about that when it is remembered that the bananas are coming to Britain.
>
> I would think that he ought to choke with embarrassment every time he eats a banana knowing that he is nourishing himself with the blood, sweat and tears of his dusky fellow men.[19]

His point was that immigrants differ, like everyone else. But for the most part immigrant landlords were painted (by both white and black tenants, as well as by the media at large) as the polar opposite of a benign and virtuous middle-class force. They were hustlers, exploiters, pimps and thugs, like Rachman's henchmen, or the gangster landlord in *Flame in the Streets*. It was clear that making the step up into home ownership conferred social power, but two very different notions of authority battled it out in the stereotype of the immigrant landlord.

Both sides of this popular black-landlord currency were created by outsiders looking in, whether tenants, social workers, housing officers, parliamentarians, or the media. The stereotypes offered little or no insight into what it might have felt like for the immigrant landlords themselves. And this was especially the case because the stereotype tended to coalesce around Caribbean (and particularly Jamaican) landlords, although they were far outnumbered by their

Asian counterparts in all immigrant areas of the country except Notting Hill and Brixton. These two 'twilight' zones stood in, in the popular imagination, for all immigrant areas, though they were in fact atypical. A 1957 survey of West Bromwich, for example, found that forty-five out of seventy-two houses owned by 'coloured persons' belonged to Asian (Indian and Pakistani) owners, even though the West Indian population was nearly twice as large as the South Asian. West Indians were far more likely to be lodgers than homeowners. In effect, the image of the hustler black landlord was an image of Notting Hill and Brixton, even of Soho – of the racy criminal underworld that outsiders liked to fantasize was thriving behind the shopfronts, the bricked-up houses and the corrugated iron.[20]

South Asian landlords were as given to exploitation as any other nationality, of course. But the kinds of power that homeownership brought them didn't fit either the aspirant middle-class assimilator type or that of gangster outsider, hustling for power on the streets. Investment in British bricks and mortar was, first and foremost, a practical response to high rents and the difficulty of finding any kind of accommodation at all. It was certainly a form of financial investment, particularly as far as the early years of frugal all-male households went. The point was not to settle in England, still less to gain status in English society, but to make money to send home, and thereby raise one's status within one's own community.

The stereotype of the Pakistani or Indian landlord was less that he was given to intimidating his white tenants with snakes and shrunken heads than that he was fond of stuffing his home full of men sleeping top to toe in rows, failed to deal with household waste and butchered chickens in his back garden. In other words he made life hell not for his white tenants but for his white neighbours. Yet in fact a large number of Asian landlords did let out rooms to a racially mixed tenantry. Mixed Pakistani, Indian, Irish, Welsh and Jamaican households were a staple feature of early 1960s sociology, and the pictures painted there – away from the pumped-up rhetoric of the newspapers in the wake of Rachman – offer a rather different perspective on the effects of the housing crisis.

The Pakistani-Irish household – comprising a Pakistani landlord living alongside a mixed Asian and Irish tenantry – crops up everywhere, in Yorkshire, the Midlands, Southall and right across London. Muhammad Anwar, writing about Rochdale in the early 1960s, recounted tales of long-standing Irish girlfriends as well as more formal, instrumental relationships between landlord and tenant: 'I have three Irishmen living in one of my houses and I sometimes go and speak to them for hours as they are all single men. I get a lot of language practice like this.' John Rex and Robert Moore argued that the multi-racial households they encountered in Birmingham's Sparkbrook in 1964 were parallel rather than integrated ethnic arenas, with the different races segregated within the rooms of the lodging house. There was clearly a good deal of truth to this. Single Irish men, like Irish couples with young children, were not lodging in overcrowded condemned housing because they wanted to but because they had no choice, in the context of an acute housing shortage. In 1956 Rashmi Desai, a Gujarati anthropologist who carried out a study of Indians living in Britain for the Institute of Race Relations, got to know a mixed Gujarati, Punjabi, West Indian and Irish household – the homeowner was a Gujarati bus conductor in Birmingham and his lodgers all worked as conductors or drivers at the same depot. The house was divided into bed-sitters and the thirteen inhabitants comprised the Gujarati owner and his nephew, three of their friends, an Indian student, a West Indian with his common law wife, an Irish woman, her husband and child, and her unmarried sister, and a Punjabi:

> The Irish family occupied the rooms on the second floor, and the West Indian couple had a room on the first floor. They both had double gas rings inside the rooms, and double beds. The Indians, with the exception of the Punjabi, used the kitchen and dining room on the ground floor. The Punjabi mixed with the others freely, but used a gas ring in his own room for cooking.

The lodging houses were homes, but ones in which the relationships between inhabitants were driven by the market. One Indian landlord charged an Irish family of five £3 10s. to live in one room (at a time when £2 was a lot to pay). He argued (with a certain amount of twisted logic) that he was doing them a favour, as they were poor people who would otherwise have to pay £7 for two rooms.[21]

Yet the stories gathered by Rex and Moore speak as much of domestic accommodation as of tension and rivalry: an Irish woman who cut through the stand-off over cleaning the communal cooker and was rewarded with chocolates by her Asian co-lodgers; the teasing of the landlord by an Irish woman who spoke to him as though he were a small child, 'to his great amusement', or another who insisted on curtseying and addressing her landlord as 'O Great King'. It is not, of course, irrelevant that the Irish – and to a certain extent the Welsh – were outsiders themselves. These tenants were racially mixed, but they all shared the experience of migration. As Rashmi Desai argued in 1963, 'Only Irish, West Indians and Pakistanis (all immigrants) willingly accept accommodation in Indian houses.' And he pointed out that racial segregation need have nothing to do with colour. While it was common to find Indian Punjabis sharing accommodation with Pakistanis, it was unheard of to find Bengalis (i.e. East Pakistanis) who were prepared to do the same. Badr Dahya similarly found 'Mirpuris, Chhachhis, Pathans and Punjabis, and, in some cases Sikh immigrants also, living together' in Bedford, Luton, Watford, Crawley and parts of London in the mid-1960s. But in all cases, East and West Pakistanis kept their distance. In Abdullah Hussein's story 'The Journey Back', two Bengalis do share accommodation with different groups of people from Pakistan, but they are tolerated only because they work for the other lodgers, and they are never allowed to forget their subordinate status, coming last in the queue for the bathroom, the kitchen and the ritual Sunday afternoon visit of the local prostitute. 'The Bengalis weren't all that naïve, but what could they do, being outnumbered six to one by the Hafizabadis and Mirpuris. So one of them ended up cooking for the Hafizabadis, while the other did the shopping for both floors. In return, they were left alone.' After all, as Rashmi Desai put it, 'an immigrant's home . . . is an immigrant's castle'.[22]

15
Teachers

Why doesn't the government make proper arrangements? Old men, sixty years old marrying twenty year old girls coming from the Punjab! Forty year old widow women are requesting unripe boys as fiancés. Nieces and nephews, mother's brother's sons, sister-in-law's sons, the whole lot are presented as their own children to be brought across. Sisters make husbands of their brothers to bring them over. Then tell me what else can one say? Then they say the government is making restrictions.

Pritam Sidhu, 'Fauji Bhadwan Singh' (1982)[1]

The 1962 Commonwealth Immigrants Act had a major effect on the character of migrant life in Britain, particularly for South Asians. There were two principal reasons for this. First, the introduction of the voucher system profoundly altered the social make-up of the migrants from India and Pakistan. Category B vouchers were reserved for people with 'specific skills and training' which were in short supply in Britain. This was code for educated people, and was designed to cut down on the numbers of low-paid workers entering the country.

The new rules did encourage those with more than purely economic ambition to make the journey – teachers, engineers, printers and craftsmen. A survey in Bradford in 1966 found that of sixty graduate migrants, only four had arrived before the 1962 Act.[2] In the first years, due to a combination of their own uncertain command of spoken English and others' prejudice against them, the voucher men mostly worked in manual jobs, rather than in the posts for which

Beating the ban: a man arrives
at London airport on a flight
from Karachi, carrying his bed
roll, 1962.

they were trained. Yet it was this generation of immigrants who
would go on to produce cultural, religious and political leaders –
newspaper men, writers, the men (and a few women) who would take
forward the work of the Indian Workers' Association and other campaigning groups, the founders of gurdwaras and mosques. They
arrived a decade later than West Indian intellectuals such as V. S.
Naipaul, Stuart Hall and George Lamming, and they were to operate
in very different circumstances. This was not only because they wrote
and campaigned in Punjabi, Hindustani and Urdu, rather than English, and their focus was necessarily on their own communities. It
was also because they entered a country where the battle lines over
'coloured' immigration had already been clearly drawn.

The second major effect of the 1962 Act, as discussed earlier, was
to consolidate family life in Britain – in effect to make migration
permanent. For many years men from India and Pakistan had put in
time in British factories and foundries, but returned home periodic-
ally to their families (often staying for up to two years), which

remained firmly rooted in their local villages. The fear of no longer being allowed back in, if they stayed away for long, led to a kind of collective decision to import family members into Britain. For the wives, children and (sometimes) parents of permanent settlers were still eligible for permits under the new Act. The numbers tell the story: 646 voucher holders arrived from India in the last six months of 1962. This increased dramatically to 8,366 in 1963, until numbers levelled off at between 2,000 and 3,000 a year. The number of dependants who made the journey in 1962 was 645, but this shot up to 6,616 in 1963, 8,770 in 1964, 12,798 in 1965 and 13,357 in 1966. It was the same from Pakistan, with a spike of voucher holders arriving in 1963 (13,526) and 9,319 dependants arriving in 1966 – an increase of more than 1,800 per cent in five years.[3]

The decision to bring over your wife and children was not prompted solely, or even marginally, by sentiment. Now that it was no longer possible to sponsor members of your extended family to work beside you it made economic sense to bring your sons instead. Sons would eventually be able to 'replace' the earning power of their fathers. And there were other, less well-foreseen economic consequences of bringing the family to England. For a start, wives and daughters could work too, either inside the family home, or – for the Indian Punjabi and Gujarati communities in particular – in factories, in hospitals and at London airport. Women's paid work was obviously to increase overall household incomes in Britain, but it also opened the door to challenges to a father's or a husband's power and authority in the family. Once women had their own incomes, and knew how to spend them, the frugal post-war bachelor years were well and truly over. Like a delayed echo of the upwardly mobile, consumerist paradise that was supposed to be the mark of working-class culture in the 1950s ('You've never had it so good!'), Asian families began to take advantage of solid wages, affordable goods and leisure opportunities to build new lives in Britain. They began spending in England rather than sending their money back home. One of the long-term consequences of this shift was that caste status – never to be knocked off its social perch entirely – began to be challenged by other kinds of status. Wealth and 'class', understood in British terms, were to become as, and sometimes more, important.

Professionals and families: these two new categories of migrants were not distinct or merely parallel consequences of the new Act. They were both to play a self-conscious part in the building of the settled Asian community in Britain, not least in realigning the relationships between financial independence, family life and sexual mores. Ironically it was those with the least financial incentive for migration – the trained teachers, printers, skilled craftsmen and engineers who arrived on category B vouchers – who were to cast the clearest eye on the economic impact of migration. They not only lived through but also dissected the effects of greater financial independence, for both men and women, on a changing social and sexual morality. And they were well placed to analyse the day-to-day murky compromises between money and morals because, although they tended to be higher caste, educated individuals who had been professionals at home in India and Pakistan, in Britain they became invisibly part of the mass of Asian migrants. Unable to land jobs in their chosen professions at least for the first years, they lived and worked instead alongside their labouring and shop-keeping brothers.

The language barrier initially created a very enclosed landscape for Asian cultural activity (as well as political and religious activity) among these first-generation migrants. Lack of confidence in spoken English meant that caste, and later class, gradations counted for little during the early 1960s, and arguably this became a strength as journalists and writers came face to face with the realities of migration for the ordinary man and woman. They had to take the dead-end jobs, along with everyone else. But beyond that, these writers were cut off from English-language audiences. There would be no V. S. Naipaul or Edna O'Brien, celebrated by an English and international readership, among this generation of Asian writers, who published in Punjabi and Urdu in ephemeral newspapers and journals both in Britain and back home. Their work mirrored the lives of the migrant men and women about whom they wrote: intensely concerned with shaping and maintaining the contours of their previous lives in a new and alien environment, keen for success, yes, but success measured by the yardstick of a purely Asian readership. Even now the majority of Punjabi stories, poems and memoirs written about England in the 1960s and 1970s have not been translated into English.

Like the wave of Caribbean writers that washed into Britain around 1950, Punjabi writers appeared to travel en masse. In 1964 Pritam Sidhu, at twenty-seven years old, was the head teacher of a private school in Patiala, in the Punjab. With a degree in English from the University of Chandigarh, and a Masters in Punjabi literature, he describes the impulse to emigrate as principally one of 'curiosity'. He applied for one of the priority vouchers for professional teachers and left his wife, Surjit, and two children, aged five and two months old, to join relatives in Hounslow. His family would join him six months later.[4]

He was not the only teacher to leave the Punjab for West London that year. Shivcharan Gill had a degree in English and Sociology from the Punjab University and a BT (Bachelor of Teacher Training), and was, also at twenty-seven, head teacher of a middle school, in Kaunke Kalan. He also decided to try out the voucher system in 1964, leaving his wife and three children with his in-laws for almost a year. Gill described his decision not in financial terms, but as the 'lure of Western life'.[5]

Like many highly educated Punjabi migrants, the Sidhus initially found spoken English a challenge. Surjit had read Shakespeare and Hardy at university, but found 'I couldn't understand the milkman, even.' Pritam Sidhu's first job, despite the teacher's voucher, was in the canteen at London airport. Later he moved to Woolf's rubber factory in Southall. Shivcharan Gill worked nearby in the British Airways Catering Department. Later he laboured alongside large numbers of fellow Indians at the Magnatex/Rockware glass factory in Greenford, and, again, at Woolf's.

There is a potent myth around Southall that the local Asian settlement started because of Woolf's – specifically that migrants were encouraged to move to the area because a manager at Woolf's, who had spent part of the war in India, was well disposed to Punjabi labour. Woolf's was a classic example of an unmodernized factory in which labourers were expected to work for low wages in very hot, dirty conditions – conditions which were to precipitate a major strike of Indian workers in 1965. As with the Midlands foundries and the textile mills in Bradford and Rochdale, it proved impossible to attract local workers to these jobs during the boom years of the mid-1950s.

According to Shivcharan Gill, who worked in the factory in the mid-1960s, the first Asian employees at Woolf's commuted from Aldgate East in the early 1950s. They were the children and relatives of migrant peddlers who had come to Britain as seamen during the 1930s, had worked building aerodromes during the war, and in the early post-war years had begun to buy up tailoring and clothing concerns in East London (as the long-settled Jewish population moved north). From about 1958 Punjabi workers were coming directly to Southall from the Punjab, bypassing East London altogether. The need for migrant workers to boost the economy was so great that there was no limit put on the number of relatives and friends that permanent settlers could sponsor, and a steady stream of Punjabi men duly arrived. It was unusual among late 1950s and 1960s male migrants not to have put in a spell at Woolf's – which employed 40 per cent of all Southall Asian men in the late 1950s – or the Mother's Pride bakery in Greenford, or on the night shift at Nestlé's, at least until something better turned up.

For the educated men on vouchers these factories were a challenge, though naturally they got the pick of the soft jobs. The white foreman at Woolf's was surprised that Pritam Sidhu knew any English at all since most of his fellow countrymen 'could speak two words'. He was given the task of collecting rubber samples from across the factory for testing. An aspiring writer, Sidhu describes the series of manual jobs he undertook as 'school for me', and a source of 'helpful material'. It gave him daily access to Indians of a different class, whom he would only have encountered from a position of authority while a head teacher back in the Punjab, and brought him into close contact with a rich oral culture. And because he spoke both English and Punjabi: 'I could read the psyche of the white man also, and see what he thought of the black man.'

The language of race and colour tells us a good deal about Sidhu's world-view. The broadly left-leaning politics of the voucher migrants made them hyper-alert to the costs as well as the benefits of migration, and much of their writing – both creative and political – focused on the experience of prejudice and racism in Britain, the corruptions and moral compromises necessary in order to succeed in an industrial economy, and the destruction of traditional family life and community born of the desire to become 'clothed in pound notes'. Migration to England raised the status of those who left in the eyes of those who stayed, and it was certainly a way of earning money, but without exception Indian writers of this first generation felt there was too heavy a price to pay for it. They shared this pessimism with the men of the Indian Workers' Association – indeed several of the writers were also active in the Association – a broadly Marxist-oriented group in these early years, whose members often had links to the Communist Party of India.

The writers formed a dedicated group that met each Saturday at the Railway Tavern in Southall (later better known as the Glassy Junction), where they would try out their poems and stories on one another, washing them down with large amounts of whisky and beer. At its height there were twenty-nine regular Punjabi members of the Progressive Writers' Association. Their shared conviction that Indian and Pakistani workers in Britain had become an exploited underclass, and were trading their culture and values for the lure of the pound note, derived in part from revolutionary Marxist politics. But it also had to do with their own personal experiences in Britain, and in particular the fact that they found themselves suddenly catapulted into the heart of the industrial proletariat. Much of their writing is marked by nostalgia and regret, contrasting the adventurous spirit with which the migrants had set out with the way they quickly became bound to shift work and overtime, fettered to the disciplines of mechanized industrial life, or – in the case of women – trapped inside isolated homes, cut off from the communal life of the village. The former subsistence farmers of the Punjab may have become wealthier, but at what cost, working from seven till seven, seven nights a week? The immigrant's alphabet read 'O is for Overtime, P is for Pound'. The number of hours a man stacked up in overtime weighed in the balance against the money he needed to pay off the debts he had incurred in getting to England, to buy land and finance improvements back home, and – if it were ever possible – to save enough so that one day he could go back.

This was life determined by arithmetic, and for many of the more privileged migrants it was a shock. There is a revealing moment in an autobiographical piece by Ranjit Dheer, who had taught at the

Government College in Muktsar before he moved to Britain, where he worked for a time in the Mother's Pride bakery. 'Here,' he says, 'you have money but lead the life of a *harijan*' – someone of the lowest caste. It wasn't just that families had to make migration pay – they also had to make it look like it was paying. Dheer described the elaborate and costly arrangements people made for taking a trip back to the Punjab, loading themselves down with cameras, tape recorders, gold bangles and expensive clothes, and having to spend extravagantly all the time they were at home:

> When there is so much money, who needs to ask where the money came from? And then who is to tell the truth? That this money is earned in factories, working day and night, twelve or fourteen hour daily shifts, pushing a broom in the airport terminal or factory, doing washing up, cleaning toilets, being a bus conductor and going out at six in the morning, in freezing weather, to deliver the post.[6]

All this may have been true, but Dheer wrote from a position of one who knew that he definitely was not a *harijan*, and for whom long hours and back-breaking work was – or should be – alien. Precisely because the voucher men had responded to the 'lure of Western life' rather than pragmatic economic need, they were more likely to be disappointed with what they found. The Dalit castes themselves, and the many intermediate castes used to hard work in their villages, were arguably no worse off in England than at home; indeed, they might find they were rather better treated in English factories than at home. And the marginal differences between rural and industrial slavery were made up for by money and opportunity. It is a telling fact that very few accounts by lower-caste Indians labouring in Britain in the 1950s and 1960s mention problems of racial discrimination. Arguably they were far too used to being discriminated against to notice.

One of the ironies of the 'middle-class', educated writers' pessimistic take on moneyed migrant life in Britain was that they depended – for publication and readership – on the existence of a new, moneyed middle class willing to support them and to invest in British-Punjabi culture in general. The newspapers which carried their stories and poems needed to carry advertisements to help balance their books – they needed, therefore, a local, middle-class and shop-owning, cinema-going, consumer-oriented clientele. It was stories about these people – their pretensions, moral compromises, successes and tragedies – that formed the core of the Punjabi literature and folk song of the 1960s.

The early migrant years of Santokh Singh Santokh – a trained printer and compositor from Bilga in Jalandhar – provides a neat gloss on this process. Santokh arrived in Britain in June 1962 on a category B voucher. He had a decent job in the city nearest to his village, Phagwara, but since one month's salary was equivalent to one day's in England, it made economic sense for him to try a stint abroad. Aged twenty-four, he had been married for five years and had two children. He left his family (they would join him three years later) to stay with his paternal aunt, who was married to a Punjabi who worked in Woolf's rubber factory. They had bought a house in Lady Margaret Road, Southall, on the rubber-factory wages. In what was becoming traditional fashion, the family kept two rooms for themselves and rented out the rest – there were eleven people living in the house altogether. When the family later moved to Slough to open a shop, Santokh was put in charge of collecting the rent from the tenants. Meanwhile he worked, and since the printing unions operated a closed shop, he worked in what were becoming the traditional places: Mother's Pride and Magnatex, as well as stints as a petrol-pump attendant and a mechanic's assistant. And in his spare time he set the print for the first Punjabi newspapers, newsletters and campaigning leaflets.[7]

The first paper printed for the Punjabi Indian migrant population in England was the *Punjab Times*, the brainchild of Gurnam Singh Sahni, president of the Sikh Gurdwara in Shepherd's Bush. The newspaper was bankrolled by eleven religious-minded Sikhs who each provided £100 of capital to get it going. The paper's more secular, and more popular, rival was *Des Pardes* (literally meaning 'home abroad'), founded by the colourful entrepreneur Tarsem Purewal (later the victim of an unsolved murder), who brought out the first issue in 1965 when he was just thirty years old.[8]

Sex and sexual relationships was the one topic that united the salacious pages of *Des Pardes* with the pessimistic and often tragic tales told by Punjabi prose writers and the exuberant lyrics of contemporary Punjabi folk songs. This should come as no surprise. The arrival of wives and children following the 1962 Act heralded the decision to consolidate life in Britain, to become immigrants rather than continue the migrant back-and-forth habits of the 1950s. And it brought profound changes to the domestic and sexual life of the Asian community.

Marriage had always been a matter of status and finance – an arrangement between two extended families concerned to stabilize or improve their standing and their prestige by making the right sort of alliance. Marriage was a question of family rather than individual ambition, let alone personal choice or desire. The financial element was openly acknowledged through the system of gifts flowing from the bride's to the groom's family. None of this disappeared in the new landscape in Britain, but it did become a great deal more complicated.

For men who already had families back in India, the new, post-1962 arrangements must have seemed relatively simple – though the shock to the system when their families actually arrived, and their bachelor days were over, may have been real nonetheless. But there were plenty of people to whom the new wave of spousal and family migration offered all kinds of opportunities: to get rid of unwanted wives (or husbands) and find new ones; to scrub out unfortunate 'mistakes' in their past and start afresh; or to make money on the side, arranging transnational marriages. There were opportunists on both sides of the continental divide. Families in the Punjab who wanted to palm off a daughter perceived as too old for marriage, or one who had blotted her copybook in the past, would accept an arrangement with an older, or less-educated, man, or one who had already been divorced. Conversely, men who in India might have found it hard to make a 'good' match held the promise of life in England in their hands. Likewise English-based families could reject dark-skinned or poorly educated men for their daughters and enter negotiations with light-skinned rural boys instead – despite the culture clash that might ensue. In effect, the promise of getting to England through marriage added a whole extra layer to what was already a very intricate business transaction. And like the dodges, partial truths and just plain lies with which European Voluntary Workers, and Irish and Caribbean migrants, peppered their passport and permit applications, it was the combination of a confident bureaucracy and lack of reliable information which made these arrangements possible.

Given a situation where most people were not issued with birth certificates, and with a thriving trade in forged papers back in India and Pakistan, it was almost impossible for the United Kingdom immigration department to disprove claims made about marriage and familial relationships, particularly when it was in the interests of both sides to keep up the fiction – both those already in England who wanted to bring people in, and those desperate to arrive. As a character in a story by Pritam Sidhu complains, the promise of being able to get to England rendered all sorts of unions viable which should not have been: old men marrying young girls, widows requesting 'unripe boys', and all sorts of distant relatives being passed off as children or fiancées, in order to get through the border. People were found with crib sheets in their luggage, having been coached for days about what to say at the airport to prove they were somebody's brother or son, or that they had previously lived in Britain and were returning to work. One man was told by an agent to claim to have lived there before the 1962 Act. He was turned back at the airport when his story unravelled, and he could not name the factories where he had worked, or the towns where he had lived. He had sold his plot of land to pay the agent and had to go back to nothing.

At the same time the government was keen to control family migrants, and there is plenty of evidence of bad faith on both sides. After the battle over the racist elements in the 1962 Act, immigration services were careful to maintain a colour-neutral front to their work, but there is no doubt that they were under pressure to curb the numbers of black and Asian family members entering the country. And the general belief that Indian and Pakistani families were bent on tricking them played into their hands. Immigrants arriving at London airport and claiming to be relatives or fiancées of permanent residents were subjected to intrusive questioning (though this was long before the notorious virginity tests of the late 1970s, which were ostensibly carried out to determine whether a woman was a genuine fiancée, or already married). A 1966 social services study at the airport (which had recently been renamed Heathrow) noted that the flights from Pakistan carried three kinds of passenger: returning residents, women with children, and unaccompanied fifteen-year-olds. Some lone children were as young as ten. A proportion of them were routinely sent back if the immigration officers were not satisfied that they were actually the offspring of the parents they claimed. Children were interviewed separately from their guardians, and questioned about their family history, the names of relations and place of residence. If the answers were inconsistent they were sent back. Or they had to answer a range of questions about their schooling and what they had done since school to see if their story matched the age they claimed to be. If the officers were unsure, they took X-rays of teeth and wrist bones to determine maturity. Given the language difficulties, and sheer fear which many of these children must have felt, it is obvious that sometimes genuine children, and genuine spouses, were sent back. But this was regarded as inevitable. 'We have heard that in Pakistan the relatives who brought the child to the airport often wait around for a couple of days in case the child should be

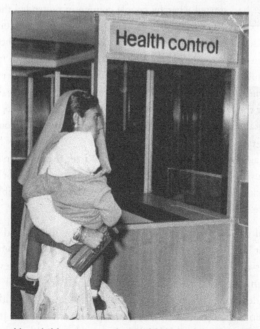

A woman and her child are sent to the Health Unit at London airport in 1965.

returned.' There was no requirement to provide a written explanation of why entry had been refused – people were sent back on the
next plane rather than given time to provide evidence that they were
who they said they were.[9]

A report on the Health Control Unit at Heathrow by the deputy
senior medical officer reveals the extent to which the doctors saw
themselves not merely as gatekeepers against disease, but as far as
possible against immigrants in general. Part of the remit of medical
officers stationed at ports of entry was to attempt to prevent NHS
tourism, and to provide a bulwark against the spread of communic-
able diseases, such as TB. Under the 1962 Commonwealth Immigrants
Act, officers had no power to refuse entry permission on medical
grounds to returning residents, or wives, or children under sixteen.
By contrast, medical examinations were routine for people travelling
on labour vouchers, as well as for fiancées and those over sixty. Age
became a battleground:

> A racket had started whereby people coming in pretended they were
> under sixteen because if they were under sixteen they could join either
> parent or an uncle or aunt, but if they were over sixteen they could
> only join both parents and they needed a labour voucher. So to defeat
> this regulation a number had pretended that they were under sixteen
> and some of them had been really old chaps! Therefore it was neces-
> sary for the doctors to examine them to look for the presence of hair,
> to look at the state of the genitalia and if there was any doubt they
> were X-rayed.
>
> Old age was a problem. It was very difficult to say a person who
> was above the age of 60. They could judge by the texture and elasticity
> of the skin and condition of the hair, but it was not possible to be
> accurate.[10]

Like all trades, this trade in bodies had its winners and its losers,
though it was sometimes hard to tell which was which. The
sixty-year-old grooms may have been smiling when they brought
their young brides home, but then they had to control them. As
Southall developed its character as a small Asian city, with its busy
market centre, shops and cinemas, along with the relative freedom to
enjoy them associated with English towns, that could prove difficult:

'On Saturday in Southall bachelors are like married men, and old married men are like bachelors. When seventeen-year-old girls are brought over to marry old men of sixty, what else can you expect?'[11] Then there was the problem of spouses changing their minds. It became rumoured that boys from the Punjab would marry anyone to get to England, and then, once they had residency, they would divorce that wife and bring another from home. By the late 1960s it had happened often enough for families to try to insert extra legal guarantees into marriage arrangements.

Moreover, it was easier to dissolve marriages which had been arranged transnationally. (Sometimes, in fact, people got married by phone, never having seen one another.) The immigration and residency regulations put in place by the British government often did not help matters. Prospective spouses who arrived in Britain (often without having met their future partners) were given a three-month temporary visa, which did not include the right to work. Full residency rights were only stamped in the passport when the marriage had been properly solemnized and the couple were living together. But problems often arose when either men or women arrived, without support, and were rejected by their future families. There were tragic cases of suicides of young women who felt the shame of returning to their families in India, and of men who were rejected after suffering accidents (which compromised their ability to work) during the three-month waiting period: 'With their British-passport-holding daughters they can barter for someone else's son and if something bad happens, if nature's rage goes against him, they sling him out like dirty rubbish.'[12]

Many of the popular Punjabi songs from this period riff off the personal and cultural clashes born of mixing up marriage with emigration, and the British government's attempts to control the marriage market through legislation. Up until the late 1960s a girl could get a husband from the Punjab without much difficulty. He might be an unsophisticated rural type, but at least there was a good deal of choice in terms of caste and health and looks. And while this pool was available fathers could look down on their fellow-immigrants' sons. And the sociologist Arthur Helweg argued that 'rather than a girl from England, families generally preferred an uneducated village girl, who was more likely to be humble and obedient towards the mother-in-law. Young men in Punjab were happy to marry the girls abroad because it gave them an opportunity to migrate.'¹³ But the 1968 Immigration Act changed the rules for girls in England, who were prohibited from sponsoring boys from the Punjab, although there was no rule against boys bringing village girls to the United Kingdom. The song-writers enjoyed the shifting balances of power:

> Taran Taran Taran!
> Dipu
> Stop looking over your shoulder.
> No more Sikhs are coming.
> No fiancés are coming now from the Panjab.
> For the government has decreed it so.
> Now be my girl-friend and let's enjoy ourselves.
> I can even buy a Zephyr or a Jaguar for you to ride in.¹⁴

She might be his girlfriend, maybe, but probably nothing more unless her parents could afford a healthy dowry. The gift of furniture or a car or a house might tip the balance in favour of an immigrant bride. Over the years the meaning of the dowry shifted from being a gift signalling the economic protection of women, to a method to gain prestige, to secure partners with wealth and status, or to compensate for 'unmarriagable' girls.

In 1969 the Labour government introduced the Immigration Appeals Act, setting up an independent tribunal for appeals but also requiring spouses and children to obtain entry certification before travelling to Britain. In practice this process was slow and costly, and the backlog of applicants in India, Pakistan and (from 1971) Bangladesh caused waiting times of over two years. But there were also plenty of more lonely, even tragic, consequences of the trade in transnational marriages, and the culture clashes they precipitated. Young girls sent as brides from India had often been well educated in Hindi and Punjabi, for example, but they joined men in England who may have had little opportunity to learn skills beyond those they would need on the factory floor. But probably the biggest problem was being isolated from relatives. Life for a woman left at home in the Punjab with her in-laws might be grim, but it was probably less desolate than

the existence of the woman brought to England to live under thumb
of her mother-in-law:

> Better that I had stayed in my village,
> Passing my days shaping the cow-dung cakes
> Better that I had stayed there, drawing water
> From the well and taking the men's food to the fields.
> Better that I had stayed in my mud house, mending and plastering its walls.
> I would at least have been queen in my own home.
> If I had not come to this country
> I would not have suffered this torture.
> O God, grant that my mother-in-law may die,
> Who demands that I hand over my unopened pay packet.[15]

Of course, if life under the thumb of your mother-in-law could be
bad, life in a nuclear family might be worse; for both men and women
the new experience of living as a couple, outside the extended family
network, could itself prove challenging. Rates of domestic violence
and female suicide were high, with feminist organizations such as the
Southall Black Sisters later arguing that there was a conspiracy of
silence about the abuses of transnational arranged marriages, for fear
of giving the British government an excuse to tighten immigration
rules still further.[16] It would take years before the issue began to be
addressed openly. And violence was only one consequence of the new
forms of intimate relationship which fusing Asian and Western marriage offered – there were also all the freedoms associated with getting
away from your elders and making up new ways of being a family in
England.

16

Scroungers

One day, however, when my heart was low, I betook myself to a labour exchange, a tastefully appointed building in Camden Town, looking like something left over from the Festival of Britain which had been spat on too often and could never be cleanly swept out. There were long queues, appearing to consist of three main classes of persons. There were the gloomy, intent and resentful representatives of the English working classes, the rightful heirs and beneficiaries of this whole set-up. There were the darkies, Maltese, Cypriots, and Irish, all in fine fettle, exchanging salutations and jokes in a variety of languages and dialects ... They had landed on these hospitable shores in full expectation of being allowed to put their hands to the plough. Finding no work available they traversed the hospitable road from the labour exchange to the National Assistance Board. In the first they were solemnly assured that there was in fact nothing at the moment; in the second they collected their money, after which they retired, the Irish to the Rowton and the adjacent pubs, there to continue their temporarily interrupted quarrels; the Cypriots to the room over the caff; the Maltese to check the girls' earnings; the West Indians to the fug of crowded, happy rooms in Notting Hill Gate where the smoke of reefers mingled with the soft sing-song of another clime and the memories of perennial sunshine.

Anthony Cronin, *The Life of Riley* (1964)[1]

Having conspicuously failed as a BBC hack, and close to destitute, the anti-hero of Anthony Cronin's satirical novel *The Life of Riley* decides to throw himself on the bounty, if not the mercy, of the British welfare system. Like the fictional Riley, Cronin spent some time in the early 1950s living in the Rowton House in Camden, so following in the footsteps of George Orwell, who had stayed there more than twenty years earlier while researching *Down and Out in Paris and London*. Unlike Orwell, however, Cronin really was hard up for accommodation, and (albeit briefly) joined the throng of his fellow countrymen in the Rowton hostel out of necessity rather than choice. While there he may well have run into Dónall Mac Amhlaigh, who was to publish his Irish-language account of life as a jobbing labourer, including a description of kipping at the Rowton, in 1960. Moreover, other writers, such as Brendan Behan and Patrick Kavanagh, also put in a stint there in the 1950s, suggesting that the line between Irish labourer and Irish bohemian was rather fine, at any rate when it came to where you slept.

The Camden Town Rowton was the largest of a string of vast institutions built by a Victorian philanthropist to provide cheap and clean lodgings for working men. Opened in 1905, it could accommodate 1,103 men in individual cubicles, each with a bed, a chair and – luxury for such lodgings at the time – a window which opened and closed. A big step up from the doss-house or the casual ward of the workhouse, the Rowtons were initially occupied by poor working men: clerks, labourers, craftsmen and apprentices. During the war the Camden Rowton was used to billet troops, and as a transit stop for evacuees; later it became a hostel for Poles and EVWs. By the mid-1950s the huge winged building in Arlington Road was largely occupied by nomadic (and, according to Cronin, raucous and untamed) Irishmen, who were silently tolerated by the long-term residents, elderly English working men who had nowhere better to go. Cronin paid a daily two shillings and threepence; by the mid-1960s it was three shillings and sixpence a night for 'a cubicle and a bed and a chamber-pot':

> There was a canteen which was comparatively safe, for the Irish scorned to eat; and there was a television room which was altogether safe, for the ranks of third Ypres veterans who sat there in caps and mufflers would, it was tacitly understood, have torn the Irish apart had they dared to intrude upon the most precious of a pensioner's remaining pleasures.[2]

The Rowton Houses did not technically form part of British post-war welfare provision – they were charitable institutions, initially intended as an alternative to privately run, overcrowded and insanitary cheap lodging houses. But anyone billeted there who was also out of work could claim unemployment benefit, or in the worst case, means-tested 'National Assistance', the replacement for relief under the Poor Law. The National Assistance Board (NAB) began life at the same time as the National Health Service, in 1948, but unlike the NHS National Assistance was in turn replaced (by Supplementary Benefit) in 1966. National Assistance was intended as help for people who slipped through other nets; it provided cash payments to the homeless, or unmarried mothers, for example, who didn't pay National Insurance contributions, and therefore were not eligible for unemployment benefit. And it provided financial top-ups for those unable to pay their rent, or afford basic food and clothing. Like the dole, National Assistance formed a front line in complaints that immigrants were abusing the welfare system, as a series of social problems – the housing crisis, unemployment in times of recession, illegitimacy, for example – were reconfigured as problems caused by immigrants.

Colonial and Commonwealth citizens had the same rights of citizenship as those who were British born, which meant that they had the same rights to social security. Popular anxiety about immigrant numbers could be rationalized as a practical problem of finite resources – surely the country's coffers could not stand up to an 'influx' or a 'flood' of newcomers who were unable or unwilling to help themselves. But the complaints about what would later be termed 'benefit tourism' also touched on more inchoate fears about the boundaries of belonging. The welfare state had been built to provide healthcare and social support to the native British, the working poor (and indeed, as William Beveridge had intended, the middle classes) who had suffered through the hungry 1930s, and fought the war, to finally be rewarded with the protections they had long deserved. By default, welfare provision was for them, not other people, and certainly not for 'foreigners'. In 1961 – in the run up to the 1962 Commonwealth Immigrants Act – a Gallup survey found that the principal reason (chosen by 46 per cent of respondents) given for opposition to 'coloured immigration' was that 'they have to be supported by our welfare services'. In 1967, long after restrictive legislation had been introduced, the number of people worried about immigrants claiming welfare had gone up to 49 per cent.[3] Right-wing popular opinion was wedded to the belief that work-shy immigrants were arriving in Britain expressly in order to leach off the state.

In fact as Anthony Cronin puts it, it was precisely because of all the sound and fury over immigrant scroungers that his alter-ego Riley decides to try his luck at the labour exchange. 'The Tory newspapers had been full of reports about the vast sums which the welfare state was disbursing to the undeserving poor', and encouraged by the adverse publicity Riley takes his chance, along with the mixed clientele of the Camden dole office: 'the darkies', the Maltese, the Cypriots and the Irish. There, however, he falls foul of a bureaucratic technicality. Since he has only a nightly, rather than a weekly, ticket for the Rowton, he is classed as homeless, and therefore ineligible for unemployment benefit. ('The Tory papers were quite wrong. Far more than private Victorian charity it [the welfare state] favoured only the deserving poor.') All he gets is a week's board in a Salvation Army hostel and five shillings pocket money. Meanwhile the canny immigrants ('my commonwealth cousins') know how to work the system, and are kept in clover.

Cronin painted his satirical stereotype of the scrounging migrant in technicolour. Not only did he (it was always a he when it was about jobs) take money from the 'rightful heirs and beneficiaries' of the welfare system, but he was insufferably jaunty and offhand as he did so. The Maltese, the Cypriots, the West Indians and the Irish were all, loosely, 'colonials': lively, talkative and pleasure seeking, Cronin enjoyed pointing up the contrast with the 'gloomy, intent and resentful' English. The rightful heirs of the benefit system, indeed of the welfare state as a whole, were solid, respectable and, most of all, 'ordinary'. They were also powerless. Indeed the English were gloomy, intent and resentful precisely because they were powerless in the face of the generosity of the welfare state's definition of the nation's working class, which appeared to include everyone.

It would be easy to fill these pages with complaints about undeserving immigrants cheating the system or, worse, getting actively preferential treatment from the council officers in charge of everything from housing to the dole. Unemployed youths in Shepherd's Bush and White City, for example, were convinced not only that black migrants, in particular, were leaping the queues for council housing and undercutting their wages ('you can't get a job in Lyons's because a black man'll go cheaper') but that they were getting a better deal in the dole office:

> I mean down the labour exchange, I mean you go in there, we were in there today, three of us, and we're standing waiting for our pay and we see one darkie go up, he drew eight – seven pounds something, we see about six whites go up, draw three pounds, another darkie go up and draw eight pound and so forth and so on. And it's nearly all blacks down there except for a few whites. Spades, I'm sorry – spades.[4]

Not only did they get more cash but they got it immediately after they arrived in England, and without having to register for work. And, though not a pressing worry for the eighteen- and nineteen-year-old Teds, many people were convinced that the (very real) failure of the state pension to increase in line with rising post-war prices was because the government was paying out too much to immigrants instead. Convictions about the newly arrived Irish were similar, despite their white skin. Irish benefit scroungers lied about the amount of rent they paid (so becoming eligible for help from the NAB), used false names at the labour exchange, and pretended they had wives and children at home in Ireland in order to cut down their rates of income tax. Fundamentally it seemed unfair that they should get anything at all, since they had not paid in to the scheme, either financially, by paying tax and National Insurance over the years, or 'morally', by living through Britain's hard times.

It should have been easy to counter the stories of hordes of immigrants relying on benefits with facts and figures. Everyone, the officials at the NAB and the labour exchanges kept insisting, had to meet the same standard of need. Migrants did have to register weekly for work at the labour exchange in order to be eligible for the dole. The percentage of newcomers receiving dole money was persistently low, particularly during the boom years, and despite discrimination in employment. Accusations that the NAB paid out for unduly high rents were also untrue, despite the fact that rents paid by black migrants usually were higher than others, as there was a premium on any accommodation which would admit them. At the end of the 1950s the London region introduced a rent cap, specifically for 'coloured' applicants, of 15 shillings a week. And in order to discourage 'unreasonable' rent claims, when an applicant for assistance was found to be living 'communally' (i.e. renting a bed in a shared room) he was not to be paid an amount to cover the rent, but a flat allowance. So, for example, an out-of-work Pakistani who paid £1 a week for his bed in a shared house in Stepney was awarded two shillings and sixpence towards the cost, since, as the NAB controller argued, it was 'an accepted practice for the coloured landlords to waive full payment of rent during periods of sickness or unemployment'. The Board itself grew tired of countering accusations of the heavy immigrant drain on resources and began to put out disclaimers, such as this weary statement from the chairman, Geoffrey Hutchinson, sent to the Tory MP for Wandsworth, Michael Hughes-Young, in April 1961:

> As regards British subjects from the Commonwealth, there is no factual basis for the idea that large numbers of them seek assistance immediately following their arrival in this country, or that they throw any substantial burden on assistance funds. Our experience is that, generally speaking, Commonwealth immigrants are keen to work and to earn the comparatively high wages they can get in this country. The vast majority of them are working and are of course paying taxes and insurance contributions in the same way as other citizens.[5]

But trading accusation and counter-accusation does not get us to the heart of the matter, which is why, given the fact that Commonwealth and Irish migrants were not unfairly creaming off benefits, so many people were convinced that they were? Seeking an answer in racism and xenophobia only gets us so far, though it is certainly not hard to find expressions of racist and xenophobic prejudice. Undoubtedly that prejudice was strengthened in moments of recession, when there were high levels of short-term unemployment, among both immigrants and the local population. At the height of the 1958 downturn just over eight thousand West Indian and Asian migrants were on National Assistance – a relatively high proportion. Two years later, with employment prospects picking up, the number had halved, but that fact received predictably little publicity. And with the rush to 'beat the ban' in 1961 and 1962 short-term unemployment among Commonwealth migrants rocketed. In Birmingham and Bradford – where there was a crisis in woollen manufacturing – they formed 75 per cent of claimants in 1962. In the same year in London, 'coloured' immigrants accounted for 20 per cent of the unemployed. That figure swiftly declined, so that by 1964 there were only 5,500 black and Asian migrants receiving assistance, less than 4 per cent of the total number of unemployed. This was despite the reluctance of many employers to hire black migrants. Yet the 'spectre' of large numbers of immigrant unemployed did not disappear so easily.

There were other reasons for the relative visibility of immigrant welfare claimants. Many of the complaints were not about unemployment benefit but the means test. 'The really sore point is that these people are on the means test and are drawing a darn sight more than our own people are getting,' complained one trade-union official during a strike at a cotton mill over the employment of Pakistani workers. This was the same complaint as that of the lad from Shepherd's Bush: whites can draw three pounds while 'darkies' get seven or eight. It may have been simply prejudice which made people come out with such claims. But it was also the case that immigrant workers generally earned a lower basic wage and were dependent on overtime to make ends meet, so that in times of recession, when overtime dried up, they became dependent on help from the state. And they often had larger families, and paid more in rent, so that they qualified for means-tested payments. Among West Indian and African migrants, more women worked, usually in low-paid jobs, which again meant that they were more of a charge on the NAB. These were all practical reasons why it may have appeared that migrants were a particular drain on the welfare services, though the answer lay in levering migrants out of low-income jobs rather than cutting their benefits. But prejudice against immigrants claiming benefits was also built in to the idea of the welfare state itself, which had been designed as a system of social security and support for 'our own people'. Put simply, the welfare system *needed* people who were not eligible for it, or who didn't 'deserve' it. The language of sponging and scrounging, and the need to conserve resources in order to look after 'our own', was integral to the whole idea of welfare.

This was the moral meaning of citizenship, after all. Those who had been on the side of Britain during the Depression and the Second World War had won the moral right to economic security. A great deal of popular anti-immigration rhetoric worked with a kind of mercenary balance sheet – those who had fought and suffered through the war were the rightful beneficiaries of the post-war dispensation. The quid pro quo felt like common sense, and was to reach its starkest, and most dangerous, articulation in Enoch Powell's quasi-mystical portrait of the Wolverhampton pensioner who had lost her husband and sons in the war and was now besieged by an army of invading foreigners. In countless popular complaints like this one, the war was remade into a myth of Britain permanently under siege. One of the effects of this was that black immigrants not only carried the history of empire into the metropolis – they 'stood for' Britain's imperial expansion, and now its contraction – but they also carried the disappointed hopes of the country's wartime past. They effectively became the symbol of not having got what you fought for. Stories of 'darkies' getting twice as much as local men in the dole office were stories of having been betrayed by the political establishment, which was willing to barter the economic security of ordinary and loyal Britons for a false ideal of post-imperial responsibility. As one of the many letters that swelled Powell's postbag later had it, 'Our British working classes have been sacrificed on the altar of a dead colonialism.'[6]

All this is to suggest that complaints about scrounging were hardly rational, let alone reasonable. The idea of the immigrant scrounger was like a fetish, or a screen onto which all sorts of post-war economic and social anxieties could be projected. But it also would be counter-productive to deny that many immigrants (like many natives) were indeed 'on the fiddle', and that this fact gave the figure of the immigrant scrounger its initial purchase. Migrants were not given to tax and National Insurance fiddles because they were either more work-shy, or less honest, than local workers, but because they were less effectively regulated by Britain's burgeoning post-war bureaucracy. Or, rather, there was a mismatch between the kinds of information that the tax and welfare people required to make a judgement on payments and deductions, and the kinds of information that could reliably be checked across borders. Ironically, the very need for 'cards', especially the National Insurance Contribution Card, facilitated certain kinds of fraud, particularly among 'nomadic' Irish workers.

The cards themselves were simple printed documents, on which the name, birthdate and address of the cardholder were handwritten, and authenticated by an official Ministry of National Insurance stamp. Employers deducted a contribution towards healthcare, future pension and unemployment provision from the wages of each employee, and bought stamps (in the Post Office) to the value of the combined contribution of both employer and employee. The stamps pasted onto the card were the proof of entitlement to benefits, and for people who were living 'at home' in Britain they were indeed an insurance against the future. If you had paid your stamps you were covered for sick pay, holiday pay, healthcare and unemployment benefit, and you could look forward to drawing your pension after the age of sixty-five, or sixty if you were a woman. If, however, you were a seasonal worker, or determined to stay in England for only a few years before settling back home, the value of future benefits was far less obvious. The great urge for migrant workers was to take or send home as much money as possible, not only by working overtime, but also by skimping on costs – paying out as little as possible on day-to-day living, and cutting down on tax and insurance payments. To get money in hand was, after all, the reason why they were away from home in the first place.

There were a number of ways of dodging tax and National Insurance payments. Irish seasonal workers employed by the big civil engineering schemes – building the hydro-electric dams in Scotland, for example – returned home to Ireland every year for the winter months. At the end of a stint in Britain they would 'sign off' and apply for tax and insurance rebates, since they were not permanent residents. When they returned to work the next year the practice was to take a new name, and repeat the process. The system of changing insurance cards was well established, and appears to have been accepted by some employers. In the late 1990s a former labour officer for the civil engineering company Costain explained the arrangements to the historian Ultan Cowley:

> Coming towards the end of the season, every man was given a £100 pay-off but we'd keep one week's wages. At the start of the next season, towards the end of March, we'd send each man a telegram to come back; if he turned up, he'd get the week's wages from last season, plus £150 start-up money. A lot of them came back all right – but with new names and new insurance cards, even though that meant they couldn't claim the back money.[7]

They could not claim back the week's pay, and they would never be able to claim a pension, but the calculation made economic sense in the short term.

False insurance cards also made it possible for men to stay working in England without having to spend a spell back home in order to get the rebate. Say Michael O'Brien worked for two years on his own cards. He would then need to spend at least six months back in Ireland in order to qualify for a rebate. Or he could park his identity as Michael O'Brien, and become Patrick Kelly instead, until he could safely resurface under his own name. This was only possible for labourers who were moving around the country on temporary jobs, and it undoubtedly increased the tendency towards nomadic lifestyles, and isolation from British society. And it made life complicated:

> Fellas was cheatin', and messin' around, and they didn't know how to do it properly; they'd go back to Ireland, and they'd come back then under their mate's name, or some relation that was in the village, and they had two ration books . . . A man would be goin' under the name of 'Flynn' in one place, and 'Murphy' in another place, and – the thing was, someone that knew them as 'Flynn' would be callin' them that in the other place, and – Oh! They'd hit a shkelp on you for that . . . So, in our time you'd be callin' them, 'Young Man', or 'Shkan' ('Skin'), or 'Cock', or 'Horse' . . . You could yell out, 'How's it goin', Horse?', and a dozen men might answer![8]

In the early post-war years, when safety was routinely ignored and accidents on site were common, men were asked to 'informally' provide their real name in case next-of-kin needed to be notified. 'Even so, a lot of men were buried anonymously.' You could come by a new insurance card by making up a name, but there was a risk that this could be checked against birth records back in Ireland, or that you would simply forget who you were supposed to be. Sometimes the fraud was more elaborate, and involved being two people at the same time: 'the practice of working on somebody else's cards was fairly widespread . . . One man I knew was working night shift on the cards of a man who had gone back to Ireland, while drawing benefit from his own in the labour exchange.'[9]

As the scams became better known, teams from the Inland Revenue began to swoop on Irish immigrants at work, or travelling to and from the building sites in vans, and ask them to state not only their name and address, but also the date they had arrived in Britain. It was easy to get caught out. One of my uncles was a carpenter who worked for many years 'shuttering' – creating the forms for pouring concrete or timbering trenches – on motorways, bridges and power stations such as Kingsnorth and Ratcliffe-on-Soar. During one stint in England in the early 1960s he used the name and birthdate of an older brother, who had stayed at home to work the farm – he could at least be sure to remember them, and his brother's existence could be proved by a birth certificate, if it came to it. But he was careful to record the exact dates when he (both of him) was supposed to have arrived and left again over a number of years, so that when he was questioned, as he was, he had the right answers.

This kind of identity swapping was so common that its usefulness seeped into other areas. Take the case of my aunt Mary. For many years Mary lived out a complicated lie in which she claimed to have used as the basis for her passport the birth certificate of an older sister who had died before she was born. It was common in those days for a new child to be given the name of a deceased older sibling. Mary 1 had been born around 1920, and Mary 2 (my aunt) around 1925. But, wanting to lop a few years off her age when embarking on a romantic attachment, Mary 2 said that her 1925 birth certificate had really belonged to Mary 1, and that she had used it to get her travel permit (to take up nursing) at the end of the war, although she was under age. She chose a new birthdate from around 1930. This meant that she was one age for the UK authorities and for the hospital where she worked, but in 'private' she could shave a few years off, a ruse which was only discovered when her sisters visited her at home with her new husband, and found birthday cards for a non-existent birthday ranged on the mantelpiece. They opened their eyes wide but kept their mouths shut.

Mary's was a sort of double bluff, a subterfuge which was not in fact a subterfuge, but only the story of one. It echoed and depended for its effect on the many 'real' identity scams which were enabled (and even encouraged) by wartime and post-war bureaucracy. The need for papers, alongside the difficulty of checking up on papers across national borders, helped precipitate a kind of market in identity. It went to the heart of one of the central contradictions of migrant life in post-war Britain. In their encounters with the elaborate bureaucracy of the UN refugee camps, with the Irish Liaison Office, with the Ministries of Labour, Health and National Insurance, the National Service Corporation Hostels, with large employers such as hospitals, mines and civil engineering companies, the migrants were little more than numbers, or bodies to be processed and put to work. Their purpose was to fill employment quotas. But that very process allowed a kind of re-making, the possibility of fabricating a new identity – and, as in the case of my aunt, not just on paper.

Another way of not paying tax and insurance was not to go on the cards at all, but to work 'on the lump', or cash in hand. Men who worked for cash would have to forgo not only holiday, pension and insurance stamps but canteens, wet-weather gear, transport subsidies and the benefits of trade-union agreements.[10] In return they got a daily rather than a weekly wage, and often worked to agreed bonuses depending on how quickly a job was finished. Because they did not pay income tax they could amass good money quickly. Many men shifted frequently between working on and off the cards. It was not unknown, of course, for British workers to work for cash in hand, but this was (and is) far more common in part-time or temporary jobs – domestic cleaners, for example, or tradesmen taking on extra jobs at weekends and in the evenings to supplement their declared earnings. But building work provided a steady and reliable niche in the twilight economy. Its huge expansion during the 1960s meant that companies could find it hard to meet the manpower needs of large contracts, and looked to unofficial subcontractors to find men who would work fast with no questions asked. Men could come over from Ireland and quickly find regular work off the books, and settle into a more-or-less nomadic lifestyle of hard work during the day, the pub in the evening, and a bed in a series of camps and lodging houses. The cost, in terms of loneliness and lack of security, would be reckoned later.

None of this was strictly scrounging, though it was evading, and it was certainly not playing by the rules of the welfare community. Stories of tax evasion, rather than benefit scrounging, were broadly corroborated by Richard Power and Dónall Mac Amhlaigh. On arrival in Birmingham in the mid-1950s Power and a friend were asked, 'How many children do you have – I mean – for the income taxes, like.' Mac Amhlaigh reported the opinion of a Glasgow tax inspector. 'There must be more than ten million people living in the Irish Republic because, according to the forms I have here, nearly every person of the age of eighteen upwards or so has over five of a family at home.' The more dependants you could claim, the larger the rebate you received.[11]

False dependants were not only an Irish thing. In fact they were a great leveller across the migrant nations, and another source of commonality between Irish and South Asian migrants in particular. Both groups, in the early post-war years, featured disproportionately large numbers of single men, for whom it made practical sense to claim rebates for the family left at home. The calculation shifted fundamentally once family members came to live in Britain. At this point not only tax breaks but all kinds of other support became – theoretically – available. Council housing for families currently living in overcrowded accommodation, free nursery places for women in low-paid work, free milk and orange juice for children under eleven, child benefit, free healthcare, free schooling. Even though the council housing and the nursery places were elusive gifts, it made financial sense for immigrants to 'buy in' to the advantages conferred by the welfare state, and to pay tax and National Insurance alongside the natives. And, increasingly, they bought in not merely financially but 'morally' – they began to identify with the national community. As Madho Ram put it of Punjabis in Wolverhampton, suddenly their children got 'money, milk and a lot of attention', and only a fool would turn their nose up at that.

Unlike the majority of Irish migrant families, Asian and West Indian couples often left some children back at home, to be brought up by a grandmother, or within the extended family. This meant that families rather than single men might be in receipt of tax breaks for non-resident children, and it proved hard to resist the temptation to bump up the numbers of family members living 'elsewhere'. One Sikh family I interviewed had two small children when they arrived in Southall in 1964. But, like other people they knew, they pretended they had left another child back in India, in order to get a better tax code. As they put it, 'after some years we wrote to the tax people that that child has died.' What was it? Fear of exposure? Guilt? Probably a bit of both. But the guilt implies that 'after some years' they had begun to identify with the redistributive aims of the welfare system. They no longer felt happy abusing it. There can be few more eloquent signs of settling down, of making the shift from being a migrant to being at home in England.

There were, of course, other ways that migrants could behave just like anyone else. They could wheel and deal and make promises they had no intention of keeping. One Punjabi folk song wryly imagines the consequences of setting store by the married man's tax allowance. This isn't exactly an arranged marriage, but it is a marriage built on a financial arrangement, and it proves to be less than fulfilling, as the female singer mourns:

In those days you used to implore me:
Let us get our marriage registered at once (and bear me children) so that
I get a more favourable code number.
The tax-man plagues me every day.
You used to touch my feet and beg me to free you from his clutches.
And now the day has come when you go
To Piccadilly every day, and spend your money.
You earn it so hardly, and spend it so uselessly.

I am a Panjabi beauty, fairer than even the fair-skinned English girls.
So why do you go to spend your nights in London?[12]

Ironically this man was cheating on his wife, rather than the state. The wife and her children were real, but the marriage, the song implies, was a sham, arranged to take advantage of tax rebates.

17

Voters

I remember, when I first moved there in 1964, I was just married and looking for a house. And I can honestly say, this is
the first time that I personally encountered people who said,
'We don't take any blacks here.' I had been living insulated
from that. I'd been a student, living in college or living in student housing. I hadn't encountered that, personally. I knew it
was going on, but this was absolutely straight, 'No blacks
here', 'We don't take any blacks', et cetera. And people
shouted at us in the street when we were going around trying
to find places, you see, myself and my white wife. You can
imagine. She was the particular object of vile remarks about
mixed race couples, and so on. So, I had a very bad introduction to the West Midlands, I must say. And I have always
thought, it may be wrong, but I've always thought that I
could understand that Powellism would have come out of the
West Midlands. I thought one could hear a particular kind
of resentment, deep resentment, almost as if we'd been left
behind by England and now we were going to be left behind
in relation to race, you know, permanently left behind. And
that's a historical resentment, latched on to race . . .

Stuart Hall (1998)[1]

The Notting Hill riots marked one of the first moments when racial
prejudice was openly, and violently, expressed in Britain. For West
Indian migrants in particular, those who had felt a compromised
sort of belonging to British culture, the riots spelled the end of uncertainty. They now knew incontrovertibly that they were 'coloured'

outsiders. And though large swathes of the population felt sympathy for the immigrants, and the liberal establishment expressed that sympathy, the government did nothing to harness it for change. A number of hopeful cross-community projects which were mooted in the immediate aftermath of the violence fell by the wayside. The extra funding for deprived areas, the house-building projects, the school pilot programmes – none of them materialized. There was no special provision for the reception, briefing, placing or housing of immigrants at all. There were no laws against racial discrimination. The focus lay on teaching the immigrants how to integrate more successfully (partly through BBC English language and culture programmes), rather than on teaching locals not to hate. And it was fear of this unchecked and growing anti-immigrant sentiment which led the Conservative government to introduce the Commonwealth Immigrants Bill in 1961.

Six years after the riots, in the 1964 general election, the success of Peter Griffiths' openly racist campaign for the Smethwick constituency dealt another blow to Britain's idea of itself as a tolerant country that was, on the whole, managing to absorb its minorities in an orderly fashion. The result in Smethwick has been seen as a turning point in the history of British racism, the first time that race and immigration explicitly formed part of a mainstream electoral appeal. Griffiths was not standing for Mosley's Union Movement or for the British National Party, but for the Conservatives. His victory, with 47.6 per cent of the vote to Patrick Gordon Walker's 42.6 per cent, defied the national swing to Labour, and it appeared to have been achieved purely by appealing to popular resentment and fear of immigrants. Interviewed by Robin Day for the BBC on election night, the Conservative peer Robert Boothby denounced the result as 'the most disgusting thing that has ever happened in British politics in, certainly in our time and probably for the last 200 years. It's revolting, Smethwick.' Harold Wilson condemned the campaign in the Commons, insisting that, 'Smethwick Conservatives can have the satisfaction of having topped the poll, of having sent a Member who, until another election returns him to oblivion, will serve his time here as a Parliamentary leper.' In fact Griffiths represented Smethwick for only two years. In the 1966 general election the constituency was won by the Labour candidate, the actor Andrew Faulds.[2]

The liberal establishment was shocked by the 1964 result, but black and Asian immigrants living in the West Midlands were less so. They had seen it coming. And at least some of them were sceptical of the amount of clear water between the two candidates when it came to matters of race anyway. When Gordon Walker stood again (and lost again) in the Leyton by-election in January 1965, a reporter for the short-lived Caribbean journal *Magnet* asked local West Indians what they thought of him.

> Mr James Roland, a 28-year-old Jamaican resident of Leyton, had this to say about why he did not vote in the by-election: 'As far as I am concerned it was a choice between Caesar and Caesar. I remember this man Mr. Gordon Walker from the days when he exiled Seretse Khama because the South African Government was putting pressure on him. I read about it back home and I don't think he changed all that much since then, and as for the other candidates, they were talking in such a soft voice about people like me that I never heard them. So who did I have to vote for?' Mr. Roland's opinions must be taken seriously because this general 'it has nothing to do with me' attitude is fairly wide-spread in the coloured community.[3]

Roland was remembering Gordon Walker's role as foreign secretary in forcing Seretse Khama into exile. Khama was a prominent royal in what was then the British Protectorate of Bechuanaland, who would later become president of Botswana. He was exiled because of his interracial marriage in 1948 to Englishwoman Ruth Williams, whom he had met while training to be a barrister at the Inns of Court in London. This capitulation to South Africa's apartheid regime was hardly what Gordon Walker was expecting, still less hoping, that his potential voters would remember.

In 1964 the Conservatives had been in power for thirteen years. They fought the election promising more of the same: stability, the protection of the family, low taxes, secure pensions. In contrast Wilson's new look, 'white heat', Labour Party promised all the fruits of modernity, investment in industry, house-building programmes and a rejection of the Conservatives' play-safe mode. The election in that

October – called a full five years after the last one – was the first to follow the passing of the Commonwealth Immigrants Act. All three of the main parties avoided making immigration central to their campaigns, avoided getting involved in what Roy Jenkins called 'coloured politics' ('one party on the side of the coloured and the other against'). Arguably this was as much about pragmatism as moral responsibility. Courting the anti-immigrant vote meant alienating immigrants, and the Commonwealth powers from which they came. But wooing the immigrants meant being branded as 'the immigrant party'. And neither Labour nor the Conservatives felt on particularly strong ground on the issue of immigration. The Conservatives had pushed through the 1962 Act in the teeth of Labour opposition, but two years later there was widespread feeling in areas of high immigration that the Act was too little, too late. It was poorly designed and impossible to enforce; in places where the main immigrant group was Irish, such as in Deptford, locals argued it was worse than useless. It had done nothing to alleviate their problems. Meanwhile Labour trod a very fine line. They had opposed restrictions in 1961, but it was political suicide to present themselves as friends of an 'open door' policy. Labour candidates in immigrant areas were reduced to bleating that most of the newcomers had arrived under the Tories. The Labour manifesto was woolly about policy too. Unlike the Tories, who professed to be worried that making discrimination illegal might give people ideas, they promised to 'legislate against racial discrimination and incitement in public places and give special help to local authorities in areas where immigrants have settled'. But they also accepted the principle of the need for restrictions on new arrivals. What they wanted, they said, was to negotiate an agreement with Commonwealth heads of state. But in the meantime, in the absence of such agreement, the Act to which they had objected should stay: 'Labour accepts that the number of immigrants entering the United Kingdom must be limited. Until a satisfactory agreement covering this can be negotiated with the Commonwealth a Labour Government will retain immigration control.' In fact, once in power, the Wilson government unilaterally tightened restrictions on newcomers from the Commonwealth.

There was tacit agreement at policy level not to play the race card. But there was nothing to stop local candidates talking up immigration. As shadow foreign secretary, Gordon Walker had fiercely denounced the Commonwealth Immigrants Bill during readings in the Commons. He had accepted that racial tension was rising in areas of high immigration, but argued that the Bill would do nothing to stop that. 'If we do nothing else but just have this Bill, the problem will get steadily worse.' Instead, what was needed was help for local authorities in immigrant-occupied areas. Peter Griffiths made the most of his opponent's soft line, insisting that 'Labour was backed by the immigrants', and that he alone spoke for local people who were weary and fearful of the immigrant burden they had been asked to bear. Griffiths campaigned on a platform of speaking truth to power. Local people wanted immigration stopped, and 'if it suits the people of Smethwick I will say it'. He proposed a ban on all immigration for five years, and deportation of criminals and the unemployed. He argued for separate school classes for immigrant children who struggled with English, and he insisted that immigrants had brought violence, crime and disease to Smethwick.

> We believe that unrestricted immigration into this town has caused a deterioration in public morals. We have no objection to a man who happens to have a coloured skin, who looks after himself and his house decently, and who works. But this town is not to be the dumping ground for criminals, the chronic sick, and those who have no intention of working.

In July 1964, as the seventeen-year-old Jamaican star Millie topped the charts with 'My Boy Lollipop', Griffiths argued in the local paper that, 'Smethwick rejects the idea of being a multi-racial society. The Government must be told of this.'

By 1964 there were 800,000 New Commonwealth immigrants living in Britain, about 1.5 per cent of the population as a whole. Smethwick was then a town of 67,000 people, of whom 4,000–5,000 (around 6 per cent) were immigrants. Just over half of the immigrants were Indian – mainly men working in the iron foundries – 37 per cent were from the Caribbean islands, and 9 per cent were from Pakistan. This figure was much higher than the national average, though there were greater concentrations – for example in Southall, where the immigrant population was more than 11 per cent. A contemporary account of the Smethwick campaign by social scientists at Birmingham University (carried out for the Institute of Race Relations) suggested that part of the hysteria over numbers may have been caused by the fact that many more immigrants arrived each day to work in the network of foundries that dotted the northern part of the town. And what was apparently the largest gurdwara in Europe stood on Smethwick High Street, attracting Sikh worshippers from across the West Midlands. The housing conditions in the area were very poor, with people living at a density of 27.4 people per acre, and more than four thousand people were on the council housing waiting list. Both Liberal and Labour candidates argued that the root cause of the problem was inadequate housing stock, but many local people blamed the immigrants. In June 1961 the tenants of Price Street had threatened a rent strike against the Labour council for rehousing a Pakistani family (whose home had been demolished under a slum-clearance scheme). Conservative councillors hurriedly sketched a policy for a ten-year residence qualification, with Griffiths arguing that 'many people who have been in this country only a few months snap up houses they know are due for demolition'. In 1963 another Tory councillor had set up 'vice vigilante' patrols through the immigrant areas. And as a researcher for the Institute of Race Relations argued, the fear and resentment of newcomers were actively amplified by the local paper, the *Smethwick Telephone*, whose pages were filled with anti-immigrant letters and opinions.[4]

One of Griffiths' electoral strengths was that he was a local man – a West Bromwich headmaster who spoke with a regional accent, he styled himself as a lone voice prepared to acknowledge the concerns of local people. And the media certainly enjoyed showcasing the locals during the campaign, or gawping at them. The BBC news aired reports in which working men said to camera: 'The blacks have come here to exploit the whites'; 'It's full of niggers. We don't want them in Smethwick. We want to get them out!' Griffiths was unapologetic about lifting the lid on this racism, arguing that in Smethwick the Conservative Party was 'acting as a safety valve – a function which otherwise might have been taken by the extreme right'. His opponents argued that what he was doing was legitimizing racist and anti-immigrant attitudes. A comparison with other constituency campaigns where immigration was an issue suggests that they were right.[5]

In Brixton, for example, where the Union Movement and Keep Britain White had been active through the 1950s, and where there had been a council-housing rent strike similar to that of Smethwick's Price Street, the swing to Labour was one of the highest in the country. Analysts argued that this was partly because the local paper, the *South London Press*, was not the *Smethwick Telephone*. Although it printed plenty of letters and articles critical of immigrants, it also gave ample space to West Indian residents objecting to prejudice and misinformation. Was part of the problem in Smethwick that the largely Asian immigrants did not fight back through the British media, but organized among themselves? The example of Southall suggests otherwise. Many of the same social ingredients were stirred up together in Southall's pot, including a local attempt to ensure that vacant properties were sold only to white buyers, and requests from residents for segregated schools. (Rejecting these requests in 1963, the minister for education, Sir Edward Boyle, laid down the principle of dispersal (bussing), with a maximum immigrant quota of one-third per school, a policy which was to prove almost as controversial.) But in Southall the immigrant card was played not by any of the main parties but by the British National Party (BNP), which had formed in 1960 through a merger between the National Labour Party and the White Defence League, and had polled well in some local elections. The BNP leader John Bean built his 'Save Our Southall' campaign around a familiar raft of measures: stop non-European migration, pay for repatriation and give no National Assistance to unemployed immigrants. Immigrants brought disease and a high birth-rate, and 'Once our stock has gone, it has gone forever,' he warned. He was helpfully explicit that the 'Northern European stock' he favoured included the Irish, the Poles and the Jews. He polled 9.1 per cent, and appears to have drawn his votes almost equally from both the Conservative and Labour candidates.[6] The difference between Smethwick and Southall was that Bean was a fringe candidate rather than a mainstream politician making political capital out of immigration. Asian immigrants in Southall knew that nearly 10 per cent of their neighbours wanted to get rid of them, and probably many more would rather they went away. But in Smethwick it was nearly 50 per cent; the Conservatives under Peter Griffiths had made it seem acceptable to hate immigrants.

A few miles from Smethwick, Birmingham's Sparkbrook (where there were an estimated 10,000 immigrants, half of whom were Irish) faced a similar housing crisis. Immigrants were crowded into large, decaying, single-room lodging houses and the locals were crowded into working-class terraces, many of which were scheduled for slum clearance. With large numbers of residents working at the Longbridge car factory there was plenty of money but few amenities. More people owned cars than had bathrooms. In 1959 the Conservatives had won Sparkbrook from Labour by a narrow majority (886 votes). But in 1964 Roy Hattersley won the seat back for Labour, with a swing of 3.3 per cent, the largest swing in Birmingham, after what was described as 'a very quiet campaign', with 'barely a hint of racialism'. The campaign successfully located the problems faced in Sparkbrook as rooted in housing rather than immigration, though one commentator suggested that the fact that the majority of immigrants – the Irish – were hard to pick out in a crowd might have had something to do with it:

> The Irish are the largest immigrant group, in Sparkbrook as in Birmingham, but in some ways they are the hardest to discuss. To many, of course, they do not appear as immigrants at all. They are the same colour as us; they've come from just across the water; they speak a kind of English. But often those living in immigrant areas regard them as their greatest trial. Whether they are from the Dublin slums or from the bog, they were not born to the highly disciplined, restrained life of the English city. They have not yet begun to adjust to their proletarian life as their respectable hosts in Sparkbrook have, and they still construe the world as a running fight between 'them' and 'us'.
>
> Nevertheless, they are not readily identifiable – a drunken Irishman looks very much like a drunken Englishman from a distance.[7]

A more plausible account was that the Irish, almost alone among post-war migrants, were actively involved in British domestic politics. Not only were they registered as voters, but they were active in the local wards. The Grenadian Labour politician David Pitt, who had stood unsuccessfully for Hampstead in the 1959 election, argued that West Indian immigrants had good reason to be suspicious of British electioneering:

> They refuse to join political parties because they are often invited to join when elections are in the offing, and they feel that the invitation to membership is merely a ruse to safeguard their vote and they strongly resent being used ... Many immigrants do not get their names on the electoral roll because they feel that they are being spied upon and the attempts to get them on the electoral roll are merely a way of trying to be sure of their whereabouts. The landlords think it is a means of trying to find out their incomes and do not put their tenants' names on the roll. The tenants believe they are safer if their addresses are not known.[8]

Arguably it was even harder to register Asian voters, who were not only keen to stay under the official radar, but often had poor English. In Southall in 1964 the Indian Workers' Association (IWA) responded to what they saw as the racism of the Southall Residents' Association (which was lobbying for white-only property sales) with a concerted effort to sign up Indian voters – and to recommend them to vote Labour. They produced pamphlets explaining the vote in Punjabi and Urdu, and gave voting demonstrations before screenings at the Dominion Cinema. They manned the polling stations with helpers who could explain the voting slips. The Birmingham IWA was active in getting the Indian vote out in Smethwick, and the two Birmingham marginal constituencies of Sparkbrook and All Saints. They produced leaflets in Punjabi, carried out advance canvassing, and on election day sent out teams to target Asian electors (whose names were easy to spot on the electoral roll) across six wards:

> During the day there were nine workers with four cars engaged specifically on the task of getting Asians to the poll; in the evening there were eighteen people and twelve cars, including two large vans. The daytime aim was to get as many women as possible to vote, and the team included three women for this purpose ... Mr Jouhl is confident that practically all Indians voted for Gordon Walker, his workers having at great pains made clear to them that the 'X' should go in the second line down.

The headline in the *Birmingham Mail* read, 'Smethwick's Immigrants Flock to the Polls'.[9]

The 1964 election marked the beginning of Asian involvement in British politics and race relations. The Indian and Pakistani Workers' Associations had initially been formed to provide support and advice for men arriving into an unfamiliar and often hostile environment. The IWA's first major campaign was to lobby the Indian government on behalf of those who had arrived on forged passports, and who were therefore unable to get on the right side of the law. By the late 1950s the problem of returning home on forged papers had introduced a new racket, which involved bribing officials in the Indian High Commission in London to renew forged passports or to issue valid ones in exchange for forged ones. In 1960 the IWA took advantage of a state visit to Britain by Jawaharlal Nehru to lobby for change, and the High Commission agreed to issue valid papers to anyone who turned in forgeries.

In the early years the IWA functioned mostly as a social support agency, an Indian citizen's advice bureau where people could get help with form filling, applications, mortgage advice and legal guidance. The leaders were mainly men who had been active in the Communist Party of India (CPI). (Those who joined the Communist Party of Great Britain (CPGB) caused a headache for British Communist leaders as they set up separate branches and held their meetings entirely in Punjabi. The men sent along from CPGB local branches listened uncomprehendingly to discussions of how to support the CPI in Indian elections.[10]) Ordinary workers were often sceptical of this political bias, and many had to be strong-armed or cajoled into joining.

> Back in the early days it was not easy to get people to join the IWA. You know Harbhajan Singh? I had a very difficult time getting him to join. He said that the IWA could do nothing, it is a waste of time; and he wouldn't join. So one day I met him in the cinema and argued with him and then I said, 'Will you give me 2/6' (the membership fee). He said, 'Yes, here it is, but I won't join.' So I took the 2/6 and enrolled him as a member.

One local organizer in the West Midlands explained how the association gathered support:

We rented a hall or a room in a pub and people would come and drink and sing. For the first half hour or so, the committee members would have to stand up and sing, but after that the other people would join and everyone would be singing. It was a very good time and everyone enjoyed it. We held three or four of these socials and after a while there would be two hundred people there, everyone enjoying themselves. Then we started a membership campaign for the IWA and everyone joined.[11]

According to Avtar Singh Jouhl, leader of the Birmingham IWA in the early 1960s, the cultural side of the Indian labour movement also attracted people associated with the left-wing folk protest movement and the Campaign for Nuclear Disarmament, including the radio balladeer Charles Parker, and folk musicians Ewan MacColl and Peggy Seeger. Other branches ran film shows to attract new members. The advantage of these new secular organizations – the Pakistani Workers' Association operated in much the same way – was that they offered men the opportunity to create new ties which cut across village lines, providing an alternative to village and caste-based community leaders. Later, as more and more migrants arrived from non-Jat groups (such as Valmiki or Ramgarhia) this secular, politicized community would be divided again, as religious groups affiliated to new caste-based temples and gurdwaras took over the role of community centres. But for a period in the early 1960s, the workers' associations held the balance of power within the Asian communities.

There were two factors which propelled the Asian labour movements forward. The first was the greater sense of security felt by the majority of workers once the Indian government lifted restrictions on the issue of passports. Once their papers were legalized they could turn their attention to campaigning against unfair dismissal and segregation in the workplace. Several factories in the West Midlands had installed separate Asian and European toilets, for example, but it was only possible to persuade men to complain about such things once they felt safe in their jobs. The second factor was yet another unintended consequence of the 1962 Commonwealth Immigrants Act. Indian, Pakistani and West Indian groups collaborated on protests against the proposed legislation. Once the Act was passed, with future right of entry to Britain now restricted and immigrants increasingly deciding to make their move permanent, it made sense for them also to accept that they were part of Britain's working class.

During the 1950s trade unions had often lodged objections to Commonwealth labour as bound to lower wages and conditions for the workforce in general. In a situation where Indian and Pakistani workers were regarded as the enemy of the British unionized worker, it made little sense for Indians and Pakistanis to agitate to join the unions themselves. (The opinions of Bradford millworkers interviewed in the early 1960s were representative: 'They stand for English workers.' 'They don't want to include us – they are prejudiced and seek to exploit us.' 'I have never heard of a union being helpful to an immigrant when he was sacked or ill-treated.'[12]) But this gradually changed, in part because immigrant workers saw the advantage of campaigning for better conditions, and in part because, facing declining membership, the unions themselves began to court Asian members. By the mid-1960s the Amalgamated Union of Foundry Workers was liaising with the left-wing Indian workers to get their compatriots to join up in the West Midlands. In 1966 the first major strike by Asian workers was organized by men protesting against the conditions inside Woolf's rubber factory, but it had taken years to get that far. As one factory worker recalled:

> There had been a lot of talk about forming a union. The feeling against it was not that it would be bad; the conditions in the factory were terrible and everyone thought that a union would help. But everyone was afraid that an attempt to organize would fail and everyone would be fired.

That was exactly what had happened in 1960. Men of the IWA had recruited 316 out of 600 workers to the union, but one of the foremen had informed the owner, who had got rid of the agitators.

> In every shop there were one or two men who were friendly with the management. They were touts for the foremen. They would find men who wanted a job and take them to the foreman. To get a job, you had to give a bribe, and the foreman would split it with the tout. Everyone

was afraid that the touts would tell the foreman who had organised the union and then the foreman would give them the sack.

In 1964 they tried again, but they made sure to sign men up to the union outside the factory, and most often in the privacy of their own homes.[13]

This increased radicalism was given articulate expression in February 1965, when Avtar Jouhl invited Malcolm X to Smethwick. The Black Power activist had been a prominent member of the Nation of Islam but by 1964 had broken away to form his own religious and civil rights organizations, Muslim Mosque, Inc. and the pan-Africanist Organization of Afro-American Unity (OAAU). In February 1965 he was in London to address the first meeting of the Council of African Organizations. Nine days before he was murdered in New York he was filmed by the BBC in Smethwick, despite the mayor, Alderman Niven, stating publicly that he did not want 'this algebraic character' stoking racial tension on the streets of his town. (He was

Malcolm X on Marshall Street in Smethwick, 1965.

accompanied on the trip by a second algebraic character, Michael de Freitas, who was introduced as Malcolm's 'Brother' Michael X, although he was to change his name to Michael Abdul Malik when he converted to Islam a few weeks later.) As the *Birmingham Post* reported, 'When asked why he had come to such a minor town, Malcolm X replied, "I have heard that the blacks . . . are being treated in the same way as the Negroes were treated in Alabama – like Hitler treated the Jews."' To the Wolverhampton *Express and Star* he complained:

> From what I understand, Colin Jordan [founder of the National Socialist Movement in 1962] can go to Smethwick and strut up and down Marshall Street and other streets preaching 'if you want a nigger neighbour vote Labour' and that's all right. As long as it is the Fascists and Nazis, it seems everything's O.K. but when I go to Smethwick there are protests. Britain has a colour problem and I give white Britons credit for realising it . . . I am just shocked that there are some people like this Mayor of Smethwick who object to my being there.[14]

Malcolm X's appearance in Smethwick took place at the same time as the Student Nonviolent Coordinating Committee organized their campaign for voting rights for African Americans in Selma, Alabama, and just one month before Martin Luther King's famous speech at the conclusion of the civil rights march to the state capital, Montgomery. United States racial discrimination was in the news, and by arguing that the black community in Britain must stand up for itself Malcolm X suggested parallels with the situation in the States. He made no distinction between West Indian and Asian immigrants, and implied that the racism they faced on account of their colour could unite them. His frank admission that 'Britain has a colour problem' was one way of insisting on the need for immigrants to campaign for their rights as black people rather than as immigrants. It was language which had, until this point, been owned by the white supremacists and it certainly made many people, including the mayor of Smethwick, uncomfortable to hear it in the mouths of black people themselves. When Peter Griffiths had won the Smethwick election four months beforehand he did so by ignoring the immigrants – his battle was not with immigrant opinion but with those in the Conservative Party who disagreed with his line on keeping them out. But

Commonwealth immigrants were beginning to organize around a consciousness of themselves as black. Why not inhabit the stereotype, and turn it back against the people who were trying to define you? Philip Donnellan's 1964 documentary about the West Indian community in Birmingham, *The Colony*, included an interview with an immigrant from St Kitts, Stan Crooke, who suggested that the experiences of the immigrants were teaching them new ways of thinking about themselves: 'The West Indian no longer considers himself a Jamaican, a Trinidadian, Barbadian, Kittian, Antiguan. We are all subtly but inexorably considering ourselves as all coloured people.'[15] Malcolm X implied that Asian migrants were also a natural part of this black alliance.

The wisdom of this stance appeared to be proved later that summer when the Labour government published its White Paper on Immigration, a document which did nothing to decrease the amount of political radicalism in the Birmingham Indian Workers' Association, and which took moderates by surprise. *The Economist* labelled it a 'Black Paper'. Commonwealth immigration was to be slashed to 8,500 category A and B voucher holders per year. Unskilled migration from the Commonwealth (the category C vouchers) was to be stopped altogether, while European and Irish immigration went on unchecked. (There had been a 30,000 net increase in migration from Ireland in 1964.) Other clauses recommended deportation of immigrants at the home secretary's discretion, with no recourse to the courts – raising protests that this would constitute a fundamental encroachment on human rights. 'Britain accepts the Colour Bar', wrote Mervyn Jones in the *New Statesman* on 6 August. He pointed out that the government was encouraging a brain drain from Commonwealth countries, while refusing entry to unskilled workers unless they were Irish. The *Spectator* called the document a 'surrender to racial prejudice, vilely dressed up to appear reasonable'. David Pitt accused the government of 'pandering to what they believe are the prejudiced views of the electorate'.

Harold Wilson was unapologetic. He argued that the White Paper was motivated neither by colour nor by racial prejudice. Instead it provided the bulwark against it. The government had a duty to act on Commonwealth immigration in order to forestall 'a social explosion in this country of the kind we have seen abroad. We cannot take the risk of allowing the democracy of this country to become stained and tarnished with the taint of racialism or colour prejudice.'[16] Like Malcolm X, Wilson was taking his lesson from the United States. The government did set up the Race Relations Board in 1965, and introduced the first of a series of laws outlawing racial discrimination in public places – including hotels and restaurants but not shops, or lodging houses, where in practice immigrants were most likely to come face to face with discrimination. But in restricting Commonwealth immigration still further Wilson's administration had accepted the basic premise that immigrants – and black immigrants in particular – were the cause of social unrest. It was easier to stop them arriving than to address the problems of discrimination and prejudice at its other source: in the ugly, depressed and intolerant mood that Stuart Hall found when he moved to Birmingham in the summer of 1964, a resentment that had 'latched on to race'.

18

Consumers

Bai, ari, ari, ari
207 di *bus* udeeke, sajj dhajj ke Kartari
Moonh dho *powder* showder laya, kiti poori tiari
12 ghante *airport* te laondi, chukdi lafafa bhaari
bus te chrhan dio ih aam jihi nai naari
sack dua doogi, ihdi *foreman* naal yaari

Awaiting for her bus no. 207, Kartari stands in her fashion-
able outfit
Her face wrapped with ample powder, all ready for incitement
Doing twelve hours shift at the airport, her pay-packet is hefty
Do let her first on the bus, sure, she is no ordinary woman
Might get you sacked, she is on friendly terms with the foreman
Southall *boli*[1]

A woman with a pay packet is a woman outside her husband's control – at least if she gets to open it herself. The apparently natural progression, or perhaps slide, from women's economic to sexual freedom is a staple of British popular culture, and from the early 1960s it became a staple of Indian culture in Britain too. Songs sung at wedding celebrations teased new husbands on their inevitable failure to maintain authority over their brides. Now that they were financially independent what could stop them doing what they wanted? The new earning power afforded to women in Britain opened up a whole new set of relationships – between women and the men with whom they worked, the shopkeepers where they spent their money, and the women friends with whom they worked who also now had money of their own. And it necessarily altered the relationships between women, their husbands and their parents. These changes were by no means regarded as entirely negative – hence the jokes. Like their English neighbours, Punjabi men liked to complain about the profligacy of their womenfolk – the way they spent money and time at the hairdressers, or in the boutiques. But men as well as women benefited from the extra cash that women's work brought in, and enjoyed the new forms of leisure that developed in response to all that disposable income: going to the cinema, eating out, buying new clothes. And it was precisely that willingness to spend which was turning Southall into a hub of urbane Asian modernity.

By the mid-1960s Southall had become associated with sophisticated city life. 'Southall is the Chandigarh of the Panjabi immigrants, not their Majha, Malwa or Duaba (the rural areas of the Panjab); *that* Panjab is in the midlands, or in Kent, in the region around Gravesend.'[2] The stereotypes were pleasingly simple. Punjabi men in the Midlands were strong types, unafraid of heavy manual labour, with a thriving, and masculine, folk culture centred on the pubs where they got together to drink, play cards and sing songs accompanied by the tumba and sarangi. Their womenfolk were well-satisfied and well-looked after. Southall, meanwhile, bred effeminate types in a world turned upside-down by women's love of shopping. (This was despite the fact that large numbers of Southall men worked as labourers in factories, and on night shifts.) In one popular song, a factory worker from the Midlands courts a young woman with the promise of getting a real man: 'Southall men are all shopkeepers. They can't appreciate your youth and beauty.' She replies by complaining of the dirt of the factories, and insists she can't do without shopping:

> She: Boy, I can't live without fashion.
> And if you won't accept this, then stay a bachelor all your life.
> I shall adopt the latest fashions with every new year that passes.
> If you are a Midlands Jat, well, I am a Southall girl.

He: In the Midlands, no man has to stay a bachelor
Because the pay-packet we bring home every week is heavy
There it is Hir who goes in search of Ranjha [i.e. Juliet who chases Romeo]
If you are a Southall girl, what of it? I am a Midlands Jat.

Songs recorded with mock horror how young women were swapping traditional dress for mini-skirts, or home-spun village ways for shop-bought cosmetics: 'Billo has forgotten her kikar tooth-stick/ And got used to Colgate's'. Rural modesty was a thing of the past – how could it survive in the city? – and the songs were nicely ambivalent about the consequences. It was one thing to be able to admire a pair of legs under a skirt; another to feel that the village boys back home were being left behind as their women got used to new freedoms. Here a young man, recently arrived in England, reports back in a letter to his friend on the awful change which has come over his lover. She struts about in Western clothes, eats sandwiches, and even drops bits of English into her conversation:

There was a time when Jai Kaur used to sit on her stool
and spin with the other girls of the village,
pleasing the young men who passed with glances from beneath her shawl.
She used to go to the fair with her anklets clinking;
but now she is a charge-hand, and like the white women she walks
provocatively, swinging her hips.
Now she goes out shopping dressed in close-fitting trousers . . .
She is no longer the innocent she once was.
She wears bell-bottoms and says 'Thank-you' and 'Sorry' at every little
thing. Stop sighing for her: it is useless to wait for her.
My friend, your white pigeon has flown from your hand.

All the fuss about fashion, make-up, 'incitement' and provocation sounds like a relatively straightforward worry that Asian women were being corrupted by Western styles of femininity. And that was certainly part of it. The concern wasn't only that girls were leaving behind their modest ways, but that village boys were surely bound to lose out in the competition with their more urbane cousins, or even with English men ('English husbands call their wives "Darling". Indian men are bad,' sings one young woman to her sister-in-law).

Shopping in Spitalfields in the early 1970s.

But at the root of the worries about modern dating and Western fashions lay another concern which was just as fundamental, about spending. Women may have been getting used to going to the cinema, eating chocolates and shopping for themselves. But they were also becoming accustomed to a whole host of other 'luxuries' that had nothing to do with leisure time, such as gas fires, prams, mops, pots, pans and, later, a vast array of plug-in labour-saving devices: Hoovers, mixers, washing machines. The teasing battle over sex played out in the popular songs was really a battle over money, and where and how it should be spent. The 'frugal' living of the early bachelor years was over – though the bachelors had had their own ways of getting rid of money, in the pub, or gambling, for example. The point of all that austerity had always been spending in the end, of course: on building two- and three-storey brick houses back home, and on buying fridges and televisions to put in them, even before there was an electricity supply. In the early 1960s the average wage of a labourer in Mirpur was the equivalent of 37 pence a week; in Birmingham it was £31. Where better to display the rich fruits of migration than back home, where money really could buy you love, or at least respect? But now that wives and families were settling in Britain that calculation was increasingly being questioned. Women were teased and criticized for their love of luxury and slavish devotion to fashion. But the fault, if such it was, lay not only with the women. For the wholesalers, shopkeepers, café-owners, travel agents, taxi-drivers and restaurateurs also wanted immigrants to spend their money in England rather than Mirpur.

The first Asian shops and restaurants catered for a very grateful set of customers who had struggled through the lean years of the early 1950s, when halal meat and traditional foods were as rare as the time it took to cook them. 'The last thing you want to do after a 12-hour shift is to go home and cook yourself some dinner,' explained one Bradford mill worker of his early years in England.[3] Nor did you want to spend your time off searching out ingredients, though it was possible to find approximations in what were then called the 'Continental Stores': 'there weren't any Asian shops in those days, there were the Jewish shops, the Polish, the Latvians – they had similar sorts of foodstuffs to what we would eat, in terms of some of the spices.⁴ Given the limited options, and limited time, the new super-markets and convenience foods were as useful to migrants as anyone else. One Pakistani living in Oxford remembered, 'During the week, for three months, we ate nothing but baked beans . . .'

Recollections of these early years offer distinctly contrary evidence about how people managed for food. On the one hand, the story is of Muslim migrants relying heavily on vegetables such as cauliflower and peas, so conscious were they of the need to avoid meat and poultry from English butchers. The first halal butcher, Haji Taslim Ali, had opened his premises in East London in the 1940s. From the early 1950s Pakistani entrepreneurs began buying up condemned houses in Whitechapel and along the Commercial Road, where they ran cafés and small restaurants serving halal meat. But outside London Muslims had to wait, as this man in Bradford recalled:

> Initially for meat there wasn't any. Then one individual discovered a process whereby he could go and buy a sheep, have it killed at the farm, and bring it over to the house and we would share it – and this sheep was obviously slaughtered in the halal fashion so everybody was eligible.

There are numerous tales – told both by immigrants and by their unhappy neighbours – of buying live chickens and slaughtering them in the back garden. On the other hand, the practice of eating non-halal meat also appears to have been widespread. Muslims would avoid pork, and Hindus beef, but lamb and chicken were condoned, and some Sikhs (who were traditionally vegetarians) apparently ate any-thing. One Punjabi Sikh who arrived in 1953 recalled:

> Things were rationed in those days, we could not get enough butter which we Indians used to think was the most healthy part of our diet, and we were working very, very hard in those days so in order to stay fit and healthy we adapted to the English diet, started eating meat. Meat does not go alone so beers and drinks followed, and we became proper Anglo-Indian gentlemen.

By the late 1950s, with rationing long over, the consumption of butter had risen exponentially – at least in Southall, where G. S. Aurora carried out his observations:

Only Indian style food is taken. During the weekdays the current vegetables or various kinds of pulses are cooked, but the Sunday dinner
consists of a meat dish, usually chicken. The consumption of butter,
which replaces *ghee* is truly phenomenal. This is largely due to the
belief that butter is the most health-giving substance. Each person
consumes around two pounds of it every week. There are two Indian
grocers who supply all the ingredients of the Indian diet. They have a
market even for the most expensive of the Indian vegetables such as
karela and *begu*n (brinjals). On an average the Indian style of cooking
makes for much cheaper meals than the English style.[5]

The first Asian grocers were part-time entrepreneurs, who sold
their goods from hired vans. They carried spices, cereals, pulses, rice,
flour, the more unusual vegetables, cooked foods, oils and kitchen
utensils. Working around their shifts in Woolf's or in the Midlands
foundries they would make a trip to a London wholesalers early in
the week, and then spend their off-time weighing and packaging
goods into small parcels, cleaning grain and (when women were
involved) cooking food for sale – samosas, for example, and Indian
sweets. The actual selling was a weekend task. A Birmingham network of Gujarati grocers, for example, all made their deliveries to
customers on Friday evenings, and at weekends, fanning out from an
initial client base in the city to small groups of migrants in outlying
towns. The food was delivered ready packaged, and customers were
used to getting several months' credit.

We can get some sense of how the system worked by comparing the
Indian peddlers and hawkers who made their money by delivering
cheap clothes and furnishings to their clients. By the late 1950s Sylheti entrepreneurs had largely taken over Jewish tailoring factories
in the East End and started their own wholesale and manufacturing
businesses – buying raw materials from India. By 1960, there were
between twenty-five and thirty wholesalers in the East End who sold
to a network of hawkers (often extended-family members) on credit.

Rashmi Desai interviewed one such hawker (a 'Mr Singh') in the
early 1960s. He had arrived in Britain in 1952, and worked first in
a clothing factory and then as a peddler, selling clothes and textiles
door-to-door four days a week. In his free time he ran a film society.

He sold on credit, offering what he argued were easy terms, and he charged no interest:

> I charge a customer from 50 per cent to 100 per cent more on my cost price depending on his reliability. Then, if he is not a reliable one, I take as big a deposit as possible. So if he does not pay me his last instalments properly, I do not bother very much, because I do not make a loss on the transaction. But most of my customers are 'regular'. I know them and they know me, hence the trouble does not arise. I do not charge them as much.[6]

The trick was to collect instalments once a week, since the smaller the instalment, the more often he was able to visit and show off his new wares. In eight years he had built up a reliable core of four hundred customers and had a turnover of £200 a week. 'He sells his goods to the West Indians mainly, but also to the poorer class of English, the Irish and to his fellow Indians.' His approach to his clients was possibly fairer than that of the home-grown tally man who appears in Nell Dunn's *Up the Junction*, dramatized for the BBC's Wednesday Play by Ken Loach in 1965; there the audience watched a West Indian immigrant being scammed into buying an overpriced suit much too small for him.

The grocers worked on a similar system, but their customer base was confined to 'fellow Indians' and for that reason the relationship between seller and buyer was as much social as commercial. Shopkeepers and their customers depend upon one another the world over, but it can be an uneasy alliance. In the case of Indian and Pakistani migrants the business association echoed the social structures of the rural village. Customers were not free to shop around with any vendor – they were patrons of a particular grocer to whom they were tied (albeit loosely) by family and village tradition. A customer could only move to a new grocer if he could explain the move in other than economic terms – for example, if the new provider was a relative. The relationship was not so different from the traditional 'tick' which operated in small towns and urban stores throughout Europe, where families always patronized the same merchant, and were rewarded with credit for doing so.

Desai described the rituals which helped mask the commercial nature of the relationship. For a start, there was no bargaining or discussion of prices. A grocer got a reputation for robbing his customers if he fell too far out of line with the prices charged by his competitors, but nobody was too concerned if he made a large profit. And the fiction of everyone doing each other a favour was maintained by talking and taking tea:

> Selling or delivering goods is a social act, much like visiting. In every house, the grocer or his assistant spends from ten to sixty minutes, or even more, enquiring about the health of the customer and his family, exchanging news and gossip from India, and delivering messages. He is offered the Gujarati hospitality, due to a visitor, which is a meal at the proper time, or tea. The grocer as a 'servant' or client must recognise the social status of his patron within the Gujarati community and must behave accordingly. Where a caste distinction exists between the patron and grocer, it must be observed.[7]

The money which flowed from the immigrant factory worker to the immigrant entrepreneur was to reshape the hierarchies of caste and status over time. It obviously suited the grocers, hawkers, café and restaurant owners to emphasize their status as retailers rather than servants of the community, and as businesses grew and shops were opened the purely financial nature of buying and selling came to the fore. The expansion of immigrant business was of course largely driven by the expansion of the community itself. As the numbers of Asian migrants grew, so did the turnover. But a major factor in allowing businesses to grow and diversify was the particular purchasing power of women. They needed so many more things.

Once wives began to set up homes in the early 1960s, and when mothers and mothers-in-law were brought over from India and Pakistan, the needs of the household became far more elaborate. Immigrants in the early years often brought cooking utensils and brass plates with them but the supply was naturally limited. Enterprising grocers began to stock an increasing range of hardware, alongside an ever-growing palette of foods to cook on it. For in these early years, Asian women in particular were captive customers to whom the grocers could sell all sorts of things which weren't particularly Asian, such as sheets, kettles, dusters, lightbulbs, Jif, Persil, Daz and Dettol. Through hawkers,

A textile shop in London, October 1955.

the immigrants could get hold of British goods and services without coming into too close contact with British society.

While selling and making money was an obvious way of doing well in Britain, so too was buying, and increasingly so. As more and more families settled in England long term, the outlay on houses, furnishings, fridges and televisions – and eventually washing machines and Kenwood mixers – became not only unavoidable, but desirable. Fathers and husbands, often new to cash themselves, accustomed themselves to their wives and daughters earning money, very often by taking on jobs done by the lowest castes in India. With poor English they had no chance of higher-grade jobs so they worked as packers for catering firms, as cleaners in hospitals, and as sweepers and lavatory attendants at Heathrow, where they took advantage of the tips left by departing international travellers. The stigma attached to traditionally 'low-caste' jobs faded away in the face of the money.

There was truth in the belief that money meant freedom, quite apart from the goods that could be bought with it. For men as well as women, cash in the pocket, or the purse, enabled a form of resistance to traditional authority within the family. A younger son or brother was more ready to call time on his overbearing elders now that he could buy a house of his own and move away from the joint family home; couples could disentangle themselves from jealous or nosey in-laws if they had money to spare. At the other end of the scale, the shops and cafés on Southall's Broadway offered young people meeting places away from eyes of parents and teachers; the town centre was a respectable place for young wives to socialize and bargain, unlike the markets at home. Yet it was certainly not the case that working women automatically gained new authority in the family. For a start, there was a huge difference between going off to work in the morning on the bus, and what was ironically called 'outworking' – supplementing the family income by making items at home.

It was not only migrant women who invested in industrial sewing machines and spent whatever time they had free from housework and childcare making clothes, lampshades, or Christmas crackers. And it was not only migrant women who were exploited. Earning 20 pence for each pair of men's trousers you sewed was slavery whether you were Asian, Cypriot or English, though only Asian women earned so little for sewing shalwar kameez, or cooking samosas and pakoras for their local stores. And for women with a poor command of English (wherever they came from) it was particularly hard to find redress, or access to any alternative employment. Some Punjabi women wrote for advice to Kailash Puri, an agony aunt who had a column in several papers in both India and the United Kingdom. Puri had been married at sixteen to a Punjabi student of palaeobotany who, in 1945, was awarded a two-year scholarship to University College London, and after a spell working in Pune, returned to England to take up a post at the University of Liverpool. Puri started publishing a magazine dedicated to women's issues while in Pune, and – despite the difficulty of finding Punjabi typesetters – she relaunched it in Liverpool in the mid-1960s. The magazine published short stories, recipes, fashion tips and Puri's advice column, which she describes as 'advice given first of all as a wife and mother'. The guidance was not so different from that offered to British women in the pages of *Woman's World* or *Woman's Weekly*, though it was certainly more local. It was of a piece with the 'Woman's Page', in the contemporary London-based Caribbean magazine *Magnet*, which outlined where new women migrants could get the best and cheapest clothes, shoes and haircuts. There was, however, nothing quite like Barbara Blake's *Magnet* column on West Indian parties (which offered quite a different picture to the complaints by noisy neighbours):

> One of the things that takes some getting accustomed to in England is the limit to the amount of entertaining that one can do in a flat or bedsitter. Most of us women come from countries where it is quite simple to give the housemaid orders to prepare dinner for a small party, or where one has enough time in the evening after work to really come up with a Cordon Bleu meal. In London, apart from the disadvantages of most flats, the price of liquor and the fact that one cannot order a delivery of toothpicks, are deterrents enough to make the most domesticated housewife tremble with fear at the thought of preparing a meal for guests.[8]

Puri's correspondents bore witness to the complex ways in which Asian women negotiated the differences between traditional and Western family values: Should I defy my parents for the man I love? How should I handle my interfering mother-in-law? Is it right to agree to an arranged marriage if I love someone else? My children have no interest in India and Indian culture – what can I do? My husband and I want to move into our own home – how can we persuade his parents? I am being bullied by my sister-in-law, who hates me. Most of the letters centred on romance and children, but there were also requests for advice from women who were being physically abused, whose husbands drank, or who felt trapped, depressed and overworked at home – who were enslaved to the sewing machine or the deep-fat fryer. This was the other side of the new world of women's earning potential, very remote from the world of fashion, make-up and freedom comically celebrated in the men's drinking songs.[9]

Folk songs about the difficulty of controlling women (wives, but also daughters) once they were earning their own money focused – obsessively – on sexual freedom, but just as threatening was the fact that women now had an economic stake in the family. There were niggling worries: now that they were earning too, what was to stop them asking their men to take an equal share in the housework, for example? But working wives could also choose to send gifts of money and goods to their own relatives back home in India, rather than their husband's relatives. This was a huge break with tradition, which apart from anything else reinforced the idea that a woman's life in England was simply luxurious.

There was also the sheer indulgence of shopping, which, at least for a time, spelled freedom rather than more drudgery. A bazaar in Bangladesh might be a shameful place for a woman to be, but not the supermarket or high street store in London. The convenience foods you could pick up in the corner shop were as useful to working migrants as to anyone else. It was true, however, that women living within strict Muslim households saw few of the benefits of urban consumerism. Although Muslim women customarily worked outside the home in London, it was far less common in Bradford or the West Midlands. And many of them did not get to go shopping either:

> My husband always came to Bradford to get the full week's meat and chicken and everything. Whenever we ran out of anything, we could always come to Bradford to get it. But we didn't have a car and I was in Purdah in those days ... it isn't nice to travel, wearing that black thing, we call it a burkha, so we always had a taxi. And we used to pay about £2 something, or £3 return, and it was a lot of money in those days. I usually came every two or three months.
>
> I wasn't allowed to go in the shops in those days. It was only men who usually go in the shop, they don't like their women going in front of everybody else, so it is his job. He used to bring everything that I needed. I just had to tell him if I was short of anything.[10]

The burgeoning Asian commercial centres in Bradford were almost uniquely male preserves during the 1960s. They were far more faithful mirrors of the Pakistani bazaar than similar Asian areas in Birmingham, Smethwick or Southall, though the mostly rural Mirpuri villagers who had settled in Bradford were probably as unused to Pakistani urban centres as to British ones. Their food and clothing had been village grown and home-made. Nonetheless the commercial centre of Bradford grew fast, especially after 1962, when immigrants knew they were here to stay.

In 1959 Bradford boasted five Pakistani-owned businesses – two grocer-butchers and three cafés. By 1966, there were 133 businesses, including 51 grocer-butchers as well as cafés, restaurants, cinemas and mosques. These were all, arguably, 'ethnic' concerns. But Pakistanis also ran travel agencies, a laundry and drycleaners, several car- and van-hire businesses, a driving school, importers and exporters, drapers and tailors, plumbers, and grocery wholesalers. There was an income-tax consultant, a herbalist, an astrologer, a bookseller, a photographer, a coal merchant and an electrical goods shop. In 1965 the first Pakistan-based bank opened in Bradford, and by the end of the decade there were two, along with several insurance companies. Newsagents sold Pakistani newspapers, magazines and Muslim calendars; the shops were hung with signs in Urdu, pictures of Mecca and Medina, verses from the Qur'an, and photographs of Pakistani nationalists such as Muhammad Iqbal and Jinnah. The newly 'ethnic' areas of Bradford must have appeared as an attempt, conscious or not, to create an exclusive Pakistani area of the city. But in the mid-1960s Sheila Allen interviewed several Bradford shopkeepers who lamented the fact that they could not encourage white locals to do business with them. The owner of the launderette, whose clientele was 50/50 'coloured' and white, was the most successful, and the landlords of two pubs were the least. Neither of them could entice white customers beyond the door ('Some English people come in and when they find me at the counter they just go out.'), and one landlord found he couldn't get a barmaid to work for him.[11]

Their entrepreneurial skills may have been rejected by the English, but they proved valuable within their own communities. Many of these men would eventually become the city's elite, taking on roles in politics, in the Pakistani literary society, and in the multi-racial Bradford Community Relations Council. As families settled there was less need for ordinary migrants to turn to people for help to fill in forms (you could get your children to do it for you). But there was more need for expert advice – on buying cars and houses, arranging mortgages, or insuring your business. It was nous and drive rather than education or traditional social standing which turned out to be the passport to wealth for Mirpuri immigrants, and while this was liberating for the first generation of newcomers, for their children it would prove a trap from which it would take a long time to disentangle themselves.

The one enterprise which did attract white locals of course was the 'Indian' restaurant – in fact almost exclusively owned and run by East Pakistani (Bangladeshi) Muslims (85–90 per cent) and Muslims from the Pakistani Punjab (most of the others). Yet curry was suspect food for most Britons right up until the late 1960s, when curry houses began to open near universities in larger cities, catering mostly for students looking for a cheap, filling meal after the pub. The other end of the market was rather more niche – restaurants, rather than curry houses or cafés, which catered for ex-colonials who missed the tastes (and perhaps the servility) of the pre-independence years. As the manager of London's Shafi put it in 1955, 'the Indian Khichris, Curries, Bombay Duck and Chutneys and other delicacies have become a regular must' for Englishmen who had lived in India. And the exotic aura of colonial India was an attraction too for the newly affluent families who wanted to serve up something new at home. How else to explain the otherwise unaccountable fact that the first ready meal (produced by Batchelors in 1961) was Vesta Chicken Curry – advertised in magazines by pictures of an attractive, sari-wearing Brahmin woman serving up your plate for you, though admittedly the curry tasted not of turmeric and chilli but of Worcester Sauce. Batchelors' punt on curry was inspired, because for the average British man and woman Asian cooking was a slowly acquired taste. In the early 1960s curry was still pretty much a dirty word. Abdullah Hussein suggested that cooking was in fact one of the ways in which South Asian landlords got rid of their tenants: 'when the whites saw us coming, they took off. The value of the houses dropped dramatically. Our people bought them up in easy installments. Most of the white tenants had left on their own; the fumes of cooking chillies eventually drove the rest of them out.' 'Indians stink of curry' was a common complaint of neighbours in all the areas where Asians settled, and it crops up continually in the sociological studies of immigrant areas in the 1960s. Early in the decade, Rashmi Desai encountered stories of English workers refusing to work with both Indians and Pakistanis because of the smell of garlic. A Sylheti immigrant who opened a café on Whitechapel's Commercial Road in 1962 was clear about the compromises which had to be made to get native Londoners through the door:

We had to sell egg and chips and other things to start with. The customers took a long time before they started trying curry – even then we would have to add milk to it to make it mild for them. At first they would always have chips with their curry, never rice. Once I had a man who wanted to fight me because he found a bay-leaf in his curry. I had to explain we added bay-leaf to give it flavouring.

Most Asian cafés and restaurants in the 1950s and early 1960s catered for Asian factory and transport workers; they were located near mills and factories, and open long hours in order to provide for people coming off the night shifts. And slowly white people began to overcome their fears about hygiene, and increase their tolerance for spice. 'Gradually we could get anything,' wrote Abdullah Hussein:

> whole wheat flour, dals, red peppers, spices, halal meat, non-halal meat, sweets made from ghee, mustard greens, bitter gourds, green chillies – you name it. Restaurants serving our kind of food opened too. Now the white people flock to them; they eat hot, spicy curry and wash it down with gallons of water. But before, merely walking through the area made their eyes water.[12]

19

Hustlers

I'll tell you a story, if I may. Many years ago when I first came
to London – I was in the British Museum – naturally. And
one of the West Indians who work there struck up a conversation with me, and wanted to know where I was from. And
I told him I was from Harlem. But that answer didn't satisfy
him. And I didn't understand what he meant. I was born in
Harlem, I was born in Harlem hospital, I said, I was born in
New York. And none of these answers satisfied him and he
said, where was your mother born? And I said, she was born
in Maryland. And I could see, though I didn't understand it,
that he was growing more and more disgusted with me . . .
more and more impatient. Where was your father born? My
father was born in New Orleans. Yes, he said, but man, where
were you *born*? And I began to get it. You know I said, well,
I said, my mother was born in Maryland, my father was born
in New Orleans, I was born in New York. He said, but *before
that*, where were you born?

James Baldwin (1968)[1]

'Where were you born?' Like 'Where are you from?' it was a question
which meant different things depending on who asked it, and required
different kinds of answer. Asked by one Punjabi-speaker or one Irish
person of another it meant which town or village do you call home,
and perhaps, where does your family live? It was the opening gambit
in a conversation which assumed affinity, and a shared experience of
migration. Asked, as in James Baldwin's story, by a West Indian of an
African American it was a question about roots – where did your

ancestors come from before they were captured and sold as slaves? The assumption of affinity was much wider; it implied a shared identity between black people across the globe.

'Where were you born?' meant something very different in the mouth of a non-immigrant. Asked of a migrant by a native Briton (in a tone ranging from the curious to the suspicious), it was a question about nationality, and ethnicity. But asked of British-born children of black immigrants, with their British accents, it wasn't a question at all but an accusation and a threat. It was a statement, not about geography but about politics. Ironically it mirrored the pan-black kinship implied by Baldwin's British Museum attendant, in that it lumped all black people together, wherever they were born. It said to black Britons, you may think you belong but we see it differently – we see difference. As the children of the post-war immigrants became teenagers in the late 1960s the question of immigration had narrowed to a question of colour. And while the children of Irish, Polish, Italian and Cypriot immigrants were identifiable because of their names, the food they ate and where they went on holiday, the children of West Indian, Asian and African immigrants could, apparently, be distinguished on sight.

For black and Asian immigrants, and their British-born children, there were two defining TV moments in 1968, which rivalled one another. Both were orchestrated for the public. When Enoch Powell gave his infamous 'Rivers of Blood' speech on Saturday, 20 April in Birmingham, it was the culmination of months of agitation and argument against the Labour government's proposed new Race Relations Bill, which was intended to expand the law to address racial discrimination in housing and employment, areas not covered by the 1965 Act. Powell made sure of maximum publicity for his speech by sending an advance copy to the local television station ATV. The cameras were at the ready to record his broad support for his Wolverhampton constituent ('a decent, ordinary fellow Englishman') who feared that the way things were going, 'In this country in fifteen or twenty years' time the black man will have the whip hand over the white man.' Powell argued that the problem was not just one of immigrant numbers, though numbers were part of it. He claimed (erroneously) that the country was welcoming 50,000 Commonwealth dependants every year, 'who are for the most part the material of the future growth of the immigrant descended population'. It was this 'native-born' black population, those who 'arrived here by exactly the same route as the rest of us' – i.e. the birth canal – who constituted the real danger in Powell's eyes. In effect he was arguing that British-born black people could, and would, claim equality with 'the rest of us', rather than accept a subordinate role in the life of the country. The numbers meant that ordinary English men 'found their wives unable to obtain hospital beds in childbirth, their children unable to obtain school places'. But the real problem was immigrant power, the demand for equal treatment. A form of 'one-way privilege' was being awarded to the newcomers, who were being granted liberty to complain about the opinions and behaviour of native Britons. Immigrant communities were being given the tools to 'agitate and campaign against their fellow citizens'. Citizens of the United Kingdom should not be 'denied [their] right to discriminate in the management of [their] own affairs'; the proposed legislation was a further blow to ordinary English men and women who 'have found themselves made strangers in their own country'.[2]

The following days saw Powell interviewed on both BBC and ITN news, and the papers were full of the speech; by Monday the Conservative Party leader, Edward Heath, had sacked him from his Shadow Cabinet and on the Tuesday (the day that the Race Relations Bill got its second reading in the Commons) a thousand East London dockers went on strike and marched to Westminster carrying signs saying 'Don't Knock Enoch', and other, similar slogans. Thousands more joined the strike in the coming days. National polls and letters to the newspapers in the weeks that followed appeared to show a majority in favour of Powell's stance. Powell himself received over 100,000 letters in April and May, mostly saying thank-you.

The letters were often attributed to multiple signatories – 359 postal workers, for example, or 30 members of a branch bank. They thanked him first of all for speaking up for ordinary workers, echoing the rhetoric associated with Peter Griffiths' victory in Smethwick four years earlier: 'at last an honest MP', 'the only man who has spoken for us', 'a man who puts country before party'. Letter-writers repeatedly insisted they were not 'racialist', since they did not believe

Dockers march to the House of Commons in support of Enoch Powell, 1968.

in the biological inferiority of non-white races. Instead they feared for British culture and traditions which could not survive under the pressure of so many newcomers, who brought with them alien ways of behaving. A surprisingly small proportion of letter-writers focused on the economic consequences of immigration – the strain on social services, or the burden on taxpayers, for example. The overwhelming focus was on cultural rather than economic losses. The boundaries of the nation had long been mapped on to Britishness – and perhaps even more closely on to Englishness – but in the new popular politics of race, the problem of those who could not or would not share that culture had been irredeemably racialized. Immigrants no longer meant all immigrants but 'Jamaicans, Indians, and God knows what other coloured people'. 'As an Englishman,' wrote one citizen to Powell, 'I would like to think that my son and grandchildren will also be Englishmen, and what's more *look like* English men and women.'[3]

Heath removed Powell from the Shadow Cabinet because he had spoken without the prior approval of the government, and because, as he explained to Robin Day on the BBC's *Panorama* programme, his words were 'inflammatory and liable to damage race relations'.

Several newspapers, including *The Times*, recorded a spike in attacks on immigrants in the immediate aftermath of the speech. A BBC opinion poll in October 1968 found that 8 per cent of immigrants felt they had suffered more discrimination since Powell's speech. And given the weakness of the 1965 legislation against racial discrimination, there was very little they could do about it. Organizations such as the Campaign Against Racial Discrimination (CARD), a broad umbrella group which was founded in 1965 in order to lobby for stronger legislation, had long argued that the 1965 Act was as good as useless. The Act criminalized discrimination on grounds of race, colour, ethnicity or national origin 'in places of public resort', such as hotels, restaurants, pubs, theatres and dancehalls. But it was still perfectly legal to post an ad for a job or a flat stating 'No Coloureds' – and there was no attempt to deal with the possibility of racism in public bodies such as the police force, or the criminal justice or education system.

One of the provisions of the 1965 Act was to set up the Race Relations Board to investigate complaints and offer mediation. In practice, most of the complaints were about being refused service in pubs and, as the Campaign Against Racial Discrimination pointed out, the 'public resort' clause actually set the bar rather high for grievances. In effect people had to feel strongly enough about the way they were treated to publicize their own humiliation. Discrimination was understood as a matter of personal attitude – whether the person was doing the discriminating or being discriminated against. The Act implied that racism could be dealt with by curbing the behaviour of racist individuals, teaching people guilty of prejudice or intolerance to do better. And it put the onus on individual victims to prove they had been hurt by that prejudice. When the policy think-tank Political and Economic Planning's *Report on Racial Discrimination* was published in 1967 it became much harder to ignore the systemic nature of discrimination. The Report detailed multiple examples of black and Asian immigrants being treated as 'second-class citizens'. These were instances in which immigrants themselves drew attention to unequal treatment, but given the reluctance of many migrants to come forward at all, CARD tried to recruit concerned citizens to gather more evidence. Their leaflet, 'How to Expose Discrimination', explained that the real problem with discrimination was that most people didn't think there was much of a problem, so that it was up to enlightened folk to prove it. There were guidelines for testing landladies and employers, including 'The Telephone Test' (get a person with an accent and one without to ring up for the same flat), 'The Letter Test' (get two people with the same qualifications, one obviously 'coloured', to apply for the same job), and other tests which required rather more effort:

> Get two members to apply for estate agents' lists, specifying exactly the same requirements of size, price, etc., and compare the lists to see that they are the same. Get coloured house-buyers or flat-hunters deliberately to apply for accommodation in previously all-white areas, or better still for housing which they *know* is up for sale or rent in such areas.

CARD's aim was to prove that discrimination was widespread, and not just an annoyance for individuals but a cause of systemic disadvantage that required intervention. It was this slow shift in understanding – towards an acceptance that black immigrants were equal citizens, rather than 'dark strangers' who had to be more or less tolerated but who could be kept in their place – to which Powell and his supporters were responding.[4]

The novelist Hanif Kureishi was a teenager in the late 1960s. His father had left Bombay in 1947 to study in London, where he had met and married an English woman. His father's family had moved from Bombay to Karachi after Partition, where they had become Pakistani. The teenage Kureishi watched his friends on the outskirts of South London become new versions of themselves too – decked out in Union Jack braces, Doc Marten boots and skinhead haircuts, they took to hunting down black and Asian immigrants and beating them:

> As Powell's speeches appeared in the papers, graffiti in support of him appeared in the London streets. Racists gained confidence. People insulted me in the street. Someone in a café refused to eat at the same table with me. The parents of a girl I was in love with told her she'd get a bad reputation by going out with darkies. Parents of my friends, both lower-middle-class and working class, often told me they were

Graffiti in London, 1968.

Powell supporters. Sometimes I heard them talking, heatedly, violently, about race, about 'the Pakis'.

Kureishi retreated from his former friends, finding refuge in reading about black liberation movements in the United States: articles on the Black Panthers, novels by James Baldwin and Richard Wright, statements by Muhammad Ali. And he recalls a TV spectacle which rivalled Powell's speech for its ability to set, or at least announce, a new agenda: the Black Power salute given by members of the US Olympic team in Mexico in October.

> A great moment occurred when I was in a sweet shop. I saw through to a TV in the backroom on which was showing the 1968 Olympic Games in Mexico. Thommie [*sic*] Smith and John Carlos were raising their fists on the victory rostrum, giving the Black Power salute as the 'Star Spangled Banner' played. The white shopkeeper was outraged. He said to me: they shouldn't mix politics and sport.[5]

The Pakistani-born writer Dilip Hiro also understood the event as signalling a radically new understanding of what it meant to be black. Seeing black Americans invoking Black Power on the television, 'millions of black people in the Western World instantly identified with them', not only those of African heritage. Arguably the pan-black alliance that began to gain ground in Britain in the late 1960s was simply echoing the logic of those who argued that black immigrants were the problem, wherever they came from ('Jamaicans, Indians, and God knows what other coloured people'). After all, Powell had specifically targeted 'Negroes', immigrant children who apparently knew no English except the word 'racialist' ('They cannot speak English, but one word they know . . .') and the Sikh community, which was campaigning in Powell's Wolverhampton constituency for transport workers to be allowed to wear turbans at work. Government officials and white supremacists alike began to use the term 'Afro-Asian' to refer not to people of mixed race but New Commonwealth immigrants in general.[6]

Comparisons with racial politics in the United States had come full circle since the 1958 riots in Notting Hill. Back then the possibility that London (or Nottingham) might have anything in common with Little Rock, Arkansas, was raised only in order to be dismissed. The Commonwealth of Nations had been built on the principles of equal citizenship and tolerance, and Britons liked to congratulate themselves (implausibly) on not being defined by a history of slavery. Ten years later it was precisely fears of ending up like America that fuelled overt anti-immigration rhetoric, including Powell's doom-laden threat that Britain would inevitably fall to rioting and racial unrest: 'that tragic and intractable phenomenon which we watch with horror unfolding on the other side of the Atlantic'. In the summer of 1967, riots and civil disturbances by mainly black protestors caused looting, destruction and the deaths of twenty-six people in Newark, New Jersey, and of forty-three people in Detroit. In early April 1968, following the assassination of Martin Luther King, there were riots across more than a hundred American cities, including Chicago, Baltimore and Washington, DC, in which thirty-nine people (thirty-four of them black) were killed. The concern of Powell's 'decent, ordinary, fellow Englishman' that the black man would soon have 'the whip hand' over the white acknowledged both that the racial histories of the United States and Great Britain were not so different after all, and that black people appeared unwilling to put up with their allotted role.

The official line was that Britain's racial problems were entirely different from those of its former colony. *The Times*, for example, insisted that,

> Nothing could do more harm than if the present troubles in America are taken to be an accurate, if enlarged, account of the problem we face here. Almost all the stereotyped images based on the American situation are utterly misleading when applied to Britain. For Birmingham, Alabama and Birmingham, England are, in the end, quite different.

Indeed part of the attraction of America's revolutionaries to young black Britons was that they behaved so differently from their parents' generation in England. When Hanif Kureishi tore down the posters of the Rolling Stones and Cream from his Bromley bedroom wall, and replaced them with pictures of the Black Panther leaders – Eldridge Cleaver, Huey Newton and Bobby Seale, sporting Jimi Hendrix haircuts and holding guns – he did so because '[t]hese people were proud and they were fighting. To my knowledge, no one in England was fighting.' But Powell's supporters convinced themselves that they soon would be.

It was obviously unreasonable to argue that Sikh bus drivers who wanted to be able to wear turbans at work were plotting the overthrow of white civilization. But American black revolutionaries had been giving speeches and making contacts in Britain which the government deemed dangerous to race relations. Soon after the 1965 visit by Malcolm X to Smethwick, Michael Abdul Malik (formerly Michael de Freitas/Michael X), along with Guyanese immigrant Roy Sawh, had founded the Racial Adjustment Action Society (RAAS) to agitate for racial equality. Bringing together Marxism, revolutionary nationalism and West Indian activism, RAAS was described in the *Observer* as an 'openly militant' group, 'born in the slums of London's Cable Street and Powis Square'. The 1966 publication by the West Indian Standing Conference of J. A. Hunte's investigation into police brutality, *Nigger Hunting in England?*, and of Neville Maxwell's *The Power of Negro Action* in 1965 seemed proof that tension was mounting. The rhetoric of Black Power – the insistence on the necessity for militant black defence against white aggression – was migrating to Britain. And in the summer of 1967, while Detroit rioted, Stokely Carmichael, former chairman of the civil rights group

Stokely Carmichael speaking at the Roundhouse, Chalk Farm, 1967.

the Student Nonviolent Coordinating Committee and an advocate of Black Power, made a ten-day visit to London, which was widely covered by the BBC, ITV and national papers.[7]

Carmichael was invited to address the Dialectics of Liberation Congress, held in July in Camden's Roundhouse. The acme of 1960s counter-cultural debate, the Congress was flagged as 'a unique gathering to demystify human violence in all its forms, the social systems from which it emanates, and to explore new forms of action'. For two weeks the proponents of radical anti-psychiatry, such as R. D. Laing, took the floor alongside Beat-generation writers (Allen Ginsberg, William Burroughs), philosophers such as Herbert Marcuse, and the proponents of various strands of revolutionary racial action: C. L. R. James, Michael Abdul Malik, Obi Egbuna and Roy Sawh. It was an entirely male line-up, as were most of the revolutionary reference points: Che Guevara, Chairman Mao, Frantz Fanon. A twenty-four-year-old civil rights activist from Derry, Eamonn McCann, spoke on discrimination against the Catholic population in Northern Ireland. He was of the highly politicized, liberal, younger generation of Irish immigrants in Britain who were rejecting wholesale what they regarded as the quietist conservatism of the post-war generation. They scorned those Irish who poured their energies into the British Labour Party at best, and at worst the emigrant County Associations ('dominated by people who craved acceptance and middle-class respectability') and the Catholic Church.[8]

The Irish radicals took their cue – and much of their language – from the American civil rights movement and, just as in the United States, there were fierce battles over whether it was better to take a reformist or revolutionary route to political change. Fionnbarra Ó Dochartaigh, who would later take a leading role in the Derry Housing Action Committee and the Northern Ireland Civil Rights Association, was, until he returned to Derry in 1966, a member of the London-based socialist and republican Connolly Association, which insisted on the parallel between the emancipation of the American South and of Catholics in Northern Ireland. But by the mid-1960s there were several alternative forums for politically minded Irish immigrants. In 1964 the Irish republican movement set up Clann na hÉireann as a support, fund-raising, and recruiting organization for the IRA in Britain – principally in Birmingham and Glasgow. The Clann ran ceilidhs and old-time dances, and started a 'Buy Irish' campaign to deepen their roots in the Irish community in Britain. One young organizer, Pádraig Yeates (the Birmingham-born son of Irish emigrants), advocated a campaign focused on aiding Irish immigrants, and publicizing discrimination against them. But the Clann also recruited volunteers who travelled to Wexford or Wicklow for military training (nicely convenient to the ferry). There was even a short-lived alliance with the Free Wales Army, which involved a cache of gelignite filched from mines in South Wales that eventually ended up dumped in a canal somewhere between Glasgow and Salford. But young Irish immigrants such as Eamonn McCann – one of the organizers of the historic civil rights march in Derry in October 1968 – were drawn to more intellectual leftist organizations, such as the Irish Communist Group and the Irish Workers' Group. Speaking in Stormont, the Northern Ireland Parliament, in 1968 William Craig, the

Ulster Unionist politician who banned the Derry march, laid part of the blame for the revolutionary civil rights demands at the door of London-based radicals:

> Of the other elements involved perhaps it is worth mentioning the Irish Workers Group, which is a revolutionary Socialist group which aims to mobilise the Irish section of the international working class to overthrow the existing Irish bourgeois states, destroy all remaining imperialist organs of political and economic control and establish an all-Ireland Socialist Workers Republic. The leader is Gerard Richard Lawless of 22 Duncan Street, London, a former member of the I.R.A. who was interned by the Government of the Irish Republic in 1957. Eamon McCann of 10 Gaston Square, Londonderry, a prominent participant in the unlawful procession, is chairman of the Irish Workers Group in Northern Ireland.[9]

Lawless was also a member of the IMG (International Marxist Group), along with Tariq Ali. In these meetings the debates focused on the ideas and dilemmas of the New Left: anti-imperialism, decolonization, nuclear disarmament, and the movement against the Vietnam War.

This was the context of the Dialectics of Liberation Congress, and in Stokely Carmichael's mouth its language was uncompromisingly combative. Taunting a speaker from the floor for failing to curb white power ('You haven't done a goddam thing to stop white violence, have you? Have you?'), he insisted on the right of black communities to use violence: 'It's my survival I'm fighting for, white boy.' There would be no change in the status quo until the 'white man' learns that 'he can die just like anybody else'. When Carmichael left London for North Vietnam the home secretary, Roy Jenkins, banned him from entering the country again as his presence was 'not conducive to the public good'. Michael Abdul Malik was deputized to give an upcoming speech in Reading in his stead. The speech, which called for the death of any white man seen 'laying hands' on a black woman, was recorded by a *Daily Express* journalist and quoted by Conservative MP Duncan Sandys in the Commons, with a call for Malik to be prosecuted under the 1965 Race Relations Act. 'I am quite satisfied,' said the judge in the September 1967 trial, 'you came down here to this peaceful town in order to make trouble, which is just what the

Act is meant to avoid.' He was sentenced to a year in prison for 'intent to stir up hatred against a section of the public in Great Britain, distinguished by colour'.[10]

Just at the point that the laws against racial discrimination were expanded and toughened, it appeared to many people they could never be enough. Indeed some argued that the legislation was designed all along to suppress black radicalism rather than white racism, and Malik's arrest and prosecution appeared to prove it. But even if the legislators were given the benefit of the doubt, the problems of racial discrimination went far deeper than the 'everyday' prejudices the law was intended to tackle. The whole idea of 'Race Relations' assumed a goal of integration, but the watchwords of the radical groups who were seeding themselves in Oakland, Chicago, Paris, London, Belfast and Derry were not integration, and not even civil rights, but international socialism, revolution and liberation. 'Integration is not our aim, it's our problem,' James Baldwin insisted at a meeting in the West Indian Students Centre in February 1968. The price of integration was assimilation, the disappearance of what was distinctive about black cultures.

For radically minded immigrants, the task was to shift the focus away from individual racial slurs and towards social and economic marginalization, the systematic disadvantage black people suffered at the hands of employers, local councils, financial institutions (insurers and mortgage companies), the police and the criminal justice system. The Black Regional Action Movement, for example, operating out of 108 Mercers Road in Tufnell Park, London, produced a roughly printed magazine called *Black Ram* through the latter half of 1968 and early 1969. The articles focused on housing, the need for black history to be taught in schools, the 1968 Guyana elections, and the case for a nationwide black strike. The first issue of the – ironically titled – magazine *Hustler* was produced at number 70 Ledbury Road in Notting Hill in May 1968, and alongside the main article on Powell ('Who Knocks Enoch'), most of the pages of this first issue were devoted to the still dire local housing situation. The magazine saw itself as a local campaigning journal, and included articles explaining to local residents 'How to use the Rent Act' against unscrupulous landlords, and keeping them up-to-date with the redevelopment of the area around Lancaster Road. The second issue included a piece on 'Your Rights' by white lawyer and local councillor Bruce Douglas-Mann, who would be elected Labour MP for Kensington North in 1970. He pointed out that according to the 1967 local housing survey, black residents were still getting a raw deal:

> They show that the average rent paid by West Indians and Africans for one-room and three-room lettings is 30 per cent higher than the average rent paid by English, Irish and Europeans; in two-room flats, rents paid by coloured immigrants are, on the average, 60 per cent higher than those paid by white people in the area.

Moreover, 75 per cent of 'coloured immigrants' were in furnished accommodation – which was not only more expensive but provided fewer rights in terms of rehousing – compared to 25 per cent of white people. There had been no significant improvement in conditions since the Milner Holland Report three years earlier (and nothing had changed when Notting Hill housing was discussed in the Commons the following year). But this issue of *Hustler* also carried an article describing recent attacks on immigrants in Wolverhampton by white people shouting their support for Powell. And over the following months, alongside star signs, African fashions and the latest soul releases, more and more space was devoted to international black revolutionary activism: articles on the anti-apartheid movement in South Africa, and on black theatre in Harlem, Andrew Salkey on 'Revolution and the Artist' in Cuba, a piece by 'black art' poet LeRoi Jones (later known as Amiri Baraka) on Black Power in his home town of Newark after the riots, and an account of the political journey of 'Black Power Michael'.[11]

Hustler's mix of culture and politics, and its underground-press style – the layout, though black and white, mirrored that of alternative pop-art magazines such as the *International Times* and *Oz* – placed it at the interface between London hippie culture and local black activism. The calls to resist rent rises, to open the garden squares to local people and to start a revolution in North Kensington echoed the rhetoric of the London Free School, which had been set up by a broad coalition of counter-cultural artists (Pink Floyd played All Saints Church Hall in Talbot Road in October 1966) and community action projects, ranging from a playschool (Michael Abdul Malik got Muhammad Ali to visit the school in Tavistock Crescent), classes in African history, rent and housing support groups, and an adventure playground on the site cleared for the construction of the Westway. Malik had his finger in most of these pies, and arguably had effected the transition from Rachmanesque rack-renter to bohemian Robin Hood with remarkable aplomb, though there were concerns that his previous reputation could not be so easily dismissed, and some local residents kept away from the London Free School because of it. And part of the reason the London Free School could operate in the area at all, occupying abandoned and condemned buildings, was because so little had been achieved in terms of improving the housing situation for the majority of residents.

The August 1968 issue of *Hustler* advertised a weekend 'Seminar on the Realities of Black Power' to be held at the West Indian Students Centre, printed a Black Power statement from the United Coloured People's Association, and covered the arrests of Obi Egbuna, Peter Martin and Gideon Dolo for the racial content of speeches they had given in Hyde Park. They were accused of inciting violence against police officers. Roy Sawh was charged under the same legislation for calling for 'coloured nurses to give wrong injections to patients, coloured bus crews not to take the fare of black people' and Indian restaurant owners to 'put something in the curry'. By January 1969 the entire magazine was devoted to Black Power. Alongside pieces on Mozambique and Vietnam, the focus was on the recent meeting of the Black Peoples' Alliance, composed of West Indian, Indian, Pakistani and African organizations and individuals, which had produced a manifesto calling for 'a militant front for black consciousness and against racialism', and repeal of the 1962 Commonwealth Immigrants Act. This was Black Power filtered through the perspective of immigrants to Britain.

Obi Egbuna was a thirty-year-old Nigerian law student who had published a novel in 1964, and had his first play, *The Anthill*, produced the following year. As a member of the Committee of African Organizations, he had helped organize Malcolm X's visit to England in 1965; in 1966 he spent several weeks with the Student Nonviolent

Coordinating Committee campaigning in the United States. In September 1967 he co-founded the United Coloured People's Association, and published a manifesto, *Black Power in Britain*, which closely mirrored arguments which had been made by Carmichael at the Roundhouse in July. Black people were not the 'initiators of violence. But if a white man lays his hand on one of us we will regard it as an open declaration of war on all of us.' Six months later he started the British Black Panther Movement, a revolutionary socialist group explicitly modelled on the US Panthers, and began editing its journal (there were three issues before his arrest), *Black Power Speaks*. The British Black Panthers were just one of a number of groups that began promoting the idea of a black working-class revolution, and which opened up the fissures between the goals of integration and liberation for black immigrants. Ambalavaner Sivanandan, then the librarian at the Institute of Race Relations in London (and who would later, as its director, take the organization on a more radical, anti-integrationist path), recalled that, 'Black Power, in particular, spoke to me very directly because it was about race and class both at once. More than that, it was about the politics of existence.'[12]

Given the violent rhetoric of many of these speeches and publications, and the explicit echoes of the aims of the American Black Panthers, it should come as no surprise that men such as Michael Abdul Malik and Egbuna were attacked in the press and in Parliament. It seemed obvious that Black Power meant disorder and social unrest, and what's more it was alien to Britain, because British culture was (flying in the face of history) not marred by a slave-owning past – or at least not one which had played out on British soil. When Malik referred to the West Indies as England's 'deep south', suggesting similarities between the experience of African Americans and of West Indians, he was condemned in the press for making inflammatory and hysterical remarks. Colin MacInnes, in the *New Statesman*, argued for caution in rejecting the analogy. Britain had created her 'deep south' overseas, and just as southern African Americans had moved to the industrial North, so West Indians had moved to the Mother Country, where they were treated with much the same disdain as black people in America. MacInnes asked the readers of the *New Statesman* to imagine themselves in their place: 'let us make the imaginative effort to see Britain as does an intelligent, if not necessarily literate or affluent, black immigrant to our country'.[13]

We get some sense of that particular black immigrant perspective from a remarkable film made in February 1968 by Horace Ové, of a meeting in the West Indian Students Centre addressed by the American novelist James Baldwin on the subject of revolutionary politics. It was the second film shot by Ové, who was not yet thirty, and who had moved to Britain in 1960 from Belmont, Trinidad (where Michael X/Abdul Malik was from), to study art. He would go on to direct *Pressure* in 1976, the first black British feature film, about the effect of police brutality on young black men, and the increasing gap in understanding and attitudes between the first generation of West Indian immigrants and their children. Ové was typical of one section of Baldwin's London audience that day – the camera shows a number of young, polo-neck-jumper-and-corduroy-jacket-wearing students, writers and artists. Andrew Salkey is there, sitting prominently at the front. But there are also people who, from their questions, are clearly working men and woman, as well as a few white and Asian faces in the crowd. Why does Baldwin use the word 'negro', one asks, rather than 'black'? Why has he written contemptuously of an African past? 'Which is better, integration or Black Power?' In fact that was a question which had been posed by ITN's *This Week* in a programme which had aired a few weeks before, in January 1968. On this occasion it was posed by a Jamaican woman who was concerned that Baldwin should appreciate the difference between being a West Indian in Britain, and being black in America:

> Now that I am in England, I am very glad that I came to England because I am more aware of the fact I'm a negro. In Jamaica I wasn't aware of the fact, because it's very cosmopolitan. And in Jamaica, I don't know if you've ever been told, we have more of a shade problem ... I never knew I was a real negro until I came to England. I know now.[14]

Baldwin's own comments that day focused on black internationalism. In Saigon, in Detroit and South Africa, 'the same war is being waged'. 'Thinking black' meant rejecting the chains of slavery, and for him the 'whip hand' was not just a metaphor. Slavery was the point of Baldwin's account of his conversation with a West Indian British Museum attendant when he first visited London ('where were you born before that?'). For, as he explained, he did not and could not know about his family history prior to the arrival in the United States. His ancestors were subject to a bill of sale which erased all information about origin, and which did so deliberately to disempower the men and women who from then on were forced to act 'under the whip'; 'we know who had the whip'. Slavery had robbed black people of their history and culture, and for Baldwin it was this fundamental rupture which necessitated a rediscovery of Black Power. Nonetheless, there is something puzzling in the story Baldwin told that day, for it was most unlikely that the British Museum attendant who struck up a conversation with him knew for certain where he himself was born 'before' he was born in Jamaica or Trinidad or Barbados. His ancestors too would have been subject to a bill of sale, which wiped out the past. What, then, was really at stake in his question to Baldwin? That as a West Indian he had a 'past' identity that he had brought with him to Britain, and that he assumed Baldwin must also have had in relation to the United States? That Baldwin must (because he was black) feel like an immigrant and hold on to a past from elsewhere?

Like the woman who explained the 'shade problem' back in Jamaica (she could barely make herself heard over the laughter of recognition), the British Museum attendant was voicing the particular character of experience for Britain's New Commonwealth population: that they were black, but they were also immigrants. Even if the West Indies (or indeed the Punjab, Mirpur and Sylhet) could be understood as Britain's deep south, they no longer lived there. At least part of their identity was bound up with where they had come from. At least part of their alienation had to be understood in geographical, rather than racial terms. It was this that made the principal difference between the first generation of migrants and their children. There were plenty of men among the first wave of immigrants who turned towards radical politics. Obi Egbuna and Michael Abdul Malik were obvious examples, but so were those such as Tariq Ali, Stuart Hall, Darcus Howe, Sivanandan, and others who were involved with the anti-Vietnam War movement, the International

Marxist Group and the *New Left Review* in the late 1960s. Enoch Powell's populist racist politics created a response among black immigrants in Britain which mirrored, and to some extent modelled itself on, the Black Power movement in the United States. The injunction to 'think black' was born of a desire to validate West Indian experience in a context where it was being belittled and unrecognized. It was telling that the writers associated with the Caribbean Artists Movement, who had arrived in Britain determined to make their mark on the metropolis, began in the late 1960s to shift their focus towards a specifically black audience. (Andrew Salkey argued, 'I began by seeking metropolitan approval. We must first seek approval of the fruits of our imagination within our society.') But 'thinking black' also involved mirroring the way immigrants were perceived by their neighbours. In the early 1950s when the first migrants arrived from Jamaica, Trinidad and Guyana, they began to acknowledge a new identity as 'West Indian'. By the late 1960s, an even more broadly defined identity had taken over. It wasn't just, as the West Indian woman who spoke to James Baldwin joked, that they had become 'real negroes', but they had become black, part of a coalition of colour which, in its struggles with a white coalition, would help redraw the map of British politics in the early 1970s. Nonetheless, even if the new consciousness of radical blackness was available to all New Commonwealth immigrants, it was certainly not availed of by all of them. There were divisions based on class, language, religion and, above all, the division between those who migrated in the post-war years, and the generation that was born in Britain.[15]

In the mid-1970s the American sociologist Thomas J. Cottle spent two years researching a book of interviews among the 'poor West Indian families of London'. Along the way he met sixteen-year-old James Coster, who was born in Hammersmith of Jamaican parents, and who would have been ten or eleven years old when Powell gave his speech, and when the American sprinters saluted Black Power in Mexico. A real-life version of one of the young men in Ové's film *Pressure*, which was made around the same time, Coster was barely willing to talk to Cottle at all, since he was white, and so talking was pointless. He looked forward to the complete transformation of the political landscape in Britain, and celebrated the revolutionary end of

A young man at the 'Black House' on Holloway Road, early 1970s.

a politics based on promises which were never kept. Because 'we don't eat promises, or live in them'. He was eloquent about his whole-sale rejection not of his parents, but of his parents' quietism, their belief in the value of respect, and respectability:

'My life is devoted to politics,' he said, 'but not any politics of the old days. All you have to do is look around and you can see what's going on. There's nothing different, or special about England. White man sits very heavy right on top of the black man. He might not think he is, but you talk to any black man and he'll tell you he is . . .

'You in America, you call what I'm saying a separatist movement. Look out, whitey, black people aren't going to talk to you no more, or listen to all your promises and deals. I don't like that word, separat-ist. All we're doing is reacting to the way white people treat us. If white people exclude us, we can do one of two things. Either we can say all right, we'll try to get by, we'll feel bad but we'll try to get by. Or we can say, before you push us out, we're going to be on our own, and be strong being on our own. We're going to show you how we don't need you, and how someday, when we're as strong as we're going to get, you're going to need us. White people don't like it when they don't know for sure what black people are thinking, and doing, and feeling. They don't like it . . .

'Everybody's going to have to learn a new way of dealing with one another. My father and mother, they still listen to all the promises. Maybe they won't change, but they can understand why things will have to change . . .'[16]

PART THREE

Pasts

20

Pasts

> My generation were in England and had no particular quarrel
> with not being of it, for the simple reason that we never broke
> our deepest sentimental links with where we had come from,
> that the Caribbean remained alive in you in England. And
> when you speak of 'home', that was home, even after thirty
> or forty years. That remained home, and also carried with it
> the fantasies of being buried at home. West Indians would tell
> you the one thing I don't want is for my bones to be laid here
> in this place. I can't be sure of it, but I doubt very much that
> that young British Black has a comparable sense of home.
>
> George Lamming (1997)[1]

Recently my parents, who are in their late eighties, moved from a
large rambling house on the outskirts of Croydon, in which they had
lived for nearly forty years, to a much smaller, more manageable one
just down the road. They found it hard. If your eye could look round
corners you could see from one house to the other, so the stress of
moving wasn't about losing a familiar neighbourhood, or having to
get used to a new local environment, different shops and bus routes.
The sadness was more existential, born of the knowledge that the
largest chunk of life was over. Their lives were contracting, both in
space and in time. It was as though less home to move about in made
it impossible to ignore the fact of less future to look forward to. And
for my mother there was an additional sadness: she could not bring
her things with her. My mother was the queen of bric-a-brac, a
sharp-eyed and dedicated hunter-out of antique- and junk-shop bar-
gains. Lunchtimes, after hospital hours and weekends would find her

searching through tat at the Missionary Mart in Croydon, or digging about in out-of-the-way Surrey antique shops in between visits to her psychiatric patients. Our house was full of furniture, china, glass, lamps, rugs, curtains, pictures, pots and pans and trinkets retrieved from these bargain raids. And because we also had a capacious cellar, nothing – not a broken cane chair or a calendar years out of date – was ever disposed of. It was simply moved aside to make room for the next thing. There is an uncannily familiar description in David Lodge's novel, *The Picturegoers*, about an encounter with another Irish family and their home in the late 1950s. The Mallorys refuse to throw anything away – souvenirs, old magazines, out-of-date calendars, 'an ancient, broken, dog's lead' which still hangs on its hook under a sign saying 'Please don't forget my walk'– so that their home becomes a museum of the family's everyday life, a place where the ordinary past continues to coexist alongside the present.[2]

Some of my mother's finds made sense to me – old plates with cracked glaze and delicate worn-out patterns, wooden side-tables, bits of old lace. And some of them seemed unimaginably ugly. I remember a large, turquoise ceramic lamp-stand in the shape of a mermaid, which my sisters and I regarded as the height of bad taste. We rolled our eyes. None of us though were quite prepared for how difficult she would find it to let go of these things. She became paralysed by the thought of choosing between them. The things she had gathered around her over more than sixty years of living in England were her history. A smaller home meant a smaller future but for her it also meant a smaller past.

I am convinced that my mother's devotion to bric-a-brac has to do with the fact that she is an immigrant. Although it mirrors the late-twentieth-century fashion for living surrounded by more or less aestheticized or kitsch versions of the past (distressed floorboards, vintage clothes), it is different in kind and certainly in degree. I suggested at the beginning of this book that when the door slammed shut on the post-war migrants' past they suffered a more extreme or uncompromising version of the universal experience of growing up. When we leave home we leave it for good. Even if we return, we cannot go back. But emigrants in the era before global mass communication left homes where the past appeared to go on without them.

They were irrevocably cut off from the history which had made them. Migrant workers – and those who believed at the time that they were migrants, rather than immigrants, and would one day be returning home – lived in a peculiarly disorienting temporal limbo where their efforts to earn money in the present were directed towards a future which they imagined as a return to the past. This was a longing for another place which was just as much a longing for another time, yet it had little in common with nostalgia. They weren't looking backwards, but forwards towards the past, even if the imagined future homecoming was limited to where their bones were to be buried. We might assume that the immigrants who accepted that they either could not or would not return home were more likely to fall prey to nostalgia, to prizing (or sometimes rejecting) the past they had lost. Yet though I know that my mother does look back wistfully to her childhood in Ireland, on which the door closed when she was just eighteen, the past which she recreated in that large rambling house was not a nostalgic projection of that childhood. Instead she surrounded herself with bits of history that had little or nothing to do with her personal story.

There were very few things in our house that were linked to my mother's childhood. I can remember three in particular. There was an oil lamp with a pink glass shade, which must once have illuminated the good room in the Irish farmhouse; there was a small ornate, Victorian glass jug, which had belonged to her mother and was perched on the mantelpiece in our sitting-room until one day I knocked it off by throwing a teddy bear and she was furious and inconsolable; and there was a picture of the Sacred Heart which hung on the wall in my bedroom when I was small. This last object was not in fact an actual relic of the past. My mother didn't bring it from home. I know this because when we went to the farm near Skibbereen for our holidays, a rival Sacred Heart hung on the wall above the settle in my grandmother's house, and underneath it shone a perpetual light, eerily red like a snake's eye, or so I imagined. Along with family photographs and calendars this was one of the very few pictures in the farmhouse. So at some point my mother bought the image of the Sacred Heart, or someone bought it for her. She must have felt ambivalent about it because she neither hung it in a public place nor put it away in a cupboard. There was no special place then for Irish bric-a-brac, or even Irish religious tat. It was bundled in with everything else. And this is why, when my sisters and I raised our eyebrows over some uniquely hideous object, we were missing the point. We were the ones with the nostalgic take on the past, happy with farmhouse-style dishes with their veneer of rustic charm, but not with ceramic mermaids. But my mother was not trying to reconstruct the past she had lost but to create her own history, and her own style, as someone who belongs in England even if Ireland, to use George Lamming's phrase, remains alive in her. Like all the immigrants I have discussed in this book, she was making her own story, one that was informed but not determined by migration. The characters I have written about here constantly shaped their own stories, which sometimes conformed to the sociological accounts of what it meant to be an immigrant – varieties of assimilation, integration, or nostalgic attachment to the homeland – but just as often did not, because everyone's bric-a-brac is by definition different and unpredictable.

Perhaps we find it easier to understand nostalgia for a lost time, a time of childhood – an experience which, after all, lies at the core of all our lives – than the messy and compromised aesthetics of the immigrant who makes his or her life elsewhere. Michael McMillan is the child of immigrants from St Vincent, who came to Britain in the 1960s, where his mother, like hundreds of other West Indian mothers, created a new kind of domestic space, a version of the Victorian parlour which was the favoured style of the colonial elite on the islands. After the ignominious struggles in rented rooms and overcrowded flats, the simple fact of having a good room in which to relax and entertain visitors spelled respectability. It was an accomplishment in itself. It said, we have arrived, and it said it loudly.

> The front room was a contradictory space, where the efficacy of the display was sometimes more important than the authenticity of the objects, such as artificial flowers, plastic pineapple ice buckets, floral patterned carpet and wallpaper that never matched, and pictures of the scantily clad 'Tina' next to *The Last Supper* . . . It was very much my mother's room, and as a second-generation, black British person from an aspirant working-class family of Vincentian parentage, I have

ambivalent memories of it. I must confess that growing up I was embarrassed about the front room's aesthetics, as it seemed in 'bad taste', or had no taste at all; in other words, it was 'kitsch' – a pejorative social code for working-class culture.[3]

Plastic-covered upholstery, swirly carpets, velvet-flocked wallpaper, the glass display cabinet, the gramophone, English seaside souvenirs, Caribbean island maps, crocheted coverings and (unaccountably) Venetian glass blow-fish: these typical furnishings referred to a lost childhood world, but they were much more emphatically about the new homes which West Indians had made in Britain. After all, owning a home in England fundamentally changed the migrant economy in which there was a division between where you made your living and where you spent it. Economic migrants sent their earnings, or large parts of them, back home. Buying a home or qualifying for a council house, putting your children through school and watching them grow up into young Britons, these were all ways of accepting you weren't going back, or not for a very long time. For Punjabi, Mirpuri and Sylheti migrants it was the same – when women arrived in the early 1960s the frugal bachelor households gave way to relatively frugal family homes. The domestic aesthetic may have been different (though 'flowers on the carpet, flowers on the walls' were part of the joy of it, as Madho Ram acknowledged in his epic poem), but the jumble of past and present souvenirs was similar. Cheap reproductions of Islamic scrolls, calendars featuring pictures of the Sikh Gurus, *The Last Supper* and the Sacred Heart jostled up against photographs of children in their school uniforms, Constable's *Hay Wain*, china dogs and the TV screen.

The temporary migrant looks forward to returning to a place which can no longer exist as it was, because it has been changed by the money the migrant has earned to make return possible. The settled immigrant has accepted that he or she is not going back, but lives in a similar temporal limbo, creating a new history in the present. Immigrants not only leave the past behind, they are also cut off from the everyday present as it unfolds in the homes they have left. They cease to be who they were, individuals recognized by a network of family, friends and acquaintances, and become merely representative of their community and their nation, whether or not that nationality conforms to who they thought they were. Calabrian villagers suddenly became Italians when they arrived in post-war Britain; Mirpuris, Sylhetis and Pakistani Punjabis all became 'Pakis' and so did many Punjabi Sikhs who held Indian passports – later they all became Asians; Jamaicans, Trinidadians, Vincentians and Guyanese became West Indian. (And then they all became black, whatever their origin. The Indo-Guyanese publisher Arif Ali, when asked with some incredulity whether it took coming to Britain to realize he was black, explained: 'Yes. In Guyana, oh no, you couldn't call me black in Guyana. What's the matter, are you mad or something? In Guyana I am an Indian or a coolie.'⁴) For all Irish labourers' obsessive insistence on the difference between Dubliners and countrymen (and women), to everyone else they were simply the Irish, just as today immigrants from Latvia, Lithuania, Romania and Poland are all simply Eastern Europeans, or sometimes simply Poles. Yet when Britain's new post-war nationalities returned to their former homes on holiday, they were none of these things. They had become foreign, no longer properly at home in Calabria, Sylhet or Guyana. They carried with them the taint of abroad – their subtle alienness always about to be betrayed by their attitude to money, their clothing, their accent or a turn of phrase.

The immigrant faced in two directions at once, and lived in two time zones. But the temporal disjunctures which lay at the heart of migration from more 'backward', 'primitive' or 'colonial' areas to the heart of industrial modernity could play out in very different ways. Ostensibly immigrants were in the vanguard compared to those who remained at home; they were on the side of money, urban life, industry, employment and consumer goods. Moreover they had the National Health Service to look after them, and their children were getting a free education, albeit not necessarily a very good one. What they lacked – a connection with home, a traditional community and a role in the future of that community – could be compensated for by strategies which varied from extended visits home to arranged marriages. The spouses, both men and women, who arrived from rural Punjab and Sylhet were often regarded as unsophisticated villagers compared with the fashionable young people of Southall and Bethnal

Green, and many of these marriages could not survive the clash of culture and expectation.

For traditional patriarchs the idea of bringing a spouse from abroad to marry one's children was a way of playing safe – buying into the known and the traditional. The strategy began to backfire as, increasingly, Asian women proved to be better educated than the teenagers and young men brought up in London and the Midlands. On the other hand there were those immigrants (particularly single men) who were always convinced they would be returning home and made little attempt to create a new world for themselves in England. They became – or they appeared to be – stuck in the past, embarrassing, or sometimes worthy, representatives of an outmoded way of life. In the early 1970s Dónall Mac Amhlaigh noted the preference among Irish labourers for conservative fashions dating from the 1940s, including starched detachable collars, which long outlasted the disappearance of that style in Ireland itself: 'Suits would be neatly pressed for the most part, and if your trouser leg was any narrower than twenty-two inches the effect was considered rather shabby.' There was of course no natural association between non-metropolitan migrants and un-fashionable dress – West Indian migrants had a reputation for par-ticularly sharp dressing. But the rural Irishman in Britain was seen as a kind of throwback, an unchanged element of rural reality, isolated from both British and Irish society, and therefore uncorrupted. Mem-oirists and ethnographers such as Mac Amhlaigh and Richard Power liked to imply that the 'real' Irish (Irish speakers, manual labourers) were to be found in the industrial cities of Britain, the last representa-tives of a now outmoded but authentic way of life.[5]

The real Ireland, however, like the real India or Pakistan or Jamaica, was not locked back in the past. Some changes were acceler-ated by emigrant remittances, and some – also in part a consequence of emigration – by the tourist boom of the 1970s, particularly in Europe. This last was a magic wand that transformed previously depopulating fishing villages and desolate beaches in seemingly arbitrary bits of Southern Europe and the Caribbean, creating such influxes of money for those who had stayed that it made it much less clear that the choice to leave had been a good one. For the emigrants themselves, particularly those who went back rarely, given the expense and difficulty of long journeys to the Caribbean and Asia, these changes must have been disorientating. There are plenty of stories of couples returning to the Punjab to stay in the new homes they have paid for, stamped with the marks of success – electricity, fridges, televisions, modern plumbing – and feeling that they no longer belonged. And for the children of those emigrants, who had never lived anywhere else than Britain, although there was less at stake in their encounter with the lost past, it was just as complicated. It may be going too far to say that they had to fake a sense of belonging, but it is certainly the case that their relationship with their parents' home had to be, to some extent, manufactured. Yet, like the manufactured quality of the typical West Indian front room, it was no less real for being made up.

Like thousands of children of post-war immigrants, we went 'home' every summer to the farm where my mother was born, and sometimes at Christmas too, for years and years. And for years after that I would take my own children on the same journey, in which we played out the contradictions of emigrant belonging. Each July back in the 1960s and 1970s, the six members of my family, plus the dog, would load ourselves into the Vauxhall Viva to drive the six hours to Swansea (before the M4 motorway was finished), to board the Swansea–Cork ferry, and then drive a further couple of hours to West Cork. When we climbed stiffly out of the car at my aunt and uncle's farm we were greeted by a gentle ritual which never failed to unsettle me. As our parents bundled off to pour the tea and open a bottle with the grown-ups, our six cousins would gather awkwardly round the four of us and one by one they would say, rather solemnly, 'Welcome home.' They were echoing their own parents, of course, and the many greetings they had heard to returning emigrants over the years. But I was not at home. At last I was released from school and the boredom of days spent lying around in the back garden or patrolling the corridors of the hospital where my mother worked, and I was on holiday. Except, apparently, not.

In fact, 'Welcome home' was not just an echo of the grown-ups. It picked up on the Irish government-led campaign to boost tourism by holding Welcome Home Week festivals in towns and villages across the country. These were mostly damp-squib affairs consisting of a parade of home-made floats down an often rather chilly main street in the middle of August. But in practice what they were acknowledging was that the emigrants returning for their holidays were really being treated as tourists, despite the homely rhetoric. (A Jamaican child migrant returning home in the 1960s found exactly the same, although the weather was undoubtedly warmer: 'I had thought of Jamaica only as paradise. Nothing was important but the sun and the beach which were the only things my parents talked about . . . But returning migrants are considered tourists. The taxi drivers are out to squeeze everybody they can get hold of. You have to stick out or they would "thief" your eyes out of their sockets.'⁶) Everywhere the point was to get travellers to spend money. Which we did. Although our encounter with 'home' was undoubtedly real – we spent most of our time holed up in the house or out in the fields with cousins with whom we built real relationships – it was also forged, constructed out of a kind of tourist brochure of styles. We were even kitted out in scratchy Aran sweaters. It would be wrong to label this nostalgia. We were simply enacting the version of being Irish which was available to us, as people who were not quite at home.

I draw on my own experience of going to Ireland on holiday not because I think it was unique but precisely because it seems to me to have been typical, at least for the children of European migrants – the Cypriots, Italians, Maltese and Irish families who went back regularly, to what were in many cases fast becoming tourist destinations. Belonging was complicated, but not longing. We borrowed our sense of longing from our parents – because they loved home, we did too. Of course it helped that the Ireland we visited conformed to our expectations of a holiday destination – an unspoilt farming landscape, open fires, rudimentary plumbing, beaches and excellent sweet shops. We did not have to contend with crowds, heat or insects like Madho Ram's horrified children on a family visit to the Punjab: 'there's no end to the flies and mosquitos there, the ants and insects torment us . . . the unemployed get shamed and shovelled around . . . there are a lot of people squashed into trains and lorries.' We did not have to try to communicate with barely remembered relatives in rubbish Punjabi or Italian. But all of us children who took part in those ritual homecomings, wherever they took place, were to some extent having to fake it. And in this we were more like our immigrant parents than we knew.

George Lamming's description of his generation of Caribbean migrants – the first-comers – draws a relatively straightforward distinction between those who stayed in touch with home imaginatively and emotionally, until the time when they could be reunited with it physically, and the next generation who do not have a comparable sense of belonging. While this is broadly true – even common sense – it underestimates the extent to which the first immigrants too had to refashion their relationship to their own past. For a start they had to renegotiate their relationship to their families, as the gap between those who left and those who stayed inevitably widened over time. Each could see in the other the alternative possibilities now closed to them, and each had to contend with the jealousies – and guilt – which went along with that. Being saddled with the responsibility of looking after elderly relatives at home while your brother or sister got to experience a new world of urban work and wealth, might look more like being protected from exhausting and atomized industrial drudgery if you looked from the other end of the telescope. The everyday tensions and rivalries between siblings were more easily fixed and codified by virtue of geographical distance. Yet the meaning of these choices (staying, or going) would change over time, as the economies of Ireland, southern Italy, Cyprus and even – though to a lesser extent – the Caribbean and South Asia, began to catch up with that of Britain.

The purpose of sending money home also changed over time. Initially, for the vast majority of economic migrants, it was the whole point of leaving, and it was meant to be temporary. But as the monthly envelopes containing £5 notes, the postal orders and the smuggled currency kept on arriving it became less a means of staving off crisis through emergency funds, and more a continuous strategy, a way of preserving a tie with home. Emigrants might complain that their role in the family had been reduced to off-site financial provider, but it was one way of staying relevant, in effect of maintaining a presence even though they were absent. Remitting became a way of life, particularly for Indian and Pakistani migrants, actively strengthening links with home. Over time, the remittances ceased to be directed to family members – to the fathers, mothers and siblings who had remained at home. Instead they went to building holiday or retirement homes for the emigrants themselves, and, through charitable giving, into high-profile religious projects (re-gilding the Golden Temple in Amritsar, for example), and philanthropic building schemes for the village community: hospitals, schools, sports facilities and sewage treatment works, but also vanity projects such as the extraordinarily elaborate gate-towers which now announce entry to many villages.[7]

The landscape in both East and West Punjab is dotted with *kothis* – *pakka* modern walled homes, often with extensive balconies, terraces and turrets – which remain locked and empty. The villages which border the Mangla lake in Mirpur feature the same large, unoccupied houses, alongside empty and half-built shops, remittance-financed businesses which have either failed, or not yet got off the ground. The price of land has soared in the area (for local earnings cannot compete with sterling savings), and apart from the brick-making and construction industries, taxi drivers and hotel owners, the economy has seen little benefit from the returning pounds. Large numbers of young men still have to migrate for work. Similarly, Jamaican 'returnee' houses, built in the cooler uplands, are instantly recognizable by their scale, extravagant architecture, and even their English-style gardens. And similarly, many of these houses remain empty, built by people who are emotionally attached to the idea of having a large and expensively furnished house at 'home', but who are unable to give up living in England. In Ireland the aesthetic priorities are rather different. There is far more cachet attached to owning a traditional farmhouse – or at least one that looks authentic – than a new-build bungalow or ranch, in part precisely because the once-booming Irish construction industry is blamed for damaging the underpopulated rural 'heritage' landscape which post-war migrants fled in the 1950s. But the investment in homes which remain empty much, if not most, of the time is the same.[8]

This investment is both financial and emotional. The emigrant-financed building of schools and clinics in remote areas of India and Pakistan makes the global economy appear necessary, and even natural. People have to go away, and stay away, in order to keep sending

money back. Individuals who build houses back home find themselves saddled with the responsibility of their continued maintenance,
but it may be that this open-ended relationship to the place they have
come from is precisely what they are looking for. Owning a house
and land – even if it is a newly built house on land which has been
bought rather than inherited – is an assertion of belonging. The elaborate turrets and balconies are not simply monuments to wealth and
status but ways of staking an ongoing claim to a very particular and
local environment. House building is an investment in a place which
has been left behind, a buying of and into nostalgia. But for this very
reason it is also a survival strategy, a way of making sense of the
impossibility of returning. Maintaining a relationship with the village or town you left many years ago is a way of acknowledging pride
in your past, but – since it is the past – it is necessarily bound up with
a sense of loss. The traditional, slower and simpler way of life the
migrant remembers exists not just in another time but in another
country. And in communities where emigration has become the norm
for young people the landscape and local environment is experienced
as something already lost, a place which will have to be commem-
orated elsewhere. All this migrants know very well, and certainly
better than those who do not have to leave their childhood communities. The experience of shifting back and forth across the dissolving
border between 'traditional' and 'modern' societies has provided
them with all the conceptual tools to become their own anthropolo-
gists. 'If I dream tonight, you can bet your life it will be about
Jamaica,' explained a twenty-eight-year-old Jamaican to Donald
Hinds in 1966. After ten years in England, a series of dead-end jobs,
and now living in a couple of rooms in a shared house with his wife
and four children, his dreams were of a return which he knew to be
impossible: 'To me the importance of Jamaica is that it is there.'[9]

The business of buying or building a house back home that you do
not plan to live in is partly backward-looking, then, but it is also ori-
entated toward the future – it acknowledges the yearning to live both
here and there simultaneously. It puts off decision to the future. It
may be for this reason that so many returnee houses remain un-
finished. Half-built houses and unfurnished homes are works-in-
progress, and so open-ended. It is more accurate to think of them not

as signifying failure (the failure of the migrant to return home) but representing hope: the hope that the future still contains possibilities. In this, of course, immigrants are just like everyone else. They may want their bones laid in the ground or their ashes scattered in the places they have come from, but until then they will keep their options open.

I began by suggesting that 'everyone was us' in the Britain which emerged out of war in the late 1940s. Wherever they had come from, people had to manage day-to-day life in the same place and, very broadly, under the same conditions. Yet the futures which the new arrivals from Europe, Asia, Africa and the Caribbean looked forward to did not often turn out as they imagined. Promises – legal, contractual, personal – were sometimes kept, but more often broken. Memoirs and recollections very often insist that the lessons learned through migration were of distance and dissimilarity, rather than resemblance and connection. And there is a strain of wry, ironic acceptance that although these were painful lessons to learn, they may also have been useful. 'Sometimes,' explained a Jamaican interviewee in Philip Donnellan's 1964 documentary *The Colony,* 'we think we shouldn't blame the people, because it's we who have come to this country and trouble them . . . If we had not come we would be none the wiser, we would still have the good image of England, thinking that they are what they are not.' Or as a Trinidadian woman argued in the same year, on the basis of her student experience in Britain, the newcomer

> has his position as a member of one of the coloured races clearly outlined for the first time; he has a whole series of class prejudices overturned; he has the colonial myth of his almost British personality completely destroyed. In the end the realization of this makes it impossible to be bitter about his stay in England. The English have at last rendered him a service.[10]

What the immigrant knows is that he or she is not at home, and truly belongs neither here nor there. Migrants are in the vanguard of an understanding not simply that 'everyone is us' but that that is so because everyone is an outsider. It is not only that post-war immigrants' contribution to British culture has opened it up to influences from elsewhere. This is not an argument about the importance of chicken tikka masala and halloumi, or mento, ska and reggae music to an expanded idea of what it means to be British, valuable though these multi-cultural strands may be. Instead, the value may lie precisely in the lesson that people find it hardest to learn, or to accept – that none of us securely belong. When indigenous Britons who still lived in largely mono-cultural communities complained about the Irish, Italians, Maltese, Cypriots, Poles, Caribbeans or South Asians who moved into their areas in the 1940s and 1950s, they were mourning their own imagined futures, which they wanted to hold on to as looking like a better version of the past they knew. It was not only the immigrants who had to learn to live in two places at once, and two time zones, but their neighbours too.

References

INTRODUCTION

1. Ruth Glass, *Newcomers* (London: Allen and Unwin, 1960), p. 237.
2. V. S. Naipaul, *The Enigma of Arrival* (London: Penguin, 1987), p. 109.
3. Muriel Spark, *The Girls of Slender Means* (London: Penguin, 1966 [1963]), p. 7.
4. On the strange temporality of migration see Ranajit Gupta, 'The Migrant's Time', *Postcolonial Studies* 1, 2 (1998), pp. 155–60.
5. For Winston Churchill's 1947 party political broadcast on emigrating Britons see Kathleen Paul, ' "British Subjects" and "British Stock": Labour's Post-War Imperialism', *Journal of British Studies* 34, 2 (1995), p. 267. On migration to the Commonwealth see also Wendy Webster, *Imagining Home: Gender, 'Race' and National Identity, 1945–64* (London: UCL Press, 1998), pp. 27–32.
6. 'What Have the Poles Done for You?' (London: British Joint Committee for Polish Affairs, 1945).
7. Joyce Eggington, *They Seek a Living* (London: Hutchinson, 1957).
8. Naipaul, *Enigma*, p. 154.

PART I: FUTURES

1. James Chuter Ede, Parliamentary Debates, HC, 7 July 1948, vol. 453, cc. 385–510. On the British Nationality Act and Commonwealth citizenship see Randall Hansen, *Citizenship and Immigration in Post-War Britain: The Institutional Origins of a Multicultural Nation* (Oxford: Oxford University Press, 2000), pp. 35–61; Nicholas Deakin, 'The British Nationality Act of 1948: A Brief Study of the Political Mythology of Race Relations', *Race* 11, 1 (1969), pp. 77–83.

I. GEOGRAPHERS

1. George Lamming, 'Journey to an Expectation', in *The Pleasures of Exile* (London: Allison and Busby, 1984), p. 212.

2. On photographs of West Indian migrants see Stuart Hall, 'Reconstruction Work: Images of Post-War Black Settlement', *Ten.8* 16 (1984), pp. 2–9; Paul Gilroy and Stuart Hall, *Black Britain: A Photographic History* (London: Saqi Books, 2011).

3. Lamming, *Pleasures*, p. 212. On advertisements for the mother country, see Elyse Dodgson, *Motherland: West Indian Women in Britain in the 1950s* (London: Heinemann, 1984), p. 10.

4. *Conversations: George Lamming: Essays, Addresses and Interviews*, eds. Richard Drayton and Andaiye (London: Karia Press, 1992), p. 48.

5. Lamming, *Pleasures*, p. 212.

6. Lamming, *Pleasures*, p. 53.

7. The son of the Trinidadian school teacher is quoted in Donald Hinds, *Journey to an Illusion: The West Indian in Britain* (London: Heinemann, 1966), p. 9.

8. For Vincent Brown's testimony see Joyce Eggington, *They Seek a Living* (London: Hutchinson, 1957), pp. 53–4.

9. The lyrics are from 'Jean and Dinah', by Mighty Sparrow. For the impact of the Second World War in the Caribbean see Harvey Neptune, *Caliban and the Yankees: Trinidad and the United States Occupation* (Chapel Hill: University of North Carolina Press, 2007); Humphrey Metzgen and John Graham, *Caribbean Wars Untold: A Salute to the British West Indies* (Kingston, Jamaica: University of the West Indies Press, 2007).

10. See Lamming's fictionalized account of his journey, *The Emigrants* (Ann Arbor: University of Michigan Press, 1994 [1954]), p. 86.

11. On the economy of the British West Indies, and on shipping, including fares and details of journeys, see Eggington, *Living*, chs 4 and 5. On the post-war economy of the West Indies see also George Cumper, *The Economy of the West Indies* (Kingston, Jamaica: University College of the West Indies, 1960); R. B. Davison, *West Indian Migrants: Social and Economic Facts of Migration from the West Indies* (London: Oxford University Press for the Institute of Race Relations, 1962), pp. 26–65; Douglas Manley, 'The West Indian Background', in S. K. Ruck, ed., *The West Indian Comes to England* (London: Routledge & Kegan Paul, 1960), pp. 3–48.

12. See Davison, *West Indian Migrants,* pp. 3–23.

13. Ferdie Martin is discussed in Eggington, *Living,* pp. 72–3. For Hazel Watson, see Ann Kramer, *Many Rivers to Cross: Caribbean People in the NHS 1948–69* (London: Sugar Media, 2006), p. 57.

14. The account of the Martinique troops appears in Lamming, *Emigrants,* p. 14.

15. V. S. Naipaul, *The Enigma of Arrival* (London: Penguin, 1987), p. 113, and pp. 136–7; for letters about the journey see V. S. Naipaul, *Letters Between a Father and Son* (London: Little, Brown, 1999), pp. 10–14; see also Patrick French, *The World Is What It Is: The Authorized Biography of V. S. Naipaul* (London: Picador, 2008), pp. 67–71.

16. On banana-boat travel see Davison, *West Indian Migrants,* p. 61; Wallace Collins, *Jamaican Migrant* (London: Routledge & Kegan Paul, 1965), p. 53. For Lucy Burnham's testimony see Kramer, *Many Rivers,* p. 62.

17. See Hinds, *Journey,* p. 26, and pp. 35–51.

18. For the analogy with the Middle Passage see Hinds, *Journey,* p. 48.

19. For migration from Monserrat see Stuart B. Philpott, 'The Monserratians: Migration Dependency and the Maintenance of Island Ties to England', in James L. Watson, ed., *Between Two Cultures: Migrants and Minorities in Britain* (Oxford: Blackwell, 1977), pp. 90–119; for eating snails in Martinique see Kramer, *Many Rivers,* p. 57.

20. Hinds, *Journey,* p. 49.

21. *Going to Britain?* (London: BBC Caribbean Service, 1959), p. 15; on the closure of stations see Hinds, *Journey,* p. 53. For a rather patronizing guide to fitting in to British society, written in the form of an autobiography of arrival by a West Indian student see H. D. Carberry and Dudley Thomson, *A West Indian in England* (London: Central Office of Information, 1950).

22. Lamming, *Emigrants,* p. 108.

23. See Kramer, *Many Rivers,* p. 62; John Western, *A Passage to England: Barbadian Londoners Speak of Home* (Minneapolis: University of Minnesota Press, 1992). One Barbadian who arrived to work for London Transport found himself easily confused: 'The other thing was that all white people looked alike to me. I had to concentrate very hard to remember at the garage who I'd been talking to the day before, what their hair was like, or their ears.' See Western, p. 56.

24. Lamming, *Pleasures,* p. 217; Stuart Hall, 'The Windrush Issue: Postscript', *Soundings* 10 (1998), pp. 188–91, p. 190; Lamming, *Pleasures,* p. 214. On migration as a version of growing up see Stuart Hall,

'Minimal Selves', in Homi Bhabha and Lisa Appignanesi, eds., *Identity and the Real Me* (London: ICA, 1987), p. 44: 'I really came here to get away from my mother. Isn't that the universal story of life?'

2. SURVIVORS

1. V. S. Naipaul, *The Enigma of Arrival* (London: Penguin, 1987), p. 154.
2. For ships and passenger lists of Polish Displaced Persons arriving from Africa and Europe see http://www.polishresettlementcampsintheuk. co.uk/passengerlist/shipsindex.htm. For stories of the protracted journey from Poland and arrival in Britain see Kathy Burrell, *Moving Lives: Narratives of Nation and Migration among Europeans in Post-War Britain* (Aldershot: Ashgate, 2006); Keith Sword, *Deportation and Exile: Poles in the Soviet Union, 1939–48* (Basingstoke: Macmillan, 1996); Keith Sword, with Norman Davies and Jan Ciechanowski, *The Formation of the Polish Community in Great Britain 1939–50* (London: University of London, 1989).
3. See Mark Ostrowski, ' "To return to Poland or not to return?": The Dilemma facing the Polish Armed Forces at the End of the Second World War': http://www.angelfire.com/ok2/polisharmy/chapter3.html. See also Zosia Biegus and Jurek Biegus, *Polish Resettlement Camps in England and Wales 1946–1969* (Rochford: PB Software, 2013).
4. See Linda McDowell, *Hard Labour: The Forgotten Voices of Latvian Migrant Volunteer Workers* (London: UCL Press, 2005), p. 50. See also Elvi Whittaker, ed., *Baltic Odyssey* (Alberta: University of Calgary Press, 1995).
5. On post-war reconstruction as it is discussed in this chapter see Tony Judt, *Post-War: A History of Europe since 1945* (London: Heinemann, 2005); see also Mark Mazower, David Feldman and Jessica Reinisch, eds., *Postwar Reconstruction of Europe: International Perspectives, 1945–1950* (Oxford: Oxford University Press, 2011), especially David Edgerton, 'War, Reconstruction and the Nationalisation of Britain, 1939–1951', pp. 29–46.
6. For the labour crisis and the case for importing Displaced Persons see Diana Kay and Robert Miles, *Refugees or Migrant Workers? European Volunteer Workers in Britain, 1946–1951* (London: Routledge, 1992); Johannes-Dieter Steinert, 'British Migration Policy and Displaced Persons', in Jessica Reinisch and Elizabeth White, eds., *The Disentanglement of Populations: Migration, Expulsion and Displace-*

ment in Post-War Europe, 1944–9 (Basingstoke: Palgrave Macmillan, 2011), pp. 229–47; J. A. Tannahill, *European Voluntary Workers in Britain* (Manchester: Manchester University Press, 1958); Elizabeth Stadulis, 'The Resettlement of Displaced Persons in the United Kingdom', *Population Studies* 5 (1952), pp. 207–37; Jacques Vernant, *The Refugee in the Post War World* (London: Allen and Unwin, 1953).

7. Judt, *Post-War*, p. 68. For developing policy in relation to the EVWs see the National Archives' Ministry of Labour and National Service files on the different recruitment schemes, especially: NA LAB 10/26 Recruitment of EVWs; LAB 26/204 Welfare; LAB 26/235 Women's Voluntary Service and EVWs; LAB 26/230 Clothing Policy; LAB 26/203 Incidence of TB in DPs and EVWs, proposal for mass radiography; LAB 8/2199 Reviews of the Working of the Private Domestic Workers Scheme.

8. For socialist approval of the Spivs and Drones Order see, 'What is a Spiv?', *The Socialist Standard*, October 1947, and Ferdynand Zweig, *Men in the Pits* (London: Gollancz, 1948), p. 112, where he outlines fears that 'parasitism' off working men will lead to the corruption of the new socialist order and welfare state. For the public information leaflet on the Control of Engagement Order see: http://www.unionhis tory.info/britainatwork/emuweb/objects/nofdigi/tuc/imagedisplay.php? irn=1551. See also Clive Harris, 'Post-War Migration and the Industrial Reserve Army', in Winston James and Clive Harris, eds., *Inside Babylon: The Caribbean Diaspora in Britain* (London: Verso, 1993), pp. 9–54.

9. LAB 8/1485 Recruitment of Women Campaign (Textile Industry), 1947 memo by D. D. MacLachlan.

10. 'A Word to the Women', BBC Light Programme, the Rt Hon. George Isaacs, 1 June 1947.

11. NA CAB 124/872 Memorandum to the Cabinet Foreign Labour Committee by A. Greenwood, 1 March 1946; see Harris, 'Post-War Migration', pp. 19–21.

12. *Economic Survey for 1947* (London: HMSO, 1947), p. 28. For discussion of the *Economic Survey* see Stadulis, 'Resettlement', pp. 211–12. Bradford Heritage Recording Unit Archive, BHRU A009/02/28.

13. BHRU B0006/01/18.

14. Kathryn Hulme, *The Wild Place* (London: Pan, 1959 [1954]), pp. 150–51.

15. The pro-Polish *News Chronicle* article appeared on 14 July 1947; similar pro-refugee material includes the leaflet 'What Have the Poles Done

for You?' (London: British Joint Committee for Polish Affairs, 1945), and a documentary film, *Code Name: Westward Ho!*, which aimed to explain the arrival of the refugees, and which is discussed by Wendy Webster in 'Britain and the Refugees of Europe 1939–50', in Louise Ryan and Wendy Webster, eds., *Gendering Migration: Masculinity, Femininity and Ethnicity in Post-War Britain* (Aldershot: Ashgate, 2008), pp. 35–51. On the 'displaced person's mind' see a 1 March 1948 memo from the Department of Labour to the Regional Welfare Officer in Leeds, LAB 26/204 Welfare.

16. See Webster, 'Britain and the Refugees of Europe', p. 36.

17. Communist anti-Pole propaganda includes Harry Pollitt's CPGB leaflet *No British Jobs for Fascist Poles*, published in London in 1946. For the attempted suicide of the Polish refugee see Jerzy Zubrzycki, *Polish Immigrants in Britain: A Study of Adjustment* (The Hague: Martinus Nijhoff, 1956). Monica Dickens, *The Heart of London* (London: Book Club, 1961); on Polish graves see NA BD 11/949 Question of Burial of Polish Civilians.

18. On the moral and physical health of DPs and the search for 'the cream', see McDowell, *Hard Labour*, ch. 4, and Kathleen Paul, 'British "Subjects" and British "Stock": Labour's Post-War Imperialism', *Journal of British Studies* 34, 2 (1995), pp. 233–76. See also Kay and Miles, *Refugees or Migrant Workers?*, p. 50, on the Foreign Labour Committee's preference for the 'exceptionally healthy and fit body' of Baltic women, and on the language of blood and stock see Wendy Webster, *Imagining Home: Gender, 'Race' and National Identity, 1945–64* (London: UCL Press, 1998), pp. 27–34.

19. For the Latvian woman who hid her pregnancy see McDowell, *Hard Labour*, p. 100; for the 'white swan thing' see p. 97. For the analogy with a 'slave market' see Margaret McNeill, *By the Rivers of Babylon: A Story of Relief Work among the Displaced Persons of Europe* (London: Bannisdale Press, 1950).

20. *Royal Commission on Population Report* (London: HMSO, 1949) Cmnd 7695. See Webster, *Imagining Home*, p. 34.

21. On 'Englishizing' the refugees see NA LAB 26/204 Welfare, and LAB 26/235 Women's Voluntary Service and EVWs.

22. Sheila Patterson, *Dark Strangers: A Study of West Indians in London* (Harmondsworth: Penguin, 1963), p. 179.

23. Oliver Ashley, 'Britain's Foreign Workers Do All Right', *Oldham Evening Chronicle*, 2 January 1950, p. 4.

3. VILLAGERS

1. John Berger and Jean Mohr, *A Seventh Man: A Book of Images and Words about the Experiences of Migrant Workers in Europe* (Harmondsworth: Penguin, 1975), p. 23.

2. John B. Keane, *Self-Portrait* (Cork: Mercier Press, 1964), pp. 32–3.

3. John Healy, *Death of an Irish Town* (Cork: Mercier Press, 1968), p. 45.

4. Des Hickey and Gus Smith, eds., *A Paler Shade of Green* (London: Leslie Frewin, 1972), p. 225; see also Interview with Michael Billington in Nicholas Grene, ed., *Talking about Tom Murphy* (Dublin: Carysfort Press, 2002), p. 96.

5. Eunan O'Halpin, ed., *MI5 and Ireland 1939–1945: The Official History* (Dublin: Irish Academic Press, 2002). On Peadar O'Donnell see Donal Ó Drisceoil, *Peadar O'Donnell* (Cork: Cork University Press, 2001); Peadar O'Donnell, 'Emigration is a Way of Keeping a Grip', *The Bell* 3, 2 (November 1941), and Peadar O'Donnell, 'Call the Exiles Home', *The Bell* 9, 5 (February, 1945).

6. Quoted in Ultan Cowley, *The Men Who Built Britain: A History of the Irish Navvy* (Dublin: Wolfhound Press, 2001), p. 134. See also Enda Delaney, *Demography, State and Society: Irish Migration to Britain, 1921–1971* (Liverpool: Liverpool University Press, 2000).

7. H. L. Morrow, 'Journey into Fear', in Leslie Daiken, ed., *They Go, The Irish* (London: Nicholson and Watson, 1944), pp. 62–71.

8. Dáil Debates, vol. 92, 14 and 16 December 1943. See also Pat Dooley, *The Irish in Britain* (London: Connolly Association, 1943).

9. For Ministry of Health debates about delousing see NA MH 55/1882 Cleansing of Irish Imported Labour 1942–49.

10. For emigration advertisements see NA LAB 8/1301 Recruitment of Nurses from Eire. Eire Government emigration policy in respect of staff for hospitals in this country (1946).

11. For the civil servant who was nervous of Italians see NA LAB 8/102 Employment of German ex-POWs in agriculture, 1948–9, Memo 10 March 1948. See also Kathy Burrell and Panikos Panayi, *Histories and Memories: Migrants and their Histories in Britain* (London: I. B. Tauris, 2006), pp. 71–2.

12. Michele Colucci is quoted in Flavia Gasperetti, 'Italian Women Migrants in Post-War Britain: The Case of Textile Workers (1949–61)', Ph.D. dissertation, University of Birmingham, 2012, p. 109. On the history of Italians in Britain see Terri Colpi, *The Italian Factor:*

The Italian Community in Great Britain (Edinburgh: Mainstream Publishing, 1991); Lucio Sponza, *Divided Loyalties: Italians in Britain during the Second World War* (Bern: Peter Lang, 2000) and 'Italians in War and Post-War Britain', in Johannes-Dieter Steinert and Inge Weber-Newth, eds., *European Immigrants in Britain, 1933–1950* (Munich: K. G. Saur Verlag, 2003), pp. 185–99.

13. See *Hidden Voices: Memories of First Generation Italians in Bedford/ Voci Nascoste: Testimonianze della Prima Generazione di Italiani a Bedford* (Bedford: Bedford Community Arts, 1999).

14. Quoted in Gasperetti, 'Italian Women Migrants', p. 102; on Miss Rathbone see pp. 117–21.

15. Quoted in Gasperetti, 'Italian Women Migrants', p. 112.

16. 'Little Italy in Bedford', *The Times*, 29 September 1960, quoted in Gasperetti, 'Italian Women Migrants', p. 63. See also, John Barr, 'Napoli, Bedfordshire', *New Society*, 2 April 1964, p. 7.

17. Raymond Williams, *The Country and the City* (Nottingham: Spokesman Books, 2011 [1973]), p. 279; Berger and Mohr, *Seventh Man*, p. 32.

18. On the legacy of partition see Pippa Virdee, ' "No Home but in Memory": The Legacies of Colonial Rule in the Punjab', in Panikos Panayi and Pippa Virdee, eds., *Refugees and the End of Empire: Imperial Collapse and Forced Migration in the Twentieth Century* (Basingstoke: Palgrave Macmillan, 2011), pp. 175–95.

19. See G. S. Aurora, *The New Frontiersmen: A Sociological Study of Indian Immigrants in the United Kingdom* (Bombay: Popular Prakashan, 1967), p. 41. On hair-cutting see pp. 43–4; see also Rashmikant Harilal Desai, *Indian Immigrants in Britain* (London: Oxford University Press, 1963), p. 77.

20. See Aurora, *Frontiersmen*, p. 42.

21. For the journey from the Punjab to Wolverhampton see Madho Ram, *Mera England da safr* [My Passage to England] (Handsworth: S. B. Kara, 1972), this translation by Beryl Dhanjal; for Naipaul's chicken meal see V. S. Naipaul, *The Enigma of Arrival* (London: Penguin, 1987), p. 122.

22. On the 'frontier' see particularly chapter 5 of Aurora, *Frontiersmen*. Aurora's fieldwork in Southall was carried out between 1957 and 1959.

4. EAST ENDERS

1. Steven Berkoff, *Free Association: An Autobiography* (London: Faber & Faber, 1996), pp. 5–6.

2. See Woodberry Down Memories Group, *Woodberry Down Memories: The History of an LCC Housing Estate* (London: ILEA, 1989); on Harrisson's report see Tony Kushner, *We Europeans? Mass-Observation, 'Race' and British Identity in the Twentieth Century* (Aldershot: Ashgate, 2004), pp. 82–102. See also William Zuckerman, *The Jew in Revolt: The Modern Jew in the World Crisis* (London: Secker and Warburg, 1937); Tony Kushner and Nadia Valman, eds., *Remembering Cable Street: Fascism and Anti-Fascism in British Society* (London: Vallentine Mitchell, 2000).

3. Alexander Baron, *With Hope, Farewell* (London: Cape, 1952), p. 48.

4. Baron, *With Hope*, p. 186. On post-war fascism see Graham Macklin, *Very Deeply Dyed in Black: Sir Oswald Mosley and the Resurrection of British Fascism after 1945* (London: I. B. Tauris, 2007), pp. 41–57; Graham Macklin, 'Police Failed Harold Pinter', *BBC History Magazine* 5, 9 (2004); Alexander Raven Thomson, *The Battle of Ridley Road* (London: Raven Books, 1947); Tony Kushner, 'Anti-Semitism and Austerity: The August 1947 Riots in Britain', in Panikos Panayi, ed., *Racial Violence in Britain, 1840–1950* (London: Leicester University Press, 1993).

5. Verily Anderson, *Spam Tomorrow* (London: Rupert Hart-Davis, 1956), p. 257.

6. On post-war Jewish settlement see Geoffrey Alderman, *London Jewry and London Politics, 1889–1986* (London: Routledge, 1989).

7. Macklin, *Very Deeply Dyed*, pp. 39–41; Morris Beckman, *The 43 Group* (London: Centreprise, 1992); Catherine Shepherd, 'Fascism in Hampstead, Parts 1 and 2', *Association of Jewish Refugees Journal* April–May (2002).

8. For the comparison between Jewish and black migrants see Yona Ginzberg, 'Sympathy and Resentment: Jews and Coloureds in London's East End', *Patterns of Prejudice* 13, 2–3 (March–June 1979), pp. 41–2. See also Barry A. Kosmin and Nigel Grizzard, *Jews in an Inner London Borough: A Study of the Jewish Population of Hackney based on the 1971 Census* (London: Research Unit, Board of Deputies of British Jews, 1975).

9. Edith Ramsay Papers, Tower Hamlets Archives, P/RAM/2/1/6, draft of article for the *Stratford Express*, May 1960. For a biography of Ramsay see Bertha Solokoff, *Edith and Stepney: The Life of Edith Ramsay* (London: Stepney Books, 1987).

10. An African Student [Derek Bamuta], 'Coloured People in Stepney', *Social Work* 7, 1 (January 1950), pp. 387–95.

11. Phyllis Young, *Report on an Investigation into the Conditions of the Coloured Population in a Stepney Area* (publisher unknown, 1944),

cited in John Marriot, *Beyond the Tower: A History of East London* (New Haven, Conn.: Yale University Press, 2011), p. 332.

12. Michael Banton, *The Coloured Quarter: Negro Immigrants in an English City* (London: Jonathan Cape, 1955), pp. 92–3.

13. Alexander Baron, *The Lowlife* (London: Black Spring Press, 2010), pp. 26–7.

14. For Kathleen see Ramsay Papers, P/RAM/3/1/15; Bamuta, 'Coloured People', p. 391.

15. See Ramsay Papers, P/RAM/2/1/5, 'Clubs and Cafes, Cable Street'.

16. Quoted in Yousuf Choudhury, ed., *Sons of the Empire: Oral History from the Bangladeshi Seamen Who Served on British Ships during the 1939–45 War* (Birmingham: Sylheti Social History Group, 1995), p. 5. See also Yousuf Choudhury, *The Roots and Tales of Bangladeshi Settlers* (Birmingham: Sylheti Social History Group, 1993) and Caroline Adams, *Across Seven Seas and Thirteen Rivers: Life Stories of Pioneer Sylhetti Settlers in Britain* (London: Tower Hamlets Arts Project, 1987).

17. Quoted in Choudhury, ed., *Sons of Empire*, p. 35.

18. For the description of housing conditions see Banton, *Coloured Quarter*, p. 107; Bamuta, 'Coloured People', p. 388.

19. Hamza Alavi, *The Pakistanis in London* (London: Institute of Race Relations, 1963), p. 1.

20. Ramsay Papers, P/RAM/3/1/2.

21. Ramsay Papers, P/RAM/2/1/12 and /3/1/13.

22. Ramsay Papers, P/RAM/2/1/5.

23. Chaim Bermant, *Point of Arrival: A Study of London's East End* (London: Eyre Methuen, 1975), pp. 249–50.

5. CARERS

1. Dónall Mac Amhlaigh, *An Irish Navvy: The Diary of an Exile*, trans. Valentin Iremonger (Cork: Collins Press, 2003 [1964]), p. 65.

2. Mac Amhlaigh, *An Irish Navvy*, p. 3 and p. 65.

3. Quoted in Peter Nolan, *A History of Mental Health Nursing* (London: Chapman and Hall, 1993), p. 110.

4. NA LAB 12/284 Recruitment of Nurses and Volunteers for Nursing in Eire: Proposed Appointment of Technical Nursing Officers to be Stationed in Eire (1944–1947). For official Irish attitudes to girls leaving to undertake nursing training in England see Clair Wills, *The Best are Leaving: Emigration and Post-War Irish Culture* (Cambridge: Cambridge University Press, 2015), particularly ch. 2. See also C. S.

Chatterton, 'The Weakest Link in the Chain of Nursing? Recruitment and Retention in Mental Health Nursing 1948–1968', Ph.D. dissertation, University of Salford, 2007; Nicola Yeates, 'Migration and Nursing in Ireland: An Internationalist History', *Translocations: Migration and Social Change* 5, 1 (2009).

5. This and the following quotations on lice and cleansing are from NA LAB 12/284.

6. Ethna MacCarthy, 'Public Health Problems Created by Louse Infestation', *Irish Journal of Medical Science* 23, 2 (February 1948), pp. 65–78.

7. 'They Treat Us Like Dirt', *Irish Democrat*, April 1951. For the choice of Baltic women over Irish see NA LAB 8/966 Recruitment of Domestic Workers from Eire; for the Jamaican who was refused nursing training see NA HO 344/105 Working Party interdepartmental correspondence. See also Chatterton, 'Weakest Link?', ch. 10; Mick Carpenter, *Working for Health* (London: Lawrence and Wishart, 1988); Donald Hinds, *Journey to an Illusion: The West Indian in Britain* (London: Heinemann, 1966), p. 75.

8. For recruitment to Runwell and Yardley Green see NA LAB 8/1301.

9. M. J. Molloy Memorandum, 'The Extermination Through Emigration Campaign', TCDMSS 8305/2; Eamon Casey, 'The Pastoral on Emigration', *The Furrow* 18, 5 (1967), pp. 245–56 (p. 256).

10. On Frimley Sanatorium see Raymond Hurt, 'Tuberculosis Sanatorium Regimen in the 1940s: A Patient's Personal Diary', *Journal of the Royal Society of Medicine* 97, 7 (2004), pp. 350–53; on hours and overtime see NA LAB 26/125.

11. On St Andrew's Hospital see Steven Cherry, *Mental Health Care in Modern England: The Norfolk Lunatic Asylum/St Andrew's Hospital c.1810–1998* (Woodbridge: Boydell, 2003), p. 236; for the University of Manchester study see *The Work of the Mental Nurse: A Survey Organized by a Joint Committee of Manchester Regional Hospital Board and the University of Manchester* (Manchester: Manchester University Press, 1955); on patients cleaning wards see especially pp. 83–5.

12. Audrey L. John, *A Study of the Psychiatric Nurse* (Edinburgh: E. & S. Livingstone, 1961), p. 94.

13. For Polish hospitals see NA MH 120/2 Polish Hospitals. I quote here from a letter of 31 January 1950, from the Lay Administrator of No. 4 Polish Hospital.

14. See Roberta Bivins, *Contagious Communities: Medicine, Migration and the NHS in Post-War Britain* (Oxford: Oxford University Press, 2015), p. 33.

15. Quoted in Bivins, *Contagious Communities*, pp. 38, 39; on overcrowding see Cherry, *Norfolk Lunatic Asylum*, p. 221.

16. Wellcome Library Archives SA/FPA/B10/35: Box 590 Immigrants.

17. British Cooperative Clinical Group, 'Gonorrhoea Study 1963', *British Journal of Venereal Disease* 41 (1965), pp. 24–9. Wellcome Library Archives SA/SMO/L20: Box 67 Health of Immigrants.

18. This and following quotations on family planning from Wellcome Library Archives SA/FPA/A21/26: Box 421 Correspondence with British Caribbean Welfare Services about provision of birth control advice to immigrant families.

19. *The Times*, 22 June 1965, Letter from Mary Park, Chief Medical Social Worker, Willesden, and George Discombe, Pathologist, Central Middlesex Hospital, Park Royal.

6. TROUBLEMAKERS

1. NA LAB 26/198 'Disturbances in National Service Corporation Hostels due to incompatibility of various nationals'. Internal Memo, 25 August 1949. The following quotations are taken from this lengthy file. For the Yugoslav infighting see Bradford Heritage Recording Unit Archive BHRU B0088/01/11.

2. NA HO 344/108 Working Party on Coloured People Seeking Employment in the United Kingdom – Report.

3. NA HO 344/103 Working Party on Coloured People Seeking Employment in the United Kingdom.

4. NA HO 344/106 Chief Constable Reports, 1953. The following quotations are taken from this file.

5. NA HO 344/105 Working Party Interdepartmental Correspondence.

6. See Virginia Noble, *Inside the Welfare State: Foundations of Policy and Practice in Post-War Britain* (London: Routledge, 2009), pp. 96–9. For police attitudes to 'work-shy' immigrants see NA HO 344/105, from which the following quotations are also taken.

7. NA HO 344/106 Chief Constable Reports, 1953.

8. NA HO 344/118 Report of Working Party on Immigration.

9. NA HO 344/106.

10. On the West Bromwich bus dispute see Mark Duffield, *Black Radicalism and the Politics of De-Industrialisation: The Hidden History of Indian Foundry Workers* (Aldershot: Avebury, 1988), pp. 27–8, and Joyce Eggington, *They Seek a Living* (London: Hutchinson, 1957), pp. 92–5. See also Simon Taylor, *A Land of Dreams: A Study of Jewish*

and Afro-Caribbean Communities in England (London: Routledge, 1993).

11. NA HO 344/106.

12. Shah's case and that of Kufait Ali below are outlined in NA HO 344/29 Pakistani Passports.

13. Quoted in Arthur Helweg, *Sikhs in England* (Oxford: Oxford University Press, 1979), p. 77.

14. See John Lambert, *Crime, Police and Race Relations: A Study in Birmingham* (London: Oxford University Press for the Institute of Race Relations, 1970). Lambert carried out his research in 1966 and 1967. On the Irish see p. 127.

7. DRINKERS

1. *A Catholic Handbook for Irish Men and Women Going to England* (Dublin: Catholic Truth Society of Ireland, 1953), pp. 13–14.

2. Fr Eamonn Gaynor, *The Shamrock Express* (Maynooth: Furrow Trust, 1962); *Irish Digest*, February 1956.

3. For de Valera on Birmingham see Mary Daly, *The Slow Failure: Population Decline and Independent Ireland* (Madison, Wisc.: University of Wisconsin Press, 2006), especially pp. 270–76; see also Enda Delaney, *The Irish in Post-War Britain* (Oxford: Oxford University Press, 2007); A. E. C. W. Spencer, *Arrangements for the Integration of Irish Immigrants in England and Wales*, ed. Mary Daly (Dublin: Irish Manuscripts Commission, 2011).

4. Oliver Reilly, 'A Worker in Birmingham', *The Furrow* 9, 4 (1958), pp. 217–24.

5. For films of the work of Irish chaplains with emigrants see *Hotel Chaplain*, Radharc Films, 1965; *Boat Train to Euston*, Radharc Films, 1965; *Oldbury Camp*, Radharc Films, 1965. See also Kieran O'Shea, *The Irish Emigrant Chaplaincy Scheme in Britain, 1957–82* (Dublin: Irish Episcopal Commission for Emigrants, 1985).

6. Archives of the Irish in Britain, London Irish Centre, 'Initial Proposal for an Irish Centre', 1948.

7. Dónall Mac Amhlaigh, *An Irish Navvy: The Diary of an Exile*, trans. Valentin Iremonger (Cork: Collins Press, 2003 [1964]), pp. 28–9.

8. Mac Amhlaigh, *An Irish Navvy*, p. 72.

9. The Archives of the Irish in Britain contain flyers and advertisements for Irish dances in the 1950s and 1960s; see also Rebecca Miller, 'Hucklebucking at the Tea Dances: Irish Showbands in Britain, 1959–

1969', *Popular Music History* 9, 3 (2014), pp. 225–47; Gearóid Ó hAllmhuráin, *O'Brien Pocket History of Traditional Irish Music* (Dublin: O'Brien, 2003); http://electricballroom.co.uk/history/.

10. Personal communications from Philomena Wills, and Gearóid Ó hAllmhuráin; Archives of the Irish in Britain, 'Initial Proposal for an Irish Centre'.

11. Richard Power, *Apple on a Treetop* (Dublin: Poolbeg Press, 1980), p. 195. See also John B. Keane, *Self-Portrait* (Cork: Mercier Press, 1964), on Irish labourers 'boasting of great feats of tunnel-digging, block-laying, and masonry', and of fights which take on mythic connotations: 'It reminded me of Cuchullain breaking his bonds' (pp. 64, 82). For representative English newspaper coverage of Irish fights see 'Mad Orgy by Irish Drunks', *Birmingham Mail*, 16 May 1956.

12. Brendan Behan, *The Dubbalin Man* (Dublin: A. & A. Farmar, 1997), p. 53.

13. For Behan's MI5 file see NA, KV 2/3181.

14. Mac Amhlaigh, *An Irish Navvy*, p. 53, p. 108; Power, *Apple*, p. 195.

15. Philip Donnellan Archive, MS 4000/6/1/42/13/C; MS 4000/6/1/42/19/C.

16. Mac Amhlaigh, *An Irish Navvy*, pp. 73–4.

17. Desmond Fisher, 'The Irishman in England', *The Furrow* 9, 4 (1958), pp. 230–35.

18. For the labour contractor see Philip Donnellan's film *The Irishmen* (1965); see also Mac Amhlaigh, *An Irish Navvy*, p. 57.

19. Interview with Michael Billington in Nicholas Grene, ed., *Talking about Tom Murphy* (Dublin: Carysfort Press, 2002), p. 96. For reviews of *A Whistle in the Dark* see Fintan O'Toole, *Tom Murphy: The Politics of Magic* (Dublin: New Island Books, 1994), pp. 9–10.

20. Philip Donnellan Archive, MS 4000/6/1/42/1/C.

21. Philip Donnellan Archive, MS 4000/6/1/42/2/C. See also Ultan Cowley, *The Men Who Built Britain: A History of the Irish Navvy* (Dublin: Wolfhound Press, 2002).

8. BROADCASTERS

1. Caryl Phillips, 'Interview: George Lamming Talks to Caryl Phillips', *Wasafiri* 13, 26 (autumn 1997), p. 13.

2. Graham Greene, *The End of the Affair* (London: Bodley Head, 1974 [1951]), pp. 160–69.

3. Anthony Cronin, *Dead as Doornails* (Dublin: Dolmen Press, 1976), p. 129. See also Daniel Farson, *Soho in the Fifties* (London: Michael

Joseph, 1987); Jonathan Fryer, *Soho in the Fifties and Sixties* (London: National Portrait Gallery, 1998); Frank Mort, *Capital Affairs: London and the Making of the Permissive Society* (New Haven, Conn.: Yale University Press, 2010).

4. Sheila Patterson, *Dark Strangers: A Sociological Study of the Absorption of a Recent West Indian Migrant Group in Brixton, South London* (London: Tavistock Publications, 1963), p. 53.

5. On the Caribbean Artists Movement see Anne Walmsley, *The Caribbean Artists Movement, 1966–1972: A Literary and Cultural History* (London: New Beacon Books, 1992). See also Lloyd Braithwaite, *Colonial West Indian Students in Britain* (Kingston, Jamaica: University of the West Indies Press, 2001) and *Colonial Students in Britain* (London: Political and Economic Planning, 1955); Bill Schwarz, ed., *West Indian Intellectuals in Britain* (Manchester: Manchester University Press, 2003).

6. For Lamming on *Caribbean Voices* see Phillips, 'Interview', p. 12. For Michael Anthony, see Walmsley, *Caribbean Artists Movement*, p. 10. See also Philip Nanton, 'What Does Mr. Swanzy Want – Shaping or Reflecting? An Assessment of Henry Swanzy's Contribution to the Development of Caribbean Literature', *Caribbean Quarterly* 46, 1 (March 2000), pp. 61–72; Glyne A. Griffith, 'Deconstructing Nationalisms: Henry Swanzy, Caribbean Voices and the Development of West Indian Literature', *Small Axe*, Number 10, 5, 2 (September 2001), pp. 1–20; Gail Low, 'Publishing Commonwealth: The Case of West Indian Writing, 1950–65', *EnterText: An Interactive Interdisciplinary E-Journal for Cultural and Historical Studies and Creative Work* 2, 1 (2001–2), pp. 71–93.

7. On Selvon see Letizia Gramaglia and Malachi McIntosh, 'Censorship, Selvon and Caribbean Voices: "Behind the Humming Bird" and the Caribbean Literary Field', *Wasafiri* 28, 2 (2013), pp. 48–54. Jan Carew is quoted in David Dabydeen, *Pak's Britannica: Articles by and Interviews with David Dabydeen*, ed. Lynne Macedo (Kingston, Jamaica: University of the West Indies Press, 2011), p. 106; on Swanzy arranging for people to earn see George Lamming, *The Pleasures of Exile* (London: Allison and Busby, 1984), p. 67. See also Glyne Griffith, *The BBC and the Development of Anglophone Caribbean Literature* (London: Palgrave Macmillan, 2016), p. 14.

8. For Naipaul in dirt and discomfort see Patrick French, *The World Is What It Is: The Authorized Biography of V. S. Naipaul* (London: Picador, 2008), p. 129; for the description of Langham House see V. S.

Naipaul, 'Prologue to an Autobiography', *Literary Occasions: Essays* (London: Picador, 2003).

9. The studio is described in V. S. Naipaul, *Half a Life* (London: Picador, 2001), p. 32.

10. The account of 200 Oxford Street is from Dabydeen, *Pak's Britannica*, pp. 112–13. Andrew Salkey's *Escape to an Autumn Pavement* was published by Hutchinson in 1960. For Diana Athill as Naipaul's editor see her *Stet: A Memoir* (London: Granta, 2000).

11. On Naipaul's attempt to write features see French, *Naipaul*, p. 183. For Swanzy's diary see Gramaglia and McIntosh, 'Censorship'.

12. H. L. V. Swanzy, 'Caribbean Voices: Prolegomena to a West Indian Culture', *Caribbean Quarterly* 1, 2 (1949), pp. 21–8. For the politics of language see Lamming, *Pleasures*, p. 182.

13. On the Mandrake Club see Dabydeen, *Pak's Britannica*, p. 66.

14. For Lamming's editorship of *Caribbean Voices* see Correspondence from George Lamming to Andrew Salkey, Andrew Salkey Papers, British Library (summer 1958). See also Stuart Hall's interview with Les Back in *Cultural Studies* 23, 4 (2009), p. 666.

15. Edward Scobie, 'Bad Taste B.B.C!', *Flamingo*, September 1969, pp. 22–4.

16. Anthony Cronin, *The Life of Riley* (London: Secker and Warburg, 1964), p. 154.

17. See Barbara Coulton, *Louis MacNeice in the BBC* (London: Faber & Faber, 1980), pp. 78–9; 'The Irish Storyteller', *Radio Times*, vol. 99, no. 1287, 13–19 June 1948, p. 9.

18. Philip Donnellan, 'We Were the BBC: An Alternative View of a Producer's Responsibility 1948–1984', unpublished typescript. Donnellan Archive, Birmingham Central Library, p. 151. See also www.philip donnellan.co.uk.

19. Cronin, *Life of Riley*, p. 157.

20. On the bucklep see Patrick Kavanagh, 'Sex and Christianity', *Kavanagh's Weekly*, 24 May 1952, pp. 7–8; for Behan on *Panorama* see Cronin, *Dead as Doornails*, p. 164.

21. On the Immigrant Programmes Unit see Gavin Schaffer, *The Vision of a Nation: Making Multiculturalism on British Television, 1960–80* (Basingstoke: Palgrave Macmillan, 2014); Darrell Newton, *Paving the Empire Road: BBC Television and Black Britons* (Manchester: Manchester University Press, 2011). For 'Make Yourself at Home' see http://www.bbc.co.uk/programmes/p0354c03; for Mahendra Kaul see http://news.bbc.co.uk/1/hi/magazine/4332380.stm.

22. On *The University of Brixton* see Rachael Gilmour ' "Welcome to the University of Brixton": Creole on the Radio', in Nadia Atia and Kate Houlden, eds., *Popular Postcolonialisms: Discourses of Empire and Popular Culture* (London: Routledge, forthcoming). For Stokely Carmichael at the Roundhouse see Rob Waters, 'Black Power on the Telly: America, Television, and Race in 1960s and 1970s Britain', *Journal of British Studies* 54, 4 (2015), pp. 947–70.

9. STRANGERS

1. George Lamming, *The Pleasures of Exile* (London: Allison and Busby, 1984), p. 81.
2. On the Notting Hill riots see Ruth Glass, assisted by Harold Pollins, *Newcomers: The West Indians in London* (London: Allen and Unwin, 1960); James Wickenden, *Colour in Britain* (London: Oxford University Press for the Institute of Race Relations, 1958); Edward Pilkington, *Beyond the Mother Country: West Indians and the Notting Hill White Riots* (London: I. B. Tauris, 1988); Robert Miles, 'The Riots of 1958: Notes on the Ideological Construction of "Race Relations" as a Political Issue in Britain', *Immigrants and Minorities* 3, 3 (1984), pp. 252–75.
3. Colin MacInnes, *Absolute Beginners* (London: McGibbon & Kee, 1960), pp. 184, 193.
4. Glass, *Newcomers*, p. 131.
5. *Manchester Guardian*, 1 September 1958, quoted in Glass, *Newcomers*, p. 132.
6. Inspectors' reports are taken from NA MEPO 9838 Notting Hill Riots; for MacInnes see *Absolute Beginners*, p. 194.
7. NA MEPO 9838.
8. NA MEPO 9838.
9. For Stuart Hall's recollections, see his interview with Les Back in *Cultural Studies* 23, 4 (2009), pp. 671–2; Stuart Hall, 'Absolute Beginnings', *Universities and Left Review* 7 (1959), pp. 17–25.
10. For Justice Salmon's verdict see Glass, *Newcomers*, p. 135. For Fenner Brockway, see Glass, *Newcomers*, p. 142, and for George Rogers see Glass, *Newcomers*, p. 150.
11. Glass, *Newcomers*, pp. 133, 135; Lamming, *Pleasures*, p. 79.
12. Lamming, *Pleasures*, p. 76.
13. On Claudia Jones in England see Marika Sherwood, *Claudia Jones: A Life in Exile* (London: Lawrence and Wishart, 1999).

14. Glass, *Newcomers*, p. 164.
15. Papers of Donald Piers Chesworth, PP2 GB370, Notes on rallies of Oswald Mosley, 24 September 1959.
16. On the danger of anti-discrimination legislation actually fostering discrimination see the speech by the government spokesman Lord Chesham, Parliamentary Debates, HL, 19 November 1958, vol. 212, col. 718. See also Glass, *Newcomers*, pp. 158–62.
17. Lamming, *Pleasures*, pp. 76, 80.

10. LOVERS

1. Wallace Collins, *Jamaican Migrant* (London: Routledge & Kegan Paul, 1965), p. 85.
2. Collins, *Jamaican Migrant*, p. 91.
3. Colin MacInnes, *City of Spades* (London: Allison and Busby, 2012 [1957]), p. 25.
4. See Leonard Sheil, 'Marriage and the Leakage', *The Furrow* 9, 4 (1958), p. 523.
5. Ruth Glass, assisted by Harold Pollins, *Newcomers: The West Indians in London* (London: Allen and Unwin, 1960), pp. 262, 265–6.
6. Michael Abdul Malik, *From Michael de Freitas to Michael X* (London: André Deutsch, 1968), p. 35.
7. For the calling cards see *Hotel Chaplain*, Radharc Films, 1965.
8. Majbritt Morrison, *Jungle West 11* (London: Tandem Books, 1964).
9. C. H. Rolph, ed., *Women of the Streets: A Sociological Study of the Common Prostitute* (London: Secker and Warburg, 1955), p. 118.
10. Michael Banton, *The Coloured Quarter: Negro Immigrants in an English City* (London, Jonathan Cape, 1955), p. 13. For the testimony of the woman from Lancaster Road see Chesworth Papers, PP2 GB370.
11. On poncing see Glass, *Newcomers*, p. 262; for schoolchildren's views of black immigrants see Stuart Hall et al., 'The Habit of Violence', *Universities and Left Review* 5 (1958); John Gosling and Douglas Warner, *The Shame of a City: An Inquiry into the Vice of London* (London, W. H. Allen, 1960), pp. 100–101.
12. On the Messina Brothers and Duncan Webb see Stefan Slater, 'Prostitutes and Popular History: Notes on the "Underworld" 1918–1939', *Crime, History and Societies* 13, 1 (2009), pp. 25–48; on Maltese immigrants see Geoff Dench, *The Maltese in London: A Case Study in the Erosion of Ethnic Consciousness* (London: Routledge, 1975); T. R. Fyvel, *The Insecure Offenders: Rebellious Youth in the Welfare State*

(London: Penguin, 1963 [1961]), p. 92. For Cyril Osborne's 1958 speech see Parliamentary Debates, HC, 29 October 1958, vol. 594, cc. 195–205; on Mosley see the report by 'Rachel' in Chesworth Papers, PP2 GB370; for MacInnes on 'doubly black sheep' see 'A Short Guide for Jumbles (to the Life of Their Coloured Brethren in England)' [1956], in *England, Half English* (London: MacGibbon & Kee, 1961), pp. 19, 22. See also Paul Gilroy, *There Ain't No Black in the Union Jack: The Cultural Politics of Race and Nation* (London: Hutchinson, 1987).

13. Glass, *Newcomers*, p. 41.

14. *The Times*, 20 May 1959, quoted in Glass, *Newcomers*, p. 56.

15. On Holland Park see Mike Phillips and Trevor Phillips, *Windrush: The Irresistible Rise of Multi-Racial Britain* (London: HarperCollins, 1998), p. 109; Sam Selvon, *The Lonely Londoners* (London: Penguin, 2006 [1956]), p. 107.

16. See Collins, *Jamaican Migrant*, p. 59.

17. Malik, *Michael X*, p. 56.

18. On looking for rooms anywhere but Notting Hill see Glass, *Newcomers*, p. 40.

19. 'Mixed Marriages', from the series *People in Trouble* (Associated-Rediffusion), broadcast 21 May 1958. Directed by Rollo Gamble. Presented by Daniel Farson.

20. *Flame in the Streets*, dir. Roy Ward Baker, 1961; *Hot Summer Night*, dir. Ted Kotcheff, for *Armchair Theatre*, ABC Television for ITV, broadcast 1 February 1959. For a somewhat more benign take on interracial romance see also *A Taste of Honey*, dir. Tony Richardson, 1961.

21. See NA HO 344/106 for the reports by Chief Constables; the article in the *Yorkshire Evening Post* appeared on 20 December 1957. See Abdullah Hussein, 'The Journey Back', in *Stories of Exile and Alienation*, trans. Muhammad Umar Memon (Karachi: Oxford University Press, 1998), pp. 77–80; see also the film adaptation of Hussein's story *Brothers in Trouble*, dir. Udayan Prasad, 1995. On 'mass prostitution' see also G. S. Aurora, *The New Frontiersmen: A Sociological Study of Indian Immigrants in the United Kingdom* (Bombay: Popular Prakashan, 1967), p. 73.

22. See Randall Hansen, *Citizenship and Immigration in Post-War Britain: The Institutional Origins of a Multicultural Nation* (Oxford: Oxford University Press, 2000), pp. 84–5.

23. G. L. C. Bertram, *West Indian Immigration* (London: Eugenics Society, 1958).

24. On interracial marriage see Glass, *Newcomers*, p. 124.

25. 'Black Marries White – The Last Barrier', ITV, 29 April 1964.

26. 'Mixed Marriages No 1. Would You Let Your Daughter Marry One?' *Man Alive*, BBC2, 2 July 1968. This programme also includes the interviews at Ridley Road market.
27. Betty Ali, see 'Mixed Marriages No 1'.
28. 'Black Marries White'.

11. BACHELORS

1. Quoted in Roger Ballard and Catherine Ballard, 'The Sikhs: The Development of South Asian Settlements in Britain', in James L. Watson, ed., *Between Two Cultures: Migrants and Minorities in Britain* (Oxford: Blackwell, 1977), p. 36.
2. Madho Ram, *Mera England da safr* [My Passage to England] (Handsworth: S. B. Kara, 1972). For an analysis and partial translation of the poem see Darshan S. Tatla, 'A Passage to England: Oral Tradition and Popular Culture among Early Punjabi Sikh Settlers in Britain', *Oral History* 30, 2 (2002), pp. 61–72. I am grateful to Darshan Tatla for providing me with a copy of the poem, which was published in a very limited edition as 50 sheets of loosely bound A4 paper, and to Beryl Dhanjal for her complete translation.
3. Dónall Mac Amhlaigh, *An Irish Navvy: The Diary of an Exile*, trans. Valentin Iremonger (Cork: Collins Press, 2003 [1964]), p. 80; Peter L. Wright, *The Coloured Worker in British Industry* (London: Oxford University Press for the Institute of Race Relations, 1968), p. 43.
4. Wright, *Coloured Worker*, p. 42. In the early post-war period the foundry workers' union (the AUFW) had agreed to allow managers to take on skilled Italian workers, while refusing Polish workers as these could become naturalized citizens and therefore couldn't be forced to leave in favour of British workers. See Mark Duffield, *Black Radicalism and the Politics of De-Industrialisation: The Hidden History of Indian Foundry Workers* (Aldershot: Avebury, 1988), p. 14.
5. Wright, *Coloured Worker*, pp. 79, 74.
6. For the manager of the engineering firm on sacking 'coloured' workers see Joyce Eggington, *They Seek a Living* (London: Hutchinson, 1957), p. 101. Wright, *Coloured Worker*, pp. 162–3.
7. On Birmid Industries see Duffield, *Black Radicalism*, p. 32; on numbered workers, see Wright, *Coloured Worker*, p. 127.
8. Wright, *Coloured Worker*, p. 136.

9. For Indian workers as cheap labour see Wright, *Coloured Worker*, p. 192; on immigrants working hard see G. S. Aurora, *The New Frontiersmen: A Sociological Study of Indian Immigrants in the United Kingdom* (Bombay: Popular Prakashan, 1967), p. 157.

10. On Punjabi oral tradition in Britain see Tatla, 'A Passage to England', and Jogindar Shamsher, *The Overtime People* (Jalandhar: ABS Publications, 1989), pp. 71–88. See also Virinder S. Kalra, 'Vilayeti Rhythms: Beyond Bhangra's Emblematic Status to a Translation of Lyrical Texts', *Theory, Culture and Society* 17, 3 (2000), pp. 80–102.

11. For the outraged manager see Wright, *Coloured Worker*, p. 140; the Birmingham study is the Fircroft Survey, Fircroft College of Adult Education Race Relations Group, 1954–55. See also Leslie Stephens, *Employment of Coloured Workers in the Birmingham Area: Report of an Enquiry* (London: Institute of Personnel Management, 1956); Aurora, *Frontiersmen*, p. 81; Dennis Brooks and Karamjit Singh, 'Pivots and Presents: Asian Brokers in British Foundries', in S. Wallam, ed., *Ethnicity at Work* (London: Macmillan, 1995), pp. 93–114.

12. For Gurbachan Gill see Darshan S. Tatla, *Gurbachan Singh Gill: A Short Biography and Memoirs* (Jalandhar: Punjab Centre for Migration Studies, 2004), p. 7. DeWitt John Jnr, *Indian Workers' Associations in Britain* (London: Oxford University Press for the Institute of Race Relations, 1969), p. 138.

13. Abdullah Hussein, 'The Journey Back', *Stories of Exile and Alienation*, trans. Muhammad Umar Memon (Karachi: Oxford University Press, 1998), pp. 77, 75. For evidence of the bribe culture in Yorkshire mills see Bradford Heritage Recording Unit Archive BHRU A0041/01/19.

12. DANCERS

1. Donald Hinds, 'The Island of Brixton', *Oral History* 8, 1 (spring 1980), pp. 49–51 (p. 51).

2. Wallace Collins, *Jamaican Migrant* (London: Routledge & Kegan Paul, 1965), pp. 59, 65, 67.

3. 'Mixed Marriages No 1. Would You Let Your Daughter Marry One?' *Man Alive*, BBC2, 2 July 1968.

4. For the Wolverhampton dancehall case, see Rashmikant Harilal Desai, *Indian Immigrants in Britain* (London: Oxford University Press, 1963), pp. 125–7. For Streatham see 'Locarno Restricts Coloured Dancers: "Bring Partners" for the Monday Night Jiving', *South London Press*, 8

August 1958, p. 7; 'They Can Go In Without Partners Now: Dance Hall Lifts Colour Ban', *South London Press*, 14 October 1958, p. 1. For the unhappy female dancer see, 'In My Opinion', *Checkers* 1, 1 (July 1948), p. 24.

5. See Lloyd Bradley, *Sounds Like London: 100 Years of Black Music in the Capital* (London: Serpent's Tail, 2013); Colin MacInnes, *City of Spades* (London: Allison and Busby, 2012 [1957]), p. 67.

6. ' "Checkers" Visits the "Met" ', *Checkers*, January 1949, p. 4.

7. MacInnes, *City of Spades*, pp. 89, 106.

8. Quoted in Bradley, *Sounds*, p. 73.

9. Quoted in Bradley, *Sounds*, p. 47.

10. Steven Berkoff, *Free Association: An Autobiography* (London: Faber & Faber, 1996), pp. 37, 134; Collins, *Jamaican Migrant*, p. 67.

11. Quoted in Bradley, *Sounds*, p. 37.

12. MacInnes, *City of Spades*, p. 154.

13. For Kitchener in Piccadilly see Mike Phillips and Trevor Phillips, *Windrush: The Irresistible Rise of Multi-Racial Britain* (London: HarperCollins, 1998), p. 103.

14. Hinds, 'Island of Brixton', p. 51.

15. 'Why the West Indian Thinks Marriage is Overdoing It', *South London Press*, 11 November 1958, p. 3.

16. NA HLG 39, Milner Holland Papers.

17. 'Tenants Complain of Jazz in the Early Hours', *Brixton Advertiser*, 26 March 1960, p. 1.

18. ' "Parties" Anger Locals', *Brixton Advertiser*, 8 October 1960, pp. 1–2.

19. Sheila Patterson, *Dark Strangers: A Sociological Study of the Absorption of a Recent West Indian Migrant Group in Brixton, South London* (London: Tavistock Publications, 1963), p. 179.

20. 'Threat to Woman', *Brixton Advertiser*, 21 October 1960, p. 1

21. Y. A. Safi, ' "The Dark Strangers" – By One of Them', *Brixton Advertiser*, 1 March 1963, p. 3.

13. BROTHERS

1. Muhammad Anwar, *The Myth of Return: Pakistanis in Britain* (London: Heinemann, 1979), pp. 196, 65.

2. See J. A. Tannahill, *European Voluntary Workers in Britain* (Manchester: Manchester University Press, 1958).

3. See Verity Saifullah Khan, 'The Pakistanis: Mirpuri Villagers at Home and in Bradford', in James L. Watson, ed., *Between Two Cultures: Migrants and Minorities in Britain* (Oxford: Blackwell, 1977), pp. 57–89; see also Virinder S. Kalra, *From Textile Mills to Taxi Ranks: Experiences of Migration, Labour and Social Change* (Aldershot: Ashgate, 2000).

4. See Anwar, *Myth of Return*, p. 106.

5. For the Bradford mill manager see Bradford Heritage Recording Unit Archive, BHRU A0043/01/04.

6. Anwar, *Myth of Return*, pp. 196–7.

7. See Khan, 'The Pakistanis', pp. 66–7.

8. For the debate on the Commonwealth Immigrants Bill see James Hampshire, *Citizenship and Belonging: Immigration and the Politics of Demographic Governance in Postwar Britain* (Basingstoke: Palgrave Macmillan, 2005), pp. 45–78. On numbers of migrants, see Paul Foot, *Immigration and Race in British Politics* (Harmondsworth: Penguin, 1965); Ian R. G. Spencer, *British Immigration Policy since 1939: The Making of Multi-Racial Britain* (London: Routledge, 1997), pp. 87–98. See also R. B. Davison, *Black British: Immigrants to England* (London: Oxford University Press, 1966), p. 3; Alison Shaw, *A Pakistani Community in Britain* (Oxford: Blackwell, 1988), p. 25.

9. Quoted in Shaw, *Pakistani Community*, p. 35.

10. Jeremy Seabrook, *City Close-Up* (London: Allen Lane, 1971), pp. 240–41.

11. See Badr Dahya, 'The Nature of Pakistani Ethnicity in Industrial Cities in Britain', in Abner Cohen, ed., *Urban Ethnicity* (London: Tavistock Publications, 1974), p. 83.

12. Elizabeth Burney, *Housing on Trial: A Study of Immigrants and Local Government* (London: Oxford University Press for the Institute of Race Relations, 1967); Dahya, 'Pakistani Ethnicity', p. 98.

13. Quoted in Shaw, *Pakistani Community*, p. 46.

14. Quoted in Shaw, *Pakistani Community*, p. 48.

15. Quoted in Anwar, *Myth of Return*, p. 197. For the ratio of Pakistani men to women see Eric Butterworth, *A Muslim Community in Britain* (London: Church Information Office, 1967).

16. Quoted in G. S. Aurora, *The New Frontiersmen: A Sociological Study of Indian Immigrants in the United Kingdom* (Bombay: Popular Prakashan, 1967), p. 162.

17. Verity Saifullah Khan, 'Purdah in the British Situation', in Diana Leonard Barker and Sheila Allen, eds., *Dependence and Exploitation in*

Work and Marriage (London: Longman, 1976), pp. 224–45. See also Verity Saifullah Khan, 'Pakistani Women in Britain', *Journal of Ethnic and Migration Studies* 5, 1–2 (1976), pp. 98–108.

14. HOMEOWNERS

1. Buchi Emecheta, *In the Ditch* (London: Allison and Busby, 1972), pp. 8–9.
2. John Davis, 'Rents and Race in 1960s London: New Light on Rachmanism', *Twentieth Century British History* 12, 1 (2001), pp. 69–92 (p. 82). I am indebted to Davis's essay for much of the background to this chapter. See also *Report of the Committee on Housing in Greater London* (Chairman, Sir Edward Milner Holland) (London: Committee on Housing in Greater London, 1965).
3. Shirley Green, *Rachman* (London: Michael Joseph, 1979), pp. 17–29.
4. Quoted in Green, *Rachman*, pp. 35–6.
5. Davis, 'Rents and Race', pp. 74–5.
6. Davis, 'Rents and Race', p. 72.
7. For details of the evidence gathered by the Committee see Milner Holland Papers NA HLG 39. For the House of Lords debate see Milner Holland Report on London Housing, Parliamentary Debates, HL, 29 March 1965, vol. 264 cc. 836–94.
8. Davis, 'Rents and Race', p. 74.
9. Wyndham Lewis, *Rotting Hill* (London: Methuen, 1951), p. 92. For discussion of the 1951 census see Betty Spinley, *The Deprived and the Privileged: Personality Development in English Society* (London: Routledge & Kegan Paul, 1953). For Michael de Freitas see Michael Abdul Malik, *From Michael de Freitas to Michael X* (London: André Deutsch, 1968), p. 56.
10. Davis, 'Rents and Race', p. 78.
11. NA HO 344/44 Policies to Aid Assimilation, 18 January 1960, Note for a meeting with George Rogers and others.
12. Malik, *Michael X*, p. 70.
13. Quoted in Davis, 'Rents and Race', p. 81.
14. Quoted in Davis, 'Rents and Race', pp. 70–71.
15. Alexander Baron, *The Lowlife* (London: Black Spring Press, 2010), p. 18.
16. Andrew Salkey, *Escape to an Autumn Pavement* (Leeds: Peepal Tree Press, 2009 [1960]), p. 68.
17. NA HO 344/44.

18. Ruth Glass, assisted by Harold Pollins, *Newcomers: The West Indians in London* (London: Allen and Unwin, 1960), pp. 58–62.

19. A. G. Bennett, letter to *South London Press*, 2 August 1957, p. 6.

20. Rashmikant Harilal Desai, *Indian Immigrants in Britain* (London: Oxford University Press, 1963), p. 27.

21. Muhammad Anwar, *The Myth of Return: Pakistanis in Britain* (London: Heinemann, 1979), pp. 198–9; Desai, *Indian Immigrants*, p. 32; John Rex and Robert Moore, *Race, Community and Conflict: A Study of Sparkbrook* (London: Oxford University Press for the Institute of Race Relations, 1967), pp. 139, 135.

22. Badr Dahya, 'The Nature of Pakistani Ethnicity in Industrial Cities in Britain', in Abner Cohen, ed., *Urban Ethnicity* (London: Tavistock Publications, 1974), p. 87; Abdullah Hussein, 'The Journey Back', in *Stories of Exile and Alienation*, trans. Muhammad Umar Memon (Karachi: Oxford University Press, 1998), pp. 75–6; Desai, *Indian Immigrants*, p. 55.

15. TEACHERS

1. Pritam Sidhu, 'Fauji Bhadwan Singh', in *Dukh Pardesan de* ['Foreign Woes'] (Amritsar: Ravi Sahit Parkashan, 1982), trans. Beryl Dhanjal.

2. Sheila Allen, Stuart Bentley and Joanna Bornat, *Work, Race and Immigration* (Bradford: University of Bradford, 1977), p. 278. The research for this study was carried out in 1966–67.

3. On numbers of voucher holders see Ian R. G. Spencer, *British Immigration Policy since 1939: The Making of Multi-Racial Britain* (London: Routledge, 1997), pp. 129–34.

4. Interview with Pritam and Surjit Sidhu, 12 May 2014. For a fictionalized autobiographical account of Sidhu's arrival and first job in England see 'Vilayet de Kamaee' ['England's Wages: Lament of the Soul'], in *Dukh Pardesan de*, trans. Beryl Dhanjal. For a critical discussion of Sidhu's stories see Jogindar Shamsher, *The Overtime People* (Jalandhar: ABS Publications, 1989), pp. 51–3. On Punjabi writers see also Darshan S. Tatla, 'A Chorus of Hushed Voices: An Introduction to Punjabi Literature in Britain', *Punjab Research Group Discussion Papers* 32 (1991), pp. 111–19; Darshan S. Tatla, 'Panjabi Poetry of the Midlands', *People to People (A Journal of the West Midlands Arts Council)*, July 1990; Darshan S. Tatla and Eleanor Nesbitt, *Sikhs in Britain: An*

Annotated Bibliography (Coventry: Centre for Research in Ethnic Relations, 1987). For other stories see Harchand Singh Bedi, ed., *Pachchon Dee Vaa* ['British Punjabi Stories'] (Amritsar: Ravi Sahit Parkashan, 2013).

5. Interview with Shivcharan Gill, 5 October 2014.

6. Ranjit Dheer, 'Nirmohi Vilayat' ['Inhospitable Britain'], from the collection *Pardesnama* (Delhi: Navyug Publishers, 1995), trans. Beryl Dhanjal. Interview with Ranjit Dheer, 20 September 2013.

7. Interview with Santokh Singh Santokh, 10 October 2014.

8. On Punjabi journalism see Shamsher, *Overtime People*, pp. 89–107. See also Jogindar Shamsher and Ralph Russell, 'Punjabi Journalism in Britain: A Background', *Journal of Ethnic and Migration Studies* 5, 3 (1976), pp. 211–21; Darshan S. Tatla and Gurharpal Singh, 'The Punjabi Press in Britain', *New Community* 15, 2 (1989), pp. 211–25.

9. See International Social Service, *Immigrants at London Airport and their Settlement in the Community* (London: International Social Service, 1967). For accounts of the working of the immigration unit see Sheila Patterson, *Immigrants and Race Relations in Britain, 1960–1967* (London: Oxford University Press for the Institute of Race Relations, 1969).

10. Wellcome Archives SA/CMO/D.106 County Councils Association Correspondence, 'How the Health Control Unit at Heathrow Airport Functions' by Dr F. J. Kinsella, Deputy Senior Medical Officer (July 1967).

11. Pritam Sidhu, from *Dharat Walaiti Desi Chamba*, quoted in Shamsher, *Overtime People*, p. 52.

12. Sathi Ludhianvi, 'Black People, White Blood', in Tarsem Neelgiri, ed., *Gori Dharti* ['White Land: A Collection of Literary Writings'] (Jallandhar: Deepak Publishers, 1979), trans. Beryl Dhanjal.

13. Arthur Helweg, *Sikhs in England* (Oxford: Oxford University Press, 1979), p. 86.

14. Shamsher, *Overtime People*, p. 82.

15. Shamsher, *Overtime People*, pp. 83–4.

16. See Southall Black Sisters, *Against the Grain: A Celebration of Survival and Struggle* (Southall: Southall Black Sisters, 1990).

16. SCROUNGERS

1. Anthony Cronin, *The Life of Riley* (London: Secker and Warburg, 1964), pp. 169–71.

2. Cronin, *Life of Riley*, p. 150.
3. Virginia Noble, *Inside the Welfare State: Foundations of Policy and Practice in Post-War Britain* (London: Routledge, 2009), p. 99.
4. Ruth Glass, assisted by Harold Pollins, *Newcomers: The West Indians in London* (London: Allen and Unwin, 1960), p. 263.
5. Noble, *Welfare State*, p. 99.
6. Camilla Schofield, *Enoch Powell and the Making of Postcolonial Britain* (Cambridge: Cambridge University Press, 2013), p. 229.
7. Ultan Cowley, *The Men Who Built Britain: A History of the Irish Navvy* (Dublin: Wolfhound Press, 2001), p. 161.
8. Cowley, *Men Who Built Britain*, p. 160.
9. Cowley, *Men Who Built Britain*, p. 160.
10. Cowley, *Men Who Built Britain*, p. 190.
11. Richard Power, *Apple on a Treetop* (Dublin: Poolbeg Press, 1980), p. 165; Dónall Mac Amhlaigh, *An Irish Navvy: The Diary of an Exile*, trans. Valentin Iremonger (Cork: Collins Press, 2003 [1964]), p. 151.
12. Jogindar Shamsher, *The Overtime People* (Jalandhar: ABS Publications, 1989), p. 81.

17. VOTERS

1. Stuart Hall, quoted in Mike Phillips and Trevor Phillips, *Windrush: The Irresistible Rise of Multi-Racial Britain* (London: HarperCollins, 1998), pp. 197–8.
2. For background on the Smethwick election see Michael Hartley-Brewer, 'Smethwick', in Nicholas Deakin, ed., *Colour and the British Electorate 1964: Six Case Studies* (London: Pall Mall Press for the Institute of Race Relations, 1965), pp. 77–105. See also Muhammad Anwar, *Race and Politics: Ethnic Minorities and the British Political System* (London: Tavistock Publications, 1986); Joe Street, 'Malcolm X, Smethwick, and the Influence of the African American Freedom Struggle on British Race Relations in the 1960s', *Journal of Black Studies* 38, 6 (2008), pp. 932–50.
3. 'White Backlash in Leyton?' *Magnet*, 13 February 1965, p. 1.
4. See Hartley-Brewer, 'Smethwick', pp. 81, 90–91.
5. 'Britain's Racist Election', Channel 4, 16 March 2016.
6. On Bean's campaign see David Woolcott, 'Southall', in Deakin, ed., *Colour*, pp. 31–53. I quote here from pp. 40–41. Satnam Virdee notes that 9.1 per cent was the largest share of the vote for a minority party in the post-war era; see Virdee, 'Anti-Racism and the Socialist Left,

1968–1979', in Evan Smith and Matthew Worley, eds., *Against the Grain: The British Far Left from 1956* (Manchester: Manchester University Press, 2014), p. 211.

7. Alan Shuttleworth, 'Sparkbrook', in Deakin, ed., *Colour*, pp. 54–76 (p. 68).

8. Rex and Moore found 'the impression of Irishness was overwhelming' at the Sparkbrook Labour Club in the early 1960s: 'The list of club members was mostly Irish. The songs that were sung were Irish. The jokes and the names given to numbers in the Bingo sessions had an Irish reference. Although the club did include some pure "Brummies", they seemed to stand out as foreigners.' John Rex and Robert Moore, *Race, Community and Conflict: A Study of Sparkbrook* (London: Oxford University Press for the Institute of Race Relations, 1967), p. 196; see pp. 191–211 for a discussion of the politics of Sparkbrook in the 1964 general election. David Pitt is quoted in Deakin, ed., *Colour*, pp. 6–7.

9. Deakin, ed., *Colour*, p. 100. See also Avtar Singh Jouhl, 'History of the Indian Workers Association', https://iwagb.wordpress.com/category/history-of-iwa/.

10. DeWitt John Jnr, *Indian Workers' Associations in Britain* (London: Oxford University Press for the Institute of Race Relations, 1969), p. 66.

11. John, *Indian Workers*, pp. 62, 52.

12. Sheila Allen, Stuart Bentley and Joanna Bornat, *Work, Race and Immigration* (Bradford: University of Bradford, 1977), p. 237.

13. John, *Indian Workers*, p. 138.

14. The *Birmingham Post* and *Express and Star* are quoted in Street, 'Malcolm X', pp. 939–40.

15. Philip Donnellan, *The Colony*, BBC, 16 June 1964.

16. On the government White Paper see Kennetta Hammond Perry, *London is the Place for Me: Black Britons, Citizenship and the Politics of Race* (Oxford: Oxford University Press, 2016), pp. 210–29.

18. CONSUMERS

1. Jogindar Shamsher, *The Overtime People* (Jalandhar: ABS Publications, 1989), p. 80.

2. Shamsher, *Overtime People*, p. 72. The following quotations from folk songs are taken from Shamsher, *Overtime People*, pp. 71–88. See also Beryl Dhanjal, 'Sikh Women in Southall (Some Impressions)', *Journal of Ethnic and Migration Studies* 5, 1–2 (1976), pp. 109–14.

3. Bradford Heritage Recording Unit, *Destination Bradford: A Century of Immigration: Photographs and Oral History* (Bradford: Bradford Libraries and Information Service, 1987), p. 44.

4. Bradford Heritage Recording Unit, *Here to Stay: Bradford's South Asian Communities* (Bradford: Bradford Heritage Recording Unit, 1994), p. 50.

5. The two statements on meat-eating are quoted in Jane Hamlett, Adrian R. Bailey, Andrew Alexander and Gareth Shaw, 'Ethnicity and Consumption: South Asian Food Shopping Patterns in Britain, 1947–75', *Journal of Consumer Culture* 8, 1 (2008), pp. 91–116 (pp. 100, 102). For two pounds of butter per person see G. S. Aurora, *The New Frontiersmen: A Sociological Study of Indian Immigrants in the United Kingdom* (Bombay: Popular Prakashan, 1967), p. 55. See also Elizabeth Buettner, ' "Going for an Indian": South Asian Restaurants and the Limits of Multiculturalism in Britain', *Journal of Modern History* 80, 4 (2008), pp. 865–901.

6. Rashmikant Harilal Desai, *Indian Immigrants in Britain* (London: Oxford University Press, 1963), p. 65.

7. Desai, *Indian Immigrants*, p. 59.

8. 'Barbara Blake on Parties', *Magnet*, 27 April 1965.

9. Interview with Kailash Puri, 10 May 2014. See also Kailash Puri and Eleanor Nesbitt, *Pool of Life: The Autobiography of a Punjabi Agony Aunt* (Brighton: Sussex Academic Press, 2013). Puri's magazine, *Roopvati*, was subtitled 'The Only Family Magazine in English and Punjabi', although in fact the majority of the articles were in Punjabi, and the advertisements, for Air India, sari fabrics, 'personal export' companies, and property agents in New Delhi promising to handle the business interests of 'overseas Punjabis', were mostly in English.

10. BHRU, *Here to Stay*, pp. 76, 77. Quoted in Hamlett et al., 'Ethnicity and Consumption', p. 107.

11. Sheila Allen, Stuart Bentley and Joanna Bornat, *Work, Race and Immigration* (Bradford: University of Bradford, 1977), pp. 263–5.

12. *Where to Eat in London* (London: publisher unknown, 1955), p. 65, quoted in Buettner, ' "Going for an Indian" ', p. 873. On the smell of curry see Desai, *Indian Immigrants*, pp. 20, 11, 65; Aurora, *Frontiersmen*, p. 88. For the Commercial Road café see Roger Ballard, *Desh Pardesh* (London: B. R. Publishing, 1996), p. 150; for white people flocking to Indian restaurants see Abdullah Hussein, 'The Journey Back', in *Stories of Exile and Alienation*, trans. Muhammad Umar Memon (Karachi: Oxford University Press, 1998), p. 63. See also

Virinder S. Kalra, 'The Political Economy of the Samosa', *South Asia Research* 24 (2004), pp. 21–36.

19. HUSTLERS

1. Baldwin tells the story in Horace Ové's film, *Baldwin's Nigger*, Infilms, 1968.
2. On Enoch Powell see Camilla Schofield, *Enoch Powell and the Making of Postcolonial Britain* (Cambridge: Cambridge University Press, 2013); Paul Foot, *The Rise of Enoch Powell: An Examination of Enoch Powell's Attitude to Immigration and Race* (Harmondsworth: Penguin, 1969); Enoch Powell, *Reflections of a Statesman: The Writings and Speeches of Enoch Powell*, ed. Rex Collings (London: Bellew, 1991); Douglas Schoen, *Enoch Powell and the Powellites* (New York: Palgrave Macmillan, 1977).
3. On letters to Powell see Diana Spearman, 'Enoch Powell's Postbag', *New Society*, 9 May 1968, pp. 667–9; Amy Whipple, 'Revisiting the "Rivers of Blood" Controversy: Letters to Enoch Powell', *Journal of British Studies* 48, 3 (2009), pp. 717–35. I quote here from p. 722.
4. On the Campaign Against Racial Discrimination see Benjamin Heinemann, *The Politics of the Powerless: A Study of the Campaign Against Racial Discrimination* (London: Oxford University Press, 1972) and ch. 6 of Kennetta Hammond Perry, *London is the Place for Me: Black Britons, Citizenship and the Politics of Race* (Oxford: Oxford University Press, 2016). For instances of discrimination see the *Report of the Race Relations Board for 1966–1967* (London: HMSO, 1967) and W. W. Daniel, *Racial Discrimination in England: Based on the PEP Report* (Harmondsworth: Penguin, 1968); for CARD advice on 'How to Expose Discrimination' see http://www.irr.org.uk.ezproxy.princeton.edu/black_history_resource/Racial_Discrimination.pdf.
5. Hanif Kureishi gives his account of growing up in South London in the 1960s in 'London and Karachi', in Raphael Samuel, ed., *Patriotism: The Making and Unmaking of British National Identity*, Vol. 2: *Minorities and Outsiders* (London: Routledge, 1989), pp. 270–87.
6. Dilip Hiro's recollection of the Olympic salute occurs in Dilip Hiro, *Black British, White British: A History of Race Relations in Britain* (London: Eyre & Spottiswoode, 1971), p. 107. His and Kureishi's recollections are discussed in Rob Waters, 'Black Power on the Telly: America, Television, and Race in 1960s and 1970s Britain,' *Journal of British Studies* 54, 4 (2015), pp. 947–70.

7. For national newspaper coverage of US race riots and the growth of Black Power in Britain see Rob Waters, 'The Significance of Michael X', M.Sc. Research Dissertation, University of Edinburgh, 2010. For accounts of Black Power in Britain see Rob Waters, *Thinking Black: Britain, 1965–1985* (Berkeley: University of California Press, forthcoming); Anne-Marie Angelo, 'The Black Panthers in London: A Diasporic Struggle Navigates the Black Atlantic', *Radical History Review* 103 (2009), pp. 17–35; Robin Bunce and Paul Field, 'Obi B. Egbuna, C. L. R. James and the Birth of Black Power in Britain: Black Radicalism in Britain 1967–72', *Twentieth Century British History* 22, 3 (2010), pp. 391–414; Robin Bunce and Paul Field, *Darcus Howe: A Political Biography* (London: Bloomsbury, 2013); A. Sivanandan, 'The Heart is Where the Battle Is: An Interview with the Author', in *Communities of Resistance: Writings on Black Struggles for Socialism* (London: Verso, 1990), pp. 1–16, and *A Different Hunger: Writings on Black Resistance* (London: Pluto, 1982); Roy Sawh, *From Where I Stand* (London: Hansib Publications, 1987); Paul Gilroy, *There Ain't No Black in the Union Jack: The Cultural Politics of Race and Nation* (London: Hutchinson, 1987). Contemporary publications referred to include J. A. Hunte, *Nigger Hunting in England?* (London: West Indian Standing Conference, 1966); Neville Maxwell, *The Power of Negro Action* (London: Privately Printed, 1965).

8. On the Dialectics of Liberation Congress see David Cooper, ed., *Dialectics of Liberation* (London: Penguin, 1968), which reproduces Carmichael's speech. For links between Irish, UK and US civil rights and revolutionary groups see Pat Dooley, *The Irish in Britain* (London: Connolly Association, 1943), and the discussion of Clann na hÉireann in Brian Hanley and Scott Millar, *The Lost Revolution: The Story of the Official IRA and the Workers' Party* (Dublin: Penguin Ireland, 2009) – I quote Pádraig Yeates on the County Associations from p. 49.

9. William Craig, 16 October 1968, Stormont Papers, Vol. 70 (1968), p. 1022.

10. See *Anatomy of Violence*, dir. Peter Davis, 1967, which includes footage of Carmichael's debate with members of the audience. On the prosecution of Malik see Gavin Schaffer, 'Legislating Against Hatred: Meaning and Motive in Section Six of the Race Relations Act of 1965', *Twentieth Century British History* 25, 2 (2014), pp. 251–75.

11. Copies of *Black Ram* and *Hustler* are available at the George Padmore Institute and Archive, Finsbury Park, London.

12. See Obi B. Egbuna, *Black Power in Britain* (London: UCPA, 1967) and *Destroy This Temple: The Voice of Black Power in Britain*

(London: William & Morrow, 1971); Sivanandan, 'The Heart is Where the Battle Is', p. 10.

13. For Colin MacInnes's defence of Michael X, see Waters, 'The Significance of Michael X', p. 31.

14. See *Baldwin's Nigger*.

15. For Andrew Salkey on 'metropolitan approval' see Rob Waters, 'Henry Swanzy, Sartre's Zombie? Black Power and the Transformation of the Caribbean Artists Movement', in Ruth Craggs and Claire Wintle, eds., *Cultures of Decolonisation: Transnational Productions and Practices, 1945–1970* (Manchester: Manchester University Press, 2016), p. 79.

16. For James Coster see Thomas J. Cottle, *Black Testimony: The Voices of Britain's West Indians* (Philadelphia: Temple University Press, 1978), pp. 71–8.

20. PASTS

1. Caryl Phillips, 'Interview: George Lamming Talks to Caryl Phillips', *Wasafiri*, 13, 26 (autumn 1997), p. 13.

2. The account of the Mallorys' lodging house is from David Lodge, *The Picturegoers* (London: Pan, 1962 [1960]), p. 34.

3. Michael McMillan's description of his childhood home appears in *The Front Room: Migrant Aesthetics in the Home* (London: Black Dog, 2009).

4. Arif Ali is quoted in Winston James, 'Migration, Racism and Identity Formation: The Caribbean Experience in Britain', in Winston James and Clive Harris, eds., *Inside Babylon: The Caribbean Diaspora in Britain* (London: Verso Press, 1993), p. 276.

5. For Dónall Mac Amhlaigh on Irish immigrant fashion see 'The Celt and his Clothes', *Ireland's Own*, 30 October 1971, p. 14.

6. The Jamaican returnee who found he was treated as a tourist is quoted by Donald Hinds, *Journey to an Illusion: The West Indian in Britain* (London: Heinemann, 1966), p. 190.

7. On philanthropic building projects in the Punjab see Verne A. Dusenberry and Darshan S. Tatla, eds., *Sikh Diaspora Philanthropy in Punjab: Global Giving for Local Good* (New Delhi: Oxford University Press, 2009).

8. For construction around Mangla lake see Virinder S. Kalra, *From Textile Mills to Taxi Ranks: Experiences of Migration, Labour and Social Change* (Aldershot: Ashgate, 2000), p. 71. On Caribbean 'returnees' see Daniel Miller, 'Migration, Material Culture and Tragedy: Four Moments in Caribbean Migration', *Mobilities* 3 (2008), pp. 397–413;

Heather A. Horst, ' "You Can't Be in Two Places at Once": Rethinking Transnationalism through Jamaican Return Migration', *Identities* 14, 1–2 (2007), pp. 63–83.

9. On nostalgia as a survival strategy see Svetlana Boym, *The Future of Nostalgia* (New York: Basic Books, 2001); Nicola Mooney, *Rural Nostalgias and Transnational Dreams: Identity and Modernity among Jat Sikhs* (Toronto: University of Toronto Press, 2011); Helen Taylor, *Refugees and the Meaning of Home: Cypriot Narratives of Loss, Longing and Daily Life in London* (Basingstoke: Palgrave Macmillan, 2015). For the man who dreamt of return to Jamaica, see Hinds, *Journey*, p. 191.

10. Philip Donnellan's *The Colony* was broadcast by the BBC in 1964; the Trinidadian woman student is quoted in Henri Tajfel and John Dawson, eds., *Disappointed Guests: Essays by African, Asian and West Indian Students* (Oxford: Oxford University Press, 1965), p. 62.

Select Bibliography

Film

Anatomy of Violence, dir. Peter Davis, 1967.
Baldwin's Nigger, dir. Horace Ové. Infilms, 1968.
Boat Train to Euston. Radharc Films, 1965.
Brothers in Trouble, dir. Udayan Prasad. BBC Films, 1995.
Code Name: Westward Ho! dir. Mary Beales. Ministry of Labour, 1949.
The Colony, dir. Philip Donnellan. BBC, 1964.
Flame in the Streets, dir. Roy Ward Baker. Rank Organization Film Productions, 1961.
Hotel Chaplain. Radharc Films, 1965.
The Irishmen: An Impression of Exile, dir. Philip Donnellan. BBC, 1965 (not transmitted).
Oldbury Camp. Radharc Films, 1965.
A Taste of Honey, dir. Tony Richardson. Woodfall Film Productions, 1961.

Manuscripts and Archives

Birmingham Central Library, Birmingham, UK

Philip Donnellan Archive, MS 4000.

Bradford Central Library, Bradford, UK

Bradford Heritage Recording Unit (BHRU).
Andrew Salkey Papers.

British Library, London, UK

London Metropolitan University Archives, London, UK

Archives of the Irish in Britain.

National Archives (NA), London, UK

Welsh Office (BD)
    BD 11 Local Authorities
Cabinet (CAB)
    CAB 124 Offices of the Minister of Reconstruction
Housing and Local Government (HLG)
    HLG 39 London Housing Survey Committee (Milner Holland Committee)
Home Office (HO)
    HO 344 Commonwealth Immigration
Security Service (KV)
    KV 2 Communism
Ministry of Labour (LAB)
    LAB 8 Employment Policy
    LAB 10 Industrial Relations
    LAB 12 Establishment Division
    LAB 26 Welfare Department
Metropolitan Police (MEPO)
    MEPO 2 Correspondence and Papers
Ministry of Health (MH)
    MH 55 Public Health Services
    MH 120 Ministry of Pensions, Hospital Management

Queen Mary Archives, University of London, London, UK

Papers of Donald Piers Chesworth, PP2.

Tower Hamlets Local History Library and Archives, London, UK

Edith Ramsay Papers, P/RAM.

Trinity College Dublin, Ireland

Arnold Marsh Papers, MS 8305

Wellcome Library, London, UK

SA/CMO Association of County Medical Officers of Health and the County Medical Officers Group of the Society of Medical Officers of Health

SA/FPA Family Planning Association

SA/SMO Society of Medical Officers of Health

Music, Radio and Television

'Black Marries White – The Last Barrier'. ITV, 29 April 1964.

'Britain's Racist Election'. Channel 4, 16 March 2016.

Hot Summer Night, dir. Ted Kotcheff for *Armchair Theatre*. ABC Television for ITV, 1959.

Mighty Sparrow. 'Yankees Gone ["Jean and Dinah"]'. *Calypso Awakening: From the Emory Cook Collection*. Washington, DC: Smithsonian Folkways, 2000 [1956]. Audio CD, Track 9.

'Mixed Marriages No 1. Would You Let Your Daughter Marry One?' *Man Alive*, dir. Rollo Gamble. BBC2, 2 July 1968.

'A Word to the Women'. BBC Light Programme, 1 June 1947.

Newspapers and Magazines

Birmingham Mail

Birmingham Post

Brixton Advertiser

Checkers

Daily Herald

Daily Mirror

Express and Star

Ireland's Own

Irish Democrat

Irish Digest

Magnet

Manchester Guardian

New Society

News Chronicle

Oldham Evening Chronicle

Picture Post
Radio Times
Reynolds News
Roopvati
South London Press
The Times
Yorkshire Evening Post

Parliamentary Papers Online

Dáil Debates: http://oireachtasdebates.oireachtas.ie
Parliamentary Debates HC: http://www.parliament.uk/business/publica tions/hansard/commons/
Parliamentary Debates HL: https://hansard.millbanksystems.com/lords/
Stormont Papers: http://stormontpapers.ahds.ac.uk/index.html

Unpublished Dissertations

Chatterton, C. S., 'The Weakest Link in the Chain of Nursing? Recruitment and Retention in Mental Health Nursing 1948–1968', Ph.D. dissertation (University of Salford, 2007).

Gasperetti, Flavia, 'Italian Women Migrants in Post-War Britain: The Case of Textile Workers (1949–61)', Ph.D. dissertation (University of Birming- ham, 2012).

Waters, Rob, 'The Significance of Michael X', M.Sc. Research Dissertation (University of Edinburgh, 2010).

Websites

Casciani, Dominic, 'And this is how you vote . . .' BBC News, 13 October 2005. news.bbc.co.uk/1/hi/magazine/4332380.stm (accessed 9/11/2016).

'Control of Engagement Order: How does the Order Affect Me?' TUC History Online. www.unionhistory.info/britainatwork/emuweb/objects/ nofdigi/tuc/imagedisplay.php?irn=1551 (accessed 4/8/2014).

'The History of Electric Ballroom'. Electric Ballroom. www.electricball room.co.uk/history/ (accessed 15/3/2016).

Jouhl, Avtar Singh, 'History of the Indian Workers Association'. Avtar Jouhl's Weblog. iwagb.wordpress.com/category/history-of-iwa (accessed 12/7/2016).

'Make Yourself at Home: Programmes for Immigrants 10 October 1965'. History of the BBC, www.bbc.co.uk/programmes/p0354c03 (accessed 5/6/2016).

Ostrowski, Mark. ' "To return to Poland or not to return?" The Dilemma Facing the Polish Armed Forces at the End of the Second World War'. Ch. 3: 'Goralu Czy Ci Nie Zal . . .', The Polish Armed Forces Decide. www. angelfire.com/ok2/polisharmy/chapter3.html (accessed 8/10/2016).

'Ships and Passenger Lists of Polish WW2 DPs arriving from Africa and Europe'. Polish Resettlement Camps in the UK 1946–1969. www. pol ishresettlementcampsintheuk.co.uk/passengerlist/shipsindex.htm (accessed 5/3/2013).

'Struggles for Justice: Racial Discrimination'. Institute for Race Relations: Black History Resources. www.irr.org.uk/black_history_resource/Racial_ Discrimination.pdf (accessed 12/4/2016).

Books and Articles

Adams, Caroline, *Across Seven Seas and Thirteen Rivers: Life Stories of Pioneer Sylhetti Settlers in Britain*. London: Tower Hamlets Arts Project, 1987.

Alavi, Hamza, *The Pakistanis in London*. London: Institute of Race Relations, 1963.

Alderman, Geoffrey, *London Jewry and London Politics, 1889–1986*. London: Routledge, 1989.

Allen, Sheila, Stuart Bentley and Joanna Bornat, *Work, Race and Immigration*. Bradford: University of Bradford, 1977.

Anderson, Verity, *Spam Tomorrow*. London: Rupert Hart-Davis, 1956.

Angelo, Anne-Marie, 'The Black Panthers in London: A Diasporic Struggle Navigates the Black Atlantic', *Radical History Review* 103 (2009), pp. 17–35.

Ansari, Sarah, 'Subjects or Citizens? India, Pakistan, and the 1948 British Nationality Act', *Journal of Imperial and Commonwealth History* 41, 2 (2013), pp. 285–312.

Anwar, Muhammad, *The Myth of Return: Pakistanis in Britain*. London: Heinemann, 1979.

—, *Race and Politics: Ethnic Minorities and the British Political System*. London: Tavistock Publications, 1986.

Athill, Diana, *Stet: A Memoir*. London: Granta, 2000.

Aurora, G. S., *The New Frontiersmen: A Sociological Study of Indian Immigrants in the United Kingdom*. Bombay: Popular Prakashan, 1967.

Ballard, Roger, *Desh Pardesh*. London: B. R. Publishing, 1996.

— and Catherine Ballard, 'The Sikhs: The Development of South Asian Settlements in Britain', in James L. Watson, ed., *Between Two Cultures: Migrants and Minorities in Britain*. Oxford: Blackwell, 1977, pp. 21–56.

[Bamuta, Derek], 'Coloured People in Stepney', *Social Work* 7, 1 (January 1950), pp. 387–95.

Banerji, S., 'Ghazals to Banghra in Great Britain', *Popular Music* 7, 2 (1988), pp. 207–13.

Banton, Michael, *The Coloured Quarter: Negro Immigrants in an English City*. London: Jonathan Cape, 1955.

Baron, Alexander, *With Hope, Farewell*. London: Cape, 1952.

—, *The Lowlife*. London: Black Spring Press, 2010.

Barr, John, 'Napoli, Bedfordshire', *New Society*, 2 April 1964.

—, 'Pakistanis in Bradford', *New Society*, 19 November 1964.

Baumann, Gerd, 'The Re-Invention of Bhangra: Social Change and Aesthetic Shifts in a Punjabi Music in Britain', *World of Music* 32, 2 (1990), pp. 81–95.

BBC Caribbean Service, *Going to Britain?* London: BBC Caribbean Service, 1959.

Beckman, Morris, *The 43 Group*. London: Centreprise, 1992.

Bedford Community Arts, *Hidden Voices: Memories of First Generation Italians in Bedford/Voci Nascoste: Testimonianze della Prima Generazione di Italiani a Bedford*. Bedford: Bedford Community Arts, 1999.

Behan, Brendan, *The Dubbalin Man*. Dublin: A. & A. Farmar, 1997.

Berger, John and Jean Mohr, *A Seventh Man: A Book of Images and Words about the Experiences of Migrant Workers in Europe*. Harmondsworth: Penguin, 1975.

Berkoff, Steven, *Free Association: An Autobiography*. London: Faber & Faber, 1996.

Bermant, Chaim, *Point of Arrival: A Study of London's East End*. London: Eyre Methuen, 1975.

Bertram, G. L. C., *West Indian Immigration*. London: Eugenics Society, 1958.

Biegus, Zosia and Jurek Biegus, *Polish Resettlement Camps in England and Wales 1946–1969*. Rochford: PB Software, 2013.

Bivins, Roberta, *Contagious Communities: Medicine, Migration and the NHS in Post-War Britain*. Oxford: Oxford University Press, 2015.

Blake, Barbara, 'Barbara Blake on Parties', *Magnet*, 27 April 1965.

Boym, Svetlana, *The Future of Nostalgia*. New York: Basic Books, 2001.

Bradford Heritage Recording Unit, *Destination Bradford: A Century of Immigration: Photographs and Oral History*. Bradford: Bradford Libraries and Information Service, 1987.

—, *Here to Stay: Bradford's South Asian Communities*. Bradford: Bradford Heritage Recording Unit, 1994.

Bradley, Lloyd, *Sounds Like London: 100 Years of Black Music in the Capital*. London: Serpent's Tail, 2013.

Braithwaite, E. R., *To Sir, With Love*. London: Bodley Head, 1962.

Braithwaite, Lloyd, *Colonial West Indian Students in Britain*. Kingston, Jamaica: University of the West Indies Press, 2001.

British Cooperative Clinical Group, 'Gonorrhea Study 1963', *British Journal of Venereal Disease* 41 (1965), pp. 24–9.

British Joint Committee for Polish Affairs, 'What Have the Poles Done for You?' London: British Joint Committee for Polish Affairs, 1945.

Brooks, Dennis, *Race and Labour in London Transport*. Oxford: Oxford University Press, 1975.

— and Karamjit Singh, 'Pivots and Presents: Asian Brokers in British Foundries', in S. Wallam, ed., *Ethnicity at Work*. London: Macmillan, 1995, pp. 93–114.

Buettner, Elizabeth. ' "Going for an Indian": South Asian Restaurants and the Limits of Multiculturalism in Britain', *Journal of Modern History* 80, 4 (2008), pp. 865–901.

—, ' "This is Staffordshire, not Alabama": Racial Geographies of Commonwealth Immigration in Early 1960s Britain', *Journal of Imperial and Commonwealth History* 42, 4 (2014), pp. 710–40.

Bunce, Robin and Paul Field, 'Obi B. Egbuna, C. L. R. James and the Birth of Black Power in Britain: Black Radicalism in Britain 1967–72', *Twentieth Century British History* 22, 3 (2010), pp. 391–414.

—, *Darcus Howe: A Political Biography*. London: Bloomsbury, 2013.

Burney, Elizabeth, *Housing on Trial: A Study of Immigrants and Local Government*. London: Oxford University Press for the Institute of Race Relations, 1967.

Burrell, Kathy, *Moving Lives: Narratives of Nation and Migration among Europeans in Post-War Britain*. Aldershot: Ashgate, 2006.

— and Panikos Panayi, *Histories and Memories: Migrants and their Histories in Britain*. London: I. B. Tauris, 2006.

Butterworth, E., 'Aspects of Race Relations in Bradford', *Race* 6, 2 (1964), pp. 129–41.

—, 'The 1962 Smallpox Outbreak and the British Press', *Race and Class* 7, 4 (1966), pp. 347–64.

Butterworth, Eric, *A Muslim Community in Britain*. London: Church Information Office, 1967.

Carberry, H. D. and Dudley Thomson, *A West Indian in England*. London: Central Office of Information, 1950.

Carpenter, Mick, *Working for Health*. London: Lawrence and Wishart, 1988.

Casey, Eamon, 'The Pastoral on Emigration', *The Furrow* 18, 5 (1967), pp. 245–56.

Castles, Stephen and Godula Kosack, *Immigrant Workers and Class Structures in Western Europe*. Oxford: Oxford University Press, 1973.

Catholic Truth Society of Ireland, *A Catholic Handbook for Irish Men and Women Going to England*. Dublin: Catholic Truth Society of Ireland, 1953.

Cavalli, Carlo, *Ricordi di un Emigrato*. London: La Voce degli Italiani, 1972.

Chaudhuri, N., *A Passage to England*. London: Macmillan, 1959.

Cherry, Steven, *Mental Health Care in Modern England: The Norfolk Lunatic Asylum/St Andrew's Hospital c.1810–1998*. Woodbridge: Boydell, 2003.

Choudhury, Yousuf, *The Roots and Tales of Bangladeshi Settlers*. Birmingham: Sylheti Social History Group, 1993.

—, ed., *Sons of the Empire: Oral History from the Bangladeshi Seamen Who Served on British Ships during the 1939–45 War*. Birmingham: Sylheti Social History Group, 1995.

Coleman, Terry, 'The Elite inside the Tunnel', *New Society*, 6 January 1966, pp. 6–8.

Collins, Wallace, *Jamaican Migrant*. London: Routledge & Kegan Paul, 1965.

Colpi, Terry, *The Italian Factor: The Italian Community in Great Britain*. Edinburgh: Mainstream Publishing, 1991.

Committee on Housing in Greater London, *Report of the Committee on Housing in Greater London*. London: Committee on Housing in Greater London, 1965.

Cooper, David, ed., *Dialectics of Liberation*. London: Penguin, 1968.

Cottle, Thomas J., *Black Testimony: The Voices of Britain's West Indians*. Philadelphia, Temple University Press, 1978.

Coulton, Barbara, *Louis MacNeice in the BBC*. London: Faber & Faber, 1980.

Cowley, Ultan, *The Men Who Built Britain: A History of the Irish Navvy*. Dublin: Wolfhound Press, 2001.

Cronin, Anthony, *The Life of Riley*. London: Secker and Warburg, 1964.

—, *Dead as Doornails*. Dublin: Dolmen Press, 1976.

Cumper, George, *The Economy of the West Indies*. Kingston, Jamaica: University College of the West Indies, 1960.

Dabydeen, David, *Pak's Britannica: Articles by and Interviews with David Dabydeen*, ed. Lynne Macedo. Kingston, Jamaica: University of the West Indies Press, 2011.

Dahya, Badr, 'Pakistanis in Britain: Transients or Settlers?', *Race* 14, 3 (1973), pp. 242–77.

—, 'The Nature of Pakistani Ethnicity in Industrial Cities in Britain', in Abner Cohen, ed., *Urban Ethnicity*. London: Tavistock Publications, 1974, pp. 77–118.

Daly, Mary, *The Slow Failure: Population Decline and Independent Ireland*. Madison, Wisc.: University of Wisconsin Press, 2006.

Daniel, W. W., *Racial Discrimination in England: Based on the PEP Report*. Harmondsworth: Penguin, 1968.

Davis, John, 'Rents and Race in 1960s London: New Light on Rachmanism', *Twentieth Century British History* 12, 1 (2001), pp. 69–92.

Davison, R. B., *West Indian Migrants: Social and Economic Facts of Migration from the West Indies*. London: Oxford University Press for the Institute of Race Relations, 1962.

—, *Black British: Immigrants to England*. London: Oxford University Press, 1966.

Deakin, Nicholas, 'The Politics of the Commonwealth Immigrants Bill', *Political Quarterly* 39 (1968), pp. 25–45.

—, 'The British Nationality Act of 1948: A Brief Study of the Political Mythology of Race Relations', *Race* 11, 1 (1969), pp. 77–83.

—, *Colour, Citizenship and British Society*. London: Panther Books, 1970.

Delaney, Enda, *Demography, State and Society: Irish Migration to Britain, 1921–1971*. Liverpool: Liverpool University Press, 2000.

—, *The Irish in Post-War Britain*. Oxford: Oxford University Press, 2007.

Dench, Geoff, *The Maltese in London: A Case Study in the Erosion of Ethnic Consciousness*. London: Routledge, 1975.

Desai, Rashmikant Harilal, *Indian Immigrants in Britain*. London: Oxford University Press, 1963.

Dhanjal, Beryl, 'Sikh Women in Southall (Some Impressions)', *Journal of Ethnic and Migration Studies* 5, 1–2 (1976), pp. 109–14.

Dheer, Ranjit, 'Nirmohi Vilayat' ['Inhospitable Britain'], from the collection *Pardesnama*. Delhi: Navyug Publishers, 1995. Trans. Beryl Dhanjal.

Dickens, Monica, *The Heart of London*. London: Book Club, 1961.

Dodgson, Elyse, *Motherland: West Indian Women in Britain in the 1950s*. London: Heinemann, 1984.

Dooley, Pat, *The Irish in Britain*. London: Connolly Association, 1943.

Duffield, Mark, *Black Radicalism and the Politics of De-Industrialisation: The Hidden History of Indian Foundry Workers*. Aldershot: Avebury, 1988.

Dusenberry, Verne A. and Darshan S. Tatla, eds., *Sikh Diaspora Philanthropy in Punjab: Global Giving for Local Good*. New Delhi: Oxford University Press, 2009.

Eade, James, *The Politics of Community: The Bangladeshi Community in East London*. London: Avebury, 1989.

—, A. Ullah, J. Iqbal and M. Hey, *Tales of Three Generations of Bengalis in Britain*. London: Swadhinta Trust and CRONEM, 2006.

Economic Survey for 1947. London: HMSO, 1947.

Egbuna, Obi B., *Black Power in Britain*. London: UCPA, 1967.

—, *Destroy This Temple: The Voice of Black Power in Britain*. London: William & Morrow, 1971.

Eggington, Joyce, *They Seek a Living*. London: Hutchinson, 1957.

Emecheta, Buchi, *In the Ditch*. London: Allison and Busby, 1972.

—, *Second-Class Citizen*. London: Allison and Busby, 1974.

Farson, Daniel, *Soho in the Fifties*. London: Michael Joseph, 1987.

Fircroft College of Adult Education Race Relations Group, *Fircroft Survey*. Birmingham: Fircroft College of Adult Education Race Relations Group, 1954–55.

Fisher, Desmond, 'The Irishman in England', *The Furrow* 9, 4 (1958), pp. 230–35.

Foot, Paul, *Immigration and Race in British Politics*. Harmondsworth: Penguin, 1965.

—, *The Rise of Enoch Powell: An Examination of Enoch Powell's Attitude to Immigration and Race*. Harmondsworth: Penguin, 1969.

French, Patrick, *The World Is What It Is: The Authorized Biography of V. S. Naipaul*. London: Picador, 2008.

Fryer, Jonathan, *Soho in the Fifties and Sixties*. London: National Portrait Gallery, 1998.

Fryer, Peter, *Staying Power: The History of Black People in Britain*. London: Pluto, 1984.

Fyvel, T. R., *The Insecure Offenders: Rebellious Youth in the Welfare State*. London: Penguin, 1963 [1961].

Gaynor, Fr Eamonn, *The Shamrock Express*. Maynooth: Furrow Trust, 1962.

Gilmour, Rachael, '"Welcome to The University of Brixton": Creole on the Radio', in Nadia Atia and Kate Houlden, eds., *Popular Postcolonialisms: Discourses of Empire and Popular Culture*. London: Routledge, forthcoming.

Gilroy, Paul, *There Ain't No Black in the Union Jack: The Cultural Politics of Race and Nation*. London: Hutchinson, 1987.

—, *Black Britain: A Photographic History*. London: Saqi Books, 2011.

Ginzberg, Yona, 'Sympathy and Resentment: Jews and Coloureds in London's East End', *Patterns of Prejudice* 13, 2–3 (March–June 1979), pp. 41–2.

Glass, Ruth, assisted by Harold Pollins, *Newcomers: The West Indians in London*. London: Allen and Unwin, 1960.

Gosling, John and Douglas Warner, *The Shame of a City: An Inquiry into the Vice of London*. London: W. H. Allen, 1960.

Gramaglia, Letizia and Malachi McIntosh, 'Censorship, Selvon and Caribbean Voices: "Behind the Humming Bird" and the Caribbean Literary Field', *Wasafiri* 28, 2 (2013), pp. 48–54.

Green, Shirley, *Rachman*. London: Michael Joseph, 1979.

Greene, Graham, *The End of the Affair*. London: Bodley Head, 1974 [1951].

Grene, Nicholas, ed., *Talking about Tom Murphy*. Dublin: Carysfort Press, 2002.

Gretton, John, 'The Lump', *New Society*, 18 March 1970, pp. 469–70.

Griffith, Glyne, 'Deconstructing Nationalisms: Henry Swanzy, Caribbean Voices and the Development of West Indian Literature', *Small Axe*, Number 10, 5, 2 (September 2001), pp. 1–20.

—, *The BBC and the Development of Anglophone Caribbean Literature*. London: Palgrave Macmillan, 2016.

Griffith, J. A. G., Judith Henderson, Margaret Usborne and Donald Wood, *Coloured Immigrants in Britain*. Oxford: Oxford University Press for the Institute of Race Relations, 1960.

Griffiths, Peter, *A Question of Colour?* London: Leslie Frewin, 1966.

Gupta, Ranajit, 'The Migrant's Time', *Postcolonial Studies* 1, 2 (1998), pp. 155–60.

Hall, Stuart, 'Lamming, Selvon and Some Trends in the West Indian Novel', *Bim* 6, 23 (1955), pp. 172–8.

—, 'Absolute Beginnings', *Universities and Left Review* 7 (1959), pp. 17–25.

—, 'Reconstruction Work: Images of Post-War Black Settlement', *Ten.8* 16 (1984), pp. 2–9.

—, 'Minimal Selves', in Homi Bhabha and Lisa Appignanesi, eds., *Identity and the Real Me*. London: ICA, 1987, pp. 44–6.

—, 'The Windrush Issue: Postscript', *Soundings* 10 (1998), pp. 188–91.

—, and Les Back, 'At Home and Not at Home', *Cultural Studies* 23, 4 (2009), pp. 658–87.

— et al., 'The Habit of Violence', *Universities and Left Review* 5 (1958), pp. 4–5.

Hamlett, Jane, Adrian R. Bailey, Andrew Alexander and Gareth Shaw, 'Ethnicity and Consumption: South Asian Food Shopping Patterns in Britain, 1947–75', *Journal of Consumer Culture* 8, 1 (2008), pp. 91–116.

Hammond Perry, Kennetta, *London is the Place for Me: Black Britons, Citizenship and the Politics of Race*. Oxford: Oxford University Press, 2016.

Hampshire, James, *Citizenship and Belonging: Immigration and the Politics of Demographic Governance in Postwar Britain*. Basingstoke: Palgrave Macmillan, 2005.

Hanley, Brian and Scott Millar, *The Lost Revolution: The Story of the Official IRA and the Workers' Party*. Dublin: Penguin Ireland, 2009.

Hansen, Randall, *Citizenship and Immigration in Post-War Britain: The Institutional Origins of a Multicultural Nation*. Oxford: Oxford University Press, 2000.

Harris, Clive, 'Post-War Migration and the Industrial Reserve Army', in Winston James and Clive Harris, eds., *Inside Babylon: The Caribbean Diaspora in Britain*. London: Verso, 1993, pp. 9–54.

Hartley-Brewer, Michael, 'Smethwick', in Nicholas Deakin, ed., *Colour and the British Electorate 1964: Six Case Studies*. London: Pall Mall Press for the Institute of Race Relations, 1965, pp. 77–105.

Healy, John, *Death of an Irish Town*. Cork: Mercier Press, 1968.

Heinemann, Benjamin, *The Politics of the Powerless: A Study of the Campaign Against Racial Discrimination*. London: Oxford University Press, 1972.

Helweg, Arthur, *Sikhs in England*. Oxford: Oxford University Press, 1979.

Hickey, Des and Gus Smith, eds., *A Paler Shade of Green*. London: Leslie Frewin, 1972.

Hickman, Mary, 'Diaspora Space and National (Re)Formations', *Eire-Ireland* 47, 1–2 (2012), pp. 19–44.

Hinds, Donald, *Journey to an Illusion: The West Indian in Britain*. London: Heinemann, 1966.

—, 'The Island of Brixton', *Oral History* 8, 1 (spring 1980), pp. 49–51.

Hiro, Dilip, *Black British, White British: A History of Race Relations in Britain*. London: Eyre and Spottiswoode, 1971.

Horst, Heather A., ' "You Can't Be in Two Places at Once": Rethinking Transnationalism through Jamaican Return Migration', *Identities* 14, 1–2 (2007), pp. 63–83.

Hulme, Kathryn, *The Wild Place*. London: Pan, 1959 [1954].

Hunte, J. A., *Nigger Hunting in England?* London: West Indian Standing Conference, 1966.

Hurt, Raymond, 'Tuberculosis Sanatorium Regimen in the 1940s: A Patient's Personal Diary', *Journal of the Royal Society of Medicine* 97, 7 (2004), pp. 350–53.

Hussein, Abdullah, 'The Journey Back', in *Stories of Exile and Alienation*, trans. Muhammad Umar Memon. Karachi: Oxford University Press, 1998, pp. 60–80.

Huxley, Elspeth, *Back Street New Worlds: A Look at Immigrants in Britain*. Toronto: University of Toronto Press/London: Chatto and Windus, 1964.

International Social Service, *Immigrants at London Airport and their Settlement in the Community*. London: International Social Service, 1967.

James, C. L. R., *Beyond a Boundary*. New York: Pantheon, 1984.

Jephcott, Pearl, *A Troubled Area: Notes on Notting Hill, London*. London: Faber & Faber, 1964.

John, Audrey L., *A Study of the Psychiatric Nurse*. Edinburgh: E. & S. Livingstone, 1961.

John, DeWitt Jnr, *Indian Workers' Associations in Britain*. London: Oxford University Press for the Institute of Race Relations, 1969.

Johnson, Buzz, *'I Think of My Mother': Notes on the Life and Times of Claudia Jones*. London: Kalia Press, 1985.

Judt, Tony, *Post-War: A History of Europe since 1945*. London: Heinemann, 2005.

Kalra, Virinder S., *From Textile Mills to Taxi Ranks: Experiences of Migration, Labour and Social Change*. Aldershot: Ashgate, 2000.

—, 'Vilayeti Rhythms: Beyond Bhangra's Emblematic Status to a Translation of Lyrical Texts', *Theory, Culture and Society* 17, 3 (2000), pp. 80–102.

—, 'The Political Economy of the Samosa', *South Asia Research* 24 (2004), pp. 21–36.

Kavanagh, Patrick, 'Sex and Christianity', *Kavanagh's Weekly*, 24 May 1952, pp. 7–8.

Kay, Diana and Robert Miles, *Refugees or Migrant Workers? European Volunteer Workers in Britain, 1946–1951*. London: Routledge, 1992.

Keane, John B., *Self-Portrait*. Cork: Mercier Press, 1964.

Khan, Verity Saifullah, 'Pakistani Women in Britain', *Journal of Ethnic and Migration Studies* 5, 1–2 (1976), pp. 98–108.

—, 'Purdah in the British Situation', in Diana Leonard Barker and Sheila Allen, eds., *Dependence and Exploitation in Work and Marriage*. London: Longman, 1976, pp. 224–45.

—, 'The Pakistanis: Mirpuri Villagers at Home and in Bradford', in James L. Watson, ed., *Between Two Cultures: Migrants and Minorities in Britain*. Oxford: Blackwell, 1977, pp. 57–89.

Kosmin, Barry A. and Nigel Grizzard, *Jews in an Inner London Borough: A Study of the Jewish Population of Hackney Based on the 1971 Census*. London: Research Unit, Board of Deputies of British Jews, 1975.

Kramer, Ann, *Many Rivers to Cross: Caribbean People in the NHS 1948–69*. London: Sugar Media, 2006.

Kureishi, Hanif, 'London and Karachi', in Raphael Samuel, ed., *Patriotism: The Making and Unmaking of British National Identity*, Vol. 2: *Minorities and Outsiders*. London: Routledge, 1989, pp. 270–87.

Kushner, Tony, 'Anti-Semitism and Austerity: The August 1947 Riots in Britain', in Panikos Panayi, ed., *Racial Violence in Britain, 1840–1950*. London: Leicester University Press, 1993.

—, *We Europeans? Mass-Observation, 'Race' and British Identity in the Twentieth Century*. Aldershot: Ashgate, 2004.

— and Nadia Valman, eds., *Remembering Cable Street: Fascism and Anti-Fascism in British Society*. London: Vallentine Mitchell, 2000.

Lambert, John, *Crime, Police and Race Relations: A Study in Birmingham*. London: Oxford University Press for the Institute of Race Relations, 1970.

Lamming, George, *The Pleasures of Exile*. London: Allison and Busby, 1984.

—, 'Migration was not a word . . .', in Richard Drayton and Andaiye, eds., *Conversations: George Lamming: Essays, Addresses and Interviews*. London: Karia Press, 1992.

—, *The Emigrants*. Ann Arbor: University of Michigan Press, 1994 [1954].

Layton-Henry, Zig, *The Politics of Immigration: Immigration, 'Race', and 'Race' Relations in Post-war Britain*. Oxford: Blackwell, 1992.

Learie, Constantine, *Colour Bar*. London: Stanley Paul, 1954.

Lewis, Wyndham, *Rotting Hill*. London: Methuen, 1951.

Little, Kenneth, *Negroes in Britain*. London: Routledge & Kegan Paul, 1948.

Lodge, David, *The Picturegoers*. London: Pan, 1962 [1960].

Low, Gail, 'Publishing Commonwealth: The Case of West Indian Writing, 1950–65', *EnterText: An Interactive Interdisciplinary E-Journal for Cultural and Historical Studies and Creative Work* 2, 1 (2001–2), pp. 71–93.

Ludhianvi, Sathi, 'Black People, White Blood', in Harchand Singh Bedi, ed., *Pachchon Dee Vaa* ['British Punjabi Stories']. Amritsar: Ravi Sahit Parkashan, 2013. Trans. Beryl Dhanjal.

Mac Amhlaigh, Dónall, *An Irish Navvy: The Diary of an Exile*, trans. Valentin Iremonger. Cork: Collins Press, 2003 [1964].

MacCarthy, Ethna, 'Public Health Problems Created by Louse Infestation', *Irish Journal of Medical Science* 23, 2 (February 1948), pp. 65–78.

McDowell, Linda, *Hard Labour: The Forgotten Voices of Latvian Migrant Volunteer Workers*. London: UCL Press, 2005.

MacInnes, Colin, *Absolute Beginners*. London: MacGibbon & Kee, 1960.

—, 'A Short Guide for Jumbles (to the Life of Their Coloured Brethren in England)' [1956], in *England, Half English*. London: MacGibbon and Kee, 1961.

—, *London, City of Any Dreams*. London: Thames and Hudson, 1962.

—, *City of Spades*. London: Allison and Busby, 2012 [1957].

Macklin, Graham, 'Police Failed Harold Pinter', *BBC History Magazine* 5, 9 (2004).

—, *Very Deeply Dyed in Black: Sir Oswald Mosley and the Resurrection of British Fascism after 1945*. London: I. B. Tauris, 2007.

McMillan, Michael, *The Front Room: Migrant Aesthetics in the Home*. London: Black Dog, 2009.

McNeill, Margaret, *By the Rivers of Babylon: A Story of Relief Work among the Displaced Persons of Europe*. London: Bannisdale Press, 1950.

Malik, Michael Abdul, *From Michael de Freitas to Michael X*. London: André Deutsch, 1968.

Manchester Regional Hospital Board and the University of Manchester, *The Work of the Mental Nurse: A Survey Organized by a Joint Committee of Manchester Regional Hospital Board and the University of Manchester*. Manchester: Manchester University Press, 1955.

Manley, Douglas, 'The West Indian Background', in S. K. Ruck, ed., *The West Indian Comes to England*. London: Routledge & Kegan Paul, 1960, pp. 3–48.

Marin, Fr Umberto, *Emigrazione Italiana in Gran Bretagna, I e II*. Rome: Centro Studi Emigrazione, 1969.

Markandaya, K., *The Nowhere Man*. New York: John Day, 1972.

Marriot, John, *Beyond the Tower: A History of East London*. New Haven, Conn.: Yale University Press, 2011.

Maxwell, Neville, *The Power of Negro Action*. London: Privately Printed, 1965.

Mazower, Mark, David Feldman and Jessica Reinisch, eds., *Postwar Reconstruction of Europe: International Perspectives, 1945–1950*. Oxford: Oxford University Press, 2011.

Metzgen, Humphrey and John Graham, *Caribbean Wars Untold: A Salute to the British West Indies*. Kingston, Jamaica: University of the West Indies Press, 2007.

Miles, Robert, *Racism and Migrant Labour*. London: Routledge, 1982.

—, 'The Riots of 1958: Notes on the Ideological Construction of "Race Relations" as a Political Issue in Britain', *Immigrants and Minorities* 3, 3 (1984), pp. 252–75.

Miller, Daniel, 'Migration, Material Culture and Tragedy: Four Moments in Caribbean Migration', *Mobilities* 3 (2008), pp. 397–413.

Miller, Rebecca, 'Hucklebucking at the Tea Dances: Irish Showbands in Britain, 1959–1969', *Popular Music History* 9, 3 (2014), pp. 225–47.

Mooney, Nicola, *Rural Nostalgias and Transnational Dreams: Identity and Modernity among Jat Sikhs*. Toronto: University of Toronto Press, 2011.

Morrison, Majbritt, *Jungle West 11*. London: Tandem Books, 1964.

Morrow, H. L., 'Journey into Fear', in Leslie Daiken, ed., *They Go, The Irish*. London: Nicholson and Watson, 1944, pp. 62–71.

Mort, Frank, *Capital Affairs: London and the Making of the Permissive Society*. New Haven, Conn.: Yale University Press, 2010.

Naipaul, V. S., *The Enigma of Arrival*. London: Penguin, 1987.

—, *Letters Between a Father and Son*. London: Little, Brown, 1999.

—, *Half a Life*. London: Picador, 2001.

—, 'Prologue to an Autobiography', *Literary Occasions: Essays*. London: Picador, 2003.

Nanton, Philip, 'What Does Mr. Swanzy Want – Shaping or Reflecting? An Assessment of Henry Swanzy's Contribution to the Development of Caribbean Literature', *Caribbean Quarterly* 46, 1 (March 2000), pp. 61–72.

Neelgiri, Tarsem, ed., *Gori Dharti* ['White Land: A Collection of Literary Writings'], Jallandhar: Deepak Publishers, 1979. Trans. Beryl Dhanjal.

Neptune, Harvey, *Caliban and the Yankees: Trinidad and the United States Occupation*. Chapel Hill: University of North Carolina Press, 2007.

Newton, Darrell, *Paving the Empire Road: BBC Television and Black Britons*. Manchester: Manchester University Press, 2011.

Noble, Virginia, *Inside the Welfare State: Foundations of Policy and Practice in Post-War Britain*. London: Routledge, 2009.

Nolan, Peter, *A History of Mental Health Nursing*. London: Chapman and Hall, 1993.

O'Donnell, Peadar, 'Emigration is a Way of Keeping a Grip', *The Bell* 3, 2 (November 1941), pp. 310–12.

—, 'Call the Exiles Home', *The Bell* 9, 5, February 1945.

Ó Drisceoil, Donal, *Peadar O'Donnell*. Cork: Cork University Press, 2001.

Ó hAllmhuráin, Gearóid, *O'Brien Pocket History of Traditional Irish Music*. Dublin: O'Brien, 2003.

O'Shea, Kieran, *The Irish Emigrant Chaplaincy Scheme in Britain, 1957–82*. Dublin: Irish Episcopal Commission for Emigrants, 1985.

O'Toole, Fintan, *Tom Murphy: The Politics of Magic*. Dublin: New Island Books, 1994.

Patterson, Sheila, *Dark Strangers: A Study of West Indians in London*. Harmondsworth: Penguin, 1963.

—, *Immigrants in Industry*. London: Oxford University Press, 1968.

—, *Immigrants and Race Relations in Britain, 1960–1967*. London: Oxford University Press for the Institute of Race Relations, 1969.

Paul, Kathleen, ' "British Subjects" and "British Stock": Labour's Post-War Imperialism', *Journal of British Studies* 34, 2 (1995), pp. 233–76.

Peach, Ceri, *West Indian Migration to Britain: A Social Geography*. London: Oxford University Press for the Institute of Race Relations, 1968.

Phillips, Caryl, 'Interview: George Lamming Talks to Caryl Phillips', *Wasafiri* 13, 26 (autumn 1997), p. 13.

Phillips, Mike and Charlie Phillips, *Notting Hill in the Sixties*. London: Lawrence and Wishart, 1991.

Phillips, Mike and Trevor Phillips, *Windrush: The Irresistible Rise of Multi-Racial Britain*. London: HarperCollins, 1998.

Philpott, Stuart B., 'The Monserratians: Migration Dependency and the Maintenance of Island Ties to England', in James L. Watson, ed., *Between Two Cultures: Migrants and Minorities in Britain*. Oxford: Blackwell, 1977, pp. 90–119.

Philpott, Trevor, 'Would You Let Your Daughter Marry a Negro?' *Picture Post*, 30 October 1954.

Pilkington, Edward, *Beyond the Mother Country: West Indians and the Notting Hill White Riots*. London: I. B. Tauris, 1988.

Political and Economic Planning, *Colonial Students in Britain*. London: Political and Economic Planning, 1955.

Pollitt, Harry, *No British Jobs for Fascist Poles*. London: Communist Party of Great Britain, 1946.

Powell, Enoch, *Reflections of a Statesman: The Writings and Speeches of Enoch Powell*, ed. Rex Collings. London: Bellew, 1991.

—, *Freedom and Reality*, ed. John Wood. London: Batsford, 1969.

Power, Richard, *Apple on a Treetop*. Dublin: Poolbeg Press, 1980.

Puri, Kailash and Eleanor Nesbitt, *Pool of Life: The Autobiography of a Punjabi Agony Aunt*. Brighton: Sussex Academic Press, 2013.

Ram, Madho, *Mera England da safr* [My Passage to England]. Handsworth: S. B. Kara, 1972 (this trans. Beryl Dhanjal).

Ramdin, Ron, *The Making of the Black Working Class in Britain*. Brookfield, VT: Gower, 1987.

Reilly, Oliver, 'A Worker in Birmingham', *The Furrow* 9, 4 (1958), pp. 217–24.

Report of the Race Relations Board for 1966–1967. London: HMSO, 1967.

Rex, John and Robert Moore, *Race, Community and Conflict: A Study of Sparkbrook*. London: Oxford University Press for the Institute of Race Relations, 1967.

— and Sally Tomlinson, *Colonial Immigrants in a British City: A Class Analysis*. London: Routledge & Kegan Paul, 1979.

Richmond, Anthony, *Colour Prejudice in Britain: A Study of West Indian Workers in Liverpool, 1941–1951*. London: Routledge, 1954.

—, *The Colour Problem: A Study of Racial Relations*. Harmondsworth: Penguin, 1961 [1955].

Rose, E. J. B. et al., *Colour and Citizenship: A Report on British Race Relations*. London: Oxford University Press for the Institute of Race Relations, 1969.

Royal Commission on Population Report. London: HMSO, 1949.

Runnymede Trust, 'Trade Unions and Immigrant Workers', *New Community* 4, 1 (1974–5), pp. 19–36.

Salkey, Andrew, *Escape to an Autumn Pavement*. Leeds: Peepal Tree Press, 2009 [1960].

—, *The Adventures of Catullus Kelly*. London: Hutchinson, 1969.

Sawh, Roy, *From Where I Stand*. London: Hansib Publications, 1987.

Schaffer, Gavin, 'Legislating Against Hatred: Meaning and Motive in Section Six of the Race Relations Act of 1965', *Twentieth Century British History* 25, 2 (2014), pp. 251–75.

—, *The Vision of a Nation: Making Multiculturalism on British Television, 1960–80*. Basingstoke: Palgrave Macmillan, 2014.

Schoen, Douglas, *Enoch Powell and the Powellites*. New York: St Martin's Press, 1977.

Schofield, Camilla, *Enoch Powell and the Making of Postcolonial Britain*. Cambridge: Cambridge University Press, 2013.

Schwarz, Bill, ed., *West Indian Intellectuals in Britain*. Manchester: Manchester University Press, 2003.

Scobie, Edward, 'Bad Taste B.B.C!', *Flamingo*, September 1969, pp. 22–4.

Seabrook, Jeremy, *City Close-Up*. London: Allen Lane, 1971.

Selvon, Sam, 'Finding Piccadilly Circus', *Guardian Weekly*, 17 December 1950, in K. Ramchand and Susheila Nasta, eds., *Foreday Morning: Selected Prose 1946–1986*. Harlow: Longman, 1989, pp. 123–6.

—, *The Lonely Londoners*. London: Penguin, 2006 [1956].

—, *Ways of Sunlight*. Harlow: Longman, 1957.

—, *The Housing Lark*. London: MacGibbon & Kee, 1965.

Shamsher, Jogindar, *The Overtime People*. Jalandhar: ABS Publications, 1989.

— and Ralph Russell, 'Punjabi Journalism in Britain: A Background', *Journal of Ethnic and Migration Studies* 5, 3 (1976), pp. 211–21.

Shaw, Alison, *A Pakistani Community in Britain*. Oxford: Blackwell, 1988.

Sheil, Leonard, 'Marriage and the Leakage', *The Furrow* 9, 4 (1958), p. 523.

Shepherd, Catherine, 'Fascism in Hampstead, Parts 1 and 2', *Association of Jewish Refugees Journal*, April and May 2002.

Sherwood, Marika, *Claudia Jones: A Life in Exile*. London: Lawrence and Wishart, 1999.

Shuttleworth, Alan, 'Sparkbrook', in Nicholas Deakin, ed., *Colour and the British Electorate 1964: Six Case Studies*. London: Pall Mall Press for the Institute of Race Relations, 1965, pp. 54–76.

Sidhu, Pritam, *Dukh Pardesan de* ['Foreign Woes']. Amritsar: Ravi Sahit Parkashan, 1982, trans. Beryl Dhanjal.

—, *Dharat Walaiti Desi Chamba*, as quoted in Jogindar Shamsher, *The Overtime People*. Jalandhar: ABS Publications, 1989.

Simpson, Julian, Aneez Esmail, Virinder S. Kalra and Stephanie J. Snow, 'Writing Migrants Back into NHS History: Addressing a "Collective Amnesia" and its Policy Implications', *Journal of the Royal Society of Medicine* 103, 10 (2010), pp. 392–6.

Sivanandan, A., *A Different Hunger: Writings on Black Resistance*. London: Pluto, 1982.

—, 'The Heart is Where the Battle Is: An Interview with the Author', in *Communities of Resistance: Writings on Black Struggles for Socialism*. London: Verso, 1990, pp. 1–16.

Slater, Stefan, 'Prostitutes and Popular History: Notes on the "Underworld" 1918–1939', *Crime, History and Societies* 13, 1 (2009), pp. 25–48.

Solokoff, Bertha, *Edith and Stepney: The Life of Edith Ramsay*. London: Stepney Books, 1987.

Southall Black Sisters, *Against the Grain: A Celebration of Survival and Struggle*. Southall: Southall Black Sisters, 1990.

Spark, Muriel, *The Girls of Slender Means*. London: Penguin, 1966 [1963].

Spearman, Diana, 'Enoch Powell's Postbag', *New Society*, 9 May 1968, pp. 667–9.

Spencer, A. E. C. W., *Arrangements for the Integration of Irish Immigrants in England and Wales*, ed. Mary Daly. Dublin: Irish Manuscripts Commission, 2011.

Spencer, Ian R. G., *British Immigration Policy since 1939: The Making of Multi-Racial Britain*. London: Routledge, 1997.

Spinley, Betty, *The Deprived and the Privileged: Personality Development in English Society*. London: Routledge & Kegan Paul, 1953.

Sponza, Lucio, *Divided Loyalties: Italians in Britain during the Second World War*. Bern: Peter Lang, 2000.

—, 'Italians in War and Post-War Britain', in Johannes-Dieter Steinert and Inge Weber-Newth, eds., *European Immigrants in Britain, 1933–1950*. Munich: K. G. Saur Verlag, 2003.

Stadulis, Elizabeth, 'The Resettlement of Displaced Persons in the United Kingdom', *Population Studies* 5 (1952), pp. 207–37.

Steinert, Johannes-Dieter, 'British Migration Policy and Displaced Persons', in Jessica Reinisch and Elizabeth White, eds., *The Disentanglement of Populations: Migration, Expulsion and Displacement in Post-War Europe, 1944–9*. Basingstoke: Palgrave Macmillan, 2011, pp. 229–47.

Stephens, Leslie, *Employment of Coloured Workers in the Birmingham Area: Report of an Enquiry*. London: Institute of Personnel Management, 1956.

Street, Joe, 'Malcolm X, Smethwick, and the Influence of the African American Freedom Struggle on British Race Relations in the 1960s', *Journal of Black Studies* 38, 6 (2008), pp. 932–50.

Swanzy, H. L. V., 'Caribbean Voices: Prolegomena to a West Indian Culture', *Caribbean Quarterly* 1, 2 (1949), pp. 21–8.

Sword, Keith, *Deportation and Exile: Poles in the Soviet Union, 1939–48*. Basingstoke: Macmillan, 1996.

—, with Norman Davies and Jan Ciechanowski, *The Formation of the Polish Community in Great Britain 1939–50*. London: University of London, 1989.

Sykes, A. J., 'Navvies: Their Work Attitudes', *Sociology* 3, 1 (1969), pp. 21–34.

—, 'Navvies: Their Social Relations', *Sociology* 3, 2 (1969), pp. 157–72.

Tajfel, Henri and John Dawson, eds., *Disappointed Guests: Essays by African, Asian and West Indian Students*. Oxford: Oxford University Press, 1965.

Tannahill, J. A., *European Voluntary Workers in Britain*. Manchester: Manchester University Press, 1958.

Tatla, Darshan S., 'A Chorus of Hushed Voices: An Introduction to Punjabi Literature in Britain', *Punjab Research Group Discussion Papers* 32 (1991), 111–19.

—, 'A Passage to England: Oral Tradition and Popular Culture among Early Punjabi Sikh Settlers in Britain', *Oral History* 30, 2 (2002), pp. 61–72.

—, *Gurbachan Singh Gill: A Short Biography and Memoirs*. Jalandhar: Punjab Centre for Migration Studies, 2004.

— and Eleanor Nesbitt, *Sikhs in Britain: An Annotated Bibliography*. Coventry: Centre for Research in Ethnic Relations, 1987.

— and Gurharpal Singh, 'The Punjabi Press in Britain', *New Community* 15, 2 (1989), pp. 211–25.

Taylor, Helen, *Refugees and the Meaning of Home: Cypriot Narratives of Loss, Longing and Daily Life in London*. Basingstoke: Palgrave Macmillan, 2015.

Taylor, Simon, *A Land of Dreams: A Study of Jewish and Afro-Caribbean Communities in England*. London: Routledge, 1993.

Thomson, Alexander Raven, *The Battle of Ridley Road*. London: Raven Books, 1947.

Vernant, Jacques, *The Refugee in the Post War World*. London: Allen and Unwin, 1953.

Virdee, Pippa, ' "No Home but in Memory": The Legacies of Colonial Rule in the Punjab', in Panikos Panayi and Pippa Virdee, eds., *Refugees and the End of Empire: Imperial Collapse and Forced Migration in the Twentieth Century*. Basingstoke: Palgrave Macmillan, 2011, pp. 175–95.

Virdee, Satnam, 'Anti-Racism and the Socialist Left, 1968–1979', in Evan Smith and Matthew Worley, eds., *Against the Grain: The British Far Left from 1956*. Manchester: Manchester University Press, 2014, pp. 209–28.

Walker, Gordon, 'White Backlash in Leyton?', *Magnet*, 13 February 1965.

Walmsley, Anne, *The Caribbean Artists Movement, 1966–1972: A Literary and Cultural History*. London: New Beacon Books, 1992.

Waters, Chris, ' "Dark Strangers" in Our Midst: Discourses of Race and Nation in Britain, 1947–1963', *Journal of British Studies* 36, 2 (1997), pp. 207–38.

Waters, Rob, 'Black Power on the Telly: America, Television, and Race in 1960s and 1970s Britain', *Journal of British Studies* 54, 4 (2015), pp. 947–70.

—, 'Henry Swanzy, Sartre's Zombie? Black Power and the Transformation of the Caribbean Artists Movement', in Ruth Craggs and Claire Wintle, eds., *Cultures of Decolonisation: Transnational Productions and Practices, 1945–1970*. Manchester: Manchester University Press, 2016, pp. 67–85.

— *Thinking Black: Britain, 1965–1985*. Berkeley: University of California Press, forthcoming.

Webster, Wendy, *Imagining Home: Gender, 'Race' and National Identity, 1945–64*. London: UCL Press, 1998.

—, ' "There'll Always be an England": Representations of Colonial Wars and Immigration, 1948–1968', *Journal of British Studies* 40 (2001), pp. 557–84.

—, 'Britain and the Refugees of Europe 1939–50', in Louise Ryan and Wendy Webster, eds., *Gendering Migration: Masculinity, Femininity and Ethnicity in Post-War Britain*. Aldershot: Ashgate, 2008.

Western, John, *A Passage to England: Barbadian Londoners Speak of Home*. Minneapolis: University of Minnesota Press, 1992.

Where to Eat in London. London: publisher unknown, 1955.

Whipple, Amy, 'Revisiting the "Rivers of Blood" Controversy: Letters to Enoch Powell', *Journal of British Studies* 48, 3 (2009), pp. 717–35.

Whittaker, Elvi, ed., *Baltic Odyssey*. Alberta: University of Calgary Press, 1995.

Wickenden, James, *Colour in Britain*. London: Oxford University Press for the Institute of Race Relations, 1958.

Williams, Raymond, *The Country and the City*. Nottingham: Spokesman Books, 2011 [1973].

Wills, Clair, *The Best are Leaving: Emigration and Post-War Irish Culture*. Cambridge: Cambridge University Press, 2015.

Woodberry Down Memories Group, *Woodberry Down Memories: The History of an LCC Housing Estate*. London: ILEA, 1989.

Woolcott, David, 'Southall', in Nicholas Deakin, ed., *Colour and the British Electorate 1964: Six Case Studies*. London: Pall Mall Press for the Institute of Race Relations, 1965, pp. 31–53.

Wright, Peter L., *The Coloured Worker in British Industry*. London: Oxford University Press for the Institute of Race Relations, 1968.

Yeates, Nicola, 'Migration and Nursing in Ireland: An Internationalist History', *Translocations: Migration and Social Change* 5, 1 (2009), pp. 1–21.

Young, Phyllis, *Report on an Investigation into the Conditions of the Coloured Population in a Stepney Area*. London: Privately published, 1944.

Zubrzycki, Jerzy, *Polish Immigrants in Britain: A Study of Adjustment*. The Hague: Martinus Nijhoff, 1956.

Zuckerman, William, *The Jew in Revolt: The Modern Jew in the World Crisis*. London: Secker and Warburg, 1937.

Acknowledgements

I am grateful to the very many people who took time to talk about their experiences as immigrants, to hunt down information and out-of-the-way stories, and to share their own thinking and research. I want to thank in particular Kuljit Bhamra, Elleke Boehmer, Chris Campbell, Claire Chatterton, Ultan Cowley, Sarah Dhanjal, Nakul Krishna, Paul Long and Linda MacDowell; my former colleagues at Queen Mary, especially Nadia Atia, Michele Barrett, Markman Ellis, Rachael Gilmour, Suzanne Hobson, Jacqueline Rose, Bill Schwarz and Nadia Valman; and my new colleagues at Princeton, especially Zahid Chaudhary, Bradin Cormack and Sophie Gee. My thanks too to the archivists at the British Library, the National Archives, the National Archives of Ireland, the British Film Institute, the Wellcome Library, Birmingham Central Library, Bradford Central Library, Ealing Central Library, Queen Mary University of London Archives, the Black Cultural Archives, London Metropolitan University Archives, Tower Hamlets Local History Library and the Library of Trinity College, Dublin. For research and translation assistance I am indebted to Sheela Banerjee, Oliver Browne, Angharad Eyre, Flavia Gasperetti, Elizabeth Robertson, Amardeep Singh, The Gentle Author and especially the incomparable Rob Waters. My thanks to Peter Straus for his lightning responses, and to Simon Winder, Maria Bedford and everyone at Allen Lane for helping to make the transition from typescript to book not merely painless but surprisingly good fun.

Early in my research I was lucky enough to come across a short study of Punjabi migrant writing published in the 1980s by Jogindar Shamsher, who had migrated from the Punjab in the mid 1950s. From his current base in Canada Jogindar introduced me to a number of writers who were active in the 1960s and 1970s, including Ranjit Dheer, Shivcharan Gill, Surjit Hans, Sathi Ludhianvi, Karam Mohan, Kailash Puri, Santokh Singh Santokh and Pritam Sidhu. They all gave generously of their time and furnished me with copies of their stories and poems. I am immensely grateful to Surjit Sidhu, who introduced me to a number of women who shared their experiences as immigrants in the 1960s with me. I also owe a huge debt of gratitude to Darshan Singh Tatla, a scholar of Punjabi literature and history. Darshan helped me to understand the cultural world of the West Midlands migrant in the 1960s, and he gave me a copy of Madho Ram's extraordinary poem, which he had found many years ago in a Wolverhampton second-hand bookshop. I could not have got very far with these materials without the kindness, wit and hard work of Beryl Dhanjal, who undertook to translate the Punjabi poems and stories for me. My visits to the home of Beryl and Ambi Dhanjal, where I was fed delicious food alongside thoughtful translations and hilarious accounts of Southall in the 1960s, were a highlight of the time I spent working on this book.

I have been blessed in my friends, who have borne with me over the years as I tried to puzzle things out. I am grateful for conversations with Ed Behrens, Catherine Berney, Nicholas Canny, Claire Connolly, Jessica Drake, Claudia FitzHerbert, Roy Foster, Luke Gibbons, Paul Hamilton, Paul Keegan, Ben Levitas, Anna Longman, Ian McBride, Barry McCrea, Helen Miles, Eve Morrison, Mary O'Callaghan, Paul O'Donovan, Diarmuid Ó Giolláin, Eunan O'Halpin, Karen Van Dyck and Kathy Watson; also my uncle Jimmy Moxley and my cousin Kevin Moxley. One particular conversation with Frances Wilson, when I was seriously stuck in 2015, made the difference between this being a book and not being one. For other kindnesses and support I thank my sisters, Siobhan Wills, Bridget Wills and Oona Roycroft; my parents, Philomena and Bernard Wills; and my children, Jacob, Luan and Philomena.

List of Illustrations

Index